AIDS: THE POLITICS OF SURVIVAL

Edited by
Nancy Krieger
Kaiser Foundation Research Institute
Oakland, California
and
Glen Margo
Private Consultant
San Francisco, Oakland

POLICY,
POLITICS,
HEALTH AND
MEDICINE
SERIES

Vicente Navarro, *Series Editor*

Baywood Publishing Company, Inc.

Amityville, New York

Printed in the United States of America.

Library of Congress Catalog Card Number: 94-372
ISBN: 0-89503-122-1 (cloth)
ISBN: 0-89503-123-X (paper)

Library of Congress Cataloging-in-Publication Data

AIDS, the politics of survival / Nancy Krieger, and Glen Margo.
editors.
p. cm. - - (Policy, politics, health, and medicine series)
Collection of previously published articles.
Includes bibliographical references
ISBN 0-89503-122-1 (cloth). - - ISBN 0-89503-123-X (paper)
1. AIDS (Disease)- -Political aspects.- -United States.
I. Krieger, Nancy. II. Margo, Glen. III. Series: Policy, politics, health, and medicine series (Unnumbered)
[DNLM: 1. Acquired Immunodeficiency Syndrome- -prevention & control- -collected works. 2. Health Policy- -collected works. 3. Politics- -collected works. WD 308 A28818 1994]
RA644.A25A3774 1994
362.1'969792- -dc20
DNLM/DLC
for Library of Congress 94-372
CIP

Acknowledgments

The editors thank Vicente Navarro for requesting the preparation of a Special Section on AIDS for the *International Journal of Health Services,* and Frontline Publications for the initial effort involved in producing *The Politics of AIDS*.

Contents

Introduction

Nancy Krieger

Shortly after the 1993 international AIDS conference in Berlin, the *New York Times* printed a telling editorial. Entitled "The Unyielding AIDS Epidemic" (1), the editorial pronounced that the conference had left a "depressing message":

> no scientific breakthrough is apt to wipe this scourge from the earth any time soon. Indeed, the existing medical weapons against AIDS are less successful now than once believed. There is little choice now but to shift the emphasis to prevention programs.

To support this stance, the editorial noted that: (*a*) "the drug AZT, long the mainstay of AIDS treatment, has only limited value for limited time—and is highly toxic to boot"; (*b*) few other drugs or vaccines seem to be on the horizon; (*c*) in the United States, AIDS is now "the leading cause of death among young men 25 to 44 years of age in 5 states and 64 cities"; and (*d*) an estimated 14 million people worldwide are infected with the AIDS virus, and this number is expected to double by the year 2000—a mere seven years from now.

In the face of "such gloom all around," the *New York Times* declared (1):

> The only immediate hope for containing the epidemic is a heavier emphasis on prevention programs. That means patient, persistent, unglamorous work yielding small gains in areas that are often controversial: better sex education, promotion of condoms, needle exchange programs for drug addicts, safer blood supplies abroad and better treatment of venereal diseases that foster the spread of AIDS.

Echoing these views, the internationally renowned journal *Science* stated that the central and "simple" message of the conference was (2, p. 1712):

> . . . back to basics. "Basics" in this case include some very straightforward—and definitely unglamourous—strategies, such as better treatment of sexually transmitted diseases other than AIDS.

Inquiring "why, in this age of instant gene cloning and pyrotechnical retrovirology, should AIDS researchers be concerned about things as scientifically mundane as gonorrhea, syphilis, and chancroid?" (2, p. 1712), the article offered two answers: HIV spreads more easily among people with these diseases and, more importantly, none of the other biomedical interventions against AIDS seem to be working.

These candid statements are as illuminating as they are disturbing. They expose fundamental assumptions underlying the framework of the late 20th century biomedical enterprise in the United States, a framework that is hampering the fight against AIDS even as it bolsters research leading to new insights about the inner workings of the immune system and the variable forms of HIV, the AIDS virus. In a frustrated and even somewhat astonished tone, these commentaries bluntly lament the fact that science alone cannot curtail the spread of AIDS. Without any sense of shame, they deride the basic work of preventing AIDS as "unglamorous" and "mundane." And, although the *New York Times* editorial concedes that AIDS prevention is difficult because it gets entangled in controversial issues, the *Science* article avoids such irksome matters entirely and focuses instead on the biological plausibility of controlling sexually transmitted diseases as a way of reducing the spread of AIDS.

Notably absent from either of these commentaries is any sense of outrage over the lives needlessly imperiled and those callously cut short by the many obstacles right-wing moralists, reactionary politicians, and entrenched research bureaucracies have placed in the way of developing sound AIDS prevention programs. Examples of such obstruction include: Congressional suppression of much-needed national surveys of sexual behavior in the United States (3); punitive legislation banning the use of federal funds to produce sexually explicit AIDS prevention materials that could be construed as "condoning" homosexuality (4); delays in expanding the case definition of AIDS to include conditions that exclusively affect women (e.g., invasive cervical cancer) (5, 6); and deliberate underfunding of research and interventions oriented to AIDS prevention (7).

Equally absent is any sense of the social inequalities that drive the spread of AIDS and how difficult they are to confront and change. The commentaries remain mute about the reasons why, in the United States, AIDS was permitted to run rampant among gay men and injection drug users and why the incidence of AIDS is now highest among blacks and Hispanics and is increasing most rapidly among women (8). And, although they note the alarming global projections of future cases of AIDS, there is no mention of any of the social conditions that foster the spread of AIDS in economically underdeveloped countries—whether it be the widespread poverty that endures as a lasting legacy of colonialism, the problems of rapid urbanization, or the contemporary "structural adjustment" policies imposed by the World Bank and the International Monetary Fund, which require drastic reductions in social and health services (9). In the world of these commentaries, such factors are of secondary importance: the solutions to health problems should instead lie in the realm of "magic bullets," of technological "quick-fix" interventions designed to eliminate or stop the transmission of specific pathogenic agents without otherwise disturbing the status quo.

The purpose of this book is to offer a corrective to these simplistic but pervasive beliefs. Its chapters present alternative analyses, each premised upon the view that politics is central to understanding, shaping, and altering the course of the AIDS epidemic. Without rejecting the necessity and utility of basic biomedical research about HIV and AIDS, the authors vividly expose why and how AIDS is not and never has been simply a scientific problem. They demonstrate the folly of presuming to attack what the biomedical model considers to be *the* cause of AIDS—HIV, the AIDS virus—without addressing the causes of the *incidence* of AIDS. And, from myriad angles, the authors dissect how social inequalities and social relationships—among and between governments, communities, and individuals—critically affect the epidemic's course. Concerned with survival, not glamour, these chapters offer concrete suggestions for research and policies that can help reduce the rate of infection and ensure the rights and well-being of those already infected.

Putting prevention first, not last, this text draws upon the insights and ingenuity of those most affected by the epidemic and links the fight against AIDS to the fight for social justice. Far from shying away from questions of politics and injustice, the authors acknowledge these inherent aspects of the AIDS epidemic, embrace the passions they arouse, and seek to put them constructively to work alongside the knowledge generated by basic research. In doing so, the authors give reason for hope, not despair. In the face of daunting odds, people committed to bettering the world have time and again devoted their full selves—heart, soul, body, and mind—to overcoming seemingly invincible foes and insurmountable barriers. In the case of AIDS, we can draw upon no less to guide our analyses and sustain our spirits as we seek to end this awful, but preventable, pandemic.

"AIDS: THE POLITICS OF SURVIVAL": STRUCTURE AND THEMES

This volume contains 12 chapters in five sections. Each section and chapter speaks to different aspects of the AIDS epidemic, as described below.

Section I: The Politics of AIDS

The first section presents an analysis of AIDS in the United States published in 1986 in a pamphlet called "The Politics of AIDS," written by Nancy Krieger and

Rose Appleman. Prepared during the midst of the second term of the Reagan administration, the pamphlet was intended to provoke debate and discussion over why—and how—the various progressive movements in the United States should become involved in the fight against AIDS.

At the time the pamphlet was published, the majority of AIDS activists in the United States were based in the gay and lesbian communities and most of the analyses about the politics of AIDS focused on homophobia (10, 11). AIDS was depicted in the media primarily as a "gay disease"; although occasional stories focused on the plight of hemophiliacs or the threats posed by prostitutes, intravenous drug users, and Haitians, the public face of AIDS in the United States was typically gay and almost always white. The pamphlet sought to challenge this partial view of AIDS and to encourage the varied U.S. progressive movements to join the lesbian and gay communities in fighting this terrible disease. Highlighting the disproportionate impact of AIDS on people of color both in the United States and abroad, the pamphlet traced the ways in which broader geopolitical trends were shaping the epidemic's course. In the United States, these included the Reagan administration's courtship and manipulation of right-wing forces to help build public support for its massive military build-up and attacks on both the welfare state and the many gains won by the progressive movements in the 1960s and 1970s; abroad, critical social and political factors included the devastating legacy of colonialism and the ongoing hardships caused by economic underdevelopment.

In the light of these political and economic realities, the pamphlet argued that the fight against AIDS would not be successful if AIDS were approached "simply" as a "gay issue" or "simply" as a "health issue." It thus urged activists of all stripes—whether based in the gay and lesbian communities, U.S. minority communities, trade unions, the health care sector, civil libertarian organizations, or left-wing political organizations—to adopt a broader framework and to become involved in what promised to be a protracted struggle. To help focus organizing efforts around AIDS, the pamphlet concluded by articulating several specific demands. These demands linked U.S. domestic and foreign policy and called upon the federal government to: (*a*) establish a centralized agency empowered to coordinate, fund, and enforce appropriate public health policy regarding AIDS research, treatment, and education; (*b*) create a national health plan guaranteeing health care for all; (*c*) end the "war on drugs" and instead implement needle exchange programs, provide adequate funding for treatment programs, create jobs, and revitalize the inner-cities; (*d*) end discrimination against lesbians and gay men; and (*e*) provide financial and technical support to Third World nations stricken by the AIDS epidemic.

Shortly after these demands were issued, they were incorporated into the AIDS platform of both the National Rainbow Coalition (12) and Reverend Jesse Jackson's inspiring 1988 presidential campaign (13). The subsequent Bush administration, however, was notable in its failure to address the AIDS epidemic, and today, despite the change in administration and some shifts in the specifics of the budgetary battles, these demands remain largely unmet.

Section II: AIDS: Community Survival in the United States

Building on the framework elaborated in "The Politics of AIDS," the next three sections contain chapters originally prepared as articles for a Special Section on AIDS published in 1990 and 1991 in the *International Journal of Health Services,* a multidisciplinary journal dedicated to publishing critical analyses of health and health care. The first of these sections, entitled "AIDS: Community Survival in the United States," includes an introduction and three chapters that elucidate the realities of AIDS transmission and prevention, especially as they pertain to racial/ethnic minorities, children, and the urban poor. The introduction clarifies what is meant by describing the politics of AIDS as the "politics of survival," and also summarizes the main points of the section's three chapters: "AIDS Prevention in the United States: Lessons from the First Decade," by Nicholas Freudenberg; "Epidemic in the War Zone: AIDS and Community Survival in New York City," by Ernest Drucker; and "Pediatric AIDS in the United States: Epidemiological Reality versus Government Policy," by Anne-Emanuelle Birn, John Santelli, and LaWanda G. Burwell.

Section III: Women and AIDS

The next section, "Women and AIDS," examines how gender relations have shaped the spread of AIDS in both economically developed and underdeveloped countries, with special attention devoted to the situation in Zimbabwe and South Africa. The introduction describes how AIDS prevention programs have typically ignored or misassessed the specific problems AIDS poses to women and then outlines the arguments presented in the section's three chapters: "More than Mothers and Whores: Redefining the AIDS Prevention Needs of Women," by Kathryn Carovano; "Women and AIDS in Zimbabwe: The Making of an Epidemic," by Mary T. Bassett and Marvellous Mhloyi; and "Human Immunodeficiency Virus and Migrant Labor in South Africa," by Karen Jochelson, Monyaola Mothibeli, and Jean-Patrick Leger.

Section IV: Solidarity and AIDS

The last segment of the original Special Section "AIDS: The Politics of Survival" is entitled "Solidarity and AIDS." Contending that "AIDS is a crisis of humanity, not 'others' " and that "solidarity is our one defense," the introduction asks the reader—you—to consider what you would do if you or your partner or your relatives or your friends were diagnosed with AIDS, and then discusses the provocative points raised by the section's three chapters: "Human

Immunodeficiency Virus in Cuba: The Public Health Response of a Third World Country," by Sarah Santana, Lily Faas, and Karen Wald; "We are All People Living with AIDS: Myths and Realities of AIDS in Brazil," by Herbert Daniel; and "Global AIDS: Critical Issues for Prevention in the 1990s," by Jonathan M. Mann. Herbert Daniel died of AIDS in 1992.

Section V: The Histories of AIDS

The final section, "The Histories of AIDS," includes a brief introduction and two chapters, one that appeared in the *International Journal of Health Services* after the Special Section was completed, and one that was published in the *American Journal of Public Health.* The introduction describes and questions how history has been invoked to understand and thereby shape the course of the AIDS epidemic. The section's two related chapters, "Thinking and Rethinking AIDS: Implications for Health Policy" and "Understanding AIDS: Historical Interpretations and the Limits of Biomedical Individualism," both by Elizabeth Fee and Nancy Krieger, critique two influential constructions of AIDS—as "gay plague" and as "chronic disease." They explore the underlying assumptions of these understandings of AIDS and argue in favor of a third, more comprehensive approach to the AIDS pandemic.

CONCLUSION

AIDS is a disease that invites commentary, requires research, and demands intervention. Inevitably linking sex and death, passion and politics, it continues to generate controversy. Appearing as a new and lethal infectious disease at a time when the biomedical establishment in the United States had shifted its focus to chronic diseases, AIDS has called into question many of the premises and verities of the biomedical model. This volume helps sharpen these questions and, in doing so, may help us develop more appropriate and effective AIDS prevention strategies.

REFERENCES

1. The unyielding AIDS epidemic [editorial]. *New York Times,* June 17, 1993, p. A16.
2. Cohen, J. Somber news from the AIDS front [news & comment]. *Science* 260: 1712–1713, 1993.
3. Hilts, P. J. Panel criticizes cancellation of study of teenage life. *New York Times,* September 25, 1991, p. A2.
4. Koch, E. Senator Helm's callousness toward AIDS victims. *New York Times,* November 8, 1987, p. 15.
5. Anastos, K., and Marte, C. Women—The missing persons in the AIDS epidemic. *Health/PAC Bull.,* Winter 1989, pp. 6–13.

6. Centers for Disease Control and Prevention. 1993 revisited classification system for HIV infection and expanded surveillance case definition among adolescents and adults. *MMWR* 41(No. RR-17): 1-19, 1992.
7. Francis, D. P. Toward a comprehensive HIV prevention program for the CDC and the nation. *JAMA* 268: 1444–1447, 1992.
8. Centers for Disease Control and Prevention. Update: Acquired immunodeficiency syndrome—United States, 1992. *MMWR* 42: 547–557, 1993.
9. The Panos Institute. *The Hidden Cost of AIDS: The Challenge of HIV to Development.* Panos Publications, London, 1992.
10. Altman, D. *AIDS in the Mind of America: The Social, Political, and Psychological Impact of a New Epidemic.* Anchor Books, Garden City, N.Y., 1987.
11. Shilts, R. *And the Band Played On: Politics, People, and the AIDS Epidemic.* St. Martin's Press, New York City, 1987.
12. National Rainbow Coalition Health Commission. Position Paper on AIDS. September 1987.
13. Issue Brief: Dealing with the AIDS Crisis. Jesse Jackson '88 position statement.

SECTION I

The Politics of AIDS

CHAPTER 1

The Politics of AIDS

Nancy Krieger and Rose Appleman

It is quite obvious that the means and methods used in prevention of disease are those provided by medicine and science. And yet whether these methods are applied or not does not depend on medicine alone but to a much higher extent on the philosophical and social tendencies of the time. . . . From whatever angle we approach these problems, over and over we find that hygiene and public health, like medicine at any age, are but an aspect of the general civilization of the time and are largely determined by the cultural conditions of that time.

H. E. Sigerist, *The Philosophy of Hygiene,* 1933

PREFACE

AIDS, the acquired immune deficiency syndrome, has become both a health crisis and a political crisis of exploding proportions.

The devastating impact of AIDS is being felt worldwide. Within the United States, the disease has inflicted its horrors on two of the country's most stigmatized groups—gay men and intravenous drug users—and has disproportionately affected minority communities. It has done so at a time when the U.S. health care system is already unable to meet the needs of the population, right-wing movements are active throughout the country, and the Reagan administration is engaged in a massive military buildup financed by savage reductions in social spending. Together, these factors have meant that the federal response to AIDS has not just been inadequate: it has been lethal. Countless lives have been unnecessarily lost or jeopardized and critical civil rights have been needlessly threatened.

To counter this damage and to reverse current government policy, the entire progressive movement must make the issue of AIDS a high priority on its political agenda. Only political action will secure an appropriate, scientific and humane response to this devastating disease, because politics permeates every aspect of prevention, research, and treatment. While scientists will be the ones to discover how AIDS can and cannot be spread, or to formulate a vaccine or find a cure, it is politics which will decide whether thousands or millions will die from AIDS. Politics, not science, will determine if people afflicted with AIDS are treated with compassion or repression, just as politics, not science, will decide if the government spends sufficient funds on education and research—or squanders scarce resources on mass testing and quarantine. Finally, politics, not science, will decide if AIDS becomes the disease to sink a crisis-ridden health care system or the spark to create a long-overdue nationalized health care program.

For all these reasons and more, the progressive movement cannot view AIDS as only a "gay issue" or a problem "the experts" must solve. Instead, AIDS has become a critical component of a progressive political program. The struggle against AIDS-related hysteria, discrimination and persecution and the fight for desperately needed AIDS education, research, and treatment have become inextricably linked to the defense of lesbian and gay rights, to the fight against rising attacks on minority communities, and to the struggle to protect and improve the health of the working class as a whole. Because politics will decide the course of AIDS, we must be part of shaping the course of these politics.

The help mobilize the progressive movement toward that end, *Frontline* newspaper sponsored a series of forums entitled "The Politics of AIDS" in various cities across the United States in the summer and fall of 1986. This pamphlet, updated through January 1987, represents an expanded version of the presentations given at those forums.

The authors of this pamphlet have both been active in the fight against AIDS for several years. Nancy Krieger most recently served as research assistant for a policy paper entitled "The Public Health Impact of Proposition 64" (California's LaRouche Initiative) issued jointly by the Schools of Public Health of a number of California universities. She is currently a doctoral candidate in epidemiology at the University of California in Berkeley and has written on AIDS and other health issues in *Science for the People, Monthly Review,* and the *American Journal of Public Health.* Rose Appleman covers the lesbian/gay rights movement and the struggle against AIDS for *Frontline* newspaper and is a member of the Line of March lesbian/gay rights commission. She has also written articles for *Coming Up!* and the *Bay Area Reporter.*

Three other individuals provided substantial assistance in preparing this pamphlet and participated in the forums from which it was developed. These were Douglas Conrad, an activist in the lesbian/gay movement in the San Francisco Bay Area; Diane Jones, a member of the Alliance Against Women's Oppression (AAWO) and a nurse on the AIDS ward at San Francisco General

Hospital, and Melinda Paras, a member of the Line of March national executive committee.

INTRODUCTION

What is AIDS? What are the politics of AIDS?

AIDS is a young white gay man in Orange County, California who is having difficulty breathing. He goes to the local hospital, is diagnosed with pneumocystis pneumonia (one of the characteristic infections afflicting people with AIDS), and is told "We don't take care of this kind of pneumonia here." Packed into a car for a six-hour drive to San Francisco, he's given an oxygen tank—only the oxygen runs out after four hours. When he arrives at the emergency room at 2 a.m., in a city with no friends or family, he can barely breathe. Three months later, he is dead, his name yet another swelling the ranks of the ever-expanding obituary section of the gay newspapers (1).

What is AIDS? What are the politics of AIDS?

AIDS is a child born to one of the 80,000 or so women intravenous drug users (IVDUs) in the New York City area. The child is delivered in central Harlem, a region where 40 percent of the women receive late or no prenatal care, where the infant mortality rate is nearly three times the national average, and where the main hospital recently suffered from a shortage of penicillin for a year-and-a-half because it could not pay its bills. The baby initially undergoes withdrawal from a heroin addiction inherited from her mother. Then, five months later, the child becomes ill with persistent diarrhea. At the hospital they discover that she's not sick with one of the typical poverty-related infectious diseases that plague malnourished inner-city infants. No, the child has AIDS—and with parents unable to care for her, hospitals too crowded to board her, and foster agencies unable to place her, no one knows where or how this child will endure what promises to be a brief, sickly life (2).

What is AIDS? What are the politics of AIDS?

AIDS is the government prediction that, in 1991, health care costs for the expected 145,000 cases will be on the order of $8–16 billion. These huge expenses will be borne disproportionately by cities in which AIDS is most concentrated, such as New York or Jersey City or San Juan or San Francisco (3). Caught between pressures for "cost-containment" and health care costs rising at twice the rate of inflation, just how are these cities to cope with AIDS patients? Where will the hospital beds be found? And how will the costs be met of the multitudes of AIDS patients lacking private health insurance—both those who lost their job-related coverage because they were fired or became too ill to work and then were redlined by private insurance companies, and those who never even had private insurance, either because they were poor enough to be on Medicaid, or if not quite that poor, were among the 35 million people in this country with no health coverage at all (4, pp. 162–168).

What is AIDS? What are the politics of AIDS?

AIDS is the week of June 20, 1986 when, in quick succession, the U.S. Justice Department gave legal sanction to discrimination based on fear of contagion of AIDS, the openly anti-gay and anti-civil liberties LaRouche Initiative secured its place on the California ballot, and the U.S. Supreme Court singled out homosexual sodomy as a crime against both nature and law, citing as evidence both Biblical injunctions and Roman law. Yet this is 1986, in a society which ostensibly sanctions the separation of Church and State.

What is AIDS? What are the politics of AIDS?

As these items indicate, AIDS has become a human tragedy, a health disaster and a political crisis of monumental proportions. Ravaging the ranks of the gay community and striking scores of IVDUs, the disease has placed new and intense demands upon a health care system already unable to meet current needs—especially those of the minority communities from which almost half the cases come. AIDS has exacerbated the political tensions of cities strapped for funds for the most basic human services.

But AIDS is even more than just another disease to add to the chronic ills which burden our society in general and which disproportionately affect minority and working class communities—such as cancer or coronary heart disease or infant mortality. AIDS has a special character in the United States because it is a *communicable* disease which literally burst into the body politic during the first year of the "Reagan Revolution" and which primarily has hit two of the most stigmatized, isolated and disenfranchised groups of our society—gays and IVDUs. As a disease and a social disaster, AIDS has dealt yet another blow to the well-being of the poorer layers of the working class, and has forced both literal and political life-and-death issues onto the day-to-day agenda of the lesbian/gay community. Consequently, the politics of AIDS cannot be understood apart from the fact that AIDS has emerged as a deadly menace in an already frightening period of rising racism, militarism and right-wing reaction.

AIDS: THE FACTS OF THE DISEASE

Because so much of the right's manipulation of the AIDS crisis has been based on a profound distortion of science, countering their agenda first requires knowing a few basic facts about AIDS.[1]

[1] Much of the technical information in this section represents a synthesis of the scientific literature, and is documented in the 1986 report *Confronting AIDS* issued by the Institute of Medicine of the National Academy of Sciences; also see Dr. Peter Selwyn's four-part series entitled "AIDS: What is Now Known" in *Hospital Practice*. The best general overview is provided by the Institute of Medicine's *Mobilizing Against AIDS*. These references, and additional resources, are listed in Appendix I.

AIDS' Impact: From Infection to Death

Though much remains unknown, a great deal has been discovered concerning this terrible disease. AIDS is caused by a virus, initially designated HTLV-III/LAV and now known as HIV, the "human immunodeficiency virus" (5). This virus attacks important regulatory cells in the immune system, the T4 lymphocytes, and it can also infect cells within the brain. By disrupting or destroying the immune system, HIV leaves the body prey to a myriad of opportunistic infections—that is, maladies caused by microorganisms which rarely create disease in persons with healthy immune systems. At present, there is no cure for AIDS, and its destruction of the immune system leads inexorably to the death of the afflicted individual.

For infection to take place, HIV must be *directly* transmitted from an infected person's blood, semen or vaginal secretions into another person's bloodstream; mere contact with skin is not sufficient. Transmission of the virus can happen in several ways: via sexual activity which leads to the tearing of membranes, through the actual exchange of blood (by shared hypodermic needles, transfusion, etc.), or from an infected mother to her unborn or newborn child. In the United States, the two most common routes of transmission are anal receptive sex and the sharing of dirty needles. Having venereal disease (VD) may also increase risk of infection, since sores may facilitate direct contact between exposed blood vessels and infected body fluids (such as semen and perhaps vaginal secretions). Because HIV will enter wherever it finds an opening, whenever particular behaviors are shared with someone who is infectious, it is a democratic creature, no respecter of color, creed or sexual orientation: AIDS is not intrinsically a "gay disease."

Above all, AIDS is *not* a casually transmitted disease: where there is no exchange of body fluids, there can be no transmission. AIDS cannot be spread by a handshake or a hug, by a sneeze or a cough, or by food prepared by a person with AIDS. If AIDS were a highly contagious disease and easily spread by any of these means (or by common insects), the AIDS epidemic would already have spread rapidly throughout the entire U.S. population, instead of occurring primarily in men 20–49 years old. As additional evidence of how hard it is to get AIDS, long-term studies of the family members of AIDS patients—and of the thousands of health care workers who have cared for them—have shown that AIDS cannot be transmitted by touching or even by sharing meals, bathrooms and beds with people who have AIDS. Based on this data, the World Health Organization (6), the United States Public Health Service (PHS) (3) and its Centers for Disease Control (CDC) (7), the Institute of Medicine of the National Academy of Science (4, p. 50), the American Medical Association (8), and the deans of all 23 Schools of Public Health within the United States (9) have all concurred that AIDS cannot be spread by casual contact in the workplace, at school or at home.

Among those individuals who do become exposed to HIV, not all necessarily develop AIDS. Like many other viruses, HIV apparently does not provoke an "all-or-nothing" response. Instead, it seems to induce a spectrum of disease, ranging from infection without any symptoms to full-blown AIDS. Indeed, current evidence suggests that between 25 and 50 percent of those infected proceed to AIDS (usually within two to five years after being exposed to the virus), while another 25 percent or so develop AIDS-Related Complex (ARC) (4, p. 91). These findings imply that perhaps a quarter or more of people infected with HIV might not become ill. Why this is so remains unknown, although researchers suspect that differences in exposures to "co-factors"—possibly other diseases or substances which can depress the immune system, such as various drugs and alcohol—may account for some of the variation in response to HIV infection (10).

Regardless of the ultimate outcome of infection, people exposed to HIV generally develop antibodies to the virus within two to eight weeks after becoming infected. In contrast to most diseases, however, these antibodies are *not* protective; they reflect the presence of HIV, but are incapable of resisting its impact. Moreover, HIV apparently produces a chronic viral infection, such that people carrying the AIDS virus are continually capable of infecting other people. Consequently, AIDS can be spread not just by people who have symptoms of the disease, but also by people who seem healthy but nonetheless are infected with HIV (4, pp. 6, 45).

To establish whether someone has been infected, a series of tests are carried out to see if antibodies to HIV are present in the person's blood. The two procedures used most often are the ELISA and Western Blot tests, with the latter used as a confirmatory procedure in persons who are positive on at least two ELISAs. The extra precaution of using three tests to determine if a person is truly infected is necessary because the implications of a positive test obviously are devastating.

Even more distressing, however, is the actual diagnosis of AIDS—news which currently is equivalent to saying that you have at most two to five years to live. But in addition to the harrowing fact of learning you have a terminal disease, many AIDS patients are also confronted by additional stresses due to the hysteria which surrounds this disease and societal contempt for both gays and IVDUs. An AIDS diagnosis can therefore trigger not only fears of death, but also the fear of being fired or evicted if your disease status becomes known—to which often is added the fear of having to reveal to non-sympathetic family, friends or co-workers that you are gay or have used IV drugs.

Among those who do develop full-blown AIDS, the actual illness can manifest itself in a variety of ways. This is because AIDS is a syndrome, rather than just one disease. Which opportunistic infection people get seems to correlate with their overall health status; among gay men with AIDS, Kaposi's sarcoma is one of the most frequent appearing diseases, while tuberculosis is more common among IVDU AIDS patients (11).

After numerous bouts with several of these infections (and in the absence of any cure), AIDS patients ultimately succumb—often due to a combination of respiratory failure and deteriorating brain function. Typically, this occurs within a year-and-a-half after symptoms first appear, but a few AIDS patients have lived as long as five years after diagnosis. The length of survival apparently depends on several factors: the stage of illness at which they were diagnosed, their state of health prior to developing AIDS, and the quality of treatment they receive. Among IVDUs with AIDS in New Jersey, for example, the average interval between diagnosis and death has been only *18 days.* According to Dr. John Rutledge, a New Jersey state health official, this is because these IVDUs "had very limited contact with our medical health services and they were just coming in and dying, sometimes on the same day" (12). Even under less adverse circumstances, however, minorities and/or IV drug users with AIDS, as compared to more affluent white AIDS patients, have on the whole become sicker and died sooner (11).

Unfortunately, the virus which causes AIDS presents formidable challenges to developing a treatment, cure or vaccine. Not only does it destroy the very immune system the body usually uses to fight off disease, but HIV also directly incorporates itself into the genetic material of the cells it infects. Treatment therefore requires drugs which can suppress replication of the virus and boost the infected person's immune system, as well as be taken for a lifetime (since the virus would never be eliminated from the infected person's body). Finding or developing safe, effective agents which can meet all these criteria will not be easy. Other properties of HIV (such as its high mutation rate) mean that designing a vaccine will also be difficult. As noted by the Institute of Medicine of the National Academy of Sciences, "the development of a vaccine against viruses like HIV has never been seriously attempted, much less achieved" (4, p. 26). Nonetheless, many researchers believe a vaccine might be made by the mid-1990s, though they caution that adequately testing it will take many more years (13).

The Origins of AIDS

At present, it remains unclear as to exactly when, where, or how AIDS entered into the human population. No data support one hypothesis advanced by certain sectors of the U.S. progressive movement: that AIDS is a consequence of CIA-inspired biological warfare. While this hypothesis is sometimes defended on the grounds that it most forcefully targets the political forces responsible for the AIDS crisis, it actually undermines a truly effective critique of the U.S. government's backward role by putting forward a headline-grabbing claim with no substantiation.

Instead, evidence suggests that AIDS first surfaced in Central Africa during the mid-1970s (14, 15). While some have attacked this hypothesis as being intrinsically racist, the actual issue is not *whether* Africa is the continent of origin, but the racist manner in which Africa is being *blamed* for the epidemic. Plausible data, in fact, indicate that HIV may have initially entered the human population through contact with the African Green Monkey, an animal already implicated as host for the Ebola, Marburg and African Yellow Fever viruses. If true, this would not be the first time a virus which was relatively harmless in one species crossed over into a different species only to trigger a new and devastating disease (16).

The International AIDS Crisis and the Consequences of Underdevelopment

AIDS is a disease which knows no borders. Although this analysis focuses on the AIDS crisis in the United States, it is important to stress that AIDS is a worldwide epidemic. The director of the World Health Organization, Dr. Halfdon Mahler, has estimated that as many as 10 million people may already be infected worldwide (17). Not only is the AIDS epidemic spreading in Africa and beginning to take hold in Asia, but cases already abound in Australia and Western Europe, a small but increasing number are being reported in Eastern Europe, and the epidemic is escalating in the Caribbean and Latin America, especially in Haiti, Puerto Rico and Brazil (18).

Depending on whether the country it strikes is developed or underdeveloped, AIDS creates distinct patterns of disease. For example, the male:female case ratio is currently about 13:1 in the United States, yet is nearly 1:1 in several Central African countries. Similarly, the two groups accounting for over 90 percent of AIDS cases in developed countries (gay or bisexual men and IVDUs) apparently represent only a small fraction of AIDS cases reported in most (but not all) underdeveloped countries (14, 15). What accounts for these differences? While some scientists have offered racist rationales ranging from "hidden homosexuality" (4, p. 75) to "exotic sexual practices" (19), in fact the real explanation lies in the economic and political domination of the underdeveloped world by the Western capitalist countries.

The high rates of AIDS which currently plague Central African countries and Haiti are intimately linked to their histories of underdevelopment. As a consequence of distorted, export-oriented economies shaped by centuries of colonial rule, these nations typically confront problems of an increasingly marginalized peasant labor force, the social disintegration of rural society, a growing migrant labor force and the emergence of squalid slums surrounding major cities—with contingent high rates of unemployment and prostitution. Lacking adequate resources to counter the diseases which flourish under such conditions, these countries suffer enormously from malnutrition, malaria, measles, tuberculosis and venereal disease (14, 20–22).

Not accidentally, evidence suggests that these interrelated consequences of underdevelopment may exert a profound influence on the distribution and spread of AIDS. That most AIDS patients from these regions are non-IVDU heterosexuals can probably by linked to poor living conditions in several ways: (*a*) the presence of societal co-factors may increase the likelihood of being exposed to HIV and/or developing AIDS (such as diseases due to poor sanitation, crowded conditions, and malnutrition); (*b*) high rates of other untreated venereal diseases (which may facilitate direct exchange of HIV-infected fluids during vaginal-penile intercourse); (*c*) the lack of adequate blood-screening tests, leading to the transfusion of contaminated blood; and (*d*) the widespread use of unsterilized hypodermic needles (due to lack of supplies and the imported "Western" practice of giving shots for every disease imaginable) (14, 15, 23). Under these conditions, it comes as no surprise that AIDS would spread in a heterosexual population, its transmission facilitated by the disastrous combination of high rates of HIV-infection in prostitutes and their use by traveling businessmen, professionals, tourists and soldiers.

AIDS has added a new and potentially disastrous component to the already jeopardized health status of people living under conditions of underdevelopment. In Haiti, nearly 150 of every 1,000 infants born die before their first birthday (as compared to 10 of every 1,000 among whites and 20 of every 1,000 among blacks in the U.S.), and the average Haitian life expectancy is only 47.5 years (as compared to 75 years for whites and 70 years for blacks in the U.S.) (24–26). AIDS now threatens to make these dismal statistics even more wretched because it is now striking men and women in their prime productive and reproductive years. By posing a severe threat to this critical sector of the population, AIDS threatens not just this generation but generations to come. This is because infected pregnant women can transmit the virus to their unborn children. The sorry fact that perhaps nearly 10 percent of pregnant women in some regions of Central Africa are already infected with HIV (4, p. 262) suggests that the future may well be bleak, populated by an ever-growing number of babies born with AIDS—children who are literally born to die.

The Toll of AIDS in the United States

In the United States, more than 28,000 people have been diagnosed in the five brief years between when AIDS first appeared in 1981 and the fall of 1986. Of those stricken, more than half have already died (27). Evidence suggests an additional one to two million people in the United States are infected, of whom perhaps as many as a third will develop full-blown AIDS. Moreover, in the next five years, the U.S. Public Health Service (PHS) predicts that the number of cases will multiply 10-fold, elevating AIDS to the category of "leading cause of death" in the United States (3). Indeed, by 1991, the PHS estimates that perhaps as many as 270,000 people will have been diagnosed with AIDS, of whom 179,000 will have died—a figure equal to nearly half the total number of U.S. World War II casualties.

At present, gay and bisexual men account for about 65 percent of people stricken by AIDS in the United States, and IVDUs constitute about another 20 percent of diagnosed AIDS cases. An additional 8 percent of AIDS patients are both IVDUs and either gay or bisexual (27). While the AIDS epidemic apparently attained fairly rapid widespread geographic dispersal among gay and bisexual men living in and traveling between the established gay communities located in various East and West Coast cites, the geographic spread of AIDS among IVDUs has proceeded more slowly. Currently, about 80 percent of IVDUs AIDS cases live clustered in New York and New Jersey. This distribution not only suggests that AIDS first entered the IVDU population in the East Coast but also that its spread from one IVDU community to another is hampered by mobility limitations imposed by addiction and living in inner cities.

The remaining 10 percent or so of the other "high risk groups" in the United States are concentrated among hemophiliacs and others dependent upon blood and blood products, as well as among the children and heterosexual partners of people at risk. But while the male:female ratio was initially about 19:1 in the early days of the epidemic, it has declined to less than 13:1—a consequence of the rise in rates of AIDS in women who use IV drugs or are partners of men in high-risk groups.

Heterosexual transmission, however, will probably not become as widespread throughout the United States as it is in underdeveloped regions. This is due to three factors: lower rates of untreated venereal disease, a substantially better level of nutrition and health, and the virtually non-existent use of unsterile hypodermic needles in medical settings. Still, within economically depressed regions—ranging from Belle Glade, Florida to inner-city ghettoes—evidence already indicates that heterosexual transmission may well become a dangerous health problem, leading to AIDS in both adults and newborns (28). The changing complexion of the disease is further revealed by new data which show that, in the large cities of the Northeast, straight IVDUs are the majority of new cases—of whom over 80 percent are minorities (2).

AIDS and Racism: A Deadly Intersection

Despite a barrage of media distortions, AIDS has *never* been a disease afflicting only affluent white gay men. True, AIDS has so far taken its most terrible toll among gay males. But it is critical to stress that neither all people with AIDS nor all gays or lesbians are either white or wealthy. From the beginning of the AIDS crisis, the disease has penetrated both minority and working class communities, and over 40 percent of those afflicted have been people of color, both gay and straight. Currently, blacks and Latinos comprise over half of the people with AIDS in New York, Philadelphia, Baltimore, Detroit, Newark, Miami and Washington, D.C. (29). Nationwide, three-fourths of the women, four-fifths of the children, two-fifths of the men and nine-tenths of the prisoners with AIDS are people of color (see Table 1; Figures 1 and 2) (30).

Approximately one-quarter of gay men with AIDS are minorities—a figure in proportion to the overall racial composition of the cities hit hardest by the disease. But adult gay or bisexual men account for only 40 percent of minorities with AIDS, as compared to 80 percent of whites with AIDS. Of the remaining

Table 1

Percentage distribution of cases of AIDS among adults (age ≥ 15 years), by race and transmission category, as of September 1986[a]

Percent of all cases[b]	Transmission category	White	Black	Hispanic	Other
66.9	Gay/bisexual male	74.3	14.8	10.2	0.7
8.0	Gay/bisexual male and IVDU[c]	64.1	22.1	13.6	0.3
17.6	IVDU[c] only	18.5	51.4	29.8	0.3
0.8	Hemophilia	86.3	5.6	8.1	0.0
0.2	Women whose sexual partner was a bisexual male	47.1	35.2	13.7	3.9
1.1	Heterosexual whose sex partner was an IVDU[c]	14.6	47.8	37.6	0.0
1.8	Blood transfusion	78.3	13.7	5.9	2.1
3.5	Undetermined	35.4	43.7	19.6	1.3
100.0		60.4	24.8	14.2	0.6

[a]Source: Centers for Disease Control. Acquired immunodeficiency syndrome (AIDS) among blacks and Hispanics—United States. *MMWR* 35: 655–666, 1986.
[b]Total number of cases: 24,102.
[c]IVDU = intravenous drug user.

60 percent of people of color who have AIDS and are straight, the vast majority became infected because either they or their lovers used IV drugs. Accordingly, as of September 1986, minority men and women accounted for *over 80 percent* of heterosexual IVDUs with AIDS and for *nearly 85 percent* of non-IVDU heterosexuals with AIDS whose main risk factor was being the sexual partner of a person who used IV drugs (30).

The disproportionate concentration of people of color among these risk groups clearly is a consequence of the deadly translation of racism to poverty and subsequent rates of drug abuse and ill health. Furthermore, as in the case of underdeveloped nations, this distribution of cases bodes ill for future generations. The sorry fact that black women account for 50 percent of all women with AIDS in the United States, while Latinas comprise another 20 percent, has already yielded a new dismal statistic: of 350 children diagnosed with AIDS as of September 1986, over 80 percent were minorities (30).

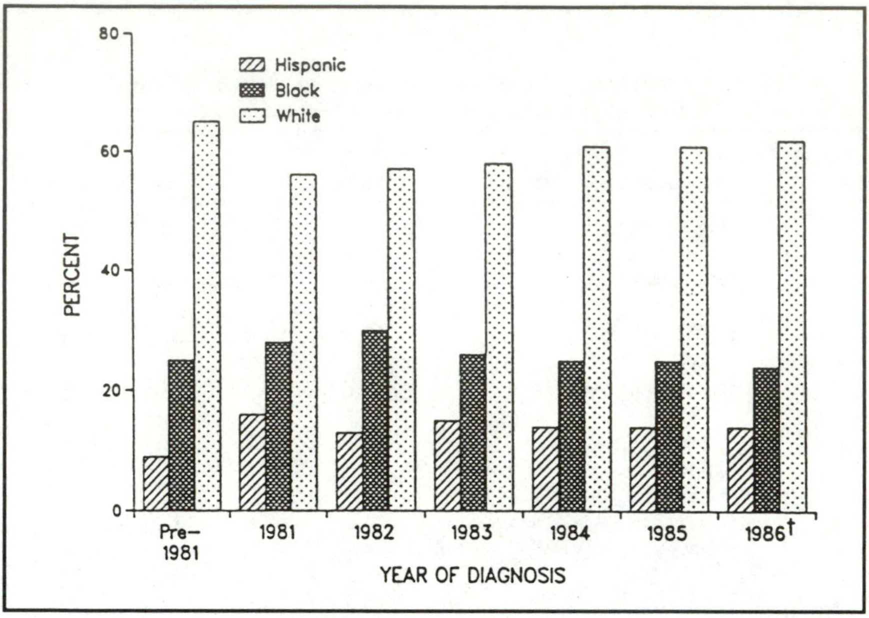

Figure 1. Percentage of acquired immunodeficiency syndrome (AIDS) cases [reported as of September 8, 1986, and excluding 153 AIDS patients (<1 percent) of other race], by year of diagnosis and race—United States, pre-1981–1986. †Incomplete year. Source: Centers for Disease Control. Acquired immunodeficiency syndrome (AIDS) among blacks and Hispanics—United States. *MMWR* 35: 655–666, 1986.

The collective impact of AIDS on the overlapping gay and minority communities has been profound. In cities where the crisis is most acute, AIDS has further endangered access to health care. The monumental cost and strain of caring for AIDS patients has fallen heaviest on public hospitals, already overburdened and ill-equipped to serve those with limited resources. In the regions where the lesbian/gay population is most concentrated, almost everyone knows someone who has died. If ever a disease demanded a massive, nationally organized and compassionate response, AIDS would be the one—and yet the reality has been the very opposite.

THE SOCIAL, SCIENTIFIC, AND POLITICAL RESPONSE TO AIDS

The societal response to AIDS has been as complex and contentious as it has been callous. Pervading the reactions of the public at large has been an utter contempt, if not hatred, for gays and IVDUs. Equally explicit has been open support for the view that these groups either "deserved" to get AIDS or somehow

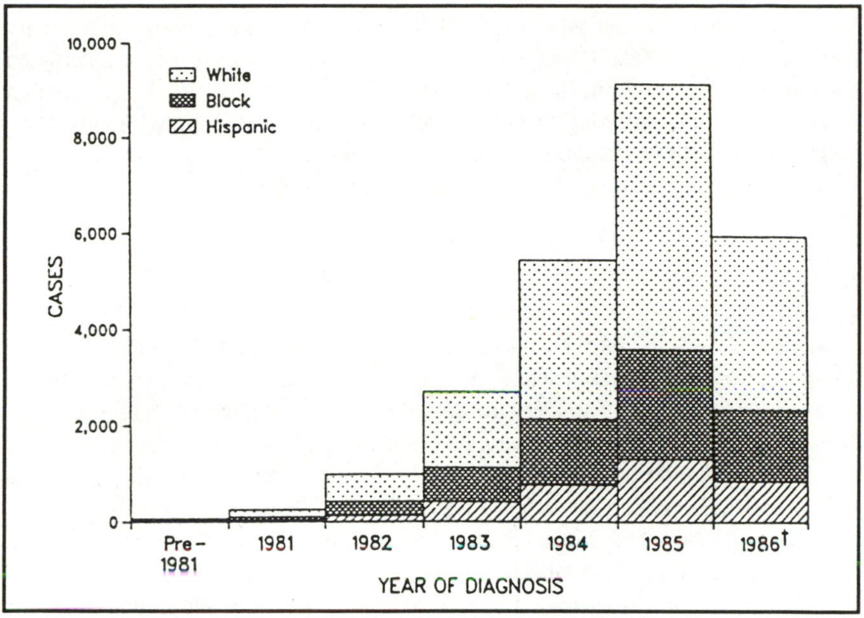

Figure 2. Acquired immunodeficiency syndrome (AIDS) cases [reported as of September 8, 1986, and excluding 153 AIDS patients (<1 percent) of other race], by year of diagnosis and race—United States, pre-1981–1986. †Incomplete year. Source: Centers for Disease Control. Acquired immunodeficiency syndrome (AIDS) among blacks and Hispanics—United States. *MMWR* 35: 655–666, 1986.

have brought this disease upon themselves via their "deviant lifestyles." Moreover, these attitudes—combined with U.S. society's strong aversion to dealing frankly with the fact that AIDS is, among other things, a sexually transmitted disease—have been shared by scientists and politicians alike, thereby profoundly affecting the types of research conducted and policies propounded. With the common question being "how can this epidemic be controlled?", these different sectors have each offered answers in accord with their basic—and often backward—beliefs about drug abuse, gays, and sexuality in general.

At the same time, the societal response to AIDS has reflected more than just prevailing social attitudes or concerns about the implications of the epidemic for the health of the populace. Just as the public reaction has been affected by the active organizing of the New Right, so too have the scientific and political responses to AIDS been influenced by factors beyond the features of the disease itself. These include not only the ways in which U.S. capitalism affects the nature and direction of scientific research, but also the current crisis of the health care system and the huge military buildup that characterizes the Reagan era. With the epidemic erupting in a society already embroiled in bitter battles over social vs.

military spending—fights which not only have pitted working class and minority communities against the Reagan administration but which have also exacerbated tactical differences within the ruling class over the best way to "keep America strong"—it is not surprising that the AIDS crisis has become an extremely symbolic, as well as cruelly concrete, social issue. Together, these crucial and diverse factors have jointly shaped the continually changing social, scientific and political response to AIDS.

The Social Response

Despite the deepening scientific understanding of AIDS, public hysteria regarding this disease has reached massive epidemic proportions. In part, this is because hysteria is a characteristic complication of epidemics, and when the disease rages for long enough, the panic finds a scapegoat. For example, the Black Death—the bubonic plague which wiped out nearly one-third of Europe in the 1400s—was blamed on the Jews, many of whom were consequently pilloried and burned at the stake. More recently, the outbreak of the plague in San Francisco in the early 1900s occurred during a time of rank anti-Chinese sentiment, such that the epidemic was wrongly blamed on the Chinese and Chinatown was quarantined.

Hysteria, Hatred and Victim-Blaming. Like any other epidemic, AIDS has its scapegoats. Yet what has given AIDS hysteria its particular virulence is that it feeds upon not only a dread of death, but a fear and loathing of homosexuals and a repugnance for IVDUs as well. Already depicted and perceived as sick, depraved, and deserving of discrimination, members of these two groups now face the charge that they are the culprits, not victims, of this devastating disease.

Indeed, the widespread public condemnation of homosexual activity and IV drug abuse has thoroughly distorted the nature and causes of these two types of behavior—as well as the differences between them. Both are portrayed by powerful forces in government, the media and the church as "sick" and "deviant" behavior, as expressions of individual pathology. But this picture is thoroughly mistaken. In the first place, being gay or lesbian is just as legitimate, valid, and socially healthy as being straight. IV drug abuse, in contrast, is destructive and unhealthy, but it must be addressed as a *social,* not an individual, phenomenon. Widespread drug addiction is a consequence of blighted lives brought to degradation and despair by an extraordinarily violent society suffused with rotting inner cities, racism, soaring unemployment, profound alienation, and the wholesale commercialization of commodities geared towards making you "feel good" via a "quick fix." And until the social forces which produce addiction in the first place are eliminated, humane treatment of the drug user is the only sensible approach. But, with AIDS now regarded as manifest "proof" of the profoundly "diseased" and "decadent" nature of "queers" and "junkies," reactionary calls to remove gays and IVDUs from the midst of so-called "civil society" have truly reached new depths.

Not surprisingly, in a society undergoing a New Right revival and already prone to victim-blaming explanations of disease causation, AIDS has more often inspired the parable of Sodom and Gomorrah than it has that of the Good Samaritan. In 1986, Reverend Charles Stanley, head of this nation's largest Protestant denomination (the 14.3 million-member Southern Baptist Convention) declared that "AIDS is God indicating his displeasure" toward homosexuality (31). In a somewhat more secular vein, Patrick Buchanan—Reagan's arch right-wing advisor—characterized AIDS as nature's revenge for unnatural sex: "The poor homosexuals, they have declared war upon nature, and now nature is exacting an awful retribution" (32). That prominent spokespersons for major faiths and the executive branch of the federal government can openly utter such damning pronouncements and yet provoke little outcry is a telling indictment of how strongly the stigmatization of high-risk groups has marked the social response to AIDS.

AIDS-Related Discrimination and Violence. Given these conditions, the hysteria and hostility inspired by AIDS has literally reached from cradle to grave, affecting every major arena of social life: school, work, housing, health care, even death itself. Rather than let their children attend classes known to "harbor" AIDS students, thousands of parents have boycotted schools. Private and federal employers have fired people with AIDS and have dismissed or refused to hire gays and others whom they suspect have or are at risk for AIDS. Landlords have used fear of AIDS as a pretext to evict or to refuse to rent to tenants they suspect might be gay. Insurance companies in numerous states have begun using "lifestyle" questions to try to screen out gay men, while others have sought legislation to permit use of the AIDS-antibody test to screen applicants directly. Moreover, not only are blood-banks experiencing dangerous shortages because of a thoroughly irrational fear of contracting AIDS via donating blood, but nurses have refused to care for AIDS patients, para-medics have refused to give artificial resuscitation to gays and others whom they think might be infectious for AIDS, and undertakers have even refused to bury people who have died of AIDS.

Fear of AIDS, combined with repugnance for those whom it strikes, has also led to widespread support for gross violations of civil rights, as well as to an increase in outright violent attacks on lesbians and gays. A December 1985 survey of 2,000 people in Los Angeles indicated that over half approved of mandatory identity cards for people who have AIDS or test positive for AIDS antibody; even more favored quarantining AIDS patients and making it a crime for them to have sex with anyone (33). In addition, 15 percent supported tattooing people who test positive or have AIDS—an idea which William F. Buckley subsequently proposed in the op-ed pages of the *New York Times* (34).

Turning these beliefs into action, during the summer of 1986 a San Francisco teenager physically assaulted a gay man with AIDS—and then had the audacity to call the San Francisco AIDS Foundation to ask if his brutal attack put him at risk for developing AIDS (35). And demonstrating that this was not an isolated event, the National Gay and Lesbian Task Force's report on "Anti-Gay Violence and Victimization in 1985" documented a rise not only in individual anti-gay acts explicitly linked to AIDS but also in anti-gay, anti-AIDS actions carried out by organized hate groups—such as the Ku Klux Klan, the Order, the Nazis and the White Patriotic Party (36).

While the general social response to AIDS has not been characterized by such outright violent attacks, it nonetheless has been marked by more hostility than compassion. Yet, to assume that the response will inevitably grow more vitriolic may be in error. A recent survey of residents in New York, London and San Francisco suggested that appropriate education campaigns can eventually induce the public to replace its initial high levels of ignorance, fear and strong anti-gay attitudes with a more informed and less reactionary stance (37). And, in a critical vote on AIDS policy in the November 1986 election, Californians defeated the LaRouche AIDS Quarantine Initiative by an almost 3:1 margin. Together, these two limited tests of public opinion indicate that the reactionary response engendered by the combination of fear of AIDS plus revulsion for its "high risk groups," though certainly potent, can be combatted and curbed.

The Scientific Response

The scientific community's reaction to AIDS was also initially hostile and inadequate, yet is now showing stronger signs of change than the general public's. This shift is due in part to scientists' growing understanding of the disease and their recognition that the spread of AIDS cannot be halted without cooperation of those at risk. It is also, however, a consequence of the ways in which the social and scientific responses to AIDS mutually create, condition and transform each other.

The Production of Scientific Knowledge. When evaluating the scientific response to AIDS, it is important first to stress that a disease like AIDS would make even the most rapid scientific progress seem agonizingly slow. The nature of the AIDS virus and what it does to the immune system requires that vast amounts of research must be conducted at the cutting edge of contemporary scientific knowledge. Without recent developments in molecular biology, virology, recombinant DNA technology, epidemiology, biostatistics and computer sciences, it would have been impossible for scientists to have discovered, isolated, characterized and created a test for the virus which causes AIDS in the space of only four years. Results simply cannot be produced on demand: determining why some people who test positive get AIDS and others remain well, or discovering how to make a vaccine or develop a treatment or a cure, are extremely difficult scientific questions. And answers to any of these would represent an extraordinarily important contribution to humanity as a whole.

It would, however, be a gross error to assume that the scientific process has been without flaws, or that it has been limited solely by obstacles within the realm of science. Quite the contrary, social, political and economic factors have negatively affected scientific work on AIDS from the outset.

One such factor was the initial reluctance of the U.S. scientific community to tackle a disease first perceived as primarily affecting gay men; interest picked up only when researchers realized that AIDS provided a unique opportunity to study how the immune system works. Underlying both of these impulses were the ways in which social conditions shape scientific inquiry in this country. U.S. scientists, as relatively privileged members of the society in which they live and work, obviously share many of this country's dominant social beliefs—be they about gays, sexuality, minorities, IVDUs, and the nature of Third World societies, or the conviction that health problems can best be solved by biomedical or technological, rather than social, interventions. These attitudes in turn influence both the types of questions scientists ask and the interventions they propose, and they have served to impede progress toward understanding and fighting AIDS.

The Pursuit of Prestige and Profit. Ironically, as soon as it became clear that AIDS would be one of the "hot" research topics of the 1980s, new problems arose—this time due to rising rivalry rather than complacent neglect. Reports of tampering, sabotage, and deliberate delay of research at the Centers for Disease Control (CDC), for example, prompted a congressional inquiry in the fall of 1986. That investigation uncovered high levels of rancor and low levels of scientific productivity resulting from a combination of administrative mismanagement and scientific feuding (38). At stake not only are prestige and potential Nobel prizes, but patents and profit as well.

Perhaps best exemplifying this problem is the current [1986] dispute between French and U.S. researchers over who first discovered the virus which causes AIDS. In this fight, the French have been seeking to secure recognition of their "contributions to AIDS research and related commercial rights"—that is, the patent rights to the AIDS antibody test, which is expected to accrue yearly revenues in excess of $5 million. French scientists were, in fact, the first to isolate (in May 1983) the virus which causes AIDS, which they named "LAV" and which they shared with the U.S. researchers. But a U.S. team was the first to develop (in May 1984) a technique for growing the virus in bulk for research purposes, utilizing a virus which they independently had isolated from U.S. AIDS patients and which they called "HTLV-III." The U.S. scientists subsequently took out a patent on the blood test in behalf of the U.S. government, a move which the French contested and finally took to court. With the suit dismissed in July 1986 (on the grounds of "no jurisdiction"), the tension between these two important research groups has only been intensified and prospects for future collaboration remain poor (39).

The profit motive may also pose as serious an obstacle to the development of a vaccine as the scientific challenge itself. Apart from complaining about research costs, the pharmaceutical industry has clearly indicated it will not manufacture an AIDS vaccine unless guaranteed a large enough market to ensure profitable returns and also freedom from liability suits (13). With several major manufacturers citing rising insurance costs as justification for halting production of critical vaccines, a spokeswoman for Genentech—one of the three major biotechnology companies working on an AIDS vaccine—bluntly stated: "no company in the country will take a new vaccine to market unless a product liability bill protecting them is passed" (40). Faced with such pressure, in November 1986 Congress approved (and Reagan signed) a "no fault" compensation bill which will be financed by a new excise tax on sales of existing vaccines. Moreover, to meet the companies' demands for a guaranteed market, the government may have to purchase specified amounts of the AIDS vaccine once it is produced. With the public hit twice to foot the bill—once as consumers and once as taxpayers—it is clear that in an economy where profits, not health, determine what will be manufactured, the production of an AIDS vaccine will depend as much on politics as it will on science.

Social Consequences of Scientific Definitions and Recommendations. The problematic nature of the scientific response to AIDS has not been solely a consequence of the drive for glory or money. Instead, it has often been expressed through the social and political implications of what, on the surface, seem like "scientific" questions—ranging from the definition of the disease and who is at risk of acquiring it to whether antibody tests should be routinely offered and how drug trials should be conducted.

Consider, for example, the term "AIDS" itself. In 1982 the CDC constructed a narrow definition which deliberately and—at that time—appropriately focused on the severe and terminal stage of the disease. This approach not only served to ensure accurate tracking of a new disease (which, at that point, was defined by exclusion, since the virus which caused AIDS had not yet been discovered) but also reflected the relative level of ignorance of the natural history of the disease. Yet, though this categorization had primarily been intended to meet epidemiological criteria, it quickly started to serve another crucial purpose: defining who was or was not eligible for Social Security disability benefits for AIDS.

As soon as it became clear that many were becoming ill without developing the opportunistic infections described in the CDC definition, a clash over terms erupted. On one side stood people suffering from these alternate manifestations of AIDS who were fighting for their rights to receive disability benefits, while on the other were researchers insisting that the scientific definition of "AIDS" must be kept consistent. Though most of the medical community eventually accepted the term "ARC" to describe these patients whose symptoms were not within the CDC's initial narrow definition, the government has continued to use the CDC's restricted guidelines to establish who could receive disability benefits. Consequently, people with ARC—no matter how sick, and regardless of whether they had lost or been fired from their jobs—are not automatically eligible for "AIDS" benefits, and instead must go through a grueling process to obtain them. Although the CDC finally expanded its classification of AIDS in 1986 to recognize the full spectrum of disease (41), it remains to be seen what impact this will have on disability eligibility criteria.

"Risk Groups," Haitians, and "Risk Behaviors." The CDC's definition of "risk group" has been equally charged. Its initial designation of Haitians as a "risk group," for example, was an act which can only by chalked up to racism. This measure provoked widespread discrimination against Haitians in the United States and devastated the tourist-dependent Haitian economy. Its alleged "scientific justification" was that a substantial number of Haitians with AIDS were non-IVDU heterosexuals. Bolstering this reasoning was the CDC's fixation on AIDS as a "gay" disease, such that it discounted the possibility of heterosexual transmission and instead labeled *all* Haitians mysteriously "at risk."

As evidence of the tenacity of this ingrained belief, the CDC clung to the category "Haitian" despite data which—as early as 1984—showed that all Haitians were *not* at equal risk and that heterosexual transmission clearly occurred in Africa (24, 42). It was not until July 1985 that the CDC finally removed "Haitian" as a risk group, acknowledging that Haitians could not be distinguished from other groups on the basis of unique risk factors (43, p. 18). And it was not until one year later, in August 1986, that the CDC finally moved non-IVDU heterosexual Haitians out of the "no identified risk" category and placed them instead into the recently expanded and more appropriate "Heterosexual Cases" risk group (which now includes "persons without other identified risks who were born in countries in which heterosexual transmission is believed to play a major role") (44, 45).

Another raging controversy about "risk groups" has been whether the CDC should refer to them at all, or should speak of "high-risk behaviors" instead. While the CDC and most researchers treat the term "risk group" as a way of describing the sectors most represented among people with AIDS, many gay organizations have opposed the use of "risk group" for two reasons. One is that it perpetuates the stigmatization of gays as a diseased or deviant group. The other is that it ignores the risk faced by men who occasionally have sex with other men yet do not identify as gay. Along these lines, the American Red Cross found that it received less antibody-positive blood after it changed its guidelines and begun urging *all* men who had sex with other men—rather than just homosexual men—not to donate (46). To turn the debate into a question of "either/or," however, is both misleading and potentially dangerous. "High risk behaviors" among "high risk groups," for example, do carry more risk than similar behaviors among "low risk groups" precisely because the AIDS virus is more common among members of "high" as compared to "low" risk groups. Consequently, while the CDC designation is not complete, it also is not wrong, for it provides necessary information needed to design appropriate intervention programs.

To Test or Not to Test: Antibody Status and Experimental Drugs. The scientific establishment and gay organizations have also clashed on questions surrounding use of the antibody test. This procedure was initially and appropriately designed to screen the blood supply. Bitter disputes, however, immediately developed over the question of testing individuals. These disputes centered on issues of confidentiality, the meaning of the test, and its relation to reducing HIV-transmission. Only after considerable protest did the CDC and public health officials accept the fact that the social consequences of even *taking* a test—that is, the implications of being labeled a "queer" or a "junkie"—meant that antibody tests *must* be either anonymous or thoroughly confidential. And only after additional agitation was it established that tests *must not* be offered without pre- and post-test counselling, given the potentially devastating effects of learning you test positive. Moreover, many in the gay community have bristled at the commonly expressed view that unless gay men definitively know their antibody status, they would not adopt "safe sex" practices. Although these tensions are far from resolved—indeed, in March 1986 the PHS recommended testing for *all* persons in any of the risk group categories (47)—at least consensus has been reached on one critical point: in addition to the confidentiality and counselling criteria, testing should be done only on a voluntary basis (4, p. 15).

In a related controversy, public health officials stirred up a storm of protest when they suggested that the same type of contact tracing employed for syphilis and other sexually transmitted diseases should be carried out with the partners of people who either have AIDS or test positive for the AIDS antibody. Their rationale was that by notifying and perhaps testing these exposed partners, it would be possible to encourage them to practice "safe sex" and thereby reduce the risk of unknowingly spreading the infection to additional partners. Other scientists, however, have joined with the gay community in pointing out that in areas where the prevalence of HIV-infection is so high that the likelihood of tracing exposure to any given individual is extremely low—as in San Francisco or New York City—contact tracing would be totally ineffective, and hence constitute an unwarranted and extreme invasions of privacy.

Many public health officials nonetheless believe that contact tracing could be an important tool in limiting the spread of AIDS in regions where only a handful of cases have been reported—such as Idaho and Montana, each of which had documented fewer than five AIDS cases by April 1986. While contact tracing perhaps might be warranted in these states and other regions with extremely low rates of AIDS, it is clear that such programs must be conducted on a voluntary basis only, with strict and severe penalties imposed for any violation of confidentiality or unauthorized disclosure of the names of the contacts. Moreover, contact tracing cannot be permitted to serve as a substitute for risk-reduction education. With consensus that these conditions must be rigorously met before implementation can occur, resolution of this issue will probably be reached soon (4, pp. 119–120).

Just as the debates about antibody testing and contact tracing started subsiding, however, another simmering dispute finally boiled over: who should have access to and how to conduct tests of experimental drugs. The bulk of the scientific establishment has argued in favor of strict adherence to the Food and Drug Administration rules which permit experimental drugs to be used only under experimental conditions. In marked contrast, many of those afflicted with full-blown AIDS, along with several prominent investigators (such as Dr. Mathilde Krim of the American Foundation for AIDS Research) have countered that it is inhumane to deny those who otherwise inevitably will die the opportunity to use any drug they can, even if they are not enrolled in a clinical trial (48). Meanwhile, in desperation, others within the gay community "tired of just being to told to wait while we die" have organized their own trials of illegal drugs (49). The active intervention of people with AIDS, supporters from the gay community and certain progressive sections of health workers has now won an important victory on this point. In a virtually unprecedented step, a panel of medical advisors to the FDA recommended (in January 1987) that azidothymidine (AZT)—the first drug of the many tested which seems to prolong the lives of AIDS patients—be licensed even though the full clinical testing of this drug has not been completed. If the FDA does license AZT, the practical implication is that any doctor will be able to give this drug to any AIDS patient, whether or not the patient is enrolled in an experimental drug trial. In addition, agreement now exists that as soon as any treatment shows some promise, future drugs must be tested against it, rather than against placebos (4, p. 219).

Towards an Appropriate Scientific Response. The spotted history of the scientific reaction to AIDS reveals one consistent pattern: almost every new discovery—be it about detecting the virus or treating the disease—has prompted heated debates between the scientific community and those with or at risk for AIDS. Because of political organizing and activism of people with AIDS and the lesbian/gay community, however, divisions between these two groups are today growing smaller and getting resolved more quickly and in more progressive directions. Indeed, as indicated by the major 1986 report issued by the prestigious Institute of Medicine of the National Academy of Sciences, agreement has been reached on several cardinal principles: halting the spread of AIDS will require a massive federally led and funded explicit education program regarding "safe sex" and "clean works" (and particularized to each of the high-risk groups) plus the provision of more IVDU treatment programs; substantially more resources must be devoted to biomedical and social science research on AIDS and should be coordinated at a federal level; discrimination against persons with or at risk for AIDS must be outlawed; and coercive measures to control the epidemic—such as forced antibody testing or quarantine—must not be permitted (4, pp. 1–3). Unfortunately, what has brought these two sectors closer together is not just an increased understanding of the disease, but rather their common opposition to the simultaneously inadequate and reactionary response of the federal government.

The Political Response

In any public health crisis involving a severe communicable disease, the state clearly must consider the health of the nation as a whole as well as the individual rights of infected and ill persons. While many political considerations apart from the disease will affect how the government reacts—such as its ability or willingness to devote resources to public health measures—its response must of necessity be guided by one central concern: how dangerous is the epidemic and how can it be controlled?

In contrast to non-contagious diseases whose impact can often be localized, no government can afford to let a lethal communicable disease get out of control. Once the state is forced to acknowledge the seriousness of the threat, it cannot afford to adopt the attitude of "let them all die"—even if the disease is primarily striking the poorest or most stigmatized sectors of society—because it cannot permit a deadly epidemic to imperil the entire population. But while the history of public health is filled with examples of governments finally acting to install sewer systems and clean water supplies in working class neighborhoods once they realized that without such measures, cholera and other water-borne diseases of the poor would continue to infect the rich, it also contains its share of leper colonies and persecution of the sick. Consequently, the question is not simply *whether* the state will respond to an epidemic, but *how* it will react.

Confronted with a lethal, sexually transmitted, blood-borne illness like AIDS and the panic it induces, a government has two options. It can allocate substantial funds to education, research and treatment and mount a massive campaign to allay public fears and prevent discrimination—the approach most scientists believe is the only one capable of halting this epidemic. Or it can permit hysteria to go unchecked, sanction the moralistic view that AIDS is the "punishment which fits the crime," and thereby create a social climate conducive to minimal research efforts and maximum utilization of coercive measures to contain the spread of the disease. And which path a government chooses—that of reason or repression—ultimately has nothing to do with science and everything to do with politics.

The Reagan Administration's Dangerous Response to AIDS. If the Reagan administration were only pursuing a course of outrageous neglect, as in the case of infant mortality and other poverty-related and "containable" health problems which disproportionately plague minority and working class communities, the

AIDS crisis would still be extremely grim. Unfortunately, it has exacerbated an already untenable situation by being in the forefront of promoting a very political, thoroughly reactionary and completely anti-scientific program to deal with AIDS, one which has given free license to state and local governments to do the same. Premised upon the notion of protecting "innocent citizens" and thoroughly shaped by backward attitudes toward gays and IVDUs, the federal government's program has consisted of an exceedingly dangerous combination of malignant neglect and opportunistic intervention. The results have been nothing less than lethal.

When, for example, was the first time the Reagan administration formally called on its experts to halt what they termed "an epidemic of fear?" That time was September 1985, a full four *years* after AIDS first appeared. What prompted this belated response? It wasn't a belated surfacing of compassion, but the fact that AIDS-provoked school boycotts were beginning to get out of hand. And what was the essential message of the press conference which the administration finally held? The government assured the U.S. people that there was no need to panic because AIDS remained confined to the gay and IVDU population (50). Or, put another way, as long as only "queers" and "junkies" were dying, as long as only black and Latino babies accounted for more than 80 percent of the infants succumbing to AIDS, the Reagan administration apparently thought AIDS was under control.

Moreover, what prompted the usually right-wing Surgeon General C. Everett Koop to issue his October 1986 report on AIDS, one which finally acknowledged that AIDS actually did pose a threat to the nation's health? It wasn't any sudden scientific breakthrough, but rather the pressing political need to scoop the Institute of Medicine of the National Academy of Science's forthcoming scathing critique of the government's "dangerously inadequate" response to AIDS (51).

Fights over Research Funding. From the outset the Reagan administration has given the unmistakable signal that the AIDS epidemic did not merit a serious response. In 1982 and 1983, rather than ask Congress to finance AIDS research, the Department of Health and Human Services (DHHS) robbed Peter to pay Paul: nearly 95 percent of all federal AIDS research money came from funds already allocated to other important health research projects (52). The same practice, though to a lesser degree, continues to this day. Moreover, not only did it take almost two years and 2,000 cases for DHHS to declare AIDS the nation's "number one health priority," but the Department's commitment was so meager that in February 1985, the Congressional Office of Technology Assessment (OTA)—usually known for exposing the various ways in which our tax dollars routinely get wasted—was forced to rebuke DHHS publicly for refusing to ask Congress for the research funds its own scientists were requesting! (53, p. 7).

The battle over AIDS budget proposals for 1986 and 1987 is even more revealing. Even considering how little the federal government spends on health research—health sciences typically receive less than 10 percent of the nearly $50 billion allocated to research each year, while more than 65 percent is given to the military (54)—AIDS funding has been inadequate. In 1986, the very same year the Reagan administration pushed through a "war on drugs" bill to the tune of $1.7 billion, it proposed only $85 million for AIDS research—less than 10 percent of the amount of money allocated to the National Cancer Institute (55). Yet AIDS is now cutting nearly as many years off the lives of single men in their prime working years as is cancer.

In the face of this obvious health crisis, Congress proposed an alternate AIDS budget which *nearly tripled* the sum Reagan was willing to spend; the final amount settled on was $234 million. And to put even this sum in perspective, the Institute of Medicine has concluded that by 1990 the government must commit at least $1 billion annually in *new* research funds, and noted that even this amount "may prove to be insufficient" to prevent the spread of HIV and to cure AIDS (4, pp. 248–249).

Battles over Risk-Reduction Education. Federal foot-dragging on research funding has been nothing short of criminal, wasting precious time and even more precious lives. Yet even in the absence of sufficient funding, scientists have established that risk-reduction education is the most effective—in fact the *only*—measure available to halt the spread of AIDS. Nor is the call for such education based simply on the belief that such intervention *might* work; proof that it does already exists. One San Francisco study of gay men, for example, found that the rate of new HIV infections dropped from 18 percent in 1983–1984 to only 4 percent in 1985, a change the researchers attributed to the adoption and popularization of "safe sex" guidelines (56). Comparable results—including declines in other sexually transmitted diseases—have also been reported in studies conducted in New York, Los Angeles, Chicago, Baltimore and Pittsburgh (57–59).

Similarly, other investigators have found that IVDUs are seeking to reduce their risk of getting AIDS by cutting down on sharing their "works" and attempting to obtain sterile needles. This trend is so strong that even drug dealers are moving to capitalize on it. In New York City, many are now successfully hawking repackaged, dirty needles at a *higher* price by promoting them as if they were "new." And beyond this, the fear of AIDS has further motivated many IVDUs to seek treatment for their addiction—only to be faced with the brutal reality that the demand for drug treatment programs far exceeds the supply.

The obvious response to these and other findings would be massive federally sponsored risk-reduction campaigns to promote "safe sex" and to treat addicts, as well as to teach IVDUs in the interim how to clean their "works" and to provide free sterile needles. Indeed, such measures have been endorsed by the National Academy of Sciences' 1986 report—which called for a sexually explicit, frank "major educational campaign" geared toward both the population at large and "high risk" groups, as well as "more methadone and other treatment programs," and "easier access to sterile, disposable needles and syringes" (4, pp. 9–13). The Academy also strongly insisted that "the most fundamental obligation for AIDS education rests with the federal government, which alone is situated to develop and coordinate" such a program (4, p. 104).

Even more to the point, such risk-reduction programs have *already been enacted* by other governments. In March 1986, for example, Switzerland distributed a free 10-page pamphlet on AIDS, printed in all four of the country's official languages, to *every* household in the nation (46). And in November 1986, the British government announced plans for an explicit $7 million national leaflet and advertising campaign to combat AIDS (60). Finally, Norway—a country with only a handful of AIDS patients—recently initiated an even bolder program targeting AIDS as a venereal disease of concern to all. Norway is doing this by utilizing billboards which are neither small nor subtle. One, displayed prominently in downtown Oslo, is several stories tall and depicts a fully erect penis dressed in a condom, with a little bowtie at the base, bearing the slogan: "Always Be Dressed for the Best. Be Prepared. AIDS is a Venereal Disease."

Likewise, to reduce both AIDS and addiction among IVDUs, the Municipal Health Service in Amsterdam has instituted a needle-exchange and free condom program, while the Australian AIDS Task Force has opted to give free sterile needles and syringes to IVDUs. Both countries have also successfully encouraged addicts to enter treatment programs (46, 61). True, nothing short of massive social change will stem the forces which lead to drug addiction in the first place, but in the interim, these efforts can help curtail the spread of AIDS among IVDUs, their sexual partners and their children. And, as noted even by the editors of the *New York Times,* "with a quarter of New York's addicts already likely to die from AIDS, a policy of doing nothing will permit the death of thousands more" (62).

Yet what has been the response of the Reagan administration? It has been to stonewall such efforts and to give a green light to lower levels of government to act likewise. Sanctioning the view that the threat of AIDS and the ravages of addiction serve as appropriate deterrents to illegal and so-called "immoral behavior," the administration apparently thinks that ignorance will halt the spread of AIDS—just as the New Right believes banning sex education will curtail teen pregnancy. Along these lines, the CDC and other public health officials have already censored AIDS pamphlets for being "too explicit" (as if people are supposed to know what "safe" and "unsafe" sex are without any hints, or how to sterilize needles without any instructions). And when the U.S. Public Health Service was questioned about the possibility of adapting the Australian AIDS IVDU program for use here, the director of its Office of Public Affairs, Shellie Langer, replied: "We don't have any evidence it would help the problem and our experts say the experience of other countries is not applicable here" (60). Or, as the Bronx District Attorney Mario Merolo put it, when asked about supplying sterile needles to addicts, "Drug abuse must . . . not be made risk free" (63).

Given this orientation, it should come as no surprise that the Reagan administration has drastically underfunded AIDS education efforts. In 1984, the PHS's Office of Public Affairs spent only $200,000 on AIDS educational materials, and in 1985 it reduced this small sum to $120,000 (53, p. 44)—in an era when one page of advertising in a major newspaper can cost $25,000, and when a major corporation will routinely spend $50 million simply to market a new detergent. The following year, 1985, only 5 percent of the federal AIDS budget went to education. When Congress proposed this be raised to 20 percent (or $68 million) in the 1986 budget, the Reagan administration sought to cut this amount by a third (64). In stark contrast, the Institute of Medicine, charging that "the present level of AIDS-related education is woefully inadequate," has warned that by 1990 the federal government must allocate *$1 billion per year* for "education and other public health expenditures" (4, pp. 97, 133). To an administration which clearly values our lives less than a company values its soap, however, combatting AIDS is apparently not worthwhile if such a battle requires explicit discussion of gay sex or IV drug use.

Passing the Buck on Providing Care. But if the Reagan administration will not take serious actions to stop the spread of AIDS, what of its efforts to assist in the care of those afflicted? While many of the problems AIDS patients face are characteristic of health care under U.S. capitalism—particularly how to pay for it—people with AIDS also constitute a patient population with unique needs, ranging from extensive counselling and practical support to home-based hospice care and the provision of housing. In a period of extensive pressure for cost-containment and retrenchment in federal appropriations for Medicaid, coverage of health care expenses for AIDS patients—of whom 40 percent, on average, rely on Medicaid funding (4, p. 162)—grows exceedingly problematic. Thus far, the bulk of the cost of the AIDS epidemic has been borne by vast amounts of unpaid labor donated by community organizations founded by gay activists, as well as by private charities and a few local governments—and *not* by federal agencies. With the crisis only promising to grow worse, current federal inaction is a guarantee of future catastrophe.

Repression: The Reaganite Prescription for Prevention. Having stymied appropriate prevention efforts and compromised health care coverage, just what has the Reagan administration been doing to curb the AIDS crisis? Chiefly, it has countenanced, if not promoted, anti-scientific discriminatory measures which not only scapegoat gays and IVDUs but also, under the guise of concern for the nation's health, constitute flagrant attacks on fundamental civil rights.

Consider, for example, the Justice Department's 1986 ruling which legitimized discrimination against persons suspected of having AIDS based on fear of contagion. To buttress its conclusion, the Justice Department not only invented scientific controversy where none exists but even totally disregarded the recommendations of the CDC—which explicitly state that employees infected with HIV should not be excluded from work because AIDS cannot be spread by casual contact in the workplace. In fact, this unjustifiable decision so completely countered public health guidelines that it was openly condemned by the Department of Health and Human Services' Assistant Secretary for Health as well as by two other groups not known for publicly challenging governmental policy: the American Medical Association and the deans of all 23 Schools of Public Health in the United States (8, 9). And as for the Reagan administration's concern about AIDS-related discrimination, it is vividly expressed by the fact that as of November 1986, the federal government had seen fit to file only *one* AIDS discrimination case—but because it waited two years to act on the complaint, the victimized AIDS patient *died 10 months before* the government even filed the charges (65).

It is the mandatory military antibody screening program, however, which epitomizes the federal government's repressive response to AIDS. Initiated in the fall of 1985, by October 1986 it had already been imposed on more than one million people. The first 750,000 tests alone cost almost $4 million. No recruit who tests positive is admitted into the service; if active-duty personnel test positive or develop AIDS and admit to either being gay or using IV drugs, they are invariably discharged (66). While the Pentagon claims testing is necessary to preserve the health of the troops (citing the highly unlikely event of battlefield transfusions) it is obvious that the true rationale is to bolster the military's longstanding anti-gay policy.

Even worse, the military's decision sets a dangerous precedent which will encourage other large institutions—such as employers and insurance companies—to utilize the test as well. As such, the Pentagon's policy signifies a massive threat to civil liberties in the nation as a whole. Indeed, in the fall of 1986 the State Department decided to follow in the military's footsteps and start its own antibody testing program, a policy which represents the first extension of forced screening to a civilian workforce. This country is already faced with its first case of a serviceman being jailed for refusing to take the test (67)—who's next?

Localized Reaction: Politicians Promote AIDS-Related Repression. Given the federal government's backward orientation, it should come as no surprise that the political response at the state and local level has primarily tended toward punitive measures. Ready to use any hot new issue to advance their careers, politicians throughout the country have been jumping onto the anti-AIDS bandwagon, simultaneously tapping into and creating yet more of AIDS hysteria and an anti-gay and "war on drugs" mentality. In 1985, Diane McGrath, a conservative Republican candidate for mayor of New York, called for closing not only gay bathhouses but also bookstores, bars and movie theaters "to protect these people from themselves." That same fall, Louie Welch, the Republican candidate for mayor of Houston, Texas, "joked" that one of his plans for combatting AIDS was to "shoot the queers" (68). Though neither won, both were mainstream candidates for the Republican Party—indicating the respectability of such chilling stances.

Indeed, elected politicians in state legislatures have been a regular source of reactionary proposals to curb AIDS. In 1986 alone, bills in at least 10 states sought to make it a crime for persons who know they have AIDS or have tested antibody-positive to infect anyone else. While none passed, all perpetuated the belief that gays and IVDUs are selfish, destructive people who would recklessly infect others. And throughout 1986, politicians repeatedly demonstrated their preference for repressive uses of the AIDS antibody test: while only three of eight proposals to prevent insurance companies from using the test to screen applicants passed, three of five proposals to test arrested prostitutes became law. And despite the fact that the CDC has repeatedly stressed that AIDS cannot be transmitted by casual contact or shared food, by 1986 politicians in more than 20 states proposed legislation to ban people who test positive or have AIDS from food-handling and educational jobs (69).

Likewise, the quarantine bills being introduced into numerous state legislatures and onto state ballots are purely political in intent and have no scientific justification whatsoever. Although quarantine is a defensible public health policy for some highly contagious deadly diseases (such as the plague), AIDS is *not* one of them. Not only is AIDS not spread by casual contact, but because people who carry HIV may be permanently infectious, quarantine would be a lifetime proposition requiring the creation of modern-day leper colonies. Consequently, on the grounds that quarantine would be both ineffective and unfeasible, every major public health organization in the United States and the National Academy of Sciences, as well as the World Health Organization, has opposed quarantine for AIDS (4, 6, 70, 71). Such unanimous scientific opposition, however, has not stopped opportunistic politicians and political groups from using quarantine as an emotional issue to build a base of support. As evidence of the receptive climate for such a strategy, in California the LaRouche AIDS Quarantine Initiative (though subsequently defeated) made it onto the ballot with nearly 700,000 signatures.

It is critical to stress, in addition, that the actual enaction of anti-AIDS quarantine measures does not hinge on passage of any of these legislative proposals. In fact, state governments already have on the books all the laws they need to invoke quarantine if they choose to do so. As the AIDS crisis deepens, it is not inconceivable to think that local governments or federal agencies under reactionary leadership might attempt to quarantine what they consider to be "high-risk geographic regions"—such as Greenwich Village or parts of the Bronx in New York and the Castro District in San Francisco. Dangerous precedents for such "solutions" already exist: during World War II, the Nazis walled in Jewish ghettoes and the United States government not only established Japanese-American internment camps but also constructed several less-well known "civilian conservation camps" in which thousands of U.S. prostitutes were incarcerated. Along these lines, one New York City judge—when hearing a case on whether a child with AIDS could be allowed to attend public school—has openly stated he could not "imagine why the city health department doesn't quarantine adults with advanced AIDS" (72).

State and local governments, moreover, have already utilized existing laws to crack down on people with or at risk for AIDS. Several cities have shut down gay bathhouses, despite the fact that these actions have eliminated important sites of public education and have done nothing to stop "high risk" sex. Others have attempted to eradicate shooting galleries in order to stop addicts from sharing dirty needles (an approach which has received the blessing of the CDC (73)), despite the fact that this is almost as useless a tactic as trying to stop drug addiction by bombing Bolivia and turning a blind eye toward the drug dealing of the Nicaraguan contras, Reagan's favorite freedom fighters. In addition, numerous jails and prisons have instituted mandatory testing for inmates, often segregating those who test positive or have AIDS. And, basing their actions on existing laws, city health department officials in San Antonio, Texas hand-delivered letters to 14 AIDS patients informing them that any sexual activity on their part would result in felony charges (74).

In sum, while several states may slowly be moving toward enacting laws to prevent housing and employment discrimination based on AIDS and a few local governments have devoted considerable funds to AIDS services (75, 76), many more have used the AIDS crisis as a vehicle to launch damaging attacks on critical civil rights. Indeed, when viewed together, the combined political response of government to AIDS at the federal, state, and local level presents a picture which can only be described as both brutal and deadly.

WHY IS THE U.S. GOVERNMENT'S RESPONSE TO AIDS SO BACKWARD?

In the United States, we are faced with a vivid and lethal contradiction: one of the wealthiest nations on earth has offered one of the meanest responses to AIDS. Rather than spearheading a massive risk-reduction education campaign or providing sufficient funds for both research and drug treatment centers, the Reagan administration has offered a program based on repression and denial. Tempting as it might be to attribute this outrageous reaction chiefly to widespread condemnation of "queers" and "junkies," to do so would be incorrect.

The choices a government makes to control any epidemic, AIDS included, depend not only upon general social attitudes toward those afflicted but also, even more importantly, upon the economic and political agenda of the ruling power at the time when the epidemic strikes. In pursuit of its agenda, a government takes on triple though not equal roles as guardian of the nation's wealth, health and values. However camouflaged behind high-sounding phrases about "serving the interests of all people equally," in capitalist society the state's preeminent purpose is to protect and expand the property and power of the wealth-controlling ruling class. At the same time, the government cannot totally disregard issues of social order or well-being, since both have an impact on this primary goal. Consequently, the reason why a disease like AIDS can provoke a genuine policy crisis is that any AIDS program—be it progressive or reactionary—of necessity forces the state to choose between its duty to defend the existing "moral order" and its obligation to protect the nation's health: either it can appease the right wing and endanger the public's health or it can follow the scientific recommendations and offend public sentiment. Ultimately, which choice the state makes depends upon the ruling class assessment of each option's political costs.

Accordingly, to comprehend the federal response to AIDS, we must consider where AIDS fits into the current context of U.S. society, taking into account the intersecting factors of dominant social values, the existence of a powerful New Right, and the overall anti-popular program of the Reagan administration. If we are to alter this nation's backward response to AIDS, we must know where to target our protest.

The Politics of Purity: Society, the State and the Political Moment

One factor contributing to the federal government's inexcusable reaction to AIDS cannot be blamed solely on either the New Right or the Reagan administration: the overall backwardness of U.S. society regarding sexuality (especially as compared to other advanced capitalist countries, particularly in Western and Northern Europe) and the volatile nature of its views on moral matters. With public passion already running high on issues such as abortion, "promiscuity," pornography, teen pregnancy and drugs, the appearance of AIDS was bound to provoke a heated response—one akin to throwing a lit match into a tank of gasoline.

Public Policy and Private Propriety. For reasons beyond the scope of this pamphlet to analyze, frank discussion of sexuality within the United States is as repressed as the commodification of sexuality is overt. While sex is used to sell everything from toothpaste to automobile tires, the advertisement of condoms on TV and school-based sex education—let alone contraceptive distribution—remain thoroughly controversial topics. One vivid consequence of this split approach to sexuality is that U.S. teenage-pregnancy rates are five times in excess of those in Western Europe (where adolescents are equally sexually active, but have much easier access to birth control (77)); another is this society's extraordinary reluctance to deal openly with sexually transmitted diseases—most of which are still viewed as shameful, if not sinful.

Accordingly, Reagan or no Reagan, the climate within the United States for explicit governmental promotion of "safe sex" for heterosexuals, let alone gays, would not be favorable. Likewise, with the public generally endorsing the view that inner-city IVDUs should be punished rather than treated for their "self-inflicted" addiction, advocacy of risk-reduction and treatment programs for either addicts or occasional users would not be easy—regardless of Reagan's "war on drugs" or Nancy's campaign to "just say no."

Yet, while present-day public opinion certainly poses an obstacle to mounting a successful AIDS prevention program, it is equally true that the state possesses the authority and resources to challenge and change these views. That it would not readily do so can be explained by its desire not to challenge deeply felt values which, apart from guiding personal conduct, serve to legitimize the government's rule and contribute to the current social and economic order. Or, to put it another way, those in power are well aware that it is easiest to govern when the beliefs of the populace correspond to the policies of the state, and most difficult when they are out of joint. Accordingly, any administration takes great care to ensure that its overall program can be justified by the dominant values it has inherited, shaped and enforced; for example, the U.S. government liberalized divorce and birth control laws only after the "family economy" was essentially an institution of the past and child labor no longer played a useful role in an increasingly skilled and less labor-intensive economy. Given these considerations, it is quite apparent that if any disease in the United States currently possessed the potential to provoke a policy crisis, AIDS would be the one.

A Classic Example: Sex, VD and World War I. To better understand the complex forces affecting AIDS policy, it therefore helps to consider an earlier and equally volatile public health and social crisis in the United States: that of venereal disease (VD) and the troops in World War I. Framed by the need of the U.S. government to participate in a war whose goal was to redivide the colonial possessions of the leading imperialist powers of the time, this issue and its resolution provide a clear example of the intricate interrelation between social mores and the political movement in establishing public health policy (78).

Toward the end of the 19th century, a strong social purity movement arose in the United States which targeted prostitution as the vice sapping the strength of the nation. Tapping into deep-seated social concerns about the changing nature of both the family and relations between the sexes in an increasingly urbanized and proletarianized society, this movement crystallized widespread personal fears and social anxieties. Yet it dealt with them not by addressing root causes within the economy, but by posing the matter as a moral issue—a type of politics which invariably makes for strange bedfellows.

The political forces in this movement were diverse and ranged from the American Medical Association and right-wing patriotic organizations (such as John D. Rockefeller, Jr.'s "American Social Hygiene Association") to feminist groups within the voluntary motherhood and suffrage movements. But while these groups differed on a variety of issues (e.g., should prostitution be outlawed or regulated?), they all agreed on one point: "the clap" served as an important enforcer of public morality. The government had no incentive to contradict this stance—until along came World War I. In wartime, the government quickly discovered it had a huge problem on its hands: what to do about the rampant VD spreading among the troops?

While the social purity forces argued that soldiers must be chaste, military pragmatists pushed prophylaxis—that is, giving out condoms and teaching soldiers how to have sex without getting VD. Ultimately, the government's version of "national security," not morality, settled the debate. With VD causing nearly 18,000 of the two million U.S. soldiers stationed in Europe to miss action on a *daily* basis, "safe sex" and not purity became official policy. In addition to setting up prophylaxis stations, the government also established the nation's first federally sponsored sex-education programs.

As soon as the war was over, however, the state reverted to its more usual "no-sex-outside-the-sacred-family" stance, withdrew its pioneering VD educational films (which it even labeled obscene!) and cut funding for VD control. Once again, VD was to be "the punishment which fit the crime"—and this was because, under prosperous peacetime conditions, the government had no need to antagonize public sentiment by pushing a new sexual ethos which contradicted the state's claim to moral authority.

The Politics of the '80s: Rising Reaction

As the case of changing VD policy 70 years ago so clearly illustrates, if general public opinion were the only factor blocking appropriate federal policy on AIDS, this obstacle could certainly be overcome by a sustained governmental effort. Unfortunately, more than just the scattered concerns of the population at large are involved. Their fears are being fanned and exploited to serve the political agenda of the New Right. Eagerly building on AIDS-inspired hysteria to bolster support for their full reactionary program, this aggressive movement has become a key actor in the national struggle over AIDS. As a result, the U.S. government's response to AIDS cannot be understood apart from the New Right's emergence as a powerful political force and its relation to the Reagan administration.

Rise of the New Right. The embattled society into which AIDS burst in 1981 already contained diverse and antagonistic movements born of the social contradictions of the times. The advances of the civil rights movement, the peace and anti-intervention movements, the women's liberation movement, and the lesbian and gay rights movement not only reflected deep-seated changes in the fabric of U.S. society, but also provoked a backlash among those who found these new conditions and progressive movements threatening. And while the actual crisis had it roots in the declining economic, political, and military position of the United States since its heyday in the 1950s, much of the battle was pitched on the traditional turf of morality. With "fundamental values" at stake, from the 1960s onwards, the terrain was set for heated conflicts over such highly charged issues as the threat of nuclear war, the propensity of the U.S. government to intervene militarily in other nation's affairs, the roots of racial discrimination and the "fairness" of affirmative action and busing for integration. Also fiercely contested were acceptable approaches to sexual behavior and the question of abortion rights, and the relationship of urban decay to teen pregnancy and drug abuse.

Out of this context emerged the New Right, a reactionary social movement based mainly among whites from the small business, professional and technical strata and the more well-to-do layers of the working class. Organized in a host of forms ranging from single-issue lobbying groups to fundamentalist churches, the U.S. New Right built its program around the reinforcement of racism under the banner of "white rights," the pursuit of militarism under the banner of virulent anticommunism, and an all-out attack on women's and lesbian/gay rights under the banner of "traditional family values." Following in the footsteps of past "social purity" movements, the New Right intentionally exploited many of the major unresolved and emotionally charged social issues wracking U.S. society. By offering apparently straightforward solutions to complex problems (is the crime rate getting too high?—that's easy: build more prisons and bring back the death sentence!), the New Right established a distinct style of organizing in which "moral issues" simultaneously functioned as "codewords" and rallying points for a comprehensive and reactionary agenda.

Based on this approach, the New Right has built itself from a handful of ideologues into a massive social movement. With their bedrock call to "defend the family" and "traditional values" and their prized tactic of powerful single-issue campaigns, New Right activists have deliberately seized upon the real anxieties and discontents of increasingly hard-hit, but previously protected and predominantly white, segments of U.S. society. The New Right has channeled the frustrations of these sectors into an organized political form.

The full array of the New Right's "single issues" reveals the scope of its thoroughly racist and jingoistic political program. In addition to leading the anti-abortion and anti-gay/lesbian movements, the New Right has also fought against affirmative action and school busing, called for more "law and order" (with "crime" a code word for "race"), fomented pseudo-populist tax revolts against social spending, and has backed every effort to reassert the international hegemony of the United States, ranging from regaining nuclear superiority to reclaiming the Panama Canal.

Not surprisingly, the New Right seized on the AIDS crisis as a political godsend. Not only did AIDS give new license to New Right demands to keep "queers" out of the schools and to throw "junkies" in jail, but it also seemed to confirm New Right declarations against "promiscuity." Merging their racist mania for "law and order" with appeals to deep-rooted and widespread anti-gay and anti-IVDU beliefs, the New Right has led the way in calling for punishment as a means of prevention. According to the New Right, mandatory testing and quarantine for AIDS are the only way "guilty" culprits (oversexed, debauched gay men and drug-crazed addicts) can be prevented from killing "innocent" victims (hemophiliacs, recipients of blood transfusions, unsuspecting heterosexual partners, and unborn children). Indeed, the New Right has matched the scientific community point-by-point in formulating a comprehensive policy for AIDS—but for every tiny step the health sector has taken toward a progressive stand, the New Right has galloped ever more rightward.

And despite the thoroughly unscientific nature of the New Right's program, it retains broad mass influence. To account for the New Right's transformation from the fringe project of a few to a movement capable of affecting national policy on AIDS, it is necessary to consider the way in which the New Right currently serves the interests of the dominant sector of the U.S. ruling class.

Reaganism in Power: War Abroad, Injustice at Home. The heightened hearing the New Right has received since the late 1970s cannot be attributed to the efforts of ring-wing organizers alone. Rather, it is a consequence of the encouragement given to the New Right by the top leaders of U.S. monopoly banks and corporations as this ruling elite and its political operatives try to grapple with growing international resistance to U.S. imperial power and control.

Ever since the 1960s, the U.S. government and transnational corporations have been confronted with an empire slipping out of their grasp. The symptoms have been widespread: the rapidly growing gains of the socialist community of nations, the mounting successes of movements for national liberation and social progress in countries of the Third World, and the increasing economic rivalry from other capitalist countries such as West Germany and Japan. For several years following the humiliating defeat of its aggression in Vietnam, Washington was unable to move decisively against these challenges to U.S. power and profit. But at the end of the 1970s the U.S. corporate class—led by its most reactionary sector—shifted to a full-scale counteroffensive. This counteroffensive acquired the popular name of "Reaganism" and has as its twin pillars a vast military buildup aimed at restoring U.S. power to intervene with force anywhere in the world and a mass austerity program—uneven across racial lines—directed against the people of the U.S. itself. That austerity program—punctuated by drastic cuts in social spending—is meant both to pay for the military buildup and to boost corporate profits and shift the country's wealth from the poorer layers of society to the rich.

To win support for cutbacks that would otherwise be unpopular, the architects of Reaganism first directed their attack against the most vulnerable sectors of society: minority and poor communities. Ideologically, the Reagan administration consciously promoted a national chauvinist and racist "all-American dream," in which the "true America" consisted of patriotic white nuclear families forced to pay precious tax-dollars to support lousy minority welfare cheats. Reaganism has also brought drastic assaults on critical civil liberties and democratic rights, and it has meant a no-holds-barred attack on the trade union movement. And, though the more liberal sectors of the ruling class have urged caution with regard to the pace and severity of this continued onslaught (based on its belief that it is easier to govern by persuasion than force), the stark reality is that whatever tactical differences exist internally, as a whole this class is basically united on the necessity of increased militarization and social austerity as the twin components of its strategy to regain U.S. hegemony in the world.

To help secure broad support among the population for this program of war and racist austerity, the dominant sector of the ruling class has given significant encouragement to the New Right. It's not that the policy makers in Wall Street board rooms and Washington offices agree with the likes of Pat Robertson on every issue, but they do find such figures useful in moving the political debate in the country to the right. And the New Right's longstanding hatred of homosexuality has played a particularly convenient role. By harping on the sacred nature of "the family" and suggesting that its decline is due to the meddling of the "welfare state," the New Right has helped the Reagan administration solve two of its problems in one blow. First this platform shifts attention away from the true reason the nuclear family is fast disappearing from the American scene, i.e., the effect of modern capitalism—for example, the need for two wages to support a household. Secondly, the New Right's program also provides ideological justification for the privatization of social problems—such as childcare, home health care for the elderly, etc.

While Ronald Reagan himself comes out of the New Right, on the way to the White House he was required to "pay his dues" to the capitalist elite and make clear that his primary loyalty would be to the ruling class. Still, more than any administration in recent history, the Reagan regime has given the New Right positions of great prestige and power. And it is largely figures emerging from the New Right who have shaped administration policy concerning the AIDS crisis.

Altogether, then, the U.S. government's backward approach to AIDS is no mere product of scattered mass prejudices. It stems, rather, from the reactionary agenda of the New Right and from an increasingly conservative ruling class intent upon imposing Reaganism on the country and on the world.

Ruling Class Disunity Concerning AIDS. Not all sectors of the ruling class are united on the Reagan administration's approach to AIDS—primarily because they do not think it will work. Like the military pragmatists faced with VD in World War I, a portion of the corporate class is not about to let a deadly communicable disease endanger the nation's well-being by threatening the health of the workforce and the survival of the health care system. Having accepted the argument that repressive measures such as mandatory testing and quarantine will do nothing to stop the spread of AIDS, they are well aware that considerable funds must be devoted to massive educational efforts, to drug treatment programs, and to research.

The *New York Times* expresses the outlook of this sector of the U.S. power structure, and has printed numerous editorials condemning what it has termed the Reagan administration's "feeble fight against AIDS" (79). The *Times* has called for explicit risk-reduction education campaigns and for distribution of sterile needles in conjunction with increased funding for drug treatment programs (80). More broadly, struggles over AIDS policies within the ruling class—as further revealed by the ongoing budget battles—have been so pronounced that even the National Academy of Sciences has described the federal government's response to AIDS as a "tug of war between the administration and Congress" (43, p. 135).

But despite the fact that the more "enlightened" wing of those who wield power oppose the worst aspects of the Reagan administration's AIDS program, this sector cannot be counted upon to develop or to implement a consistently progressive or even scientific AIDS policy. This is because they are not motivated by the interests of those most afflicted by or at risk of getting AIDS, but rather are seeking to protect the economic health of the corporate class.

Concrete evidence of the liberal elite's vacillation in the fight against AIDS is already widespread. This sector has already refrained from challenging the mandatory antibody testing program implemented by the military—a stance which once again demonstrates how they cannot be trusted to defend lesbian and gay rights. Moreover, despite their obvious concerns about the economic toll of AIDS, no major ruling class figure has yet proposed a nationalized health program as a possible solution to the health care crisis which AIDS currently is compounding. Instead, like their more reactionary brethren (with whom they differ on tactics, not goals), they will not advocate any policy which either qualitatively undermines U.S. military might and authority or which excludes the private sector from the profitable health care industry. Sharing the same central economic, political and military aims as the Reagan administration—and confronted by the same skyrocketing federal deficit, international economic woes, and rising domestic demands on this country's ever-shrinking social programs—this more liberal wing has clearly indicated that these larger concerns will of necessity frame and constrain the types of funds and efforts it is prepared to devote to combatting AIDS.

Relying on a Progressive Popular Movement. To ensure the implementation of an appropriate, scientific and compassionate AIDS program, it will therefore be necessary to build a broad people's movement capable of anchoring a protracted and difficult political battle. Such a popularly based movement will, of course, have to find ways to work with the more liberal sectors of the ruling class, but must retain its independent perspective and its commitment to defending the rights of those with or at risk for AIDS. And this movement must be built so it not only includes the lesbian and gay community, but also U.S. minority communities, trade unions, workers in the health care sector, civil liberties advocates and the organized left.

While the beginnings of such a popular movement are starting to emerge, it is clear that the gay and lesbian community has thus far shouldered the bulk of the fightback against AIDS. And it has done so on every front imaginable. On the social front, the gay and lesbian community has conducted countless educationals and written innumerable editorials and letters to counter public hysteria. On the scientific and medical front, it has demanded adequate and appropriate research and treatment, and has also provided endless hours of care and support for people with AIDS. And, on the political front, it has fought repressive legislation, battled for anti-discrimination laws, and lobbied for sufficient funding. When necessary, the gay and lesbian movement nationwide has taken to the streets, in demonstrations to protest the Supreme Court's sodomy ruling, in annual candlelight vigils to commemorate those who have died of AIDS, and in yearly Gay Pride marches to celebrate and defend its very existence in defiance of both this dread disease and a sanctimonious society which would prefer gays and lesbians did not exist at all.

With the growing recognition that AIDS poses a profound threat to the political as well as literal well-being of this nation, additional forces have begun to join in the struggle against both AIDS and repressive AIDS policies. The American Civil Liberties Union has already participated in numerous cases regarding AIDS-related discrimination. In addition, several unions have conducted AIDS educationals for their members and opposed repressive AIDS legislation; one example is the Service Employees International Union (SEIU), whose members are concentrated not only in the health sector but also in the very service jobs for which mandatory antibody testing has been proposed. New organizations such as the National Minority AIDS Council have joined alongside gay groups, such as Black and White Men Together, to tackle AIDS in minority communities.

Finally, people from the public health, medical and scientific communities have become an increasingly important advocate of an appropriate AIDS policy. Mincing no words, the National Academy of Sciences has clearly warned that this nation must devote at least $2 billion per year on AIDS intervention and research programs by 1990 if the current AIDS crisis is to be prevented from turning into an utter catastrophe (4, pp. 1–3).

It will take more than good intentions and common interests, however, for these diverse sectors to create a strong and broad political movement united not only against the Reagan administration's repressive AIDS policy but in favor of a comprehensive, progressive AIDS program. What it will require is active organizing based on clearly specified pro-working class, pro-lesbian/gay, and anti-racist demands—and it is in articulating and fighting for such demands that the organized progressive forces in the U.S. can make a significant and unique contribution.

AIDS' CHALLENGE TO THE PROGRESSIVE MOVEMENT

As every scientific and political fact concerning AIDS demonstrates, this disease is not "simply" a "gay issue," it is not "simply" a "health issue"—it is everyone's issue, a critical component of the agenda of the *entire* people's movement. Because AIDS is a terminal, communicable disease which has primarily afflicted gay men and IV drug users in a society riddled with discrimination against gays and engaged in an all-out "war on drugs," and because AIDS coincidentally struck at the very moment when the New Right was beginning to gain increased support from the dominant sector of the U.S. ruling class, AIDS has developed into one of the most complex, multifaceted problems facing our society today. Exacerbating already existing tensions, AIDS has become an extremely dangerous political and public health phenomenon, and has squarely placed on our agenda the crisis of the health care system under U.S. capitalism, the rising attacks on minority communities, and the defense of lesbian and gay rights.

Because of these things, AIDS poses a particular challenge to self-consciously progressive and left forces. That challenge can only be met by aggressively combatting all the prejudices and myths surrounding AIDS, by drawing out the connections between the AIDS crisis and all the other dimensions of U.S. capitalism's current crisis, and by raising a set of demands that can most effectively focus a broad and massive popular fightback.

To fight against AIDS, we cannot rely on voluntary action or "self-help" strategies, but instead must force the federal government to respond to this crisis in a scientific and compassionate manner. We must demand that the government establish a centralized agency empowered to create and enforce appropriate public health policy, as well as to coordinate and fund not only AIDS research and treatment programs but also massive educational efforts to counter the spread of AIDS and its contingent epidemic of fear. Beyond multi-lingual and culturally sensitive leaflets and pamphlets on what AIDS is and how its spread can be minimized via "safe sex" and "clean works," we must demand that the government subsidize even more visible educational approaches utilizing billboards, TV specials and commercials, radio shows and public service announcements and also newspaper articles and ads.

In addition to sponsoring such programs for the entire population, the federal government must also embark on a public campaign to "destigmatize" and guarantee adequate services to those sectors of society at highest risk for AIDS—gays and IVDUs. As part of this, we must demand that the state not only implement a nationalized health plan but also increase funding for programs which can help reduce the health crises in minority and working class communities which AIDS is now compounding. And in solidarity with those fighting to overcome the legacy of underdevelopment, we must demand that the U.S. provide substantial financial and technical support to Third World nations stricken by this epidemic—for without this assistance, AIDS will assuredly kill millions of their people and jeopardize future generations to come.

To fight against AIDS, the progressive movement cannot simply tolerate lesbians and gays, but must take up active defense of the right to be gay, the right to be lesbian. We must demand that public schools provide sex-education courses which not only frankly discuss the realities of AIDS as a preventable venereal and blood-borne disease but which also acknowledge that being gay is as valid an identity as being straight. Additionally, we must halt the government's reactionary policy of mandatory screening in the military, challenge its attempts to legalize discrimination based on fear of contagion, and fight to overturn the Supreme Court's sodomy ruling in order to secure constitutional protection of the rights of lesbians and gays.

To fight against AIDS, we must expose the government's "war on drugs" and demand that the state in the short term provide sterile needles to addicts while it simultaneously increases funding for treatment programs—which, at this very moment, are turning away more people than they can help. More than this, we must challenge the government's lie that substance abuse is the cause, rather than a symptom, of urban decay. And as part of the fight against AIDS, we must call for jobs for inner-city residents, particularly for the young, we must call for an end to dreams deferred by the deadening effects of racism and poverty.

Finally, in calling for more human services, in calling for more jobs, in calling for social justice as we fight against AIDS, we must indict the Reagan administration's expansionist military program as the prime culprit preventing a more rapid resolution of this crisis. The funds which can and should be going into AIDS education, treatment and research programs are being gobbled up by the current U.S. military buildup. Ronald Reagan and the forces he represents are sacrificing lives every passing hour as they strive for the return of the "good old days" when Washington could "send the marines" at a moment's notice to defend U.S. corporate investments around the world. Without a major dent in their runaway military budget and imperial aspirations, the breakthroughs that are so urgently needed in the fight against AIDS will be delayed again and again.

The politics of AIDS are playing out in the midst of the crisis of contemporary capitalism; in the midst of an unprecedented "peace-time" military buildup accompanied by an assault on the conditions of life of the working class as a whole and its minority sectors in particular; in the midst of a health care crisis of astronomical proportions; and in the midst of a New Right revival and attacks on the rights of lesbians and gays. Under these circumstances, the fightback against AIDS has become a critical part of the overall progressive political struggle of our generation.

REFERENCES

1. Resident, University of California, San Francisco. Personal Communication, 1986.
2. Selwyn, P. A. What is now known. II. Epidemiology. *Hosp. Pract.,* June 15, 1986, pp. 127–164.
3. U.S. Public Health Service. Coolfont Report: A PHS plan for prevention and control of AIDS and the AIDS virus. *Public Health Rep.* 101: 341–348, 1986.
4. Committee on a National Strategy for AIDS of the Institute of Medicine. *Confronting AIDS: Directions for Public Health, Health Care and Research.* National Academy Press, Washington, D.C., 1986.

5. Coffin, J., et al. Human immunodeficiency virus (letter). *Science* 236: 69, 1986.
6. Division of Communicable Diseases, World Health Organization. AIDS and the WHO Collaborating Centers: Memorandum from a WHO meeting. *Bull. World Health Organ.* 63: 1003–1007, 1985.
7. Centers for Disease Control. Recommendations for preventing transmission of infection with HTLV-III/LAV in the workplace. *MMWR* 34: 681–695, 1985.
8. *New York Times,* July 12, 1986, p. 7.
9. Association of Schools of Public Health. News Release: Public Health Deans Critical of Justice Department's Ruling on AIDS. June 26, 1986.
10. Selwyn, P. A. AIDS: What is now known. IV. Psychosocial aspects, treatment prospects. *Hosp. Pract.,* October 15, 1986, pp. 125–162.
11. Maayan, S., et al. Acquired immunodeficiency syndrome (AIDS) in an economically disadvantaged population. *Arch. Intern. Med.* 145: 1607–1612, 1985.
12. *New York Times,* July 24, 1986, p. 9.
13. Francis, D. P., and Petricciani, J. C. The prospects for and pathways towards a vaccine for AIDS. *N. Engl. J. Med.* 313: 1586–1590, 1985.
14. Biggar, R. J. The AIDS problem in Africa. *Lancet* I: 79–82, 1986.
15. Quinn, T. C., et al. AIDS in Africa: An epidemiologic paradigm. *Science* 234: 955-963, 1986.
16. Seale, J. AIDS virus infection: Prognosis and treatment. *J. R. Soc. Med.* 78: 613, 1985.
17. Mahler, H. Opening speech. Presented at the Second International Conference on AIDS, Paris, June 23–25, 1986.
18. Proceedings of the Second International Conference on AIDS, Paris, June 23–25, 1986.
19. *New York Times,* December 28, 1985, p. 14.
20. Doyal, L. *The Political Economy of Health.* South End Press, Boston, 1981.
21. Sanders, D. *The Struggle for Health: Medicine and the Politics of Underdevelopment.* MacMillan, London, 1985.
22. Rosenbert, M. J., Schulz, K. F., and Burton, N. Sexually transmitted diseases in Sub-Saharan Africa. *Lancet* II: 152, 1986.
23. Fischl, M. A., and Scott, G. B. The acquired immunodeficiency syndrome among Haitian adults and infants: An update. In *Advances in Host Defense Mechanisms,* Vol. 5, edited by J. I. Gallin and A. S. Fauci, pp. 109–129. Raven Press, New York, 1985.
24. Barry, M., Mellors, J., and Bia, F. Haiti and the AIDS connection. *J. Chron. Dis.* 37: 593–595, 1984.
25. Frank, E., et al. AIDS in Haitian-Americans: A reassessment. *Cancer Res.* 45: 4619s-4620s, 1985.
26. Department of Health and Human Services. *Health Status of Minority and Low-Income Populations,* pp. 41, 67. DHHS Publication No. (HRSA) HRS-P-DV 85-1. U.S. Government Printing Office, Washington, D.C., 1985.
27. Centers for Disease Control. *AIDS Weekly Surveillance Report,* November 24, 1986.
28. Centers for Disease Control. Acquired immunodeficiency syndrome (AIDS) in Western Palm Beach County, Florida. *MMWR* 35: 609–612, 1986.
29. *San Francisco Chronicle,* October 26, 1985.
30. Centers for Disease Control. Acquired immunodeficiency syndrome (AIDS) among blacks and Hispanics—United States. *MMWR* 35: 655–666, 1986.
31. *Oakland Tribune* Associated Press, January 18, 1986, p. A-8.
32. Weeks, J. *Sexuality and Its Discontents,* p. 48. Routledge & Kegan Paul, London, 1985.
33. *New York Times,* December 20, 1985, p. 14.

34. *New York Times,* March 18, 1986, p. 27.
35. *Oakland Tribune,* September 12, 1986, p. C-7.
36. *New York Native,* May 19, 1985, p. 1.
37. *San Francisco Chronicle,* August 27, 1986.
38. *New York Times,* December 10, 1986, p. 15.
39. *New York Times,* July 1, 1986, p. 22.
40. *Oakland Tribune,* June 24, 1986, pp. B-1, B-8.
41. Centers for Disease Control. Classification system for HTLV-III/LAV infections. *MMWR* 35: 334–339, 1986.
42. Altema, R., and Bright, L. Only homosexual Haitians, not all Haitians. *Ann. Intern. Med.* 99: 877–878, 1983.
43. National Academy of Sciences. *Mobilizing Against AIDS: The Unfinished Story of a Virus.* Harvard University Press, Cambridge, Mass., 1986.
44. *New York Times,* August 1, 1986, p. 7.
45. Centers for Disease Control. Update: Acquired immunodeficiency syndrome—United States. *MMWR* 35: 17–21, 1986.
46. Population Information Program. AIDS—A public health crisis. *Popul. Rep. [L]* 6: L-193–L-228, 1986.
47. Centers for Disease Control. Additional recommendations to reduce sexual and drug abuse-related transmission of human T-lymphotropic virus type III/lymphadenopathy-associated virus. *MMWR* 35: 152–156, 1986.
48. Krim, M. A chance at life for AIDS sufferers. *New York Times,* August 8, 1986, p. 23.
49. *Oakland Tribune,* October 10, 1985, pp. A-1, A-14.
50. *New York Times,* September 20, 1985, pp. 1, 11.
51. *Village Voice,* September 30, 1986, pp. 14, 16.
52. *Oakland Tribune,* October 25, 1985, p. C-9.
53. U.S. Congress, Office of Technology Assessment. *Review of the Public Health Service's Response to AIDS: A Technical Memorandum.* OTA-TM-H-24. U.S. Government Printing Office, Washington, D.C., 1985.
54. U.S. Bureau of the Census. *Statistical Abstracts of the United States, 1985,* Ed. 105, p. 576. U.S. Government Printing Office, Washington, D.C., 1985.
55. U.S. Department of Health and Human Services. *NIH Data Book 1985.* NIH Publication No. 85-1261. U.S. Government Printing Office, Washington, D.C., 1985.
56. Winkelstein, W., Jr., et al. Reduction in Human Immunodeficiency Virus Transmission in San Francisco, 1982–1985. Presented at the Second International Conference on AIDS, Paris, June 23–25, 1986.
57. Stevens, C. AIDS Virus Infection in Homosexual Men in New York City. Presented at the Society for Epidemiological Research, 19th Annual Meeting, Pittsburgh, June 18, 1986.
58. Martin, J. L. Sexual Behavior Patterns, Behavior Change, and Occurrence of Antibody of LAV/HTLV-III among New York City Gay Men. Presented at the Second International Conference on AIDS, Paris, June 23–25, 1986.
59. Chmiel, J., et al., and the Multi-Center AIDS Collaborative Study. Prevention of LAV/HTLV-III Infection through Modification of Sexual Practices. Presented at the Second International Conference on AIDS, Paris, June 23–25, 1986.
60. *Oakland Tribune* Associated Press, November 12, 1986, p. A-9.
61. *New York Times,* May 30, 1986, p. 13.
62. *New York Times,* November 11, 1986, p. 22.
63. *Guardian,* November 6, 1985, p. 3.
64. *New York Times,* July 6, 1986.

65. *New York Times,* August 9, 1986, pp. 1, 8.
66. *New York Times,* October 29, 1985, pp. 1, 13.
67. *New York Times,* June 24, 1986, p. 8.
68. *New York Times,* October 26, 1985, p. 11.
69. International Government Health Policy Project. *A Synopsis of AIDS-Related Legislation Introduced in the 1986 State Legislative Sessions.* George Washington University, Washington, D.C., 1986.
70. Benenson, A. S. (ed.). *Control of Communicable Diseases in Man,* Ed. 14, p. 5. American Public Health Association, Washington, D.C., 1985.
71. Association of State and Territorial Health Officers. *Guide to Public Health Practice: HTLV-III Antibody Testing and Community Approaches.* Recommendations from a Consensus Conference, Bethesda, Md., August 1–2, 1985.
72. *New York Times,* October 7, 1985, p. 22.
73. Centers for Disease Control. Additional recommendations to reduce sexual and drug abuse-related transmission of human T-lymphotropic virus type III/lymphadenopathy-associated virus. *MMWR* 35: 152–156, 1986.
74. *New York Times,* October 18, 1985, p. 11.
75. *New York Times,* September 17, 1986, p. 11.
76. Arno, P. S. The nonprofit sector's response to the AIDS epidemic: Community-based services in San Francisco. *Am. J. Public Health* 76: 1325–1330, 1986.
77. *New York Times,* December 10, 1986, pp. 1, 51.
78. Brandt, A. M. *No Magic Bullets: A Social History of Venereal Disease in the United States Since 1880.* Oxford University Press, New York, 1985.
79. *New York Times,* July 14, 1986, p. 16.
80. *New York Times,* November 7, 1986, p. 26.

APPENDIX I: RESOURCES[2]

Suggested Readings

ON AIDS:

The best available general overviews are:

National Academy of Sciences. *Mobilizing Against AIDS: The Unfinished Story of a Virus.* Harvard University Press, Cambridge, Mass., 1986.

Selwyn P. A. AIDS: What is now known. *Hosp. Pract.* 1986.

I—History and Immunovirology. May 15, pp. 67–82.

II—Epidemiology. June 15, pp. 127–164.

III—Clinical Aspects. September 15, pp. 119–153.

IV—Psychosocial Aspects, Treatment Prospects. October 15, pp. 125–162.

And the most comprehensive is:

Committee on a National Strategy for AIDS of the Institute of Medicine. *Confronting AIDS: Directions for Public Health, Health Care and Research.* National Academy Press, Washington, D.C., 1986.

[2] All publications and organizations are as listed in the original 1986 publication.

ON THE POLITICS OF HEALTH CARE:

Doyal, L., *The Political Economy of Health.* South End Press, Boston, 1981.

Sanders, D. *The Struggle for Health: Medicine and the Politics of Underdevelopment.* MacMillan, London, 1985.

Periodicals

The Advocate
6922 Hollywood Blvd., 10th floor
Los Angeles, CA 90028
(213) 871-1225
Biweekly national newsmagazine. The gay community's answer to *Time.*

Gay Community News
167 Tremont St.
Boston, MA 02111
(617) 426-4469
Weekly newspaper, national coverage with local emphasis. Collectively produced, progressive. Anti-racist orientation; strives for balance of lesbian/gay male perspectives.

Health PAC Bulletin
Health Policy Advisory Center
17 Murray St.
New York, NY 10007
(212) 267-8890
Quarterly; progressive analysis of all aspects of health policy, including growth and dimensions of the medical/industrial complex; the movement for affordable, accessible care; occupational health; the health workforce; AIDS. Health PAC has also published various pamphlets and educational materials and is becoming a membership organization so it can play a stronger role in linking health-care activists.

Science for the People
897 Main St.
Cambridge, MA 02139
(617) 547-0370
Bimonthly magazine that aims to popularize a progressive view of science and technology. Covers a range of issues including biotechnology, occupational health, impact of military/corporate financing on research, science in the Third World.

The Nation's Health
c/o American Public Health Association
1015 15th St. NW
Washington, DC 20005
(202) 789-5600
Follows spectrum of public health issues, including AIDS policy, funding, legislation. Monthly newspaper of the American Public Health Association. APHA is the major organization of public health professionals—researchers, health care providers and administrators. Caucuses within APHA, including socialist, lesbian/gay and

public hospitals caucuses, have worked to bring a progressive perspective on AIDS to the organization as a whole. For information on caucuses, contact APHA at the address above.

Organizations

U.S. Public Health Service AIDS Hotline
1-800-342-AIDS (good anywhere in the U.S., including Alaska and Hawaii; 24 hours a day, 7 days a week)
Four-minute capsule of basic AIDS information (definition, transmission, testing, risk reduction.) Provides second toll-free number for follow-up questions; has lists of public clinics, doctors, sites for anonymous HIV antibody testing; some pamphlets available.

National Gay/Lesbian CrisisLine/AIDS 800
1-800-221-7044 (good anywhere in the U.S. 3–9 p.m. E.S.T., Monday through Friday)
A project of the Fund for Human Dignity, the education foundation associated with the National Lesbian/Gay Task Force. Basic AIDS information and counseling; assistance with a range of lesbian/gay concerns.

CAIN: Computerized AIDS Information Network
1213 N. Highland Ave.
Los Angeles, CA 90038
(213) 464-7400, ext. 277 (general information number)
1-800-544-4005 (subscription information)
Database comprising a broad spectrum of AIDS information: general AIDS facts, lists of service providers, educational materials (including audiovisual aids, some of which are available on loan), news articles and abstracts.

National Association of People With AIDS
1012 14th St. NW, Suite 601
Washington, DC 20005
(202) 347-0390
Advocacy/support organization formed by and for people with AIDS (PWAs) to give PWAs a stronger voice in community-based service delivery, federal and state policy setting, and media treatment of the AIDS crisis. Represents a collective of 14 local PWA groups and a resource for formation of new groups. Publishes *Hints,* a booklet for the newly diagnosed, and a quarterly newsletter.

Project Inform
25 Taylor St., Room 618
San Francisco, CA 94102
1-800-334-7422 in the San Francisco Bay Area
1-800-822-7422 elsewhere in the U.S.
Provides information on use of available experimental drugs in the treatment of AIDS and ARC, how to obtain these drugs, histories of their use, clinical trial status, customs procedures. Provides physician referrals.

National AIDS Network
1012 14th St. NW, Suite 601
Washington, DC 20005
(202) 347-0390
Membership organization by and for AIDS education/service providers. Primary resource on the national level, and a link to local work. Acts as an information clearinghouse and source of technical assistance. Publishes a bi-monthly newsletter and a national directory of AIDS organizations. Recently established a minority affairs section.

AIDS Action Council
729 8th St. SE, Suite 200
Washington, DC 20003
(202) 547-3101
National lobbying/advocacy organization. Represents the more than 230 AIDS service organizations across the country. Primary role is to fight for adequate funding for AIDS research, education, care. Publishes a bi-monthly legislative update and a national directory of support services for PWAs. Key resource for federal funding questions.

National Gay/Lesbian Task Force
1517 U St. NW
Washington, DC 20009
(202) 332-6483
Focuses on lobbying and public education. Lesbian/gay community advocate at the federal level on AIDS and a full range of civil rights issues. Public education aims at raising consciousness, dispelling myths about lesbian/gay lives and concerns. Also acts as information clearinghouse for lesbian/gay activists. Sponsors two organizing efforts: The Privacy Project, for sodomy law repeal; and an anti-violence project.

National Minorities AIDS Council
P.O. Box 2490
Washington, DC 20013
Telephone: c/o Craig Harris, (202) 543-1953
New organization forging links among groups taking on the AIDS crisis in minority communities. Provides technical assistance in developing programs, especially education/prevention efforts, sensitive to needs of minority community. Works with AIDS service organizations, government bodies, minority community-based health and social service organizations. Clearinghouse for culturally sensitive and appropriate educational materials and prevention strategies. Acts as an advocate for minority AIDS projects with the federal government.

Women's AIDS Network
333 Valencia, 4th Floor
San Francisco, CA 94103
(415) 864-4376
Support group for women doing AIDS work. Advocacy, resource development for programs for women affected by AIDS. Source of up-to-date information on women and AIDS, has produced two pamphlets on women and AIDS, one specifically for lesbians. Monthly newsletter; meets in San Francisco Bay Area; national connections.

National Coalition for Black Lesbians and Gays
P.O. Box 2490
Washington, DC 20013
(202) 265-7117
National organization with 11 chapters/organizing efforts. Political/educational organization aiming to raise consciousness, nurture development of culture and community among Black lesbians and gay men. Sponsored national conference on "AIDS in the Black Community" in 1986; publishes a quarterly magazine, *Black/Out.*

National Association of Black and White Men Together
584 Castro St., #140
San Francisco, CA 94114
National gay inter-racial and explicitly anti-racist organization. Thirty independent chapters, mostly in major cities. Sponsors varied educational, social, cultural and political activities. Political focus is on fighting racism within the gay community.

National Lesbian/Gay Health Foundation, Inc.
P.O. box 65472
Washington, DC 20035
(202) 797-3708
Educational foundation created to increase awareness of all lesbian/gay health issues. Clearinghouse for gay health movement, affiliated with nearly two dozen gay caucuses and associations from various health and mental health professions. Sponsors annual National Lesbian/Gay Health Conference and AIDS Forum. Compiling national survey of lesbian health care needs. Published in 1984 *Sourcebook on Lesbian/Gay Health Care* which includes a national directory of AIDS and lesbian/gay health care services, bibliographies, essays; second edition due summer, 1987.

American Association of Physicians for Human Rights
P.O. Box 14366
San Francisco, CA 94114
(415) 558-9353
National organization of doctors and medical students committed to the elimination of anti-gay discrimination in the health professions, and delivery of unbiased, informed and understanding medical care for gay men and lesbians. Published position papers on AIDS issues (e.g. HIV testing). Members are active in AIDS education, research, etc.; a valuable network to tap for speakers, research and treatment information and physician referrals.

National Gay Rights Advocates/AIDS Civil Rights Project
540 Castro St.
San Francisco, CA 94114
(415) 863-3624
Involved in educational efforts and precedent-setting litigation to improve the legal status of people with AIDS and ARC. Published *The AIDS Practice Manual: A Legal and Educational Guide;* also two pamphlets, *AIDS and Your Legal Rights* and *Pros and Cons of the HTLVIII Antibody Test.*

Health and Medicine Policy Research Group
220 S. State St., Suite 1330
Chicago, IL 60604
(312) 922-8057
Work has local focus, national implications. Studies a range of urban health problems such as infant mortality; environmental hazards such as leaded gas, decaying public hospitals. Develops policy proposals; works with existing organizations and coalitions or helps build new ones to push for implementation. Has published a journal, *Health and Medicine,* which is consolidating with *Health PAC Bulletin* as of winter, 1987 (back issues still available).

Coalition for a National Health System
c/o Anthony DiMarco
116 Laburnam Crescent
Rochester, NY 14620-1836
(716) 442-1684
Coalition of individuals working to regenerate movement for a national health system. Sponsored successful referendum in Massachusetts recommending national health system; working on similar measures elsewhere. Planning a national conference for late spring, 1987. Works closely with the Gray Panthers.

Service Employees International Union (SEIU)
Health & Safety Department
1313 L St. NW
Washington, DC 20003
(202) 898-3385
Publishes brochure, *AIDS and the Health Care Worker,* and *The AIDS Book: Information for Workers,* which includes the general Centers for Disease Control guidelines for workplace AIDS prevention and detailed workplace guidelines for many of the occupations organized by SEIU.

American Federation of State, County and Municipal Employees (AFSCME)
Research Department
1625 L St. NW
Washington, DC 20036
(202) 429-1215
Three fact sheets on AIDS: General, for healthcare workers and for correction officers. Video: Excerpts from AFSCME conference on AIDS in the workplace. Developed infectious disease contract language, and petitioned OSHA to establish a hazardous exposure standard for blood and body fluids.

Resource groups that deal with IV drug abuse, particularly as it relates to AIDS, tend to be organized on a local level rather than regionally or nationally. Many local drug abuse programs are forming AIDS committees and vice versa. Listed are programs that serve as models for intervention.

Pride Institute
14400 Martin Drive
Eden Prairie, MN 55344

1-800-547-7433
Residential treatment center for lesbians and gay men with substance abuse problems; national model.

AIDS Education Project
Montefiore Medical Center
111 E. 210th St.
Bronx, NY 10467
(212) 655-7619
Publishes materials on connections between IV drug use and AIDS. Its 1986 pamphlet, *AIDS and Drug Abuse,* will be published in Spanish in spring of 1987.

Street Outreach AIDS Prevention Project (SOAPP)
A project of the Health Education Resource Organization (HERO)
101 West Read St.
Baltimore, MD 21201
(301) 685-1180
Example of an effective outreach to IVDUs. Former IVDUs take AIDS prevention information, condoms, etc. wherever they can find their prospective clients—street corners, bars, shooting galleries, etc. HERO is a multifaceted AIDS project that runs a hotline, community education, professional training, non-medical support services. Targets the varied groups affect by AIDS.

APPENDIX II: GUIDELINES— SYMPTOMS OF AIDS, "SAFE SEX," AND "CLEAN WORKS"

Symptoms of AIDS
(adapted from the San Francisco AIDS Foundation)

- Unexplained, persistent fatigue.
- Unexplained fever, shaking chills, or drenching night sweats lasting longer than several weeks.
- Unexplained weight loss greater than 10 pounds.
- Swollen glands (enlarged lymph nodes usually in the neck, armpits or groin) which are otherwise unexplained and last more than two months
- Pink to purple flat or bruised blotches or bumps occurring on or under the skin, inside the mouth, nose, eyelids or rectum. Initially they may resemble bruises but do not disappear. They are usually harder than the skin around them.
- Persistent white spots or unusual blemishes in the mouth.
- Persistent diarrhea.
- Persistent dry cough which has lasted too long to be caused by a common respiratory infection, especially if accompanied by shortness of breath.

Sexual Practices and Risks of AIDS
(adapted from the San Francisco AIDS Foundation)

Safe

Massage, hugging, cuddling
Mutual masturbation
Social kissing (dry)
Body-to-body rubbing (frottage)
Voyeurism, exhibitionism, fantasy

Possibly Safe

Tongue kissing
Vaginal intercourse with condom
Anal intercourse with condom
Cunnilingus*
Fellatio with condom
Fellatio without condom, stopping before climax*
*Also considered "possibly unsafe" or "unsafe"

Unsafe

Vaginal intercourse without a condom
Anal intercourse without a condom
Blood contact (including menstrual blood)
Fellatio without condom; semen or urine in mouth
Anilingus ("rimming")
Hand in rectum ("fisting")
Sharing sex toys that have contact with body fluids

Clean Works
(adapted from the AIDS Project of the East Bay)

There are two methods to sterilize a needle and syringe.
(1) BOIL the works (the best method)
- boil water in pot with enough water to cover the works
- separate the plunger and needle from the syringe
- drop all three parts into the water
- boil for *15 minutes*

(2) SOAK the works in Rubbing Alcohol or Bleach[3]

- pour rubbing alcohol or bleach into a clean glass
- pull rubbing alcohol or bleach into syringe through needle
- let works soak in the glass for *15 minutes*
- rinse alcohol or bleach out of works with tap water

[3] Rubbing alcohol is no longer recommended.

SECTION II

AIDS: Community Survival in the United States

Introduction

Nancy Krieger and Glen Margo

. . . you must go on, I can't go on, I'll go on.
Samuel Beckett, *The Unnamable*

Survival. The word connotes endurance, and beyond that, defiance. It is a word of determination, a word marked by time and by sorrow, a word enmeshed with mourning, and a word that bespeaks hope. To survive is to live as those surrounding you die. It is to continue, by chance or design, after some shattering event cuts the very flow of time into "after" and "before." Bearing witness to severed ties, the fact of survival at once underscores our connections to others as it highlights the fragile nature of these bonds.

Yet, although the act of surviving involves both personal loss and personal resolve, survival itself is a profoundly social phenomenon. More than a matter of simply individual luck or will, survival has always been contingent upon the most basic requirements of human existence, the most basic structures and values of human society. Food and shelter, work and rest, family and friends, reproduction and sexuality, health care and social services: the survival of present and future generations is affected by each, and all in turn are inherently linked to the functioning of the economy and the political priorities of the state. The possibility of survival cannot be divorced from the politics of survival—and nowhere has this become more evident than in the now raging global epidemic of AIDS, the acquired immune deficiency syndrome.

AIDS burst into the world's view in 1981. That year, the first case was diagnosed in the United States (1). Ever since, AIDS has posed stark questions of

Originally published in the *International Journal of Health Services* 20(4): 583–588, 1990.

survival, questions that concern not only who has died, but who shall live. Driving these questions are four striking features of the AIDS epidemic (2–4):

- Its lethal nature.
- Its three modes of transmission (sexual intercourse with an infected partner; exchange of infected blood; from an infected mother to her fetus or infant).
- Its concentration among men and women aged 20 to 44, the prime productive and reproductive years.
- Its disproportionate effect on, hence increased stigmatization of and discrimination against, oppressed and marginalized populations: women and men in Third World countries; people of color within the United States; gay and bisexual men; intravenous drug users and their partners plus children; sex workers, and prisoners.

At least 5 million people in 152 countries scattered across all five continents are estimated to be infected by the human immunodeficiency virus (HIV): 2.5 million in Africa, 2 million in the Americas, 500,000 in Europe, and about 100,000 in Asia and Oceania (5). At issue is the survival not only of these individuals, but of entire families, communities, regions, and perhaps even nations (4).

Numbing numbers alone, however, define neither the scope nor the mandate of the response to AIDS. The task of prevention, the provision of care, the search for a cure—throughout the history of public health, these have never been simply technical exercises (6). Instead, they are activities fundamentally shaped by social priorities, by the availability of resources, and by the multiple agendas of those who set and react to these priorities, who control and contest these resources. Screening blood for HIV is hardly a possibility in nations whose annual health budgets amounts to only $0.30 per capita (U.S. dollars) (4)—yet in some of these countries the military budget outstrips social spending by a ratio of more than 10 to 1 (7). Nor is it a simple matter, even in much wealthier nations, to secure resources for and prevent discrimination against persons with AIDS when the epidemic is concentrated among gay men, intravenous drug users (IVDUs), and people of color, for hatred of homosexuality, contempt for the "undeserving poor," and racism run deep (3, 8). Representing the outcome of intense struggle among the different forces grappling with the epidemic, the social response to AIDS is neither inevitable nor monolithic, and is always shaped by each society's cultural legacy and its historic and present position in the world economy.

In the case of AIDS, moreover, it has become increasingly clear that diverse stakeholders differ drastically in how they have been affected by, define, and thus aim to resolve the epidemic of crises linked to this disease. The cast of characters is as varied as the interests they represent, and includes: people who are seropositive for HIV or have AIDS, their families and the communities from which they come, other AIDS activists, public health professionals, health care providers, health insurance companies, the pharmaceutical industry, banks, the legal system, the prison system, the military, the education system, religious institutions, international development agencies and nongovernmental organizations, governments, politicians, and the public at large. Although some in public health may see AIDS as primarily a public health problem, it is important to remember that for others the epidemic has provided new grounds for empire building, whether it be through boosting scientific or political careers, battling over turf and money in the fast-growing AIDS industry, winning converts through evangelical aid agencies and crusades, promoting political parties and organizations, or protecting national security (3, 7, 8). Much more than AIDS is at the issue in the AIDS epidemic.

Even where AIDS *is* the legitimate focus of concern, the specific form assumed by battles over policies and programs depends on how the "problem" is posed and what theories of disease causation are invoked, for the solutions ventured rarely transcend the paradigms that guide their birth. At issue is whether AIDS is seen primarily as a moral issue, a medical disease, a complex public health problem, or a threat to economic productivity and development. At stake are competing systems of ethics and values, opposing views of social justice. Given this context, it is not surprising that AIDS- related conflicts routinely erupt around such basic issues as democratic and human rights, the right to health care, reproductive rights, and the allocation of funds for health research and health services. Hinging upon all these debates are not only the livelihood and lives of people infected by HIV, including those ill with AIDS, but also the funding and implementation of AIDS prevention and research programs, whose survival often is as precarious as that of the people whose interests they allegedly serve.

If the worldwide fight against AIDS is to succeed, and if widely divergent national programs are to be united into a comprehensive and integrated approach, then our understanding of the different social, political, and economic issues involved, both domestic and international, necessarily will have to be as sophisticated and detailed as our knowledge of the HIV genome and the pathogenesis of the disease. Only by incorporating both types of insights will we be able to comprehend—and perhaps ultimately interrupt—the dynamics of the social production and reproduction of the AIDS epidemic.

Adding to the urgency of this task is the rapidly changing world situation. Times of turmoil—of economic instability, of altered migration patterns, of changing mores—have always proved fertile ground for the propagation of epidemics (6). The thawing of the cold war; the upheavals in Eastern Europe and the Soviet Union; the looming economic consolidation of Western Europe; the plans of major aid donors to divert substantial funds from Third World programs to Eurocentric political initiatives; the intensified conflicts in South Africa, the Middle East, and Latin America; the rising significance of the Pacific Rim; the declining economy of the United States—all undoubtedly will influence the future course of not just AIDS, but other diseases as well.

In a world whose social order is changing before our eyes, AIDS insistently brings new meaning to the age-old question of what it is we must do to survive—as individuals, as families, as communities, as nations, as members of an interdependent world. In one short decade, the politics of AIDS has become the politics of survival. Within our lifetime, AIDS has cleaved the course of time: we all now live in this age of AIDS. If our survival and that of future generations is to be less a matter of chance and more one of conscious and just design, it is imperative that we refine our understanding of the complex problems created by the AIDS epidemic and the context in which they unfold. Only on the basis of this knowledge can we develop viable and constructive interventions.

AIDS: COMMUNITY SURVIVAL IN THE UNITED STATES

Section II concerns AIDS and the survival of communities. Addressing different aspects and implications of the AIDS epidemic, the three chapters in this section consider, through concrete analysis, the question of AIDS and the politics of survival within the United States. Vividly examining the ways in which a wide range of social, political, economic, and cultural factors have influenced the epidemic's course, all three clearly articulate why and how these factors must be taken into account when designing and implementing AIDS prevention and control programs.

In Chapter 2, "AIDS Prevention in the United States: Lessons from the First Decade," Dr. Nicholas Freudenberg cogently delineates the limits of traditional public health strategies in tackling the epidemic, and suggests additional avenues for action. For example, providing educational information is not enough; instead, we need interactive communication and interventions that empower people and enable them to take ownership of and sustain community-based efforts to prevent AIDS. Other failures, many of which can be attributed to the biomedical tunnel-vision that has guided AIDS policy during this first decade, include: restricting AIDS funding to intervention programs that address *only* AIDS, separating treatment and prevention services, not acknowledging the widespread distrust of political and scientific officialdom, and focusing on individual behavior change rather than the social and political factors that shape behavior.

As we enter our second decade of AIDS, Freudenberg urges us to take heed of the costly lessons learned from the gay and black and Latino communities now devastated by this epidemic. To Freudenberg, a central question we must ask is how we can turn the vision of a world without AIDS into a primary tool for community involvement and action. As we work to prevent AIDS, our daily activities, our planning and policy formulations, must be rooted in social justice and equity. But, as Freudenberg forcefully reminds us, we are not simply fighting AIDS: we are also striving to build a better world in which the unjust conditions that foster its spread no longer exist.

Chapter 3, by Dr. Ernest Drucker, "Epidemic in the War Zone: AIDS and Community Survival in New York City," builds on Freudenberg's observations, and analyzes the epidemic's grip on the city's poorest communities and its dire implications for their future. Emphasizing the social epidemiology of AIDS and its potential to diffuse outward to a world beyond the urban epicenter, Drucker points out that populations at risk are created by socioeconomic conditions and in turn are better defined by social characteristics than by biological susceptibilities. In a city polarized between the wealthy and the poor, between whites and people of color, the volatile factors of social class and race, joined with gender and age, and their association with the behavioral determinants of risk for AIDS—sexuality and drug use—form the context of this epidemic.

Chapter 3 also highlights how the AIDS epidemic has intersected with concurrent crises that already threaten community survival in that beleaguered city. Overwhelmed public hospitals, the lack of affordable housing, high levels of unemployment and incarceration, and a shortage of slots in drug abuse treatment facilities together set the stage for and are exacerbated by the AIDS epidemic. In the face of enormous social destruction and cruel competition for scarce resources, Drucker asks: how can we better mobilize and expand the pool of people dedicated to fighting for the survival of their communities? As one response, Drucker cites examples of successful community-based AIDS interventions in the South Bronx that draw on the often untapped strengths of extended family networks among the urban poor. Instead of trying to create comprehensive social services de novo, Drucker suggests, we would perhaps do better integrating AIDS programs into existing institutions that utilize these and other extant social ties. Even so, Drucker notes, our efforts will be hampered until city, state, and federal officials are forced to muster the political will required to release urgently needed resources to combat this epidemic.

The question of political leadership and accountability is also addressed by Anne-Emanuelle Birn, John Santelli, and LaWanda Burwell in Chapter 4, "Pediatric AIDS in the United States: Epidemiological Reality versus Government Policy." Examining issues raised by HIV infection among several different age groups—infants and toddlers, young school-age children, and teenagers—the authors contrast the high degree of governmental involvement in school placement policies with the relative absence of effective programs geared to the children at greatest risk: those at the youngest and oldest extremes of the pediatric spectrum.

In particular, Birn and coauthors point out that by 1992 AIDS will be one of the five leading causes of both infant and childhood mortality in the United States, with the vast majority of HIV-infected infants and toddlers located in poor, urban minority communities. Representing the second generation placed at risk by this epidemic, virtually all of these seropositive children are born to mothers who became infected either through their own or their partner's use of drugs. Yet, instead of promoting programs to reduce the risk of AIDS infection among this group of women or bolstering foster care initiatives to look after these children, governmental agencies at the local, state, and federal level have been more concerned with issues regarding school attendance by primarily white and middle-class HIV-infected children. And, as Birn and coauthors describe, once in school, policy problems associated with AIDS are far from over. For example, moralistic obstacles presently impede implementation of explicit AIDS education programs on safer sex. One consequence is increasing HIV transmission among adolescents, as reflected by the rapidly rising rate of AIDS among young adults in their early 20s. Until and unless AIDS interventions grapple with the problems of childhood poverty and the realities of teen sexuality, Birn and colleagues argue, these grim trends will only worsen.

The glaring gap between public policy and the hard data presented by these three chapters makes the struggle for survival of present and future generations a pressing concern. The problems described and potential strategies proposed are relevant to AIDS activists not only within the United States but worldwide.

REFERENCES

1. Pneumocystis pneumonia—Los Angeles. *MMWR* 30: 250–252, 1981.
2. Institute of Medicine, National Academy of Sciences. *Confronting AIDS: Update 1988*. National Academy Press, Washington, D.C., 1989.
3. Krieger, N., and Appleman, R. *The Politics of AIDS*. Frontline Pamphlets, Oakland, Calif., 1986.
4. The Panos Institute. *AIDS and the Third World*. New Society Publishers, Philadelphia, 1989.
5. Mann, J. M. Global AIDS into the 1990s. *World Health*, October 1989, pp. 6–7.
6. Rosen, G. *The History of Public Health*. MD Publications, New York, 1958.
7. Hancock, G. *Lords of Poverty: The Power, Prestige and Corruption of the International Aid Business*. Atlantic Monthly Press, New York, 1989.
8. Carter, E., and Watney, S. (eds.). *Taking Liberties: AIDS and Cultural Politics*. Serpent's Tail, London, 1989.

CHAPTER 2

AIDS Prevention in the United States: Lessons from the First Decade

Nicholas Freudenberg

As the end of the first decade of the AIDS/HIV epidemic in the United States approaches, it is appropriate to take stock of what has been accomplished, what has been learned, and what needs to be done to prevent the further spread of this epidemic and to care for those already affected. For the past years, much of the effort has been dominated by crisis: the urgent need for AIDS education, particularly for groups not reached by mainstream media; the delayed reaction to the epidemic on the part of federal, state, and local governments; and the failure to acknowledge that AIDS was a problem of women, African-Americans, Latinos, and other ethnic groups as well as gay white men. This crisis orientation was perhaps a necessary response to a real emergency, but the price for our lack of planning is high: too many programs duplicate some services while leaving other needs unmet; too few educational programs have been evaluated; and nearly nine years after the first case of AIDS was diagnosed, the United States still lacks consensus on many of the basic public health, moral, and social questions related to AIDS prevention. As a result of these failures, people who might have been protected became infected, communities that might have been spared experienced the full impact of this epidemic, and people who might have lived have died.

The urgent question facing public health workers and community activists in the United States today is whether they can learn enough from the gay and black and Latino communities that have already been devastated by the epidemic to take effective action now, or whether two years hence other communities around the nation will also face high infection rates and climbing death tolls. Two factors will determine the answer to this question. One is the quality of the leadership and the

Originally published in the *International Journal of Health Services* 20(4) 589–599, 1990.

quantity of resources provided by the federal government for AIDS prevention in the next few years. The other is the skill and commitment that AIDS educators and activists demonstrate in developing, implementing, and evaluating effective AIDS prevention programs. In this chapter I will review some lessons from the experiences of AIDS educators during the past nine years, identify some problems that are blocking further progress, and suggest some directions for the future.

THE IMPACT OF AIDS EDUCATION

Since AIDS/HIV disease was first identified in the early 1980s, educational activities designed to change attitudes, knowledge, and behavior have been carried out. These include distribution of pamphlets, community education, mass media coverage, one-to-one counseling, condom distribution, telephone hotlines, demonstrations, lobbying, civil disobedience, and hundreds of other activities (1). Although it is seldom possible to distinguish the impact of any single intervention, data from several sources and a number of recent literature reviews make it possible to make some broad generalizations about the effect of AIDS education.

Most of the population of the United States now has fairly accurate information about how HIV is transmitted and how to protect themselves. Surveys of adolescents, drug users, prostitutes, and the general population show that the overwhelming proportion of people have most of the essential facts on AIDS (2–6). Moreover, surveys of the U.S. population by the National Center for Health Statistics suggest that the proportion of the population with such accurate knowledge continues to increase (7). For example, the proportion of people who said it was definitely true that a pregnant woman could pass HIV on to her baby increased from 69 percent in August 1987 to 80 percent in August 1988. This high and growing level of accurate knowledge about AIDS constitutes a triumph for AIDS education and demonstrates, particularly, the power of the media in reaching people.

But it would be a mistake to be complacent about the successes in providing information. Significant portions of the population continue to believe that mosquitoes, sharing food with someone infected with HIV, using public toilets, or being sneezed on can transmit infection (7). Such misconceptions contribute to the discrimination that people with AIDS, or those perceived to be at risk of infection, often encounter.

Some sectors of the population have not yet fully benefited from educational campaigns. For example, a study in Arizona by Dr. Antonio Estrada and colleagues (8) found that Native Americans living on reservations were less knowledgeable about AIDS than urban Native Americans, and that Latinos less acculturated into U.S. society were less knowledgeable than more acculturated Latinos. A study in San Francisco found that although white, black, and Latino high-school students knew that AIDS was sexually transmitted, fewer blacks and Latinos than whites knew that condoms could protect against transmission (9).

People with less formal education continue to lack some vital facts. While 92 percent of the U.S. population with more than 12 years of education believes that it is definitely or probably false that you can tell if someone has HIV infection just by looking at them, fully 25 percent of those with less than 12 years of education do not know the answer to this question (10). Identifying and addressing such gaps in knowledge is a critical task for AIDS educators in the years to come.

Attitudes toward AIDS have also changed, but here it is more difficult to assess their significance. In August 1987, 60 percent of the U.S. population believed its risk for becoming infected was low; a year later this proportion increased to 75 percent (7). Does this reflect an accurate assessment of risk and a reduction in unnecessary anxiety, or have the media made people think that only gay men or IV drug users are at risk? Substantial segments of the population continue to have punitive attitudes toward people with AIDS, believing that the condition is a punishment for immoral behavior (3). Such attitudes make it harder to convince people that AIDS is a problem for everyone, whether one is personally at risk or not.

Other attitudes also shape the social environment for AIDS prevention. Public opinion polls show strong support for government-supported education: as early as 1985 a national poll showed that 74 percent of the respondents supported production and distribution of explicit safer-sex educational materials. A 1987 Louis Harris poll showed that 60 percent of American adults supported television advertising of condoms (1). However, despite broad public support for AIDS and sex education in schools, development and implementation of these programs have been blocked repeatedly by a vocal minority of religious leaders and conservatives. In New York City, for example, a film on AIDS for high-school students was withheld for more than a year because it did not sufficiently stress abstinence.

In the arena of public opinion, substantial support can be found for both humane and punitive policies. While much of the public would be willing to support more intensive prevention efforts, there is also backing for more coercive measures to control the epidemic. Polls show that somewhere between 25 and 40 percent of the population would support quarantine, mandatory HIV testing, banning of HIV-infected children from schools, and other such policies (3).

AIDS education programs have contributed to a variety of changes in behavior. Let us first look at behavior related to education itself. By December 1988, 62 percent of the respondents to the National Center for Health Statistics survey reported that they had discussed AIDS with their children aged 10 to 17. About 60 percent reported that their children had received education on AIDS at school, indicating substantial progress in changing the behavior of school systems (10). As noted, however, school programs are often unable to use the clear and explicit language that would help young people protect themselves. Substantial portions of the population reported watching public service announcements, reading pamphlets on AIDS, or talking with a friend about AIDS. Only 3 percent, however, had discussed AIDS with a health professional (10). These data confirm that many people have taken action to get AIDS information but fewer have participated in more intensive interventions.

When we turn to evidence for reductions in risk behavior the data present a complex story. One repeated finding is that accurate information is not by itself a predictor of behavior change (2, 5). It may be a necessary condition, but it is certainly not sufficient. Gay men have shown the most significant changes in sexual behavior. According to Marshall Becker of the University of Michigan, the reductions in risky behavior among some groups of gay men "may be the most rapid and profound response to a health threat which has ever been documented" (5). Some studies show that perhaps 90 percent of urban gay men have made some changes in their sexual behavior to reduce the risk from HIV infection. But this tells only half the story. Many men who have sex with men do not consistently practice safer sex. They may use condoms more, have unprotected anal intercourse less, and have fewer partners, but only a small minority always follow safer sex guidelines (2, 5, 11). This suggests the critical importance of ongoing support for risk reduction, often called "relapse prevention" (12). Moreover, there is some evidence that the changes observed in large, organized urban gay communities with a high incidence of AIDS have not occurred in gay populations in low-incidence areas, among gay men of color, or among those still "in the closet" (2, 5, 13, 14). The gay community's experience with AIDS demonstrates that it is possible to make dramatic changes in sexual behavior in a relatively short time; however, ongoing interventions are needed to sustain these changes over time.

For drug users, the news is also mixed. Based on their review of the literature, Des Jarlais and Friedman (15) of the New York State Division of Substance Abuse Services concluded that more than half the IV drug users who have participated in studies have made some changes in their risk behavior related to AIDS. Somewhat more than half have made changes in their drug habits, either getting off drugs or using clean needles more often, and somewhat less than half have changed their sexual behavior, either by using condoms or reducing the number of partners. Fewer are practicing these changes consistently, emphasizing the need for ongoing education and support. Not only intravenous heroin users but also crack users who combine crack with injected cocaine, heroin, or other drugs, and who often have many sex partners and may trade sex for drugs, are at high risk for HIV infection (16, 17). This is an ominous development that puts hundreds of thousands, especially young people, African-Americans, and Latinos in urban areas, at risk of HIV infection. A major challenge for AIDS educators is to help their constituents understand the crack–AIDS link and to help communities develop effective programs to combat crack addition.

Less evidence is available on behavior change among populations other than gay men and drug users, but several studies show that very few adolescents, whether high-school students, dropouts, or college students, are protecting themselves against HIV (2, 5, 9). Those who now use condoms for casual sexual encounters often stop using them with regular partners.

The ray of hope in these findings is that those groups that have been most intensively targeted for education—gay men and drug users—have shown the most dramatic changes in behavior. Thus, similar efforts for other populations might lead to similar results. A more pessimistic view is that only high death tolls will convince a population that changes in behavior are needed. Failing to act decisively now guarantees that only the second explanation will be tested. Given the current patterns of HIV infection, choosing this path is nothing short of genocide against people of color. As Harvey Fineberg, Dean of the Harvard School of Public Health, has observed, "the best we can do in AIDS education offers no guarantee of success. To do less invites failure" (18).

OBSTACLES TO PROGRESS

From the data summarized above and from interviews with more than 100 AIDS educators around the country and several dozen community AIDS workers in New York City, six major obstacles to more effective AIDS education are apparent (1, 19).

1. *Too much AIDS education seeks only to provide information.* Because of the success of previous efforts, most people now know the basic facts about AIDS. It is time to move on to the question of behavior and the social environment in which that behavior occurs. Those information campaigns that continue should be targeted at specific subgroups identified as lacking relevant knowledge and at reinforcing existing knowledge rather than teaching people what they already know. These should be local efforts with a high level of involvement of the target population. Paying Madison Avenue advertising companies millions of dollars for public service announcements, as several government agencies are doing, will probably not buy much in AIDS prevention.

2. *Too many AIDS education programs rely on one-way communication.* Changing drug and sexual behaviors requires engaging people on the most intimate subjects of their lives. As noted by Ruth Rodriguez, formerly with the Hispanic AIDS Forum in New York City, "confianza," or trust, is an essential characteristic of an effective relationship between educator and learner. Such trust cannot develop if information flows only one way, from the educator to the learner. Rather, it necessitates an interaction in which learners teach about their community, culture, and values, and teachers listen so that they can anchor education in an existing framework. Too much of AIDS education has been what the Brazilian educator Paulo Freire (20) calls "banking education" in which the teacher deposits knowledge in the supposedly empty head of the students where it can be withdrawn on demand. Many AIDS educators working in ethnic communities have developed useful models for involving community residents in planning and implementing AIDS prevention programs (1, 21, 22).

3. *Too many AIDS prevention programs focus narrowly on AIDS as a single issue.* The vast majority of funding for AIDS prevention has been restricted to

programs that address only AIDS. A number of factors contributed to this narrow approach: the fact that AIDS was a new problem needing new resources, the success of AIDS activists in convincing Congress to appropriate money for AIDS, a tradition of categorical funding for single diseases, and an unwillingness to look at the political and social roots of many of our society's ills. But while more federal dollars for AIDS are urgently needed, the narrow categorical approach has several adverse consequences.

First, people do not experience AIDS as a separate problem. As a nurse working in a church-based program in the South Bronx said, "There's a whole death list in this community. AIDS is just one more thing besides loss of jobs, education, housing and health care." In many communities, AIDS is not the first issue people want to address. By having the flexibility to start with infant mortality, sexually transmitted diseases, substance abuse, inadequate schools, or lack of housing, AIDS educators can increase their chances of engaging people and creating a relationship in which AIDS can be discussed. Moreover, many of the pressing problems facing our communities are directly connected to AIDS: drug abuse, teen pregnancy, and lack of primary and preventive health care.

Second, categorical AIDS prevention programs are not likely to work without access to drug treatment; treatment for sexually transmitted diseases; contraceptive, abortion, and prenatal care; and comprehensive sexuality, drug, and health education in schools and communities (23). To create high-quality AIDS education programs without providing people with the means to change their behavior is like building a house with no foundation: it will inevitably collapse.

Third, AIDS-specific funding leaves programs vulnerable to shifting political winds. How long will the government or foundations make support of AIDS prevention a priority? As the epidemic becomes concentrated in African-American and Latino communities, can communities continue to depend on a mostly white, mostly male, mostly wealthy Congress and White House to provide the needed resources? By setting up separate AIDS organizations and programs, they become sitting ducks for conservatives who want to use the epidemic to advance their conservative political agenda.

4. *AIDS programs lack a comprehensive approach to prevention and treatment.* Few AIDS services integrate prevention and treatment. In reality the two are inseparably intertwined. For example, good AIDS education in prisons helps to prevent discrimination against inmates with AIDS, encouraging them to get needed treatment. Support groups for HIV-positive people help them to initiate and maintain the behavior changes that will prevent them from infecting others. But too often prevention and treatment compete for limited resources. As the number of infected people grows, and as the inadequacies of the United States' medical care system become more apparent, officials are likely to cut money for prevention in order to expand treatment. Unless AIDS workers can make the case for an integrated system of care, these pendulum swings between prevention

and treatment will continue, each leaving in its shadow deaths that could have been prevented.

5. *Too few AIDS education programs acknowledge and address the distrust that many people feel toward government, scientists, and health officials.* According to a 1989 National Center for Health Statistics survey, 28 percent of their sample of the U.S. adult population was doubtful about AIDS information provided by federal health officials; another 6 percent of respondents did not know whether to believe what they are told. For those with less than 12 years of education, the proportion in these two categories rises to 44 percent (10).

A federal government that has dismantled many programs serving poor people over the last nine years, a Supreme Court that has thrown out important affirmative action precedents and restricted the rights of poor women to get abortions, state governments whose spending for prisons increased at three times the rate of spending for public assistance, and federal health programs that will pay for a woman to get sterilized but not for an abortion—together create a social climate in which many low-income people may not want to hear what the government has to say about their sexual and drug behaviors. How people perceive the government and health authorities profoundly influences whether they will listen to, hear, or follow the messages offered. Many of those most in need of AIDS education—drug users, gay men, homeless people, street kids, workers in the sex industry—have not had much positive experience with governments. Public health officials may need to support organizations very distant from government, even critical of it, if these populations are to be reached. Funders, however, are often unwilling to take these risks.

6. *Most AIDS prevention programs focus too much on individual behavior and too little on the social and political factors that shape that behavior.* To reduce the incidence of HIV infection, AIDS education programs need to help people change their sexual and drug habits. But sexuality and drug use are complicated behaviors, deeply rooted in cultural, social, economic, and political ground. To attempt to change the behavior without changing the social environment in which that behavior occurs ignores much of what we know about health education. It also reinforces a tendency all too common in public health programs to blame the victims of disease rather than the perpetrators of the social conditions that create illness (24–26).

Take a "simple" behavior such as using a condom. What influences the decision to use one? It includes what one thinks about how people are supposed to relate to each other, especially about sex; whether one believes acting now will pay off in the future, or if one even has a future. It includes how friends will react, what religion says, and what using a condom means about the kind of person one is. For a woman, it means thinking about how a male partner is going to react if she asks him to use a condom. So AIDS education programs that tell people about the benefits of condoms, show people how to use them, and then hand them out only begin to address the problem.

Interviews with community groups working on AIDS in New York City reveal two central issues that AIDS prevention programs have to address (19). One is gender relations, how our society and culture define what it means to be a man or a woman. The profound inequality between men and women in every culture within our society contributes to the sexual double standard, in which men can do what they want sexually and women cannot; it contributes to women's economic dependence on men, limiting their ability to negotiate equal, mutual relationships; it forces women to have major responsibility for child care and health, including the protection of fetuses. Each of these directly increases the risk of HIV infection. For too long AIDS educators have been unwilling to tackle sexism head on because it is too divisive. But there is no more powerful force influencing sexual behavior, and if sexism is off limits, the ability to change how people have sex is very limited. The question is not whether to discuss sexual inequality but how to raise it in a way that respects the particular dynamics of each culture.

The second central issue is how to respond to the current epidemic of drug use. Two common attitudes are first, a pessimism that anything at all can be done, and second, a desire to lock up every pusher and user and throw away the keys. Neither offers a useful strategy for AIDS prevention, and both reflect the lack of creative thinking and leadership on the drug problem from any level of society.

These are both obviously enormous issues with no promise of simple answers. Neither can be addressed at the individual level. The goal has to be to engage communities in dialogues on these two questions. Such a dialogue is an essential condition for sustained behavior change; the success of some gay communities in initiating such discussions has contributed to dramatic declines in the incidence of HIV infection. AIDS educators need to help other communities to create a social environment where people can talk about these issues, debate different points of view, and question their own beliefs and values. This is a very different task from handing out condoms, teaching addicts to clean their "works," or explaining safer sex guidelines, which, while necessary, will not be enough to contain the spread of HIV.

Every neighborhood has organizations that can initiate these discussions. In Washington Heights in Upper Manhattan, for example, social clubs for Dominicans provide an ideal opportunity to talk to men about families and health and surviving in a new country. In a black neighborhood in Brooklyn, day care mothers have invited friends and neighbors into their living rooms to watch a video on AIDS, then talk about how to protect themselves. In the South Bronx, a social action group based in several local churches brought together younger and older women to talk about changing values in families and about men and sex.

What these organizations share is an ongoing, intimate, and trusting relationship with their members. The important lesson for funders and policy makers is that all community organizations are not the same. Those groups that represent elites in a community may have a better track record on fiscal management and write more professional proposals, but it is unlikely that they know how to talk to people in their neighborhood about drugs, sex, and what it feels like to be poor. They probably are not the ones to organize people to demand the services and programs needed to contain this epidemic. Community-level workers need to look for and support those grassroots organizations connected to ordinary people. Funders and policy makers need to convince their agencies that taking some risks with these groups is essential if AIDS prevention is going to move forward in poor and minority populations.

FUTURE DIRECTIONS

How can AIDS prevention programs address these obstacles? First, programs must come from within the culture of the target population and at the same time challenge cultural values that put people at risk of HIV. Too often, AIDS educators have adopted a simplistic view of culture. Either culture is seen entirely as an obstacle to risk reduction ("Why do 'those people' act in such self-destructive ways?"), or it is seen as a fixed entity that must be respected no matter what. This viewpoint allows AIDS prevention workers to accept machismo, homophobia, or racism without question. In reality, all cultures are dynamic and heterogeneous. The strong grandmother is as much a part of Latino culture as the macho man. Black churches have traditions of both acceptance of and harsh condemnation of homosexuality. The challenge for AIDS educators is to identify elements of the culture that can support prevention and risk reduction, and to help populations to question other elements that increase risk. Nor is culture ever divorced from a socioeconomic matrix. As De La Cancela (22) has observed, effective AIDS prevention programs need to address the interactions between culture, economics, and politics.

Second, AIDS prevention must be integrated into other programs serving community needs. Every group initially responds to AIDS with denial. But by showing the concrete connections between AIDS and substance abuse, teen pregnancy, infant mortality, inadequate education, and poverty, AIDS educators can help communities to find an appropriate place for AIDS on their political agenda. Government agencies and other funders need to find ways to ensure that their money is being spent on AIDS without so restricting agencies that they have trouble enlisting the trust and support of their constituents.

Third, grassroots organizations that are already connected to people's everyday lives should be enlisted in the AIDS prevention effort. Many governments have made remarkable progress in funding community organizations that they would barely have spoken to a few years ago. But too often the funded groups are still one level removed from the lives of people at risk of HIV infection. While some organizations need significant funding to develop AIDS programs, many grassroots groups also need training, help in thinking through the issue, and small-scale financial support for such activities as child care for participants, producing flyers, and mailings. Funding needs to be more flexible so that these groups can also be helped. Our ability to raise the issues of gender relations and substance abuse depends on finding and strengthening those groups best qualified to raise these questions.

Fourth, AIDS educators working at the community level should support those individuals and organizations that take a more political approach to AIDS. The future direction of this epidemic depends as much on what happens in the political arena as it does on new discoveries in the laboratories or on hospital wards. Some are more comfortable simply providing a service, but people are also needed who can fight for legislation and demonstrate for more resources. The emergence of a group like ACTUP (AIDS Coalition to Unleash Power) in the gay community demonstrates how militants can reinforce and deepen the work of the earlier organizations, which now devote most of their energy to providing vital services to people with AIDS. It would be a tragedy if every group concerned with AIDS in African-American and Latino communities became so dependent on government money to provide services that it was forced to give up the opportunity to link the fight to control AIDS with other struggles for social justice. Government will inevitably use its financial power to limit the scope of AIDS prevention programs; AIDS activists cannot leave this control uncontested.

Finally, the AIDS prevention effort has to be connected with a vision of a better world. Let's face it: a world where everyone uses a condom every time they exchange bodily fluids or where every drug user cleans his or her works just doesn't turn many people on. It is not enough to sustain the incredible energy, commitment, anger, and love that most AIDS workers put into their work every day. It is not enough to mobilize communities to protect themselves. Yet by focusing on individual behavior change, AIDS educators do not offer people more. If they do offer more, it is the negative image of protecting oneself from a deadly disease—also not enough to sustain concerted effort.

The reality is that a world without AIDS, or a world with this epidemic under control, will look very different. AIDS educators and activists need to help people visualize this world and connect their daily activities to making it happen. It will be a world where every one is entitled to comprehensive education about sexuality, drugs, and health; a world where those who need treatment for drug addiction can get it on demand; a world where basic health care is a right, not a privilege; a world where gay men and lesbians, women and people of color, are not discriminated against; a world where alternatives to drug use exist for the young people of this country; a world where no one has to die on the streets because there is no home for them. That is the world AIDS activists work for when they try to teach people about AIDS. That is the kind of world people are willing to fight and live for. That is the world we can create together that will give some meaning to this terrible epidemic.

REFERENCES

1. Freudenberg, N. *Preventing AIDS: A Guide to Effective Education for the Prevention of HIV Infection*. American Public Health Association, Washington, D.C., 1989.
2. Turner, C. F., Miller, H. G., and Moses, L. E. (eds.). *AIDS, Sexual Behavior and Intravenous Drug Use*. National Academy Press, Washington, D.C., 1989.
3. Blake, S., and Arkins, E. B. *AIDS Information Monitor. A Summary of National Public Opinion Surveys on AIDS 1983 through 1986*. American Red Cross, Washington, D.C., 1988.
4. Selwyn, P. A., et al. Knowledge about AIDS and high-risk behavior among intravenous drug users in New York City. *AIDS* 1: 247-254, 1987.
5. Becker, M. H., and Joseph, J. G. AIDS and behavioral change to reduce risk: A review. *Am. J. Public Health* 78(4): 394–410, 1988.
6. National Center for Health Statistics, Dawson, D. A., and Hardy, A. M. AIDS knowledge and attitudes of Black Americans—Provisional data from the 1988 National Health Interview Survey. Advance data from *Vital and Health Statistics*, No. 165. U.S. Department of Health and Human Services, Public Health Service, Hyattsville, Md., 1989.
7. HIV epidemic and AIDS: Trends in knowledge—United States, 1987 and 1988. *MMWR* 38(20): 353–363, 1989.
8. Estrada, A., et al. *Survey of Knowledge, Attitudes and Behaviors Related to HIV/AIDS of Ethnic Minorities in Arizona*. Arizona State Department of Health, Phoenix, 1989.
9. DiClemente, R., Boyer, C., and Morales, E. Minorities and AIDS knowledge, attitudes and misconceptions among black and Latino adolescents. *Am. J. Public Health* 78(1): 55–57, 1988.
10. National Center for Health Statistics, Dawson, D. A. AIDS knowledge and attitudes: August 1988—provisional data from the 1988 National Health Interview Survey. Advance data from *Vital and Health Statistics*, No. 163. U.S. Department of Health and Human Services, Public Health Service, Hyattsville, Md., 1989.
11. Martin, J. L., Garcia, M. A., and Beatrice, S. T. Sexual behavior changes and HIV antibody in a cohort of New York City gay men. *Am. J. Public Health* 79(4): 501–503, 1989.
12. Marlatt, G. A., and Gordon, J. R. *Maintenance Strategies in the Treatment of Addiction*. Guilford, New York, 1985.
13. Calabrese, L. H., et al. Persistence of high risk sexual activity among homosexual men in an area of low incidence of AIDS. *AIDS Res.* 2(4): 357–361, 1986.
14. Jones, C. C., et al. Persistence of high risk sexual activity among homosexual men in an area of low incidence of AIDS. *Sex. Transm. Dis.* 14: 79–82, 1987.
15. Des Jarlais, D., and Friedman, S. The psychology of preventing AIDS among intravenous drug users. *Am. Psychol.* 43(11): 865–870, 1988.
16. Chaisson, R. E., et al. Cocaine, Race and HIV Infection in IV Drug Users. Paper presented at the Fourth International AIDS Conference, Stockholm, June 12–16, 1988.
17. Friedman, S. R., et al. Crack Use Puts Women at Risk for Heterosexual Transmission of HIV from Intravenous Drug Users. Paper presented at the Fourth International AIDS Conference, Stockholm, June 12–16, 1988.
18. Fineberg, H. V. Education to prevent AIDS: Prospects and obstacles. *Science* 239: 592–596, 1988.
19. Freudenberg, N., Lee, J., and Silver, D. How Black and Latino Community organizations respond to the AIDS epidemic. *AIDS Educ. Prevent.* 1(1): 12–21, 1989.
20. Freire, P. *Pedagogy of the Oppressed*. Herder and Herder, New York, 1970.

21. Williams, L. S. AIDS risk reduction: A community health intervention for minority high risk group members. *Health Educ. Q.* 13(4): 407–421, 1986.
22. De La Cancela, V. Minority AIDS prevention: Moving beyond cultural perspectives toward sociopolitical empowerment. *AIDS Educ. Prevent.* 1(2): 141–153, 1989.
23. Cates, W., and Bowen, G. S. Education for AIDS prevention: Not our only voluntary weapon. *Am. J. Public Health* 79: 871–874, 1989.
24. Ryan, W. *Blaming the Victim*. Vintage Press, New York, 1971.
25. Crawford, R. You are dangerous to your health: The ideology and politics of victim blaming. *Int. J. Health Serv.* 7(4): 663–680, 1977.
26. Freudenberg, N. Health education for social change: A strategy for public health in the U.S. *Int. J. Health Educ.* 24(3): 138–145, 1981.

CHAPTER 3

Epidemic in the War Zone: AIDS and Community Survival in New York City

Ernest Drucker

Even in the best of times epidemics mean serious trouble for a large city. And, for New York City (NYC), these are not the best of times. The AIDS epidemic, which has already claimed over 15,000 lives here (1), is an unparalleled disaster for this city. Riding on waves of prior neglect, it illuminates an interrelated set of problems which, by themselves, could threaten the survival of any urban area: a large, neglected, and angry underclass; deteriorated housing and municipal infrastructure; high rates of school failure and unemployment; and the inevitable consequences—disease, crime, and broken families.

The political will and the organizational energy needed to "do the right thing"—to accept responsibility for the victims of a disordered social structure—appear to be absent. Although great wealth is evident throughout the region, financial resources are said to be unavailable for the most pressing tasks at hand; New York State and NYC each claim billion dollar deficits, and the federal government is not willing to help. So, while the political process grinds ahead at a glacial pace, the price of social failure is paid on the streets of run-down neighborhoods in the Bronx, Brooklyn, and Manhattan. This chapter begins with an examination of the grip that the AIDS epidemic already holds on NYC's poorest communities and its dire implications for the city's large underclass population. And, lest we imagine that this problem will remain confined to poor inner-city populations, I will also present evidence of the inevitable diffusion of AIDS outward to a wider world beyond the urban epicenter. Finally, I will explore the possibility of mobilizing those human resources that are still available in NYC to help blunt AIDS' fearsome impact and restrict its further spread.

Originally published in the *International Journal of Health Services* 20(4): 601–615, 1990.

AIDS IN NEW YORK CITY, 1981–1990

By late 1990, NYC will have had over 25,000 reported cases of AIDS. With less than 3 percent of the nation's population, NYC accounts for almost 20 percent of all AIDS cases in the United States (2). Yet, even this stark measure of the disproportionate impact of the epidemic understates both the extent and the character of the problem. For it is the devastating impact of AIDS on particular neighborhoods and communities of the city that really distinguishes this phase of the epidemic.

AIDS, like most epidemics, is not best understood as a single outburst of infection or disease affecting an entire population or region with equal force. Because the human immunodeficiency virus (HIV) is a blood-borne, sexual, and perinatally transmitted infection—one based on patterns of intimate contact—AIDS spreads at different rates through different communities and the distinct subpopulations that inhabit them. Populations at risk are better defined by social and behavioral characteristics than by any biological susceptibilities: social class, race, age, and their association with the behavioral determinants of risk for AIDS—sexuality and drug use—form the context of this epidemic. Further, in NYC it is the specific geographic patterning of these factors that places so many of its communities at such high risk. Geographic and demographic differences in prevalence of HIV, based upon these social characteristics, determine the probable risk of infection for others in the same communities, even for those not in the original risk groups.

As the infection establishes itself in these groups and communities over time, it first deepens in each, producing endemic levels. We can see this in the high rates of infection within the specific risk groups (e.g., gay men or drug users) and in the geographic concentration of these cases in specific neighborhoods. Then, depending on each group's or community's position in the larger social order (i.e., its sexual or drug-using contact with those outside), AIDS spreads beyond the local communities to the city as a whole and, ultimately, to the wider population beyond the urban epicenter.

The dynamism of this process can be seen in the changing characteristics of AIDS cases reported in NYC over the last few years. These form the most visible face of the disease and are generally perceived as *the epidemic*. It is individuals sick with full-blown AIDS that we are most directly aware of, and, in the aggregate, these cases have the most immediate impact on the community and its health care and social service systems. At first it is the acceleration of the incidence of AIDS cases in NYC that is most dramatic. It took almost five years—from 1981 to 1985—for the first 5,000 AIDS cases in NYC; the second 5,000 took only one and a half years, and the next 5,000 only 14 months. In 1991 we expect over 10,000 new cases and 7,000 to 8,000 deaths (1).

Table 1 presents the incidence of AIDS cases and known mortality among adults in NYC for the period 1981–1990. This rapid growth in the incidence of

AIDS cases sends shock waves through the communities most severely affected. Quite quickly, people in these areas and risk groups come to know personally someone who is sick and, soon thereafter, several people. This phenomenon, which the sociologist Kai Erickson likens to a natural disaster, was seen first and most dramatically in some of the gay communities of NYC and San Francisco, for example, Fire Island and the Castro, where young gay men "buried" 30 or more friends in just a few years (3). But it is also now visible in the rapid appearance of AIDS in places such as the Bronx. Between 1982 and 1985, AIDS hospital

Table 1

Known mortality among adult AIDS cases, by period of diagnosis, New York City[a]

		No. of cases	Percent known dead[b]
1981	Jan–June	40	90%
	July–Dec	100	93%
1982	Jan–June	178	90%
	July–Dec	304	91%
1983	Jan–June	461	90%
	July–Dec	533	91%
1984	Jan–June	776	84%
	July–Dec	949	85%
1985	Jan–June	1,233	83%
	July–Dec	1,423	82%
1986	Jan–June	1,813	81%
	July–Dec	2,124	79%
1987	Jan–June	2,393	72%
	July–Dec	2,426	65%
1988	Jan–June	2,851	56%
	July–Dec	2,640	47%
1989	Jan–June	2,351	31%
	July–Dec	1,705	10%
1990	Jan–June	41	7%
	Totalc	24,383	63%[d]
	Total cumulative deaths	15,364	

[a]Source: New York City Department of Health. *AIDS Surveillance Update*. New York, February 2, 1990.

[b]Reporting of deaths is incomplete.

[c]Table totals include 42 cases diagnosed prior to 1981, 38 of whom are known to have died.

[d]1,929 additional death dates, identified through semiannual death certificate match, were added in this report.

admissions in the Bronx rose rapidly and clustered in the poorest areas of the South Bronx (4) (Figure 1).

NYC, however, soon saw another even more striking development in the pattern of AIDS cases, as the center of the epidemic began to shift away from the original risk groups. In August of 1988, for the first time, newly reported cases of AIDS among intravenous (IV) drug users and their sexual partners in NYC outnumbered those of homosexual and bisexual men (1). More cases of AIDS related to drug use also, of course, signified a change in the relative prevalence of AIDS among heterosexuals, African-Americans and Hispanics, and women and infants. These trends have continued since August 1988, and the differences widen with each month.

Yet, even these appalling figures on AIDS cases and deaths do not give the best portrait of the epidemic's significance for the population of NYC. Ultimately, it is the underlying cause of AIDS—the HIV infection—that offers the most complete and revealing picture of both the current epidemic in the city and its probable future course. There is a very large group of HIV-infected adults in NYC, estimated at between 150 and 250 thousand people (5). The sheer size of this group is central for assessing the impact of AIDS on NYC as a whole. Further, the uneven geographic and social distribution of this large population of HIV-infected people determines the epidemic's short-term impact on local communities. It does this first by affecting incidence, the rate of new HIV infections. Whether by sexual transmission, needle sharing, or pregnancy and childbirth, HIV's spread is ultimately driven by the background prevalence levels. Most HIV-infected individuals in NYC do not know their infective status; fewer than 10 percent have tested positive. This group will, for many years, represent a substantial risk for transmission to others in NYC, mostly through unprotected heterosexual intercourse and continued widespread IV drug use. These behaviors are unlikely to change rapidly, given the city's inability to discuss human sexuality or treat drug use.

The second aspect of this early phase of the epidemic's course in NYC has to do with the rate of progression of the 200,000 individuals already infected toward full-blown AIDS and related symptomatic states. The long and variable latency of the virus, a median elapsed time of eight to ten years between infection and the appearance of full-blown AIDS (6), plays a crucial role in interpreting HIV prevalence data. If infection by HIV antedates the appearance of AIDS by almost 10 years, the timing of the spread of the original epidemic of HIV infection, and the age characteristics of those newly infected, must be reinterpreted. Both are pushed back to an earlier period, and what we see as AIDS cases now are the result of a pattern of epidemic spread long past. This latency, which determines the timing of new AIDS cases, also shapes the demand that the epidemic will place on a number of vital resources in the community—family support structures, health and social services, foster care and housing—all of which are affected today by infections transmitted a decade or more ago. Even our most successful efforts at prevention will not deter this element of AIDS' impact.

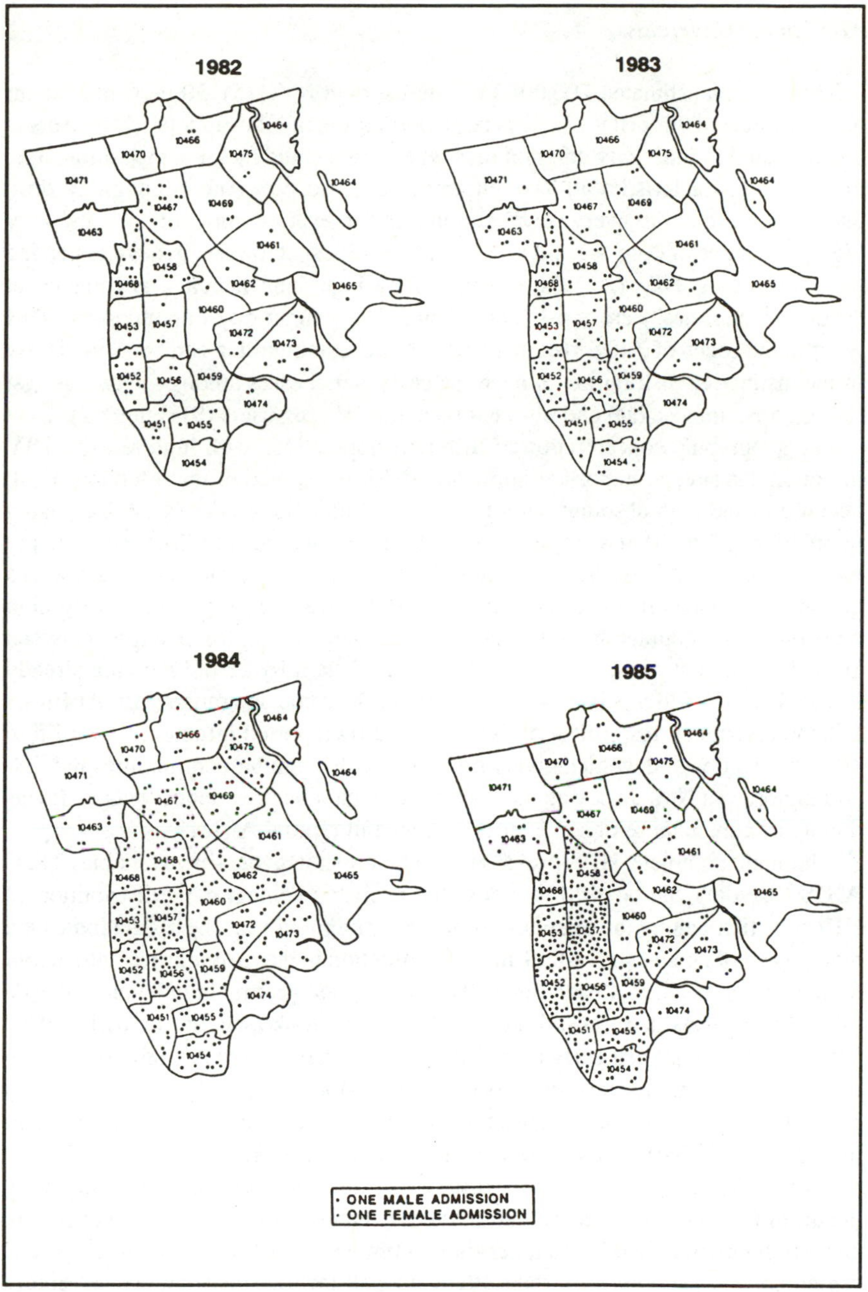

Figure 1. Hospital admissions for immune disorders in the Bronx, by zip code, among people aged 25 to 44. Source: New York State Department of Health.

AIDS in the Underclass

There are an estimated 200,000 IV drug users in NYC (5), 50 percent of them already infected with HIV (7). This large population of HIV-infected drug users is concentrated in inner-city communities where ethnic and racial composition, age, and social characteristics all have enormous significance. And although IV drug users can be found in every social stratum and in every community (8), the very high prevalence of drug use and its association with specific risk behaviors needed for transmitting HIV (i.e., the sharing of syringes and needles, attendance at "shooting galleries") are most focused in NYC's inner-city communities. This geographic focus of AIDS risk in specific NYC communities can be seen clearly in the distinctive distribution of even the early AIDS cases among the two largest risk groups: homosexual and bisexual men and IV drug users (9) (Figure 2).

The geographic concentration of different populations with high rates of HIV infection has several important implications for the spread of the infection. First, because of the high absolute rate of HIV infection among NYC's IV drug-using population (50 to 60 percent) and the high prevalence rates of drug use in many inner-city communities, the geographic concentration of drug use coincides with a geographic concentration of HIV-infected individuals. This produces very high rates of overall population prevalence. In the South Bronx, for example, between 10 and 20 percent of the *entire population* of 25- to 45-year-old men are already infected, as are 5 to 8 percent of all women in the same age range (10). At Bronx Lebanon Hospital this projection is confirmed by reported infection rates of 5 to 10 percent among all women giving birth (11). Other similar communities in NYC and in northern New Jersey appear to have comparable prevalence levels—levels that approximate those of some areas of East and Central Africa.

Although complete HIV prevalence data are not generally available, NYC AIDS case data can be used to model the probable demographic distribution of HIV infection among the populations of these communities. These data indicate a median age of people with AIDS and HIV infection in the early thirties, with about 80 percent in the 25 to 45 age range. The eight to ten year median latency of HIV infection suggests that transmission for this group took place in the early 1980s while most were in their early or mid-twenties. Gender and race/ethnicity are also quite specific. Among IV drug users with AIDS, about 75 percent are male and 85 percent African-American or Hispanic, a pattern that is most powerfully evident in pediatric AIDS cases: over 90 percent are among minorities (1).

Social networks, in which both drug use and sexual contact most frequently occur, are predicated on these demographic features: race/ethnicity, age group, and neighborhood. Within the inner-city communities of NYC, both drug use and sexual contact patterns, with their attendant risk for transmission, are extremely local in nature. "Shooting galleries" are a neighborhood institution; drug "copping" and sharing networks are usually based on teenage gang membership (itself usually bound to "turf") or on social relations originating in early

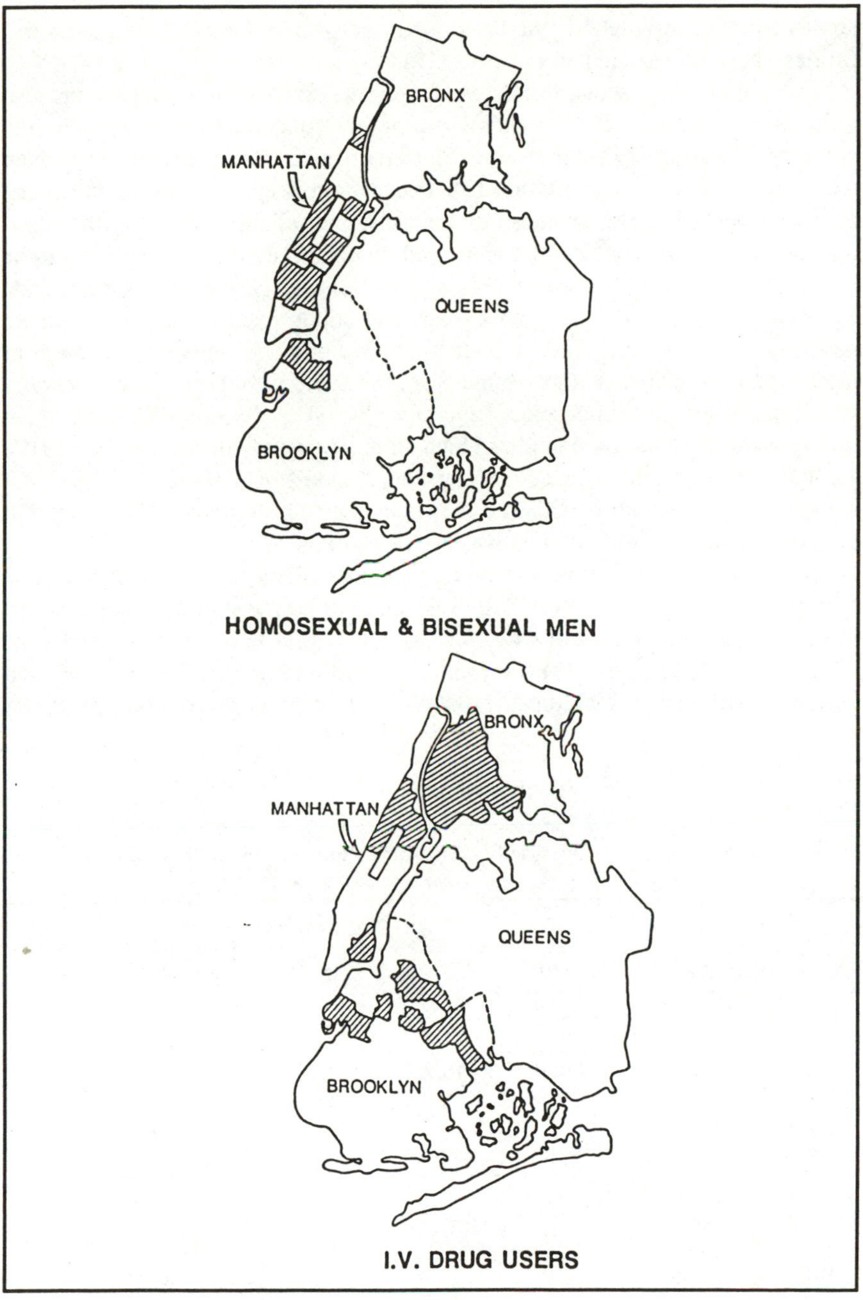

Figure 2. Distribution of AIDS cases in New York City, by zip code of residence, 1981–84. Source: reference 9.

adolescence. "The block" is the basic urban geographic unit for drug sales territories, social clubs, and party circuits (12).

In addition to these social structures of drug use, sexual contact patterns are also quite local in nature. These patterns are highly concordant by age, race, and ethnicity. Table 2 shows the results of a study of over 400 South Bronx women receiving first trimester abortions (13). This pattern is apparent in the frequency of sexual contacts between those of the same race/ethnicity and the increased likelihood of sexual contact with men aged 25 to 45 (i.e., those most likely to be HIV infected) as the woman reaches age 25 herself. This high risk for sexual exposure to HIV, associated with the age and ethnic patterns of sexual contact patterns, is further reinforced by geography. In our study, almost 50 percent of these women's sexual partners came from the same postal zip code, generally within a quarter of a mile radius (five city blocks) of the home of the woman interviewed. In such communities, high population prevalence levels of HIV among males in the sexually active years can lead to levels of HIV infection that are sustained over long periods (i.e., to endemicity), irrespective of the fact that the original mode of transmission was needle sharing.

An early indication of this developing HIV endemicity in the inner city can be seen in the results of New York State's program of HIV testing for all newborns. In 1988, close to 2 percent of women delivering babies in the inner-city areas of NYC were HIV infected (14). Between one-third and one-half of these women lacked any history of IV drug use themselves, and this proportion appears to

Table 2

Heterosexual contact patterns of South Bronx women receiving first trimester abortions (N = 429): Characteristics of current sex partners (CSP)[a]

	Age of woman				
Characteristic of CSP	<20	20–24	25–29	30–34	>35
Age:					
Median	21	26	30	34	39
Range	15–30	19–55	20–55	23–60	28–56
Percent aged 25–34	12%	46%	64%	69%	17%
Percent same race/ ethnicity as woman	90%	86%	93%	93%	84%
Zip code of residence of CSP:					
Same as woman's		41%			
Same + adjacent		59%			
Within South Bronx		70%			
Within Bronx		82%			

[a]Source: Drucker, E., et al. Abstract A604. Fifth International Conference on AIDS, Montreal, June 4–9, 1989.

be rising (15). In all likelihood, these women were the sexual partners of previously infected drug-using men. But, of course, even those women who did have histories of IV drug use were, almost universally, *also* the sexual partners of men (sometimes many men) who were IV drug users. Thus, it becomes extremely difficult to attribute these women's infection to one exposure or the other, since they were dually exposed for sustained periods of time to both risks for infection.

The relative importance of cases of AIDS among women differs dramatically by geographic region of the country. Thus for the United States as a whole, fewer than 10 percent of people with AIDS are women, whereas in the South Bronx, Harlem, and Newark, over 25 percent are female (1, 2). Aside from high rates of perinatal transmission within certain areas, high HIV prevalence rates among women also imply the potential for transmission to male sexual partners who may not themselves be drug users. The efficiency of sexual transmission of HIV is greater from males to females (as is the case with most sexually transmitted diseases), but some evidence now exists to suggest that the bidirectional transmission seen in Africa and the Caribbean is occurring in NYC (16, 17).

Diffusion Outward

Although the most noticeable initial effect of high levels of HIV infection in the population of urban minority communities may be a sharp rise in the incidence of new infections within these specific neighborhoods, the situation is not static. In relatively short order (i.e., within several years), there must be some diffusion of infection to adjacent areas. Recent data from the screening of U.S. military applicants illustrate this (18). The geographic areas showing the most rapid increase in the rate of HIV infection among recruits are the counties immediately adjacent to those urban areas with the highest absolute prevalence levels of HIV (i.e., the suburban counties surrounding NYC, San Francisco, Miami, and Dallas/Fort Worth). Even within high-risk groups, such as IV drug users, this pattern of geographic diffusion can be seen graphically. For example, the rates of HIV infection among methadone patients in several Connecticut towns are an inverse function of automobile mileage from NYC (19). This pattern of diffusion is based on the manner in which people buy drugs in central city areas and then transport them back out to the suburbs and to outlying districts. The travel involved in purchasing drugs may accompany exposure to HIV through needle sharing (to sample wares) or drug-associated sexual contacts in another locale. And, of course, the geographic overlap of drug-using and needle-sharing networks and the small but significant nonexclusivity of race/ethnicity among sexual contacts foster wider diffusion of any infectious agent.

Finally, an important additional mechanism for the geographic diffusion of HIV beyond the inner city is associated with migration patterns and the characteristics of social and family networks, many of which bridge geographically distant areas.

These social networks create a powerful surrogate of actual proximity, and function to bring populations of some quite distant localities into frequent and intimate association with populations living in AIDS-endemic urban areas. For NYC, the most dramatic instance of this phenomenon can be seen in the Puerto Rican population, which has the highest rates of HIV infection of any ethnic group (20, 21). This group's close and on-going ties with the island of Puerto Rico, through continued residence of many family members of origin and easy and inexpensive travel, assure a steady stream of travelers. This pattern may be amplified by the special problems associated with particular risk factors for HIV, for example, drug use. Drug users often move in response to pressures associated with their addiction, traveling home to Puerto Rico to get off drugs or to escape legal problems stemming from criminal activities in NYC. This mobility is a clear mechanism for increasing the risk of transmission of HIV beyond those circumscribed local communities with high prevalence levels of HIV infection.

A similar pattern can be seen for the African-American population of Northeastern cities with family roots in the Southeastern United States (Virginia, Georgia, and the Carolinas) or, for Chicago, with roots and connections in the Mississippi Delta and the deep South (Mississippi, Louisiana, and Alabama). In the Atlantic states, there is also an important role of migrant farm labor. Clusters of AIDS cases (implying pockets of infection) are already evident in Georgia and South Carolina (2) and, recently, these Southern cases have been shown to be undercounted or underreported by as much as 50 percent (22), suggesting that the problem may be even more advanced. These examples of the ways in which social patterns of HIV prevalence determine potential geographic diffusion suggest that the current high concentration of HIV infection in the heterosexual minority populations of some U.S. inner-city communities is no assurance of invulnerability for adjacent regions or even for very distant ones.

IMPACT ON HEALTH SERVICES

An immediate consequence of the growing AIDS case incidence in NYC is its impact on the city's hospitals and health care system. By the end of 1989, over 2,000 people with AIDS, or suspected AIDS, occupied hospital beds in NYC each day (23). The city's total medical/surgical bed capacity had been reduced by 8,000 beds to 27,000, over the course of the last decade. This left the NYC hospital system with no "excess" capacity to deal with any new demands that might be placed upon it. Of course, all the old demands, the needs of the very old and the very young (its traditional users), did not diminish. And several significant new burdens, other than AIDS care, were placed on the system in the 1980s: demands associated with the deinstitutionalization of patients from New York State psychiatric hospitals in the 1970s; high rates of homelessness; more premature infants requiring neonatal intensive care; longer-stay "boarder babies"; and most recently, the impact of increased drug traffic and its associated violence (24). All have increased the background demands on the health care system, especially its most scarce and expensive resource: acute-care hospital beds. In January of 1989, over 1,000 patients were "held" in emergency rooms each day, awaiting admission to hospital beds (25). To this is added the AIDS epidemic. On a regular basis, since 1985, approximately 20 to 25 percent of all those individuals diagnosed and still alive with AIDS in NYC have been in the hospital on any given day (26). Finally, the severity of illness associated with most AIDS hospitalizations, and the increased acuity of care required for such patients, means that AIDS patients represent more demand than "average" patients.

As we climb toward an expected annual incidence of 8,000 to 10,000 new AIDS cases per year in NYC, by 1992 or 1993, we can expect as many as 4,000 of the city's beds (i.e., nearly 1 in 6) to be occupied by AIDS patients (5). In addition, another 1,000 to 2,000 beds may be occupied by patients never diagnosed as having AIDS, as defined by the Centers for Disease Control (CDC), but hospitalized with HIV-related conditions such as pneumonia or tuberculosis (27). In the Bronx (28), we found a 130 percent increase in pneumonia hospitalizations among adult men between 1982 and 1986. These were apparently HIV-related and accounted for a number of additional hospital days equal to 42 percent of those accounted for by AIDS cases themselves during the same period. Another study (29) found that Blue Cross patients diagnosed with AIDS utilized significantly more outpatient and hospital services even *prior* to their diagnosis—an amount equal to 20 percent of their utilization after diagnosis—but their conditions were never noted as "AIDS-related" when they occurred since they preceded formal diagnosis with CDC-defined AIDS.

The hospital system of NYC is already under intense stress associated with the institution of diagnosis related groups and what have become chronic staffing shortages. Negotiated wage increases in several key staff areas—especially nursing—will lessen the buying power of health dollars in NYC at the same time as the city's financial resources are reduced and fewer health care workers choose to work in the city's hospitals (30). Further, these staff shortages are not evenly distributed between voluntary and municipal hospitals and the very different communities they serve. NYC's municipal hospitals carry the heaviest burden of the city's AIDS cases (23); have the largest number of staff vacancies in nursing, medicine, and other skilled categories; and have the weakest support infrastructure (e.g., social services, counselors). At Lincoln Medical and Mental Health Center in the Bronx, 97 beds were recently put out of service because the NYC Health and Hospitals Corporation could not find enough nurses, and a new fully equipped AIDS unit in the same hospital has never been opened for the same reason.

Finally, a particularly troubling and unusual aspect of the U.S. AIDS epidemic is a result of the legislated association between drug addiction and criminality. Because of the increased arrest rate and imprisonment of drug users in NYC (over 250,000 are arrested each year), large numbers with HIV infection are entering the state's prison system. Studies conducted by the New York State Department of

Corrections indicate that 20 to 25 percent of *all* new inmates are HIV infected (31). Among its 50,000 prison inmates, New York State can expect 2,000 new cases of AIDS in the coming year—there is already one AIDS death per day within that system. Prison health services are chronically understaffed and have great difficulty in attracting capable individuals, given the traditional place of prison health services on the margins of medicine and public health. Yet, that system will have to mount health care services to care for a population with AIDS greater than that of many large cities in the United States and Europe.

Early Intervention—The Expansion of Responsibility

The impact of the AIDS epidemic in NYC, and our inadequacies in meeting its demands, are most evident in relation to acute hospital care services, but this problem enlarges with the promise of early medical intervention and prophylactic treatment of HIV infection (32, 33). Instead of "just" having 10,000 people to treat for full-blown AIDS, we now have over 100,000 HIV-infected people eligible for the potential benefits of early intervention with AZT, pentamidine, DDI, and the other new drugs that will surely emerge over the next few years. These drugs may only serve to defer, rather than prevent, future hospitalization, yet they unquestionably offer promise to improve the length and quality of life of those infected with HIV. Such treatments do, however, require very substantial levels of medical service not currently available to most of the populations that would be most in need of them (i.e., inner-city drug users and their families) (24). Thus AIDS invokes a set of new problems closely linked to many old ones—the maldistribution of health care services as a function of social class—a problem already well recognized in the United States, but one that never seems to improve.

COMMUNITY SURVIVAL

One of the AIDS epidemic's effects on any community with high rates of infection and disease is to increase competition for scarce resources: health care, social services, foster care, housing. The last is especially crucial, as the work of urban ecologists and urban anthropologists demonstrates. Aside from the obvious difficulties of discharging homeless AIDS patients from hospitals, the sheer magnitude of the problem is staggering. Studies of drug users (with and without AIDS) find that many are homeless or marginally housed (34). At Rikers Island, the NYC jail that admits 140,000 per year, 18 percent of men slept in the street the night before their arrest, and close to 45 percent did so within the last three months (35). Huge homeless populations of the city (50 to 60 thousand) (36) overlap with the drug-addicted, and these, in turn, with HIV infection and illness. Each night 36,000 stay in city residences, shelters, and hotels—and there are at least that many more on the streets. Another 100,000 occupants of the city's 185,000 public housing units are doubled up and sharing space intended for a single family. The average waiting time for public housing is one year to 18 months for "priority cases" (e.g., those families burnt out of their homes) and 10 to 20 years for "others" (i.e., there is *no* availability for "others"). The vacancy rate for apartments in NYC renting for under $300 per month is essentially zero. Although a new 5 billion dollar building renewal plan is now underway in NYC to create 90,000 new units of renovated housing over the next three to four years, little is provided in the way of social support, child care, drug-addiction treatment, or local health services for these communities. One can predict that these new buildings will shortly deteriorate, because without such services, their tenants' problems (drug use, mental illness, etc.) will soon overwhelm them (37).

Housing destruction also devastates urban communities by destroying the coherent social networks that sustain poor families and permit some modicum of functioning in a hostile environment. Until this social fabric is healed or reconstructed through stable housing, it becomes virtually impossible to prevent continued high prevalence levels of socially determined conditions: infant and perinatal mortality, drug addiction and alcoholism, and violence. The provision of adequate housing is a necessary precondition for a decent life under normal circumstances, but in the midst of this epidemic it becomes a precondition for survival itself.

Local Initiatives

If all of NYC's major institutions are buckling under the stress of AIDS, and budgetary allocations are meager for the upcoming period, how will the city respond to this crisis? NYC faces a deficit of close to 1 billion dollars per year, and a larger figure is given for New York State. Inpatient medical services for people with AIDS in NYC will cost close to 7 billion dollars over the next three to five years—double that figure if early intervention programs are mounted. The prospects for an effective governmental response are poor, given unwillingness on the part of the federal government to invest the kinds of money needed to make a difference. Without doubt, therefore, enormous social destruction will take place in NYC over the next five years. But a few modest programs, coming out of local initiatives, suggest that something can be done to minimize the disaster.

In communities throughout the city, local people are coming forth to give the compassionate care needed for people with AIDS. Many are, in a sense, already "paid" through existing social welfare arrangements—Aid to Families with Dependent Children, Medicaid, Food Stamps, Housing Subsidies. These people, with all their disabilities, understand all too well that it is their own families that are dying of AIDS. And, in our experience, they are eager to help. It makes far more sense to acknowledge and supplement this existing network of family, neighbors, and friends—to recognize the critical role that they already play in coping with many of NYC's most serious problems—than to try to construct utopian "comprehensive" social service systems. The individuals with the formal training are simply not there, and the municipal institutions needed to produce services are unavailable. A notable exception is the many churches that have opened their doors to the problem—establishing shelters, home-visiting programs, feeding programs, and, in some cases, AIDS ministries that train and field volunteers to help with hospital and home care. In the Bronx a growing body of volunteers has been recruited from among patients' families and neighbors. Many are themselves former drug users who are willing to visit neighborhoods shunned by home health workers (38).

Families and Social Support

Ultimately, community survival is closely linked to family survival. Local initiatives that support the development and strengthening of social and family networks by locating and reinforcing natural support systems are essential. If one looks, such supports are already evident in many poor communities to a surprising extent, perhaps to a degree equal to or exceeding that of the gay community in San Francisco. Poor people have always had to rely on mutual support and assistance and do so without many of the advantages of the often more affluent gay population—its income, education, and more stable living conditions.

Approaches that build upon family support networks may be the only hope for those communities facing the full force of the AIDS epidemic in NYC. Social welfare theory has always paid lip service to preservation of the "family unit," but, in practice, tends to disempower the actual family members who might hold things together if they were assisted in doing so. As AIDS cuts a swath through family after family—some have four or five members already sick with the disease and more infected—it is crucial that we provide support for these families and groups of families with AIDS. Neighborhood health teams, home visiting, block health stations, expanded child care services, and financial assistance should all be directed to decentralized community-based organizations employing local residents who are deputized as community health workers. Some streets will have scores of people sick with AIDS. These must be encapsulated in a protective system of services that relies on healthy members to help the sick, and provides outside expertise to work on-site rather than expecting patients and families to come to where health professionals are more comfortably ensconced in their clinics and hospitals.

Any failure to take the necessary measures to provide adequate care for the sick will assure an unabated spread of infection. Without early detection, counseling, and medical treatment of asymptomatic HIV-infected individuals, the likelihood of their infecting others is and will remain great. Thus, humane clinical care is the natural complement of an effective public health policy toward AIDS. And, if we cannot marshall the political will to intervene in what is today perceived as the plight of "the other," the insistent reality of AIDS will assert itself and, soon enough, it will become apparent that AIDS is everyone's problem.

REFERENCES

1. New York City Department of Health. *AIDS Surveillance Update*. New York, February 28, 1990.
2. Centers for Disease Control. *HIV/AIDS Surveillance Report*. Atlanta, February 1990.
3. Shilts, R. *And the Band Played On: Politics, People, and the AIDS Epidemic*. Penguin Books, New York, 1988.
4. Drucker, E. Unpublished data analysis, based on New York State Hospital Reporting System, 1982–1986.
5. New York City AIDS Task Force. *Report*. New York City Health Systems Agency, New York, 1989.
6. Hessol, N. A., et al. Prevalence, incidence, and progression of human immunodeficiency virus infection in homosexual and bisexual men in hepatitis B vaccine trials, 1978–1988. *Am. J. Epidemiol.* 130: 1167–1175, 1989.
7. DesJarlais, D. C., et al. HIV-1 infection among intravenous drug users in Manhattan, New York City, from 1977 through 1987. *JAMA* 261: 108–112, 1989.
8. Eisenhandler, J., and Drucker, E. Estimating the Prevalence of IV Drug Use and HIV Infection among Subscribers of a Large Private Health Insurance Plan in the New York Area. Abstract presented at the Sixth International Conference on AIDS, San Francisco, 1990.
9. Krystal, A., and New York City Department of Health AIDS Surveillance Group. The AIDS epidemic in New York City, 1981–1984. *Am. J. Epidemiol.* 123: 1013–1025, 1986.
10. Drucker, E., and Vermund, S. H. Estimating population prevalence of human immunodeficiency virus infection in urban areas with high rates of intravenous drug use: A model of the Bronx in 1988. *Am. J. Epidemiol.* 130: 133–142, 1989.
11. Ernst, J. Personal communication, based on unpublished data from the Bronx Lebanon Hospital Center, New York, 1990.
12. Williams, T. M. *The Cocaine Kids: The Inside Story of a Teenage Drug Ring*. Addison-Wesley, Reading, Mass., 1989.
13. Drucker, E., et al. Heterosexual Contact Patterns of 429 Pregnant Non-I.V. Drug Using Women in the South Bronx, New York, in 1988. Paper presented at the Fifth International Conference on AIDS, Montreal, June 4–9, 1989.
14. Novick, L. F., et al. HIV seroprevalence in newborns in New York State. *JAMA* 261: 1745–1750, 1989.
15. Abrams, E. Personal communications, based on unpublished data. Harlem Hospital Center, New York City, 1990.
16. Chiasson, M. A., et al. Risk factors for human immunodeficiency virus type 1 (HIV-1) infection in patients at a sexually transmitted disease clinic in NYC. *Am. J. Epidemiol.* 131: 208–220, 1990.
17. Steigbigel, N., et al. Heterosexual Transmission of Infection and Disease by the Human Immunodeficiency Virus (HIV). Paper presented at the Third International Conference on AIDS, Washington, D.C., June 1–5, 1987.
18. Gardner, L., et al. Spatial diffusion of the human immunodeficiency virus infection epidemic in the United States, 1985–1987. *Ann. Assoc. Am. Geographers* 79: 25–43, 1989.
19. D'Aguila, R., et al. HIV Seroprevalence among Connecticut Intravenous Drug Users in 1986. Paper presented at the Third International Conference on AIDS, Washington, D.C., June 1–5, 1987.
20. Selik, R. M., et al. Birthplace and the risk of AIDS among Hispanics in the United States. *Am. J. Public Health* 79: 836–839, 1989.

21. Menendez, B. S., et al. AIDS mortality among Puerto Ricans and other Hispanics in New York City, 1981–1987. *J. Acquired Immune Deficiency Syndromes*, 1990, in press.
22. Conway, G. A., et al., Underreporting of AIDS cases in South Carolina, 1986 and 1987. *JAMA* 262: 2859–2863, 1989.
23. Health Systems Agency. *New York City AIDS Task Force Report.* New York City Department of Health, New York, 1989.
24. Bigel Institute for Health Policy and the United Hospital Fund of New York. *New York City's Hospital Occupancy Crisis: Caring for a Patient Population.* United Hospital Fund, New York, 1988.
25. Vladeck, B. Worst-case scenarios. *President's Letter.* United Hospital Fund, February 1990.
26. Drucker, E., et al. Hospital Utilization Patterns and Changes for the Case of Inner-city AIDS Patients: By Risk Group, Sex, and Race/ethnicity. Paper presented at the Third International Conference on AIDS, Washington, D.C., June 1–5, 1987.
27. Stoneburner, R. L., et al. A larger spectrum of severe HIV-1 related disease in intravenous drug users in New York City. *Science* 242: 916–919, 1988.
28. Drucker, E., et al. Increasing rate of pneumonia hospitalizations in the Bronx: A sentinel indicator for human immunodeficiency virus. *Int. J. Epidemiol.* 18: 926–933, 1989.
29. Eisenhandler, J. The HIV Experience of Empire Blue Cross and Blue Shield. Unpublished paper, December 1989.
30. Lambert, B. In spite of crisis, New York lacks basic services for AIDS patients. *New York Times*, January 3, 1989.
31. Greifinger, R. New York State Department of Corrections Data. Presented at the Fourth Montefiore Symposium on AIDS, New York City, January 23, 1990.
32. Arno, P., et al. Economic and policy implications of early intervention in HIV disease. *JAMA* 262: 1493–1498, 1989.
33. Volberding, P. A., et al. Zidovudine in asymptomatic human immunodeficiency virus infection. *N. Engl. J. Med.* 322: 941–949, 1990.
34. Drucker, E., et al. IV Drug Users with AIDS in New York City: A Study of Dependent Children, Housing and Drug Addiction Treatment. Report to the AIDS Service Delivery Consortium, New York City, July 20, 1988.
35. Zoloth, S., and Michaels, D. Personal communication, based on unpublished data. New York City, 1990.
36. Ron, A., and Rogers, D. E. AIDS in the United States: Patient care and politics. *Daedalus J. Am. Acad. Arts Sci.* 118(2), 1989.
37. Raske, S. F. Homeless plan called meager for New York. *New York Times*, December 4, 1989, p. B1.
38. Poust, B., et al. An Inner-city Volunteer Program Utilizing Community AIDS Education as a Vehicle for Recruitment. Paper presented at the Fifth International Conference on AIDS, Montreal, June 4–9, 1989.

CHAPTER 4

Pediatric AIDS in the United States: Epidemiological Reality Versus Government Policy

Anne-Emanuelle Birn, John Santelli, and LaWanda G. Burwell

Pediatric acquired immune deficiency syndrome (AIDS) is a complicated disease, socially, biologically, and politically. For its sufferers, mostly residents of poor, minority, inner-city communities, AIDS is not a unique affliction but only another in a long series of insults. Deficient housing, unemployment, poor nutrition, decaying social and municipal services, illiteracy, drug use, oppressive social conditions, and inadequate prenatal care have all contributed to unacceptable levels of death and disease.

Pediatric AIDS affects three age groups with distinct transmission paths: (*a*) infants and young children who became infected through perinatal transmission; (*b*) school-age children, the majority of whom acquired the human immunodeficiency virus (HIV) through blood transfusions (mostly hemophiliacs); and (*c*) teenagers who, like adults, acquired the disease through sexual activity or intravenous (IV) drug use.

In this chapter we examine the demographic distribution of pediatric AIDS in the United States and analyze the public policies for each age group. Here, the social context of AIDS is of paramount importance; poverty looms as the powerful partner to pediatric AIDS. In spite of this clear connection, government actions have failed to confront the underlying causes and consequences of childhood, household, and community poverty. The analysis will emphasize the nature and implications of the contradiction between the epidemiological reality of pediatric

Originally published in the *International Journal of Health Services* 20(4): 617–630, 1990.

AIDS and the response of state, local, and federal governments through funding, targeted programs, and other forms of legislation.

EPIDEMIOLOGY OF PEDIATRIC AIDS

Pediatric AIDS cases constitute approximately 2 percent of the United States total, but cases among children pose a growing concern. As of December 1989, 2,456 cases of AIDS had been diagnosed among people under the age of 20 (1). It has been estimated that by 1992, AIDS will be one of the five leading causes of both infant and childhood mortality in the United States (2, p. 12). Table 1 presents the distribution of pediatric and young adult AIDS cases by age. AIDS cases in children under 5 years old, most of these due to perinatal (vertical) transmission, represent 68 percent of cases among children and adolescents. Although AIDS is rare in adolescents, the large number of AIDS cases among 20- to 29-year-olds implies considerable transmission among teenagers (3).

The earliest cases of pediatric AIDS in the United States were reported in 1982 and strongly suggested both in utero (4) and transfusion-related transmission. By 1985, the basic epidemiology of HIV transmission in children was established (5). The probable routes of transmission for pediatric AIDS patients under the age of 13 are shown in Table 2. Approximately 57 percent of total pediatric cases and 73 percent of perinatal cases are related to IV drug use (6). Most mothers identify IV drug use as a likely route of transmission, involving either their own drug use or that of sexual partners (7).

Pediatric cases have occurred disproportionately in poor, inner-city populations with high rates of drug use and sexually transmitted diseases (STDs) (8). Recent reports from New York City have also identified crack houses, where sex is commonly exchanged for drugs, as an important new locus of transmission (9). The chance of a newborn becoming infected with HIV if the mother is infected

Table 1

Age distribution of reported cases of AIDS and percentage change, United States, 1988 and 1989[a]

	Reported cases			
Age, yr	1988	1989	Percent of total 1989 cases	Percent change, 1988 to 1989
<5	465	525	1.6%	+13%
5–9	100	92	0.3%	–8%
10–19	154	150	0.4%	–3%
20–29	6,646	7,002	19.9%	+5%
All ages	32,196	35,238	100.0%	+9%

[a]Source: reference 3, p. 82.

Table 2

Pediatric AIDS patients under 13 years of age, by exposure category (probable route of transmission) and race/ethnic group, United States, 1981–1988[a,b]

	White	Black	Hispanic	Other	Total
Total no.	321	707	308	8	1349
Exposure category					
Mother					
IV drug user	22%	47%	50%	—	42%
Sex with IV drug user	10%	15%	21%	—	15%
Sex with person at risk (non-IV drug user)	8%	4%	4%	—	5%
Coagulation disorder	19%	1%	4%	—	6%
Transfusion recipient	29%	5%	11%	—	12%
Other risk factor	9%	23%	6%	—	16%
No identified risk	3%	5%	4%	—	4%

[a]Source: reference 6, p. 233.
[b]Owing to rounding, totals may exceed 100%. Dashes indicate numbers too small to calculate meaningful percentage.

was first estimated to be between 20 and 60 percent (10), but more recent estimates have put the risk closer to 30 percent (11); the risk may be lower if the mother is asymptomatic or only in the early stages of infection (10). Maternal HIV infection does not seem to suppress fertility (12).

Pediatric AIDS is vastly overrepresented among U.S. ethnic and racial minorities, particularly African-Americans and Hispanics (13) (Table 3). Although African-American children comprise only 15 percent of U.S. children, 53 to 55 percent of perinatal cases have occurred in African-Americans (2, p. 13; 13). Similarly, 10 percent of U.S. children are Hispanic, yet 20 to 22 percent of pediatric AIDS cases have occurred among Hispanics. Only one-quarter of pediatric AIDS cases have occurred in white infants. Most perinatal cases have occurred in New York, New Jersey, and Florida in poor, urban areas, closely paralleling the epidemic in women and heterosexuals (5).

AIDS in school-age children (5 to 15 year olds) is rare, accounting for 0.2 percent of total U.S. cases, although school children represent 16 percent of the total U.S. population (14, p. 8). More recent data (through December 31, 1989) show that AIDS in children aged 5 to 17 years accounts for 0.45 percent of total U.S. cases (15). Most school-age cases of AIDS and HIV infection have been linked to transfusions occurring before May 1985, when universal screening of blood supplies began. The hemophiliac population has been particularly devastated, with 35 to 70 percent of adult and pediatric patients infected (16). Patients with hemophilia often receive replacement therapy blood

Table 3

Racial/ethnic distribution of AIDS cases compared with total U.S. population, 1981–1988[a,b]

	White	Black	Hispanic	Other	Total
U.S. population	80%	12%	6%	3%	100%
AIDS cases					
Adult/adolescent					
Males	62%	24%	13%	1%	100%
Females	29%	54%	16%	1%	100%
Children (<13 years)	25%	55%	20%	<1%	100%

[a]Source: reference 13, p. 18.
[b]Excluding U.S. territories.

products derived from thousands of blood donors. In contrast to perinatal AIDS cases, most transfusion-related infections have occurred in young, white males, the group most likely to have hemophilia. These cases have received a great deal of publicity, yet they represent only 6 percent of pediatric AIDS cases under age 13 (6, p. 233).

The reported number of adolescent AIDS cases severely underestimates HIV infection in this age group. Because of the long latency period after infection, most adolescents who acquire the infection do not become symptomatic until they reach their twenties. Twenty-one percent of AIDS cases occur among 20- to 29-year-olds, many of whom became infected as teenagers (14, p. i). High rates of unprotected sexual activity, high rates of STDs, frequent partner changes, and experimentation with drugs increase adolescents' likelihood of becoming infected (14, pp. 14–23). Sexual contact with infected adults is probably the major route of transmission. For adolescent women these infected sexual partners are often IV drug users; for adolescent men, homosexual or bisexual adult males.

Transmission patterns for adolescents are similar to adult patterns, but sociodemographic trends are magnified, with the proportion of cases among the poor and minorities far overrepresented. For example, HIV seroprevalence in military recruits (mostly men in their late teens and early twenties) is 3.9 per 1000 in blacks versus 0.9 per 1000 in whites (14, p. 9).

Although both publicity and policy have focused on school-age children, the great majority of pediatric AIDS cases have occurred at the extreme ends of the pediatric age spectrum.

PERINATAL AIDS

Infants and toddlers with AIDS are part of a series of national problems for which neither the U.S. government nor local governments have made a commitment to launch comprehensive prevention and treatment efforts. The social conditions that contribute to the epidemic of perinatal AIDS in the United States are "manifested in the problems of illicit drug use, teenage pregnancy, sexually transmitted diseases and inadequate health and social services for poor people" (17).

Poverty emerges as the critical cofactor for AIDS and for most other causes of infant, childhood, and adolescent mortality. In 1988, the U.S. government calculated the poverty level as an annual income of $12,091 for a family of four (18). By this definition,[1] more than one-fourth of U.S. children are poor. Although the percentage of children in poverty fell over 40 percent during the 1960s and 1970s, since 1979 childhood poverty has risen 25.6 percent, with the largest increases among children under 5 years (20, pp. 242–246). A cursory budget analysis offers an explanation for these trends. From 1980 to 1990, the national defense budget increased by 54.2 percent, while federal spending on social programs declined by 16.4 percent (20, pp. 240–241). Between 1978 and 1986, direct federal appropriations for maternal and child health centers declined by almost half (21, p. 44).

This scenario has resulted in an increase in childhood death and disease, with minority youngsters suffering the greatest insults. The United States had one of the lowest infant mortality rates in the world in the 1950s, but by 1987 the country's rank dropped to 22. In 1987 the infant mortality rate for African-Americans (17.9 per 1000 live births) was over twice the rate for whites (8.6 per 1000) (22). AIDS, like virtually every other illness, affects poor communities disproportionately.

Despite the reality that perinatal AIDS is growing rapidly as a cause of infant mortality, national prevention efforts have not been adequate. Only two of the numerous Public Health Service prevention initiatives target the prevention of maternal infection and drug abuse (23). A specific example of relative priority of funding for prevention of perinatal transmission is found within the Centers for Disease Control (CDC). In the CDC Division of STD/HIV, 2.9 percent of the 1989 budget was allocated to perinatal prevention demonstration projects, and 4.3 percent was allocated to services for HIV- infected hemophilia patients (24), even though screening of the blood supply has virtually removed the likelihood of transmission to hemophiliacs since 1985.

The connection between perinatal AIDS and illicit drug use links it with one of the most intractable social problems in the United States. It is estimated that there are 350,000 to 400,000 IV drug users in the United States (25). In states with the highest rates of HIV infection such as New York and New Jersey, over 60 percent of IV drug users test positive for the virus (26). Drug treatment resources were not

[1] The federal poverty level is a highly problematic tool. It measures poverty in absolute terms, without reflecting the difficulties that stem from relative levels of deprivation. Beeghley (19) has shown that the poverty line uses several definitions of poverty, double counts income, and "misunderstands the nature of public assistance."

sufficient for the number of drug abusers before the AIDS epidemic, and the availability of drug treatment continues to be a barrier in the battle against AIDS (27). Because male IV drug users can infect their partners, both male and female drug use contribute to the prevalence of perinatal AIDS.

In the particular case of pregnant women who are drug users, treatment options are extremely limited in most U.S. cities. The complexity of tracking pregnant women who are substance abusers has made some medical providers, hospitals, and treatment programs wary of treating these patients. In addition, some states have policies that exacerbate the problems of providing care to pregnant drug abusers. Florida received national attention recently for prosecuting women whose babies are compromised by maternal drug use (28). This type of policy will not improve the likelihood that women who do not have a history of using health care services will come forward for treatment for themselves or for their infants.

The New York State policy of refusing to discharge newborns to substance-abusing mothers has led to a large increase in the number of children kept in the wards of public hospitals, such as Harlem Hospital (29). Hegarty and colleagues (30) conducted a chart review of 37 children who received inpatient care for AIDS or an AIDS-related condition between 1981 and 1987. Nearly one-third of those children were "boarder babies"—infants remaining in the hospital after birth due to lack of any placement alternatives once the child was medically cleared for discharge.

Hospital wards cannot continue as infant households. Infants should not be separated from mothers who are undergoing drug treatment; supportive foster families must be found for the balance of boarder babies. Availability of foster care placement for minority children has not been adequate, especially for children with physical and mental handicaps and other medical problems (31). A few programs, such as the Baltimore Association for Retarded Children, focus on foster care for medically fragile children, demonstrating that the provision of supportive services, such as training and specialized social workers, can increase the availability of foster homes (32). Policies that discriminate against drug-using pregnant women, and against their newborns and toddlers, are unacceptable.

Much of the success of AIDS prevention and services in the gay male community has been the result of organized efforts within that community. Friedman and Casriel (33) suggest that the absence of self-organization by IV drug users and their partners has impeded attempts to reduce the spread of HIV. Gay men had already organized to promote change in their social status before the AIDS epidemic. There is no such history of organization among U.S. drug users, although there has been social organizing in Europe.

As of January 1, 1989, more than 600 community-based AIDS organizations were in operation in the United States (34). These groups range from small, shoe-string operations to large agencies; however, the larger, more organized efforts continue to focus on gay men and persons with AIDS, rather than on minorities (especially women) and prevention. Although growing in number, the initiatives for racial minorities and IV drug users and their partners continue to be too fragmented to address the magnitude of the problem.

It is in prevention efforts that the ambivalence of U.S. values and attitudes regarding sexuality and drug use becomes most poignant. Perinatal prevention initiatives tend to focus only on the woman of child-bearing age; however, perinatal and pediatric AIDS are family issues. Immediate and extended family members are important care providers and conveyers of acceptable behavioral norms.

To affect perinatal transmission means to intervene not only in expressions of sexuality but also in fertility and pregnancy. Counseling an HIV-infected woman that she has a 30 percent chance of having an infected child and then expecting her to seek an abortion can accentuate the cultural differences between patient and practitioner. Intervention programs cannot be successful if they reflect the cultural orientation and world view of the providers and not the clients. Obstetricians have reported that many women who know they are HIV-positive and who have already had an HIV-positive child (or children) continue to conceive and complete pregnancies (35, 36). Practitioners must understand the extent to which childbearing is valued, especially when the risk of infant mortality is high.

Further, the decision to abort a potentially infected fetus presents a "double-edged sword" because of restrictions on Medicaid coverage of abortions in the majority of U.S. states (35, p. 51). Over the last decade the controversial right-to-life movement, which vociferously opposes the performance of abortion, has pressured most states to ban government funding of abortion. Thus abortion remains a delicate issue. On the one hand, it must be made a realistic option for low-income women; on the other hand, pregnant HIV-positive women must be allowed to decide for themselves whether or not to carry their babies to term.

The families who bear and must care for perinatally infected infants and toddlers are often recipients of publicly funded medical care services. Historically, the women, men, and children affected by AIDS—mostly poor people of color—have been underserved by the medical and educational systems of this country (37). AIDS may have drawn renewed national attention to their needs; however, their issues of survival have not changed. Although the children contracting AIDS by perinatal transmission are viewed as innocent victims, their drug-using parents are not perceived in this manner (38). These children are often too sick at too early an age to raise issues of placement in the general public school population; thus the infants and toddlers infected perinatally have not received the same public attention as school-age pediatric cases. For the parents of many children infected perinatally, the technicality of their own serostatus (particularly if they are asymptomatic) is not as much a priority as drug dependence, housing, income maintenance, or family crisis. Advocacy for their children or even for themselves is not possible in the context of such a fragile hold on basic needs for survival.

Prevention efforts must be community-based, culturally relevant, and appropriate to the families at risk for perinatal transmission of AIDS. Drug prevention and treatment must become a priority, not only through expanding the number of programs, but also by developing innovative approaches to multiple drug addictions and by providing support for drug-affected families. Programs for pregnant women and their partners must be developed, allowing drug-addicted and recovering women to remain with their children. Finally, community-based prevention projects must be supported through government funding, with existing agencies (such as local health departments) offering technical assistance and local grassroots organizations providing cultural sensitivity in outreach strategies and materials.

SCHOOL-AGE CHILDREN WITH AIDS

The public school attendance of HIV-infected children provoked irrational fears about transmission in the school, and these hysterical reactions have been encouraged by the media. A handful of early cases in which children were publicly excluded from schools exacerbated these sentiments. One such case, which received an enormous amount of national publicity, was that of Ryan White, a 13-year-old boy who contracted HIV infection from a blood transfusion for hemophilia. Although Indiana had a policy for the school placement of children with AIDS and the state board of health concluded that White could attend school, his access to public school was denied from 1984 to 1986. The superintendent of White's local school district denied him entrance, and the litigation that followed, including petitions from parent groups seeking to bar his admission to school, was covered extensively in the national press (39). The school placement of children with AIDS became a forum in which the national hysteria concerning transmission by casual contact could be exhibited.

School placement for HIV-infected children is essentially a civil rights issue. The controversy over school placement of HIV-infected children has pitted the rights of access to public education, nondiscrimination, and confidentiality against the protection of the public's health. Despite early uncertainty, by 1986 it was becoming clear that casual transmission does not occur or is extremely uncommon (40). In August 1985 the CDC issued guidelines on school placement of HIV-infected children (41); in March 1986 the American Academy of Pediatrics communicated a similar set of guidelines (42). Based on the epidemiological evidence available at that time, both sets of guidelines enunciated a number of principles:

1. In general, infected school-age children should be allowed to attend school in an unrestricted setting.
2. Some children, such as preschoolers and children with neurological impairments, may need a more restricted setting.

3. In determining an individual educational placement, a team approach should be employed, using representatives of health and education departments along with family members.
4. Staff knowledge about a child's HIV status should be based on a "need to know," and a child's right to privacy should be respected.
5. Universal hygiene precautions should be adopted by schools.
6. Mandatory or universal screening is not warranted.
7. Education about HIV/AIDS should be encouraged for parents, students, and educational staff.

Although not implemented in every community, these guidelines have greatly lessened fear and confusion and have enabled local policy to be formulated on a rational basis using available scientific knowledge. Some of the specific recommendations have now become outdated (e.g., requiring a restricted setting for preschoolers), but the general principles have offered valuable guidance.

The media emphasis has slighted the many successful school placement programs that exist around the country. Ironically, the best gauge of success of these local programs is the absence of media coverage. The CDC and the American Academy of Pediatrics provided leadership by promulgating guidelines for school placement of HIV-infected students. Many local school systems, including those in New York, San Francisco, and Baltimore, have responded by developing sound school placement policies, protecting the rights of these children to attend school (43, 44). The success of these policies has resulted from the courage of principals, teachers, parents, and local departments of public health.

Along with these guidelines from national health authorities, a history of protecting the civil rights of handicapped children has directly contributed to the protection of HIV-infected children. Public Law 94-142, the Education for All Handicapped Children's Act (1975), sets forth the principle of a free and appropriate education in the least restrictive environment possible. The Rehabilitation Act of 1973 (Section 504) prohibits discrimination in any federally funded program against an otherwise qualified person solely on the basis of a handicap. While not all HIV-infected children are viewed as handicapped or in need of special education services, many infected children have been protected by these laws (45). The early school placement cases involved mostly middle-class children whose parents assumed advocacy roles for their rights. Protections such as the Education for All Handicapped Children's Act and Section 504 of the Rehabilitation Act gave involved parents and advocates a legal context in which to defend their children's rights to public education (46, 47).

The most important outcomes of a school placement policy for HIV-infected children are to protect the right to education, to allay public fears, and to prevent discrimination. Even though the media and local governments exaggerated the epidemiological scope of AIDS among school children, the controversy over school placement has ultimately contributed positively to clarifying the public's understanding about casual transmission. School placement policies were initially created to protect staff and noninfected children from children with the disease. Experience has taught us that HIV-infected children pose little threat to others in the school building (48).

Remaining issues on school placement include the continued assurance of HIV-infected children's right to education, protection of confidentiality, and whether or not school personnel "need to know" about an HIV-infected child. In many cases HIV- infected children have important health needs, involving immuno-suppression and the administration of AZT by school personnel, that will have to be addressed in the school setting. Local leaders have a continuing obligation to protect the educational rights of HIV-infected children where irrational fears resurface.

AIDS AND ADOLESCENCE

Adolescents may be the third largest group to be infected with HIV, after gay men and IV drug users (14). AIDS among adolescents shadows the patterns among young adults. Adolescents differ from adults, however, in their degree of economic and social dependence, in their developmental immaturities, and in their disenfranchisement. Teenagers are especially vulnerable in a society that contributes grossly insufficient resources to their health, education, and well-being. Because most adolescents attend school, they also form a potentially captive audience for AIDS prevention and education efforts. Nonetheless, education policies have failed to explicitly address the realities surrounding adolescent AIDS.

The CDC's publication, "Guidelines for Effective School Health Education to Prevent the Spread of AIDS" (49), relies on information-based, traditional approaches to health education, despite ample evidence that new knowledge has little impact on adolescent sexual behavior or drug use behavior. School-based AIDS prevention programs are saddled by moral strictures and federal restrictions. The rise of religious fundamentalism in the United States during the 1980s has led to repeated assaults on sex education and on AIDS prevention efforts in the schools. Jesse Helms, a prominent moral and political conservative in the U.S. Senate, successfully lobbied for a 1988 law that prohibited the funding of "materials and activities that promote or encourage, directly, homosexual sexual activities." In addition, federally funded prevention programs are expected (under threat of funding withdrawal) to promote abstinence from sexual activity outside a monogamous marriage and to promote abstinence from IV drug use (50). This law bars explicit educational approaches for gay men, adolescents, and other groups, and inhibits the promotion of protective measures, such as the use of condoms. A forced climate of puritanism has impeded the ability of schools to advocate the responsible use of condoms by sexually active teenagers or from openly addressing issues of other forms of contraception and abortion.

If the nation's most prominent public health agency is politically obstructed from issuing explicit guidelines, the ability of schools to carry out effective education strategies is also minimized. Thus, most schools do not encourage social skills training, such as how to convince a partner to use a condom. Despite the fact that the majority of high-school students in this country are sexually active, dispensing of condoms through the public schools is in general forbidden. Even the rapidly growing number of school clinics are rarely allowed to dispense condoms or contraceptives. Currently, only 12 percent dispense such supplies (51).

Notwithstanding the well-publicized efforts by former Surgeon General Everett Koop and others, national and school-based efforts have been much more successful in changing knowledge and attitudes about AIDS than in changing high-risk behavior (52–56). Early AIDS surveys of adolescents in San Francisco and Massachusetts documented several gaps in knowledge about AIDS (52, 53). A 1986 survey from Connecticut has demonstrated that adolescents are now much better informed, but increased knowledge is not being translated into increased condom usage, intentions to use condoms, or other behavior changes (54). In that study only 4 percent of students reported that they learned about AIDS from a teacher. Likewise, the vast majority of adolescents in New York understand the risks of unprotected sex but most fail to modify their behavior (55). A follow-up survey in Massachusetts between 1986 and 1988 documented small changes in condom usage, but gaps between knowledge and behavior persist (56). The survey showed a small decline in drug use, particularly IV drug use, but an increase in the percentage of adolescents who were sexually active. Self-reported condom use increased from 2 to 19 percent, but 37 percent of sexually active teenagers said they never used condoms and 33 percent only used them sporadically. In 1988, 60 percent of students had received formal instruction about AIDS, up from 43 percent in 1986 (56). Thus, education campaigns have had little success so far in encouraging teenagers to behave differently.

Are AIDS education and prevention worth pursuing at all? The answer depends on the nature of the strategies and the availability of alternatives. Allan Brandt (57, 58) has suggested several directions for AIDS prevention based on his examination of the history of syphilis prevention. First, modifying sexual behavior is more likely to be effective than outright prohibition. Efforts based on moral injunctions and provoking fear are more likely to fail than programs designed to provide intensive education, widespread provision of condoms, and confidential testing. Teenage pregnancy researcher Freudenberg (59) has pointed out that the social and political obstacles to AIDS education are exacerbated by the confusion between moral and public health agendas; social conservatives have used the opportunity to preach a "morality" that has little relevance for teenagers who are already sexually active. The most damaging aspect of this ideology is that morality lessons are promoted as a substitute for health and social services; indeed, they serve as a justification for diverting resources.

Community-based health educators have taken the lead in promoting innovative ways to change behavior by using the media, challenging personal attitudes of invulnerability, and employing social skills training to induce a partner to use a condom. Explicit forms of health education were initially developed by community-based AIDS prevention organizations in the gay community and have begun more recently in minority communities. These groups have not been afraid to confront issues frankly and directly; in the gay community especially, empowerment has stemmed from community control over education and prevention. Unfortunately, school-based AIDS education continues to be assaulted by powerful outside forces that ensure the irrelevance and ineffectiveness of school policies on AIDS.

In the end, school-based strategies aimed at individual behavioral change are flawed for two reasons. First, political and moral forces in many school districts have blocked the explicit discussion of AIDS prevention. More importantly, behavioral approaches to alleviating social and socioeconomic problems are slow to take effect and only modestly successful. Decades of experience with teen pregnancy prevention have shown that fulfilling work and life opportunities—secure alternatives to poverty and inadequate prospects—are ultimately the most effective means of preventing teen parenthood. Failure to address adolescent sexuality and life options for adolescents will only contribute to the increase of HIV infection in adolescents and their future offspring.

DISCUSSION

Pediatric AIDS is rapidly becoming a leading cause of death for infants and children. Despite an early understanding of the epidemiological scope of the disease, policies, funding, and public attention have not reflected this understanding. Government policy-makers and the media initially ignored and then devoted a disproportionate share of attention to this problem. However, rather than focusing on the overwhelming majority of pediatric cases—HIV acquired through perinatal transmission—powerful public opinion shapers have dedicated their concern to a handful of cases, involving primarily middle-class children who acquired the disease through blood transfusions. The media's technique of rallying public sympathy around a "typical" middle-class child who suffers random misfortune may be contrasted with its coverage of perinatal AIDS, which is portrayed as the result of the immoral, illegal behavior of entire communities.

Unfortunately, the federal government has contributed to the prejudice against poor and minority groups by categorizing "risk groups" and assigning behavioral culpability for the acquisition of disease. Not only is this approach an incentive for discriminatory practices, but it also represents a void in the understanding of the pressures and stresses faced by the poor. As David Dinkins, the former mayor of New York City, has pointed out, "AIDS is not only the product of certain risk activities, but also of social and economic conditions . . . " (60, p. 47).

The issues surrounding perinatally transmitted AIDS continue to be neglected in the policy arena, largely because they are issues of poverty. Dr. Margaret Heagerty, director of pediatrics at Harlem Hospital Center, asserts, "children with AIDS in this hospital are, by definition, poor." Notwithstanding the desperate straits of many urban public hospitals, "medical care is in many ways the simplest of the needs of the children of this community with AIDS. They and their families need resources outside the hospital in the form of housing, home care, respite care" (61, pp. 57–58). The acutely inadequate social infrastructure for poor families is as much the origin of the AIDS epidemic as is the human immunodeficiency virus. Deteriorating housing, racism, sexism, joblessness, malnutrition, inaccessible health care, and inadequate social services add up to a brutal environment of despair, disease, and premature death. Unfortunately, as U.S. society continues to view diseases as discrete events with a specific biological etiology, poor people die young and suffer lives that are marked by pain and disability.

Despite the controversies it generated, the school placement of HIV-infected hemophiliacs represented a resolvable issue. The parents of this small group of children assumed strong advocacy roles; civil liberties organizations called upon existing laws protecting handicapped children to champion the rights of HIV-infected youngsters to attend school. National health authorities issued sensible guidelines to assist local jurisdictions in implementing school placement policies. Once blood supplies were systematically screened, prevention for future transfusion recipients was virtually assured.

Nonetheless, school placement is becoming a more complicated issue. As perinatally infected children are attaining school age and more HIV-infected teenagers are being identified, the beneficiaries of effective school placement policies are changing. The problem of pediatric AIDS is growing most dramatically in minority and disadvantaged communities, whose school systems have already been ravaged by chronic underfunding. New school placement issues are emerging: education while the child is in the hospital and expanded health and special education services while the child is in school.

The schools provide an important setting for prevention. For teenagers especially, effective strategies that overcome conservative barriers to explicit education must be developed. We must empower school-based health educators to provide effective health education strategies, like those used by their community-based colleagues.

To prevent and address pediatric AIDS in its social context, the United States must make battling childhood poverty the nation's top policy priority. Prevention of pediatric AIDS must be both sensitive and relevant to communities in which the greatest threat to survival is poverty, not AIDS. Ultimately, issues surrounding pediatric AIDS only reinforce the long-term position of child health advocates: the best investment a society can make is a sincere commitment of resources to improve the health, education, and welfare of its children.

REFERENCES

1. Centers for Disease Control. Automated Data Reporting System. February 5, 1990.
2. Novello, A. C., et al. *Final Report: Secretary's Work Group on Pediatric HIV Infection and Disease*. Department of Health and Human Services. U.S. Government Printing Office, Washington, D.C., 1988.
3. Update: Acquired immunodeficiency syndrome—United States, 1989. *MMWR* 39(5): 81–86, 1990.
4. Rubinstein, A., and Bernstein, L. The epidemiology of pediatric acquired immunodeficiency syndrome. *Clin. Immunol. Immunopathol.* 40: 115–121, 1986.
5. Rogers, M. F., et al. Acquired immunodeficiency syndrome in children: Report of the Centers for Disease Control national surveillance, 1982–1985. *Pediatrics* 79: 1008–1014, 1987.
6. Update: Acquired immunodeficiency syndrome—United States, 1981–1988. *MMWR* 38(14): 229–236, 1989.
7. Peterman, T. A., et al. The challenge of human immunodeficiency virus (HIV) and acquired immunodeficiency syndrome (AIDS) in women and children. *Fertil. Steril.* 49(4): 571–581, 1988.
8. Osterholm, M. T., and MacDonald, K. L. Facing the complex issues of pediatric AIDS: A public health perspective. *JAMA* 258: 2736–2737, 1987.
9. Kerr, P. Crack and resurgence of syphilis spreading AIDS among the poor. *New York Times*, August 29, 1989.
10. Pape, J. W., and Johnson, W. Perinatal transmission of the human immunodeficiency virus. *PAHO Bull.* 23(1–2): 50–58, 1989.
11. Blanche, S., et al. A prospective study of infants born to women seropositive for human immunodeficiency virus type I. *N. Engl. J. Med.* 320: 1643–1648, 1989.
12. Selwyn, P. A., et al. Prospective study of human immunodeficiency virus infection and pregnancy outcomes in intravenous drug users. *JAMA* 261: 1289–1294, 1989.
13. AIDS and human immunodeficiency virus infection in the United States: 1988 Update. *MMWR*. 38(S-4): 1–38, 1989.
14. Hein, K. *AIDS in Adolescence: A Rationale for Concern*. Carnegie Council on Adolescent Development Working Papers, Washington, D.C., 1988.
15. Stehr-Green, J. K. The Division of HIV-AIDS Surveillance, Centers for Disease Control. Personal communication. May 1990.
16. Centers for Disease Control. *Human Immunodeficiency Virus I Infections in the United States: A Review of Current Knowledge and Plans for Expansion of HIV Surveillance Activities*, p. 2. Atlanta, 1987.
17. American Public Health Association. Special Initiative on AIDS. *Report No. 6: Pediatric HIV Infection*. Washington, D.C., 1989.
18. U.S. Department of Commerce. *Money Income and Poverty Status in the United States: 1988*. Current Population Reports, Series P-60, No. 166. Advance Data from the March 1989 Current Population Survey. U.S. Government Printing Office, Washington, D.C., 1989.
19. Beeghley, L. Illusion and reality in the measurement of poverty. *Soc. Probl.* 31(3): 322–333, 1984.
20. Children's Defense Fund. *A Children's Defense Budget FY 1989: An Analysis of Our Nation's Investment in Children*. Washington, D.C., 1988.
21. Office of Technology Assessment. *Healthy Children: Investing in the Future*, p. 44. Publication OTA-H-345. U.S. Government Printing Office, Washington, D.C., 1988.
22. National Center for Health Statistics. *Health United States 1989*. U.S. Department of Health and Human Services, Publication No. (PHS 90-1232). Hyattsville, Md., 1990.

23. Donahue, A. H., et al. HIV infection in women: An inventory of Public Health Service initiatives. *AIDS Public Policy J.* 4(2): 120–124, 1989.
24. Centers for Disease Control. Division of STD/HIV. *Annual Report, Fiscal year 1989*. Atlanta, 1989.
25. Brown, L. S., and Primm, B. J. Intravenous drug abuse and AIDS in minorities. *AIDS Public Policy J.* 3(2): 5–15, 1988.
26. Longshore, D. Reaching populations at higher risk for AIDS. *AIDS Public Policy J.* 4(2): 101–105, 1989.
27. Des Jarlais, D. C. Policy issues regarding AIDS among intravenous drug users: An overview. *AIDS Public Policy J.* 3(2): 1–4, 1988.
28. Sachs, A. Here come the pregnancy police: Mothers of drug-exposed infants face legal punishment. *Time* 133(21): 104, 1989.
29. Abrams, E. Personal communication. Harlem Hospital, April 5, 1990.
30. Hegarty, J. D., et al. The medical care costs of human immunodeficiency virus-infected children in Harlem. *JAMA* 260: 1901–1905, 1988.
31. American Public Health Association House Committee Report. Public health problems fuel surge of children in foster care.*The Nation's Health* 20(1): 1, 11, 1990.
32. Baltimore Association for Retarded Children. Personal communication, April 5, 1990.
33. Friedman, S. R., and Casriel, C. Drug users' organizations and AIDS policy. *AIDS Public Policy J.* 3(2): 30–36, 1988.
34. Kawata, P. A., and Andriote, J. M. The national AIDS network: Promoting community-based AIDS services. *AIDS Public Policy J.* 4(3): 164–167, 1989.
35. Mitchell, J. L. Women, AIDS and public policy. *AIDS Public Policy J.* 3(2): 50–52, 1988.
36. Selwyn, P. A., et al. Knowledge of HIV antibody status and decisions to continue or terminate pregnancy among intravenous drug users. *JAMA* 261: 3567–3571, 1989.
37. Prasad, N. A system view of health care for the poor. *J. Natl. Med. Assoc.* 81(2): 169–176, 1989.
38. Yankauer, A. AIDS and public health. *Am. J. Public Health* 78: 364–366, 1988.
39. Kass, F. C. Schoolchildren with AIDS. In *AIDS & the Law: A Guide for the Public*, edited by H. L. Dalton, S. Burris, and the Yale AIDS Law Project, pp. 66–80. Yale University Press, New Haven, 1987.
40. Friedland, G. H., et al. Lack of transmission of HTLV-III/LAV infection to household contacts of patients with AIDS or AIDS-related complex with oral candidiasis. *N. Engl. J. Med.* 314: 344–349, 1986.
41. Education and foster care of children infected with human t-lymphotropic virus type III/lymphadenopathy-associated virus. *MMWR* 34(34): 517–521, 1985.
42. American Academy of Pediatrics. Committee on School Health/Committee on Infectious Diseases. School attendance of children and adolescents with human t lymphotropic virus III/lymphadenopathy-associated virus infection. *Pediatrics* 77: 430–432, 1986.
43. Michael, S. Personal communication. New York City Health Department, April 1990.
44. Bradley, B. Personal communication. San Francisco Health Department, April 1990.
45. Fraser, K. *Someone at School has AIDS: A Guide to Developing Policies for Students and School Staff Members who are Infected with HIV*. National Association of State Boards of Education, Alexandria, Va., 1989.
46. Jones, N. L. The Education of All Handicapped Children Act: Coverage of children with acquired immune deficiency syndrome (AIDS). *J. Law Educ.* 15(2): 195–206, 1986.
47. Klindworth, L. A., et al. Pediatric AIDS, developmental disabilities, and education. *AIDS Educ. Prevent.* 1(4): 291–301, 1989.

48. Rogers, M. F., et al. Lack of transmission of human immunodeficiency virus from infected children to their household contacts. *Pediatrics* 85: 210–214, 1990.
49. Centers for Disease Control. Guidelines for effective school health education to prevent the spread of AIDS. *MMWR* 37(S-2): 1–14, 1988.
50. Departments of Labor, Health and Human Services, and Education, and Related Agencies Appropriations Act, 1988. Public Law 100-202, Title 5, Section 514.
51. Donovan, P., and Waszak, C. *School-Based Clinics Enter the '90s: Update, Evaluation and Future Challenges*, p. 7. Center for Population Options, Washington, D.C., 1989.
52. DiClemente, R. J., Zorn, J., and Temoshok, L. Adolescents and AIDS: A survey of knowledge, attitudes and beliefs about AIDS in San Francisco. *Am. J. Public Health* 76: 1443–1445, 1986.
53. Strunin, L., and Hingson, R. Acquired immunodeficiency syndrome and adolescents: Knowledge, belief, attitudes, and behaviors. *Pediatrics* 79: 825–828, 1987.
54. Kegeles, S. M., Adler, N. E., and Irwin, C. E. Sexually active adolescents and condoms: Changes over one year in knowledge, attitudes and use. *Am. J. Public Health* 78: 460–461, 1988.
55. Goodman, E., and Cohall, A. T. Acquired immunodeficiency syndrome and adolescents: Knowledge, attitudes, beliefs, and behaviors in a New York City adolescent minority population. *Pediatrics* 84: 36–42, 1989.
56. Hingson, R., Strunin, L., and Berlin, B. Acquired immunodeficiency syndrome transmission: Changes in knowledge and behaviors among teenagers, Massachusetts statewide surveys, 1986 to 1988. *Pediatrics* 85: 24–30, 1990.
57. Brandt, A. M. The syphilis epidemic and its relation to AIDS. *Science* 239: 375–380, 1988.
58. Brandt, A. M. AIDS in historical perspective: Four lessons from the history of sexually transmitted diseases. *Am. J. Public Health* 78: 367–371, 1988.
59. Freudenberg, N. Social and political obstacles to AIDS education. *SIECUS Rep.* 17(6): 1–6, 1989.
60. Dinkins, D. N. Testimony. In *Pediatric AIDS Hearing*, Hearing before the Select Committee on Narcotics Abuse and Control, House of Representatives, July 27, 1987. SCNAC-100-1-10. U.S. Government Printing Office, Washington, D.C., 1988.
61. Heagerty, M. C. Testimony, In *Pediatric AIDS Hearing*, Hearing before the Select Committee on Narcotics Abuse and Control, House of Representatives, July 27, 1987. SCNAC-100-1-10. U.S. Government Printing Office, Washington, D.C., 1988.

SECTION III

Women and AIDS

Introduction

Nancy Krieger and Glen Margo

Around the world, more and more women—principally poor women of color—are being diagnosed with and are dying of AIDS, the acquired immune deficiency syndrome (1–4). At the same time, ever increasing numbers of women are becoming infected by HIV, the human immunodeficiency virus. As uncertainty and illness disrupt the daily routines and kinship ties upon which survival so heavily depends, lives that are often already difficult grow even harder. And, as these women become ill, and as they die, their families and communities not only mourn but are left desperately seeking ways to fill the many roles that these women—like any other women—have always assumed: as caretakers within their families and among their friends; as mothers, sisters, daughters, wives, and lovers; as cooks and housekeepers; as peasant farmers and wage earners; and as vital members of their neighborhoods and nations (1–4).

Yet, despite the growing dimensions of this crisis, we continue to confront what is perhaps the most glaring omission in the global effort to control AIDS: the absence of appropriate and effective AIDS prevention programs that target and involve *all* women potentially at risk of HIV infection (1). To help us understand why this gap exists and what we must do to close it, the chapters in Section III focus on women and AIDS. Using the same approach of social critique and historical perspective employed in Section II, the authors argue that much more than poor planning underlies the neglectful approach to women and AIDS. Instead, the priorities and policies that put women last—and the factors that increase their risk of HIV infection—are the concrete and deadly expression of social, political, economic, and cultural conflicts that contribute to women's oppression and are deeply embedded in the diverse societies where AIDS has taken root.

Originally published in the *International Journal of Health Services* 21(1): 127–130, 1991.

Chapter 5, "More than Mothers and Whores: Redefining the AIDS Prevention Needs of Women," by Kathryn Carovano, cuts to the heart of the matter: the inequality of the sexes and the control of women's sexuality. Examining the situation of women in both economically underdeveloped and developed countries, Carovano posits that women with the least control over their bodies and their lives are at greatest risk of HIV infection. At issue is not only women's economic and social powerlessness, but a sexist ideology that defines and dichotomizes women as either "good" or "bad," as "mothers" or "whores." According to this view, women exist to meet the needs of men and the demands of motherhood. Translated into AIDS prevention programs, Carovano asserts, this framework has resulted in emphasizing the threat that "bad" HIV-infected women (e.g., sex workers) pose to men, and that "good" HIV-infected women (e.g., monogamous mothers) pose to their current or future offspring. Utterly ignored, if not deliberately negated, is the possibility that women might be autonomous, sexually active beings whose right and need to be protected from HIV infection is as legitimate and necessary as that of children and men.

To build her case, Carovano carefully reviews the alarming epidemiology of AIDS among women (more women are expected to become ill with AIDS during 1990 and 1991 than during all of the 1980s), and emphasizes the epidemic's disproportionate toll on poor women and women of color. She further notes that the true dimensions of this crisis are masked by underreporting of AIDS and HIV infection among women. Three factors contribute to this problem: the lack of access to health care among the poor, the exclusion of "female" conditions (e.g., pelvic inflammatory disease) from official diagnostic criteria for AIDS, and the persistent attitude among physicians that "most women are good girls who don't get AIDS." Analyzing the implications of these data for AIDS prevention programs geared to adolescent women, "women of reproductive age," and women in the sex industry, Carovano concludes that passive education and condoms are not enough. Instead, we must not only involve women at risk directly in the design and implementation of AIDS prevention programs, but must also develop women-controlled preventive technology (which ideally would protect against HIV infection during heterosexual intercourse while permitting conception to take place, if desired). And, more fundamentally, we must also work to eliminate the social and economic barriers that deny women equal control over sexual decisions.

Elaborating on many of these themes, in Chapter 6, Mary Bassett and Marvellous Mhloyi examine "Women and AIDS in Zimbabwe: The Making of an Epidemic." The question these authors address is *why*—as opposed to just *how*—AIDS in Africa has become a widespread sexually transmitted disease, with 80 percent of cases due to heterosexual intercourse and perinatal transmission. At issue is not just the biological properties of HIV, but the social structures that support its spread. To Bassett and Mhloyi, the pattern of AIDS in Africa—and particularly the high risk of infection among women—cannot be understood apart from the legacy of colonialism and the insidious combination of traditional and European patriarchal values.

In a concise historical analysis of Zimbabwe, Bassett and Mhloyi dissect the social misery and dispossession that occurred under colonialism. They clearly document how such factors as land expropriation and the creation of a migrant male labor force have indelibly stamped everyday life, including family structure and the very roles of women and men. These conditions—conjoined with the present realities of rapid urbanization, rural impoverishment, and high levels of military mobilization—in turn simultaneously fostered new patterns of sexual relations (characterized by multiple partners) and established the basis for the epidemic spread of sexually transmitted diseases. Add AIDS to this scenario, and the result is a crisis of overwhelming proportions. Yet, rather than retreat to fatalism, the authors offer a ray of hope. Just as historical circumstances, and not innate characteristics of "African life" or "human nature," created the current contours of the AIDS epidemic, so too can active interventions alter the epidemic's course. Echoing Carovano's proposals, the steps they urge are clear: not only must we provide education about HIV transmission, but we must also increase women's limited options—by developing alternatives to condoms and by promoting women's employment.

The hypothesis that a society's gender relations and economic structure can encourage high-risk sexual behaviors that efficiently transmit disease over a broad geographic area is further explored by Karen Jochelson, Monyaola Mothibeli, and Jean-Patrick Leger in Chapter 7, "Human Immunodeficiency Virus and Migrant Labor in South Africa." Using powerful evidence obtained from carefully compiled interview data, the authors vividly demonstrate how the migrant labor system forced upon workers in the South African mines constitutes a major risk factor for the transmission of HIV and other sexually transmitted diseases (most of which were unknown in precolonial Africa). By disrupting familial bonds, the migrant system not only establishes a pool of male workers who often turn to exchanging money or gifts for sex, but also creates a network of women who turn to prostitution to survive. Members of each group in turn often take these diseases back to rural areas when they return to visit their families and kin. The result: endemic infection, aggravated by the high rates of other ailments—such as malnutrition, malaria, and parasitic disease—that are all too common in impoverished regions.

Yet, as Jochelson and colleagues describe, rather than address the obvious social factors that feed the epidemic's growth, the South African government has opted to conduct a two-pronged program that is bound to fail. First, it has attempted to expatriate all migrant workers who test positive for HIV, which does nothing to stop HIV transmission and instead bolsters its spread into other areas. Second, the government's campaign to encourage condom use has promoted intense distrust among the miners, partly for cultural reasons and because the official literature revives hated memories of past racist population control initiatives. As an alternative approach to curtailing HIV transmission, Jochelson and colleagues propose a fundamentally different strategy. Like Carovano, and Bassett and Mhloyi, they argue that AIDS education must not only be designed with the active involvement of those at risk, but must also be provided by organizations people can trust—such as unions, the African National Congress, and other grassroots groups—and not by management or official government agencies. They also call for an end to the migrant system of labor itself, for as long as it continues, so too will the spread of AIDS and other sexually transmitted diseases.

Taken together, the three chapters in Section III offer a strong indictment of purely educational approaches to ending the AIDS epidemic. Only by recognizing the socioeconomic and cultural determinants of both disease and sexual behavior, and only by incorporating these insights into our AIDS prevention programs, will we have a chance to curb the spread of this lethal disease. Unless we grapple with the basic issues of sexuality, power, and survival—of what it is that ordinary and often powerless women and men must do to raise their families and to live from day-to-day—we are unlikely to succeed in our fight against AIDS.

REFERENCES

1. Panos Institute. Women and children last? *World AIDS* 1(7): 4–5, 1990.
2. Danziger, R. Women and AIDS. *World Health*, October 1990, pp. 14–15.
3. Reider, I., and Ruppelt, P. (eds.). *AIDS: The Women*. Cleis Press, San Francisco, 1988.
4. Anastos, K., and Marte, C. Women—The missing persons in the AIDS epidemic. *Health/PAC Bull.*, Winter 1989, pp. 6–15.

CHAPTER 5

More Than Mothers and Whores: Redefining the AIDS Prevention Needs of Women

Kathryn Carovano

In the spring of 1989, while I was working in Lima, Peru, a group of feminist women organized a meeting so that I could talk with them about women and AIDS. We talked a lot about the risks to women and about what they thought could be done, and we got into a discussion of options: the condom and non-penetrative sex. Frescia, a health educator there, told me this story:

> We had just finished a health promotion program with a group of women and we asked them to fill out an evaluation form. One of the women who was very good during the training was taking a long time to finish the questionnaire, so I asked her if she was having trouble with it. She told me that she was having a hard time reading it, so I asked her if maybe she needed to use glasses. She said yes, that she had had her eyes tested ten years ago, and the doctor had prescribed glasses for her. She had bought a pair but lost them a few months later. To explain why she had never gotten a new pair she said, "My husband told me that I was so stupid that he would never buy me another pair of glasses." So just imagine this woman asking her husband to use a condom or consider having nonpenetrative sex.

Around the world, women are at increasing risk for AIDS. At the root of this risk is women's lack of control over their bodies and their lives. As Herbert Daniel (1), a writer and activist living with AIDS in Brazil has pointed out, "Like every other epidemic, AIDS develops in the cracks and crevasses of society's inequalities. We cannot face the epidemic if we try to hide the contradictions and conflicts which it exposes."

Originally published in the *International Journal of Health Services* 21(1): 131–142, 1991.

As the AIDS epidemic continues to unfold, we are being forced to confront once again one of society's more glaring inequalities—the inequality of the sexes. The relative lack of control by women in relation to men, particularly in the context of sexual relations, places them at increasing risk for AIDS. Those women with the least control, generally poor women of color, are those who face the greatest risk. In order to develop effective AIDS prevention programs, we must confront the challenges that this "crack" exposes and develop programs that give women control over their sexuality and over their own lives. A first step toward developing prevention programs for women is to recognize that women are primarily at risk for AIDS because they are sexually active, and that their sexual activity goes beyond the simplified realms of sex for procreation or sex for money. Sex for some is for pleasure. And for many women, sex is simply part of survival.

Throughout the world, women's sexual identities have long been defined on the basis of their reproductive capacity and, to a lesser degree, their involvement in commercial sex. Motherhood legitimizes a woman's sexuality—and very often her life—while prostitution provides women with a means of survival, though with a heavy stigma. Women in many societies have traditionally been identified sexually as either mothers or whores, "good girls" or "bad girls." In examining current AIDS prevention efforts for women, one finds that this dichotomy dominates and is being utilized as a framework to identify the risks posed to and by women. Many societies regard the sensuous, sexual woman as "bad" and, in essence, only "bad girls" are perceived to be at risk for AIDS. "Good girls," in contrast, are viewed as asexual or their sexuality is relegated to the socially sanctioned realm of sex for procreation, which is seen as unrelated to HIV transmission. Both "mother" and "prostitute" are definitions for women that are based on their relationships to others; "As women we are so often defined by who leans on us. Being needed names us" (2). In the context of AIDS, these definitions reflect the needs of men and children, and it is in their relationship to the HIV-infected woman that she becomes a concern or threat. The focus on these particular identities, "mother" and "prostitute," among the many that define women leads one easily to the hypothesis that efforts to prevent AIDS among women have been the result not of a concern for women, but rather a concern that is primarily about protecting the health of men and children.

The impact of this thinking is reflected by the fact that to date, most AIDS prevention programs for women have been designed exclusively to reach women in the sex industry. Women engaged in prostitution have been identified as one of the principal "reservoirs" for HIV and, as such, a "risk group" that threatens the "general population." Faced with increasing numbers of children at risk for AIDS as a result of rising infection rates among women, new programs are also being formulated to target prenatal women. Unfortunately, those women—and they are most of us—who do not fall into one of these limited spheres are being largely ignored by program planners and implementing agencies working in AIDS prevention. Not surprisingly, the numbers of AIDS cases reported among women continue to grow at alarming rates.

THE EPIDEMIOLOGY OF AIDS AMONG WOMEN

According to the World Health Organization, of the estimated 600,000 people who developed AIDS in the 1980s, over 150,000 were women. During the next two years, 500,000 more people will develop AIDS and of these, 200,000 are expected to be women. In other words, more women are expected to become ill with AIDS during 1990 and 1991 than developed AIDS during the last decade (3).

These figures are alarming as they stand, yet the actual number of women who have died or are living with AIDS is undoubtedly far greater even than these numbers convey. Underreporting of AIDS cases is a recognized problem throughout the developing world, and underreporting of cases among women is a problem everywhere. Problems of reporting cases among women result from factors as varied as women's lack of access to health care, the exclusion of "female diseases" in the diagnostic criteria for AIDS, and the persistent attitude among many physicians that "good girls don't get AIDS." Despite these problems, data still show that women around the world are being diagnosed with AIDS in ever increasing numbers and most of them are poor women of color, whether they are living in Newark, Bangkok, Nairobi, or Rio de Janeiro.

In the United States, the proportion of the total AIDS cases occurring among women rose from 7 percent of cases reported before 1985 to 11 percent of cases reported during the first half of 1989 (4). In Frankfurt, West Germany, the percentage of HIV-infected patients who are women rose from 4 percent in 1984 to 25 percent in 1988 (5). Throughout much of sub-Saharan Africa, women represent 50 percent or more of AIDS cases, and similar ratios have been reported in some parts of the English-speaking Caribbean. Studies conducted among pregnant women have revealed seroprevalence rates of 10.5 percent in Port au Prince, Haiti, and 24 percent in Kampala, Uganda (3). In Latin America and Asia, women currently make up a small but growing percentage of reported cases. The growth of pediatric AIDS cases reveals the ripple effect of HIV infection in women; according to James Grant (6), Director General of UNICEF, over 90 percent of pediatric AIDS cases are the result of perinatal transmission. AIDS accounts for up to one-third of all deaths to children in some African cities, and in some parts of New York City, one of every 100 babies is born with HIV infection (7). UNICEF has projected that the average infant mortality rate in ten East and Central African countries will rise from a current rate of 164 deaths per 1000 to 185 per 1000 by the year 2000; prior to the introduction of HIV, these rates had been projected to fall to 130 per 1000 during the next decade. In addition, UNICEF has estimated that in these countries, as many as 5 million children will have lost their parents to AIDS by the end of the decade (6). A survey conducted in 1989 in the Rakai district of Uganda—the region hardest hit by AIDS—found that 23,351 children had already lost one or both parents, the majority of them to AIDS (8).

These alarming statistics indicate the need to develop AIDS prevention programs that provide information and sexual empowerment to all sexually active women. The remainder of this chapter will look at the risks that AIDS poses to specific segments of the population of women, beginning with young, adolescent women.

ADOLESCENT WOMEN

If knowledge were power, then adolescent women would probably be among the least powerful—and in fact they are when it comes to their ability to protect themselves against HIV infection.

The guiding philosophy in dealing with adolescent sexuality in many cultures is "if you don't talk about sex they won't do it." This logic, however, is critically flawed. Adolescents are sexual beings at varying stages of self-awareness and understanding. Many of them do and will continue to engage in sexual intercourse despite lack of access to any accurate information about sex. Unfortunately, if you do not talk to them, they will almost undoubtedly also engage in "unsafe sex." Sex can and does occur without much understanding; "safe" sex requires an ability to distinguish between risky and nonrisky sexual activities *and* an ability to choose safer sex.

Whether or not you talk about it, teens clearly are having sex. Many women—and most men—have their first sexual relations prior to marriage, usually during their teens, and most often those first encounters are unprotected. Research in family planning has revealed that the quality of reproductive health information is generally low among adolescents. This is a reflection in part of the lack of social acceptance of providing sex education and contraceptive services to teens in many countries. In the developing world, contraceptive services are often available only to married women, and in some situations, only to women who have already borne one or more children (9).

In most of the world's countries, births to women under 20 represent a significant proportion of all births; in Swaziland a study conducted in 1985 reported that over 30 percent of children were born to women between 15 and 19 years of age (10). According to evidence from the World Fertility Survey, the average fertility rate for women aged 15 to 19 in developing countries is 8.7 percent of the global total (11, Table 21, p. 33). High levels of adolescent pregnancy and teenage abortions reported in Japan (12), Nigeria (13), and Baltimore, Maryland (14), reflect the reality of high levels of sexual activity and low levels of correct contraceptive use among adolescents.

Given the sexual practices of teens, the threat of AIDS cannot be ignored. In the United States in 1989, 26.3 percent (n = 4,306) of the AIDS cases reported among females occurred among women between 20 and 29 years of age (15). Given the long incubation period for AIDS, the majority of these women may very well have been infected during adolescence. A survey conducted in 1988 in a New York City shelter found that 18 percent of the girls in the study tested positive for HIV antibody (16). In some African cities where infection rates among sexually active adults have reached 30 to 40 percent, the risk of exposure through sexual contact is extremely high. Young women tend to have their first sexual encounter later than their male peers, hence even their first contact could place them at risk for HIV. In Uganda, older men are reportedly looking to young school girls instead of prostitutes for "AIDS-free sex" (17).

AIDS prevention programs for adolescent women and girls, in school, while increasingly common in developed countries, are still extremely rare in the developing world. The need for such programs is critical, though given the very early school drop-out rates of many girls in developing countries, school-based programs alone are not enough. On average, 44 percent of ever-married women in the developing world have received no formal education and of those who have, only 7 percent have ten or more years of schooling (11, p. 217). Out-of-school programs will be critical in reaching young minority women in many developed countries as well.

Adolescent women, like everyone else, need to be given information that offers them choices and is based on an understanding of their sexual behavior. Studies of adolescents who have received sex education have shown that they are not likely to engage in sex any sooner or any more frequently than their uninformed peers, but they are more likely to use contraceptives (18). Sex education and AIDS information is not an aphrodisiac, but rather a basic tool for adolescent health and survival. To deny adolescents access is to leave them powerless and at high risk for HIV.

"WOMEN OF REPRODUCTIVE AGE"

The first woman to be diagnosed with AIDS in Mexico (in 1985) was a 52-year-old housewife living in Mexico City; her only known "risk" behavior was having unprotected sexual intercourse with her husband (19). The vast majority of women with AIDS and HIV infection are between the ages of 20 and 45 and are frequently referred to as "women of reproductive age." As neglected as young women have been, even more neglected are women over 20. Although these women are generally better informed about sexuality and family planning and perhaps more able to make mature choices about their sexual behavior, they are also at increasing risk for AIDS and yet remain largely uninformed. To date, this group—if not involved in prostitution—has probably received the least attention of all sectors of society.

The primary reason for the lack of programs for this population is the false notion that these women are not at risk. These are the "good girls" who are generally perceived to be loyally monogamous or asexual and hence not at risk for

HIV. Only when pregnant or considering pregnancy are most women in this population directly confronted with their potential risk of contracting AIDS, and generally in the context of society's concern for their unborn children. Many women with HIV infection in both developed and developing countries learn that they are infected only after one of their children is diagnosed with AIDS; in the United States an estimated 60 percent of HIV-infected women find out about their seropositive status only once their children are diagnosed with AIDS (20). Routine screening of prenatal women is increasingly becoming the norm in many developed countries, including the United Kingdom, where legislation passed in November 1989 makes it a requirement for all pregnant women (21).

Ironically, despite the identification of this population as "women of reproductive age," the only advice given is that if they perceive themselves to be at risk, they should protect themselves from AIDS using methods that prohibit conception. The limited means available to prevent the sexual transmission of HIV have exposed the contradiction between disease prevention and women's reproductive roles. As discussed earlier, condoms and nonpenetrative sex are currently the only means available to sexually active men and women to prevent HIV transmission. In addition to providing protection against the sexual transmission of HIV, both methods also inhibit conception, an added advantage for some, but a critical flaw for those wishing to conceive.

Noreen Kaleeba (22), Director of the AIDS Support Organization in Uganda, made real this dilemma when she described her experience counseling a young woman considering pregnancy. Her client's reasons for not adopting measures to protect herself from HIV despite recognizing her potential risk included the following: "Babies and condoms don't go together, nonpenetrative sex is no sex at all for a man, and it is a woman's responsibility to bear a child." Motherhood brings status, security, and validation to many women's lives. In many cultures women are told that the purpose of their existence is to bring forth new life, especially male, and that their value depends on bringing it forth (23, p. 159).

In many cultures, there is no social place for women who are unable or choose not to have children. "Because there is no alternative social or personal identity for women separate from parenting, women's risk of infection is greater" (24). In other words, as long as there is no valid role for women who choose not to parent children, measures to prevent HIV infection that negate the importance of that role will have only limited impact. To provide women exclusively with HIV prevention methods that contradict most societies' fertility norms is to provide many women with no options at all. The need for research and development of an effective virucide to prevent HIV transmission without impeding reproduction is critical if we are to provide a real choice to many women.

Women need to be able to protect themselves from HIV without being forced to forfeit the option to bear children. In an ideal world, mutually faithful monogamy would allow women to protect themselves and have healthy children, but this is not the reality of relationships for most of the world's population. To force women to rely on abstinence, nonpenetrative sex, condoms, female condoms, and potentially even spermicides is to ignore the importance placed on women's reproductive roles.

WOMEN IN THE SEX INDUSTRY

In January 1990, the *Prensa Libre*, a leading newspaper in Guatemala, published a plea to national police from the regional health director of Esquintla to undertake a national search for a young Salvadoran woman who had left the city. The article provided her name, a description of her appearance, and information about where she had most recently worked. The justification for the search: the young woman in question was a prostitute who had tested positive for HIV. The objective of the search: to find this woman and put her under "medical surveillance" in order to control the further spread of HIV in Guatemala.

Throughout the world, AIDS prevention programs have been developed targeting women in the sex industry. While there are many programs that have been developed with the clear intention of protecting women working in what is potentially a high-risk trade, there are also countless cases of scapegoating and abuse. Prostitutes have repeatedly been referred to as "reservoirs for transmission" and blamed for "spreading AIDS." This is a reflection of the "bad girl" vision of woman as temptress, while men are simply viewed as innocently responding to natural urges. Prostitutes are seen as encouraging men to stray, hence they are held responsible for their own and others' disease. It is worth noting that despite this portrayal of prostitute-as-vector, as of January 1989, in the United States, ". . . there [had] been no documented cases of men becoming infected through contact with a specific prostitute" (25).

Prostitution has existed in every society for which there are written records and continues to exist as a result of sexual double standards that limit women's economic options and means of sexual expression. It is, by definition, the exchange of sexual services for money or goods, and thus logically, most women who enter voluntarily into prostitution do so primarily for economic reasons (26). As Simone de Beauvoir (27, p. 620) points out in *The Second Sex*:

> The truth is that in a world where misery and unemployment prevail, there will be people to enter any profession that is open; as long as a police force and prostitution exist, there will be policemen and prostitutes, more especially as these occupations pay better than many others. It is pure hypocrisy to wonder at the supply that masculine demand stimulates; that is simply the action of an elementary and universal economic process.

According to a report in the *New African*, economic problems compelled many Ghanaian women to seek income through prostitution; these women currently constitute the population at highest risk for AIDS in Ghana (28).

Considerable effort has been focused on developing AIDS prevention programs targeting women in the sex industry. To date, this work has involved five principal approaches, which can be summarized as follows:

- Methods that truly seek to provide women with information and tools that will allow them to protect themselves, or at least give them a better chance at doing so.
- Methods that seek to evade the risk posed by HIV by providing sex workers with job training and alternative employment opportunities.
- The harassment and/or arrest of women as a means of theoretically eliminating prostitution.
- Routine HIV antibody testing of legally or semi-legally registered prostitutes.
- Combinations of one or more of these approaches.

Of these approaches, only the first has proven appropriate or effective in preventing the spread of AIDS to prostitutes. The others either scapegoat women, are unrealistic, or overlook prostitutes entirely to focus instead on the protection of male clients. A common flaw found in almost all efforts thus far is a lack of focus on the education of both clients and/or noncommercial partners, and a lack of recognition that not all sex is "work."

Women involved in prostitution face many of the same challenges in their intimate—as opposed to commercial—sexual relations as do their "nonworking" peers (29). Efforts to promote behavior change among prostitutes have shown that the greatest area of resistance is in women's relationships with their steady and/or noncommercial partners. "Although most prostitutes [in the United States] expect to use condoms with their customers, most do not use them with their primary partners" (25). Additionally, numerous studies have shown that, more frequently than not, prostitutes are mothers as well as whores. A survey conducted among 100 female sex workers in metropolitan Manila found that 31 percent of them were married and 62 percent were supporting children; 14 percent were raising children with no support from their spouse or family (30). A survey of 47 women in Nairobi, Kenya, found that all of them had at least one child, though 95 percent were unmarried (31). Approaches that negate the mother—and lover—in the whore have not been and will not be effective in preventing the further spread of HIV to women.

The first step toward developing effective prevention programs for women in the sex industry must be a recognition of the diverse population of women involved in prostitution and the complexity of their lives. Women's situations vary depending on multiple factors such as number of dependents, age, legal status, general health and appearance, where they work (e.g., street, brothel, bar), drug-use practices, voluntary or forced involvement in prostitution, and sexual behavior. Many of these factors will affect the degree of control that sex workers experience in their sexual encounters and will determine whether it is more appropriate to provide training in safe sex negotiation or condom use techniques that will leave clients unaware.

For those women who choose or are forced to work in the sex industry, the risk posed by AIDS is potentially high and the need for information and skills great. "Women in general and sex workers in specific have little trust in the 'good intentions' of outsiders" (32), and programs that include sex workers in their design and implementation have proven most likely to succeed.

REPRODUCTIVE DECISION-MAKING FOR WOMEN LIVING WITH HIV AND AIDS

As HIV continues to spread among women, the need for prevention and support programs for women and their children with HIV disease is also growing. HIV-positive women need to have access to quality information about HIV transmission and disease management. They also need to receive quality counseling that will assist them to make informed choices about future sexual behavior and fertility.

Women with HIV disease need to understand the potential risk of pregnancy and repeated exposure to HIV to their own health. Studies remain inconclusive on the issue of the affect of pregnancy on an HIV-infected woman's health, though the majority suggest that it may have little impact. In addition, women need information about the risk of transmitting the virus to their unborn children. Current estimates of vertical transmission rates range from 30 to 50 percent (33), a risk that may or may not be deemed acceptable to an HIV-infected woman and/or her partner. One popular anecdote is of a poor, black seropositive woman who upon being accused by her physician of making an irresponsible decision in choosing to bear a child responded: "Fifty percent is the best odds I've been given since I was diagnosed as carrying this virus" (34). Perception of risk is relative, and on the basis of a woman's or couple's view of this risk, they must be free to choose whether or not to bear children.

Throughout the world, millions of women who are subfertile or infertile live in dread of divorce or social ostracism because they cannot bear children (9, p. 6). "Women's status as childbearer has been made into a major fact of her life. Terms like 'barren' or 'childless' have been used to negate any further identity" (23, p. 11). The argument that suggests that HIV-positive women should not bear children identifies them, in essence, as barren.

In many parts of the developing world in particular, women make reproductive decisions with a view to children as security investments. Studies have shown that "the higher the level of infant mortality, the greater fertility necessary to achieve the [security] goal" (35). As infant mortality levels increase as a result of HIV, we may witness more rather than fewer births to women with HIV disease. A survey conducted among 58 women with HIV infection in Kinshasa, Zaire, supports this possibility by documenting that 71 percent wanted more children within the next two years and 5 percent were already pregnant (36). In Port au Prince, Haiti, a study found that pregnancies were as common among HIV-infected women as among a control group of uninfected women (3). The argument that HIV-infected women should receive "directive counseling" to avoid or terminate pregnancy denies the complexity and real importance of motherhood in many women's lives.

For HIV-infected women who choose to bear children or who have already delivered children who are infected with HIV, health care programs need to be integrated to provide concurrent care for women and children. If a woman has to travel to two separate clinics to receive care for herself and her child, the woman's health can be expected to suffer. Women have traditionally given priority to their children's health care needs over their own, and there is no evidence to suggest that AIDS has changed this pattern (37).

CONCLUSION

Women of all ages are primarily at risk of contracting AIDS through sexual contact with an infected partner. Most women currently lack needed information, tools, and the power over their own bodies and lives to enable them to reduce their risk. A review of available data leaves a feeling that we must find a "magic bullet" that will give women the technological means to protect themselves, or there must be a revolution to finally give women equal control over sexual decisions.

Women are more than mothers and whores, and the core issue is about "women's right to be sexual, to separate sexuality from procreation" (23, p. xvii) and to be in control of their own sexual decision-making. For those women who do not seek to conceive, condoms and nonpenetrative sex do exist as potential alternatives. However, the general problem of powerlessness and lack of control by women in sexual decision-making is highlighted when considering either option, particularly condoms. Women who attempt to introduce condoms into a relationship are often perceived as overly "prepared" for sex, not trusting of their partner's fidelity, unfaithful themselves, or even HIV-infected (38, 39). For women in the sex industry, a condom may mean accepting a lower fee for service or blurring the distinction between work and love. For all women, condoms and nonpenetrative sex, unlike most other contraceptive technologies available today, both require male cooperation, which implicitly means male control. Women tend to choose contraceptive methods that their male partners are not "inconvenienced" by and often are not even aware of. Evidence from the World Fertility Survey of current contraceptive users shows that the mean level of pill use is 31 percent throughout the developing world, a rate that far exceeds that of any other modern method, including condoms, which are reportedly used by only 7 percent of the population (11, p. 146). From family planning we know that while many men support controlling the size of their families, few assume primary responsibility for the prevention of pregnancy.

Alternative, women-controlled preventive technology is critically needed, but in the mean time, prevention education programs are also needed that begin to make all sexually active women aware of their potential risk for AIDS. Studies conducted in the United States have shown that while women are relatively knowledgeable about AIDS and endorse condoms as an important way to prevent the spread of HIV, they do not use them, in large part because they do not perceive *themselves* to be at risk (40). This lack of risk awareness, which is certainly not unique to U.S. women, is largely a reflection of the false notion that women are not at risk—a perception that must be challenged if effective programs are to be developed.

Efforts to prevent the spread of AIDS to women must therefore focus on empowerment, on the "repossession by women of our bodies" (23, p. 285), which will require both social reform and technological support. Acknowledging the risks faced by women and providing them with targeted prevention information are desperately needed, but alone will not enable many women in both developed and developing countries to protect themselves from HIV infection. Supporting efforts to develop women-controlled preventive technology that provides women with real choices is also critical, given the reality of many women's lives.

In order to be effective, AIDS prevention programs for women must be developed in a context of understanding the social and economic barriers that result in the powerlessness that characterizes many of the women affected by AIDS in both the developing and the developed world. It is time to go beyond the simple vision of women as either mothers or whores to a recognition of the diversity of women's sexual roles and the risks they face, often for reasons that go far beyond their individual control. The "risk group" approach tends to deny the multiple factors that place women at risk of contracting HIV and to ignore the complexity of implementing change in many women's lives. To ensure this understanding, the women being targeted must be involved at every stage of policy and program development. Only then can women's needs begin to be understood and met in ways that will allow them to effectively protect themselves from AIDS.

REFERENCES

1. Daniel, H. *Vida Antes da Morte/Life Before Death*, p. 37. Escritorio e Tipografia Jaboti Ltda, Rio de Janeiro, Brazil, 1989.
2. Moskowitz, F. *A Leak in the Heart: Tales From a Woman's Life*, p. 99. David R. Godine, Boston, 1985.
3. Mann, J. Women, Mothers, Children and the Global AIDS Strategy. Paper presented at the International Conference on the Implications of AIDS for Mothers and Children, Paris, November 27, 1989.
4. Current trends: First 100,000 cases of AIDS—United States. *MMWR* 38: 561–563, 1989.
5. Staszewski, S. Epidemiology of HIV Infection in Women from Frankfurt Area. Poster presented at the Fifth International Conference on AIDS, Montreal, June 7, 1989.

6. Grant, J. UNICEF's Present Policy and New Approaches. Paper presented at the International Conference on the Implications of AIDS for Mothers and Children, Paris, November 27, 1989.
7. New York State Department of Health. *Status Report: HIV Seroprevalence Study*. Albany, N.Y., July 1988.
8. U.S. Department of State. Pediatric AIDS Prevention Under FY90 Child Survival FRA. Unclassified Cable. American Embassy, Kampala, Uganda, December 5, 1989.
9. Germain, A., and Ordway, J. *Population Control and Women's Health: Balancing the Scales*, pp. 1–15. International Women's Health Coalition, Washington, D.C., June 1989.
10. Gule, G. Z. *Youth Education and Services for Health and Family Life: Situation Analysis in Swaziland*, p. 28. International Planned Parenthood Federation, Africa Region, July 1985.
11. United Nations. *Fertility Behavior in the Context of Development: Evidence from the World Fertility Survey*. New York, 1987.
12. Hayashi, K. Adolescent sexual activities and fertility in Japan. *Bull. Inst. Public Health* 32(2–4): 88–94, 1983.
13. Nichols, D., et al. Sexual behavior, contraceptive practice and reproductive health among Nigerian adolescents. *Stud. Fam. Plann.* 17: 110–116, 1986.
14. Governor's Task Force on Teen Pregnancy. *A Call to Action: Final Report, Governor's Task Force on Teen Pregnancy, State of Maryland*, p. 56. Annapolis, September 1985.
15. Centers for Disease Control. AIDS cases by sex, age at diagnosis, and race ethnicity, reported through June 1898, United States. In *HIV/AIDS Among Racial and Ethnic Populations*, p. 3. Atlanta, June 1989.
16. Foley, M. J. Women health policymakers: Interview with Dr. Mathilde Krim. *The Network News* (National Women's Health Network) 13(6): 52, 1988.
17. Ojulu, E. Ugandan prostitutes are now wiser. *New African*, September, 1988, p. 34.
18. Youth in the 1980s: Social and Health Concerns. *Popul. Rep* [*M*] 12: M-349–M-388, 1985.
19. Lifshiz, A. Inmunodeficiencia adquirida en un sujeto de bajo riesgo: primera mujer en Mexico. In *Revista Medica*. Instituto Mexicano de Seguro Social, Mexico, June 1986.
20. Low income minority women and AIDS. *The Network News* (National Women's Health Network) 13(5): 6, 1988.
21. Sherr, L. Changes in the Impact of AIDS on Obstetrics Staff. Paper presented at the International Conference on the Implications for AIDS for Mothers and Children, Paris, November 29, 1989.
22. Kaleeba, N. Management of Mothers, Children and Families in Developing Countries. Paper presented at the International Conference on the Implications of AIDS for Mothers and Children, Paris, November 28, 1989.
23. Rich, A. *Of Woman Born: Motherhood as Experience and Institution*. W. W. Norton, New York, 1976.
24. Reid, E. Women and AIDS. In *National AIDS Bulletin*, pp. 20–23. Australian Federation of AIDS Organizations, August 1988.
25. Cohen, J. Overstating the risk of AIDS: Scapegoating prostitutes. *Focus: A Guide to AIDS Research* 2(4): 1–2, 1989.
26. Alexander, P. On Prostitution, pp. 1–20. Unpublished monograph. The National Task Force on Prostitution, February 1987.
27. de Beauvoir, S. *The Second Sex*. Random House, New York, 1952.

28. Yeboah-Afaria, A. Ghananian prostitutes fight AIDS with condoms. *New African*, January 1989, p. 54.
29. Worth, D. Sexual decisionmaking and AIDS: Why condom promotion among vulnerable women is likely to fail. *Stud. Fam. Plann.* 20: 297–307, 1989.
30. MacDonald, G. KAP Survey of a Purposive Sample of Male and Female Sex Workers in Metropolitan Manila, the Philippines. Internal AIDSCOM Monograph. Academy for Educational Development, Washington, D.C., January 1989.
31. Katsivo, M. N. Social Characteristics and Sexual Behavior of Women in the High Risk Behavior Category. Paper presented at the Fifth International Conference on AIDS, Montreal, June 7, 1989.
32. Stephens, C. Women Working as Prostitutes: Participatory/Consensus-Based Planning for the Provision of Mobile, Prevention, Risk-Reduction, and Seroprevalence Activities. Paper presented at the Fifth International Conference on AIDS, Montreal, June 8, 1989.
33. Hauer, L. B. Pregnancy and HIV Infection. *Focus: A Guide to AIDS Research* 4(11): 1–2, 1989.
34. Arras, J. D. HIV Infection and Reproductive Decisions: An Ethical Analysis. Paper presented at the Fifth International Conference on AIDS, Montreal, June 6, 1989.
35. Cain, M. Women's status and fertility in developing countries: Son preference and economic security. *World Bank Staff Working Paper, No. 682, Population and Development Series*, No. 7, pp. 1–68. World Bank, Washington, D.C., 1984.
36. Hassig, S. Contraceptive Utilization and Reproductive Desires in a Group of HIV-Positive Women in Kinshasa. Paper presented at the Fifth International Conference on AIDS, Montreal, June 7, 1989.
37. Riley, M. Project Director, Children's HIV & AIDS Model Program (Project CHAMP), Children's National Medical Center/Academy for Educational Development, Washington, D.C. Personal communication, May 9, 1990.
38. Worth, D., and Rodriguez, R. Latina women and AIDS. *SIECUS Report* 15(3): 5–7, 1987.
39. Bledsoe, C. The Cultural Meaning of AIDS and Condoms for Stable Heterosexual Relations in Africa: Recent Evidence from the Local Print Media. Paper presented at IUSSP Seminar, Kinshasa, Zaire, February 27, 1989.
40. Valdiserri, R. O., et al. The relationship between women's attitudes about condoms and their use: Implications for condom promotion campaigns. *Am. J. Public Health*, 79: 499–501, 1989.

CHAPTER 6

Women and AIDS in Zimbabwe: The Making of an Epidemic

Mary T. Bassett and Marvellous Mhloyi

The AIDS epidemic in Africa, first reported in 1983 among patients from Central Africa who sought medical care in European centers (1), has now reached major proportions. In some urban areas, the prevalence of infection by HIV, the human immunodeficiency virus, in the adult population is approaching 20 percent (2–4). The burden on health services is already being felt: in Ivory Coast, where the first person with AIDS was diagnosed as recently as 1985, over 40 percent of hospitalized patients in the capital city are seropositive (5). Popular concern about the disease reflects these figures. In Uganda, where the wasting syndrome "Slim Disease" was described in the early 1980s, a community-based survey found AIDS to be identified as the number one health problem. Affecting young people who have successfully survived the risks of death in early childhood, AIDS is causing deaths in an economically important age group (15 to 45 years) that was previously relatively protected from mortality. Perinatal transmission threatens hard-won gains in the reduction of infant mortality. Though dwarfed by the big killers—malnutrition and parasitic and bacterial infections—AIDS is having an important and still-evolving effect on health, and poses a substantial threat to present and future generations.

Efforts to halt the epidemic of AIDS in Africa will fall short if we fail to consider the diverse components, both social and biological, that contribute to its spread. Drawing on our joint experience as a clinician/epidemiologist and a social scientist in Zimbabwe, we will explore how current patterns of AIDS transmission in our country—and in Africa more generally—are driven by a combination of factors stemming from the intersection of traditional culture with our colonial

Originally published in the *International Journal of Health Services* 21(1): 143–156, 1991.

legacy and present-day political economy. In particular, we will examine how social conditions have shaped the course of AIDS through their effects on sexual relationships within and outside fast-changing family structures. By focusing on the particular situation of women in Zimbabwe, and by highlighting how the epidemic is perpetuated by patterns of trade, migrant labor, and sexually transmitted diseases, we hope to suggest a broader framework for comprehending and preventing AIDS in Africa.

UNDERSTANDING AIDS IN AFRICA: THE DIFFERING EXPLANATIONS

Early in the epidemic, investigators working in Africa noted that AIDS was occurring about as often in women as in men. This was in striking contrast to the pattern seen in North America and Europe (now called "Pattern 1"), where male predominance reflected the fact that the initial major risk group in these regions was homosexual men. The different epidemiological profile of AIDS in central and eastern Africa, however, supported the hypothesis that heterosexual intercourse was the major mechanism of transmission in these parts of Africa. Because of the subsequent large numbers of infected women, perinatal transmission also took on significant public health importance. It is generally estimated that these two mechanisms—heterosexual intercourse and perinatal transmission—account for 80 percent of AIDS cases in Africa. In Zimbabwe, where blood supplies have been screened for HIV-1 since 1985, the proportion attributable to these two routes of spread is certainly even higher. Blandly labeled "Pattern 2," this pattern of spread has been regarded as ominous and threatening ever since it was first described.

Since the initial studies of AIDS in Africa, our appreciation of the modes of transmission has expanded, but the basic framework remains unchanged: AIDS in Africa is a sexually transmitted disease with no special risk groups. In this chapter we suggest that an understanding of the full dimensions of the AIDS outbreak in Africa, what Jonathan Mann (6) has described as the "third epidemic," requires that the discussion be broadened. We need to go beyond the supposedly neutral terms of "risk group" and "risk factor" to examine the social context in which the epidemic has taken hold and is spreading. Any epidemic sustains itself largely because of the social organization that supports its propagation, not simply because of the biological characteristics of the "causative agent." In the case of HIV, the single most important biological feature, from a public health point of view, is the long period (years) of asymptomatic infection during which transmission can occur. Although lethal, HIV is relatively noninfectious: who gets infected and who does not has more to do with socially determined behavior than with pathogenicity. Just as much as HIV is a requirement for the AIDS epidemic, so too are the social relations that mold, even determine, the setting of each individual's exposure and susceptibility to infection.

What is it about Africa that explains its particular mass pattern of disease? Behind the "how" of transmission lies a "why" which haunts the understanding of AIDS in Africa. Addressing these issues has important implications for control of the epidemic. We will focus on the more difficult question of "why," in part because we believe much of the "how" has already been explained. Our central thesis is that the stage on which this epidemic is unfolding has been set by the social realities of Africa: the migrant labor system, rapid urbanization, constant war with high levels of military mobilization, landlessness, and poverty.

In Africa, traditional cultures are filtered through the facts of colonization and the market economy, both of which have transformed traditional family roles. The history of social misery and dispossession under colonialism has left its stamp on the facts of everyday life: how the family is organized, the role of women, and the role of men. In this sense, the traditional cultures of precolonial societies no longer exist. Instead, culture represents an adaptation of tradition to the changing society. In recent years, the world economic crisis has eroded many of the social gains of independent African countries. This, in broad strokes, is the setting in which the AIDS epidemic is occurring.

The heterosexual transmission of AIDS in Africa poses a frightening specter to the West. Although heterosexual transmission had been identified in North America prior to the description of AIDS in Africa (7), the number of such cases was small and, though growing, remains small. Western explanations for the heterosexual pattern in Africa have been marked by both media hysteria and scientific racism. Images of the dark continent, harboring dangerous diseases, inhabited by people whose social interactions are propelled by sexual frenzy, have long been engraved in the Western view of Africa. Eminent scientists proclaimed the origin of the epidemic to be Africa before data to substantiate their hypothesis were definitive (8). Work on genetic markers for susceptibility rapidly found its way into print (9). Even data on cranial capacities, a relic of eugenic science, were trotted out to explain African susceptibility (10).

This cultural assault, coupled with the fear of loss of needed foreign currency in tourist revenues and investment, was followed by an unfortunate delay in, and even suppression of, the African public health response to the AIDS outbreak. To admit the existence of the AIDS epidemic became tantamount to admitting the inferiority of African ways of life. This was particularly galling when it was clear that the vast majority of cases were initially diagnosed in the United States. The weight of numbers has now stripped away African preoccupation with the intrigues of international science. Researchers in Africa, in both the social and biological sciences, with the support of their governments, have turned their attention to the ways in which the epidemic can be slowed.

WOMEN AND AIDS IN AFRICA: REASONS FOR PARTICULAR CONCERN

Our focus in this chapter is particularly on women. This emphasis derives from several concerns. First, women in Africa are being portrayed as the dangerous vector of the AIDS outbreak. For example, in terms of epidemiological investigations, this has meant an emphasis on study of female prostitutes to the exclusion of other women. The devastating level of infection documented in some groups of women who sell sexual services is wrongly interpreted to mean that without them, the epidemic would not be occurring. Usually, as Padian (11) has pointed out, all we know is that these women, infected by their clients, are experiencing the brunt of the epidemic. Usually, because we have not identified or studied the men who use prostitutes, we do not know the extent of HIV infection among this group of men. Although it is plausible that female prostitutes contribute to the spread of HIV, we do not know the extent to which the propagation of the epidemic depends upon them.

If not depicted as a dangerous source of infection, women are of interest to those conducting AIDS research or designing interventions mainly when in their pregnant state. Numerous surveys record the prevalence of HIV infection among prenatal women. Information on the extent of infection in this group is important for charting the course of the epidemic. Still, the image of women becomes one of contaminated vessels bearing condemned babies. Because of the shorter natural history of infection in children, a woman may be identified as seropositive because of a sick child, before she herself shows signs of being ill. This reinforces the notion that the mother is solely responsible for the child's serostatus.

These negative portrayals alone are reason enough to examine the position of women in this epidemic. Dangerous precedents exist for the curtailment of women's rights in the face of outbreaks of other sexually transmitted diseases (12). But the position of women is important for still other reasons. The limited control that women have to determine their own lives forms parts of the social substrate of the current epidemic, as we will describe in more detail. The subordination of African women in patrilineal societies places them at a special disadvantage with regard to their ability or willingness to intervene and reduce their own risk of HIV infection. For many women, faced with divorce or dire poverty on the one hand and the risk of HIV infection on the other, the choice becomes one of "social death" or biological death. No one involved in caring for HIV-infected women in Zimbabwe, and presumably elsewhere, can fail to be struck by the limited options women have in negotiating their sexual relations.

Appreciation of these constraints should inform our efforts in developing intervention strategies. In many settings, women in the younger age groups are actually experiencing higher levels of infection than men. In Zaire, women have a higher prevalence of HIV infection until the age of 35 (13). In Ghana, among those diagnosed with AIDS, women outnumber men (14). Ghana's female predominance, Neequaque (14) suggests, may result from women returning home to Ghana when they are ill, after having engaged in sex work in neighboring Ivory Coast.

Unfolding behind these statistics are family tragedies with wrenching human dimensions:

- An elderly woman is carried into the clinic by her daughters. She is wasted by chronic diarrhea which, compounded with severe peripheral neuropathy, has left her unable to walk. She has been tested for HIV but has not been informed of her diagnosis. In privacy, she is told that she has AIDS and that her prognosis is poor. Does she want to go home or come into hospital? "I will go home," she says. Should we discuss the diagnosis with her children? "Are they in danger?" she asks. No. Then she will keep it to herself. And her husband? Well, he comes around only now and then, and she is staying with her elder daughter. What does he do for a living? He is a long-distance truck driver. "He provided well for the family," she says, "driving up and down and bringing us money and bringing us AIDS." She thanks us for explaining what is happening to her and goes home.
- A young woman of 24, her pretty face scarred by a rash, comes to the clinic with her 1-year-old child, the third born. The child is well dressed, for clinic day. He clings to his mother. I pat his head and feel his neck: he has enlarged lymph nodes and looks small for his age. She asks, "Can I please have another HIV test?" Her husband sent her and the boy home to her parents when told of her HIV status. He will only take her back if the test is negative. He is not providing any support. No, he refused testing, saying he is fine. The first two children are fine, they have been kept by the paternal grandmother. She has not seen them in six months.
- A women in her mid-30s, divorced and caring for her two children, frankly states that she supplements her income by having "friends." The children are brought in for testing: they are negative. They are living with their maternal grandparents, she supports them. Can she get her partners to use condoms? She has tried and they refuse. What arrangements can she make for the children if she gets sick? She shakes her head: "My children will suffer."

These cases illustrate that, in Africa, as everywhere, women are the caregivers. They take the larger responsibility for the maintenance of family health and care of the sick. Women are caring for the sick children, sick husbands, and sick relatives who have AIDS. Care for a sick child must carry on in the face of her own illness and an uncertain future for (usually) both parents (15). How can we support this role? Will traditional coping mechanisms within the extended family hold up?

In their role as caregivers and as consumers of family planning techniques, women may be more accessible than men to health care providers. But as a locus of change in this epidemic, women may have the most limited options.

Prescriptions to control the spread of AIDS must take into account these constraints and include efforts to increase women's options.

TRACING THE SPREAD OF AIDS IN AFRICA: THE ROLE OF TRADE, MIGRANT LABOR, AND URBANIZATION

The path of the AIDS epidemic among both women and men in Africa cannot be understood apart from the realities of commerce and civil strife. Data suggest that the epidemic first became established in the central African countries of Zaire, Ruwanda, and Burundi. Early sporadic cases may have been identified as early as the 1960s in Zaire (16), with the epidemic form beginning to appear in the mid-1970s. AIDS was next identified in Uganda, to the east, and in Zambia, to the south. Following the routes of trade and population movement, the epidemic soon spread even further east, to Kenya and Tanzania, and also further south, to Zimbabwe and Malawi. Together, these countries form the large hinterland of South Africa's labor reserve. That infection travels in the wake of trade is shown by the experience of the small town of Kasensero in southern Uganda, located along the truck route to the capital of Kampala. Recent reports suggest that up to half of all deaths in this town are attributable to AIDS (17). Undoubtedly the tremendous social disruptions experienced during Uganda's recent war-torn years have also contributed to the spread of the virus.

Within Zimbabwe, data support a north-to-south spread. In 1985, for example, 3 percent of blood donors in the northern city of Harare were seropositive, compared with 0.05 percent in the city of Bulwayo, to the south. South Africa, the southern tip of the continent, continues to report low rates of infection (below 5 percent), but the doubling time of the incidence of infection is six months (18). While no evidence of HIV seropositivity was found in 1987 among attenders at a South African clinic for the treatment of sexually transmitted diseases (STDs), by 1988 the prevalence had risen to 1.1 percent among women and to 0.6 percent among men (19).

The populous west coast of Africa, belonging to a different axis of trade and commerce connections than east-central Africa, has been affected by AIDS more recently. For example, Nigeria—where one in five Africans live—has relatively few cases of AIDS. But seroprevalence data suggest that the virus is present in the Nigerian population: one survey found that about 1 percent of prostitutes were infected (20). In addition, the identification of a second human immunodeficiency virus (HIV-2) in Senegal in 1985 adds another dimension to the epidemic in west Africa.

In all, 43 of Africa's 50 countries have reported cases of AIDS to the World Health Organization. Some 80 percent of these cases have occurred in nine nations at the center of the epidemic; these countries account for about one-sixth of Africa's population (21). But it would be shortsighted to describe the epidemic as geographically limited. Once HIV is present in a population, the incidence of infection can undergo exponential spread. In Zimbabwe, blood donor data suggest a rapid rise in HIV infection in recent years. In 1985, an average of 2.3 percent of donations tested positive on a single ELISA (enzyme-linked immunosorbent assay), but the figure in some urban areas five years later exceeds 15 percent. In Ivory Coast, the prevalence rose from 1 to 4 percent in two years (22); among prenatal women in Lilongwe, Malawi, it rose from 3 percent in 1986 to 18 percent in 1989 (23); in Bangui, Central African Republic, it rose from 2 percent in 1985 to 7 percent in 1989 (24). In the absence of aggressive intervention efforts, rapid spread of the virus seems likely.

Researchers often remark that HIV infection seems to be an urban rather than a rural problem (25). Much of Africa's population presumably should be protected, since the majority (from 60 to 90 percent) still is rural. But data suggest that significant rates of infection nonetheless are occurring in rural areas: 12 percent in a community sample in rural Uganda (26), 4.9 percent in a sample including prenatal women and donors from rural Tanzania (27), and 3.2 percent among hospital patients in rural Zimbabwe (28). Sparing of these regions seems a function more of the level of technological development (roads, bus transport, etc.) than of any "cultural barriers" to infection due to the strength of "traditional" values in rural areas. Undisrupted traditional culture simply no longer exists, particularly in regions where migrant labor was forcibly introduced at the turn of the century. At present, rates of urban migration in Africa are the highest in the world. In Zimbabwe, which has a good infrastructure and where movement between town and rural areas is frequent, many researchers do not expect the rural–urban gradient to be sustained. The history of Zimbabwe serves as an example of the role of recent colonial history, particularly in the settler colonies, in establishing the social context of the epidemic.

UNDERSTANDING THE EPIDEMIOLOGY OF AIDS IN ZIMBABWE: THE POLITICAL ECONOMY OF FAMILY STRUCTURES

Zimbabwe became independent in 1980 after a long and bitter war against the settler regime that left at least 20,000 dead (29). Its period of colonization lasted nearly a century. White "pioneers" in search of gold entered the territory from South Africa in the 1890s. The final uprising in opposition to the European incursion was defeated in 1897. When gold failed to materialize, the settlers turned to agriculture, and the expropriation of African lands rapidly followed. Land alienation served the dual function of expanding the commercial agricultural sector and creating a labor pool among the now landless peasants. The forced entry of African men into the cash economy was furthered by the introduction of a hut tax that required cash payment. By the 1930s, the law of the land decreed that whites—who comprised less than 5 percent of the population—own half of the land, while the original inhabitants—who comprised 95 percent of the population—be relegated to the remaining half. This "other half," then called the "Tribal Trust Lands" and now called the "communal areas," consisted of the least arable lands.

Prior to the colonial period, traditional Zimbabwean societies were patrilineal (30). Marriage was, and is today, accompanied by payment of a bride-price in compensation to the wife's family for loss of her labor and reproductive capacity, and also as a token of esteem and affection from one family to another. In Zimbabwe, the bride-price has taken on new economic meaning in a market economy. Payment is substantial and may take years to complete. In precolonial times, women returned to their natal family only if divorced. The commitment implicit in married life was not to male sexual fidelity, but to financial support of the wife and offspring (who became part of the male lineage). If wealth permitted, men could have more than one wife. These additional wives did not displace the older wives, who instead maintained their status as senior wives and also could share in the labor of more junior wives. Having multiple wives, however, is beyond the financial capability of most men: according to a 1982 study, under 5 percent of married women in Zimbabwe were in polygamous unions (31).

Patriarchal values parallel the patrilineal system of inheritance and dominated Zimbabwe's traditional societies. Women's entitlement was limited, but it was not nonexistent. For example, women were entitled to the earnings of their own handwork, to plots on which to grow family foods, and to certain gifts of motherhood (30). These limited protections were further curtailed during the colonial period, when European settler society introduced its own patriarchal values. Codification of European-identified "traditional" law reduced women to perpetual minority status in the guardianship of either their fathers or their husbands. Property rights were extremely limited, as were rights even to their own children. Surveys in the early 1980s showed that about half of households in rural areas of Zimbabwe were de facto headed by women (32). But responsibility does not translate into control. Women did not become owners of either land or the products of their labor. While many of the legal barriers to women's equality were overturned in a series of laws passed after Zimbabwe's independence in 1980, decades of legally entrenched social inequality will take time to overcome.

Barriers to women's equality in Zimbabwe, however, stem not simply from patriarchal values but also from the land hunger created by European expropriation. Severe overcrowding in the most unproductive areas meant that women rarely were awarded land in their own right. As men left to work in the towns and on large-scale farms and mines, women and families were left behind to manage as subsistence farmers. Rural women's labor also increased, as it extended to tasks originally performed by men. A study of peasant woman's "typical" workday suggests that it extends from 4:30 a.m. until 9 p.m. In 1982, of an estimated 780,000 families in the peasant sector, nearly a third (235,000) operated on this split-family strategy (33).

As family separation became a feature of life, the rules of sexual relationships outside marriage also changed. Husbands formed other liaisons in town. These relationships might even supersede the rural wife, leading to divorce or a reduction in remittances. The impact on the rural families left behind could be catastrophic. Loss of cash income from the towns placed women-headed households at a far higher risk of having malnourished children; in one study, the risk was found to increase sixfold (34). The rural income might even be used to supplement urban expenses. Those men who could not afford to maintain urban wives opted for more casual arrangements. These multiple relationships, often referred to as modern-day versions of polygamy, actually differ considerably from the polygamous unions of Zimbabwe's traditional culture, described above.

In sharp contrast to the practice of polygamy in the precolonial era, the multiple relationships that arose in the urban setting of the colonial and postcolonial Zimbabwean society are not rare: they are practically universal. Obviously, this has required a change in where both women and men live, as well as in their patterns of sexual interaction. Although urban female migration initially was restricted both legally and by the lack of employment prospects, some women migrated to meet the demand for sexual services created by the artificial settlement of men without their families. An urban woman, particularly one divorced or unmarried, became almost synonymous with a prostitute. This stereotype is strong and has found its way into the AIDS control program. An early poster depicted a woman in a miniskirt and high-heeled boots, dragging on a cigarette, and the caption exhorted men to remain faithful to their families. (The poster concept, we are told, was developed by women!)

In Zimbabwe, as in other parts of Africa (35, 36), the exchange of sex for money or for other goods and services covers a broad range of arrangements. Many are not socially considered to be prostitution. Some of these women sell single sexual encounters. Probably more common are situations in which men pay for ongoing sexual and domestic services. These may range from sporadic payments to stable live-in partnerships. The definition of a prostitute therefore becomes somewhat arbitrary. Women who live apart or are divorced from their husbands may supplement their low incomes with gifts from male friends. Most would not enter into liaisons without financial compensation, and none would consider themselves prostitutes. In addition, some women who work as seasonal laborers support themselves off-season by selling sex. Others sell sex to meet a specific obligation, such as school fees. Younger women, even those of school age, may trade sex for the status of an older lover who can give them otherwise inaccessible goods or experiences (meals in hotels, riding in an expensive car, and so on). These men are popularly known as "sugar daddies." Finally, employed women may be forced to exchange sex for job security.

Popular belief holds that these patterns are well established in towns, but rural life also offers the opportunity for commercial sex. Rural "growth points" (rudimentary business centers), army camps, and similar locations provide the setting for such exchanges to occur. It is also widely believed that some urban women, particularly professional women, are both willing and have the opportunity to "balance the score" with their errant husbands. Whatever the extent of this practice, strong social sanctions exist against women engaging in extramarital sex. Although hardly any data exist on contemporary sexual relations in Zimbabwe, it seems safe to state that few women feel they are in the position to have sexual relations without some sort of benefit, whether social (including marriage) or material. For the vast majority of women, sexual relationships occur in the context of marriage (37, Table A.2.2, p. 65). By the age of 20 to 24 years, 75 percent of women in Zimbabwe have been married, in line with the traditionally sanctioned requirement that childbearing occur within marriage.

AIDS AND SEXUALLY TRANSMITTED DISEASES IN ZIMBABWE: AN IMPORTANT CONNECTION

The changing nature of marital and extramarital sexual relationships in Zimbabwe has profoundly influenced patterns of transmission of not only AIDS, but other STDs as well. The link between these STDs and AIDS is twofold. Serving as a marker of sexual activity outside the family unit, the presence of STDs indicates likely areas where AIDS may spread. In addition, data suggest that STDs may be a cofactor for HIV infection (15, 38), as discussed below.

At present, STDs are common in Zimbabwe. Last year, over 900,000 cases of STDs were treated nationwide (39). With the population estimated at 10 million (and assuming one case per person), this averages out to treatment of nearly one-quarter of the adult population! Popular ideas about STDs suggest that little stigma is attached to male infection. Having an STD is almost a rite of passage into manhood, proof of sexual activity: "A bull is not a bull without his scars." Consistent with both data and belief, a study on HIV infection among male factory workers found that a history of prior STD was common among both seropositive and seronegative men: 100 and 75 percent, respectively (40). Other risk factors, now documented in numerous studies of AIDS in Africa, were also more common in the HIV-positive group, e.g., multiple partners, a history of payment for sex. What was unexpected was the high prevalence of high-risk activities among the seronegative men: 40 percent reported an STD in the previous year, and the majority (67 percent) had paid money for sex. Seropositive men were more likely than seronegative men to report a history of genital ulcer. In the light of these data, one can hardly characterize the seronegative comparison group as "low risk."

Many investigators now believe that the enhanced risk of heterosexual transmission of AIDS in Africa may largely be explained by high rates of concurrent infection with another STD (15, 38, 41). Of particular concern is chancroid, an STD that is common in Africa but not in the West. In Zimbabwe, about half of genital ulcer disease is due to chancroid. The important role of such ulcers in HIV transmission is biologically plausible. Both disruption of the mucosal barrier and the presence of HIV-infected white blood cells would explain the increased likelihood of infection. In our clinic in Harare, where we have been seeing patients referred for HIV infection for a number of years, we found that among those couples in which the male partner was the index case, a history of genital ulcers was three times more likely among men in couples where HIV infection was concordant rather than discordant (15).

The focus on genital ulcers as an important cofactor for HIV transmission has both positive and negative features. While it offers new approaches for intervention programs, it also shifts emphasis from the broader social context of STD occurrence to more narrow medical concerns. Certainly any intervention that results in reduced rates of STDs, such as increasing public awareness about the availability of treatment for STDs, will also mean a diminution of HIV transmission. It is said that some women now inspect men for signs of genital ulcer before agreeing to have sex, a strategy that may be particularly useful for women engaged in commercial sex. The focus on genital ulcer also is appealing because it seems to eliminate all of the value-laden issues that accompany interpretation of other risk factors, such as multiple partners and prostitute contact. Zimbabwe's Ministry of Health has generated protocols for STD treatment, and the nation's independence made access to medical care effectively universal. Nonetheless, the number of cases of STDs in Zimbabwe increases yearly. To reduce the problem of HIV transmission to the problem of controlling genital ulcer is to search for a "technological fix" that fails to address the social factors that jointly underlie both problems.

As suggested by our work in Harare (15), it is against this background of high rates of STDs that AIDS transmission occurs, and in most cases it is the male partner who introduces HIV infection into the family unit. In our clinic, we ask married patients to bring their spouses. About half of the partners eventually appear for screening. The main reason that other partners do not come is because they live elsewhere, usually in the rural areas. Among the initial 75 couples, reported risk factors for AIDS were more prevalent among men that women, who universally denied having multiple partners. Only in two couples was the wife seropositive and the husband seronegative. In both cases, the wife had an identifiable risk factor (blood transfusion, first marriage to a partner who died of an AIDS-like illness). Although we do not know the duration or timing of infection in the couples we have studied, the paucity of female-positive/male-negative couples supports our impression that wives are most often placed at risk by their husbands. Moreover, because women in general are more likely to use health services than men, referral patterns seem unlikely to explain the small number of women as the index cases.

We are seeing more women now, usually referred because of HIV-related illness in a child. Often the mother has been tested without the involvement of the husband. Increasingly, the husband declines screening and sometimes rejects the mother and child. These are the realities of AIDS experienced by women in Zimbabwe.

AIDS PREVENTION IN AFRICA: PROSPECTS FOR THE FUTURE

We have discussed how sexual relationships in Zimbabwe and, by extension, other parts of sub-Saharan Africa are far more complex than the term "promiscuous" implies. To halt the current epidemic spread of AIDS, we will have to reckon with these patterns as we encourage changes in individual behavior—so far the only universally available "weapon" to combat this disease. The fact that historically produced social conditions have created situations that promote behavior which we now call "high risk" should not be taken to mean that this behavior is inevitable, or that only a complete social transformation will permit meaningful interventions to reduce transmission of HIV. Instead, our point is that the pattern of sexual relations, which places many people at risk for HIV infection, is not due to some "natural proclivity" of African men or to some inherent feature of "human nature," but is social in origin, and so can be changed. In Zimbabwe, the twin legacies of the patriarchy and colonialism seem the most important factors in shaping family structure, sexual relations, and the risk of HIV infection. If we do not take this into account, we cannot hope to develop specific and effective interventions to halt the spread of AIDS.

A first and urgent step in AIDS prevention is to ensure that people are provided with information and resources necessary to diminish their chance of being infected by HIV. As far as possible, the public health campaign should be rooted in organizations that people know and trust. Schoepf and coauthors (42) report that in Zaire, people initially joked that AIDS was an "imaginary syndrome invented by Europeans to discourage African lovers." This attitude betrays a distrust of outside prescriptions for changes in sexual behavior, prescriptions that were initially seen as part of population control programs. Clinics, schools, and the radio are all natural places for information to be made available. In settings where the government is not trusted, other organizations become particularly important: the trade union movement, women's groups, grassroots organizations—all need to be convinced of the importance of adding AIDS prevention to their agenda.

The campaign should bring information about HIV transmission and prevention into everyday life in forms accessible to a population in which many people are illiterate and a biological understanding of disease is virtually absent. A series of articles on AIDS in Zimbabwe's national newspaper in 1987 was replete with such terms as "killer lymphocytes," "T4 cells," and the like, and required a university-level biology background. Decades of experience in health education can be brought to bear on developing methods of getting across information about AIDS in ways that are popular, nonjudgmental, and hopeful. For example, a leading musician here recently came out with a song about AIDS, as have musicians in Zaire, Uganda, Zambia, and elsewhere.

For most people, celibacy or a single lifetime partner are not realistic options. Efforts should therefore focus on reducing transmission. In practice this means limiting the number of partners and using condoms. Condoms cost only a few cents each, but providing them in adequate numbers to the sexually active population of the continent will still run into millions of dollars. Most African governments are facing cuts in social expenditures as a result of structural adjustment, and many cannot afford the cost of condoms or, indeed, the overall public health campaign. International aid will continue to be vital in AIDS control.

Adopting the use of condoms is more complicated than learning how to use them (42). While the distribution, and presumably use, of condoms appears to be increasing (43), a recent national survey of Zimbabwean men found that only 35 percent said they had ever used condoms (44). Most viewed condom use as appropriate for prostitutes, but not within marriages or other stable arrangements. As we have suggested, women are in a weak position to dictate how sex takes place. As seroprevalence increases and individuals are more likely to know personally someone with AIDS, more women may be willing to risk abuse or divorce to reduce their risk of infection. Further complicating matters is the fact that many women want to have children. Clearly acceptable alternatives to condoms need to be found that allow women to control use and possibly permit conception. Some possibilities have been outlined by Stein (45).

Unfortunately, we have little direct experience with such a broad public health program. So far, attention in Zimbabwe has focused on individual counseling and case identification. Blood donors who test positive are not informed of a "problem" (unless they ask) and are permitted to continue to donate blood (which subsequently is discarded). Research activities have been subject to careful and lengthy scrutiny. Posters about AIDS on clinic walls are now three years old. The pace is picking up, but progress is slow. Reports from other centers (46, 47) support some optimism about people's ability to change high-risk behaviors.

We have had ample time to reflect on the social implications of the AIDS epidemic. We have agonized as we see patients who are infected and who had no knowledge of their risks. Fathers as well as mothers suffer when their children become sick or, though seemingly well, carry a death sentence in their small bodies. For all the hardships of womanhood in Africa, there is no doubt that children are universally cherished. To protect their future may be the strongest incentive in the campaign to reduce HIV transmission.

REFERENCES

1. Clumeck, N., et al. Acquired immunodeficiency syndrome in African patients. *N. Engl. J. Med.* 310: 492–497, 1984.
2. Nationwide community based serological survey of human immunodeficiency virus type 1 (HIV-1) and other human retrovirus infections in a central African country. Rwandan HIV seroprevalence study group. *Lancet* 1: 941–943, 1988.
3. Carswell, J. W. HIV infection in healthy persons in Uganda. *AIDS* 1: 223–227, 1987.

4. Malbye, M., et al. Evidence for heterosexual transmission and clinical manifestations of human immunodeficiency virus infection and related conditions in Lusaka, Zambia, *Lancet* 2: 1113–1115, 1986.
5. DeCock, K. M., et al. Rapid emergence of AIDS in Abidjan, Ivory Coast. *Lancet* 2: 408–411, 1989.
6. Mann, J. M. Social, cultural and political aspects: An overview. *AIDS* 2(Suppl.): S207–S208, 1988.
7. Harris, C., et al. Immunodeficiency in female sexual partners of men with the acquired immunodeficiency syndrome. *N. Engl. J. Med.* 308: 1181–1184, 1983.
8. Sabatier, R. *Blaming Others: Prejudice, Race, and Worldwide AIDS*. The Panos Institute, Washington, D.C., 1988.
9. Eales, L. J., et al. Association of different allelic forms of group specific component with susceptibility to and clinical manifestations of human immunodeficiency virus. *Lancet* 2: 277–283, 1987.
10. Rushton, J. P., and Bogaert, A. F. Population differences in susceptibility to AIDS: An evolutionary analysis. *Soc. Sci. Med.* 28: 1211–1220, 1989.
11. Padian, N. Prostitute women and AIDS: Epidemiology. *AIDS* 2: 413–419, 1989.
12. Schoepf, B. G. Methodology, Ethics, and Politics: AIDS Research in Africa for Whom? Unpublished manuscript.
13. Quinn, T., et al. AIDS in Africa: An epidemiologic paradigm. *Science* 234: 955–963, 1986.
14. Neequaque, A. R., Osei, L., and Mingle, A. A. Dynamics of HIV epidemic: The Ghanian experience. In *The Global Impact of AIDS*, edited by A. Fleming and M. Carballo, pp. 9–15. Alan R. Liss, New York, 1988.
15. Latif, A. S., et al. Genital ulcers and transmission of HIV among couples in Zimbabwe. *AIDS* 3: 519–523, 1989.
16. Sonnet, J., et al. Early AIDS cases originating in Zaire and Burundi (1962–1976). *Scand. J. Infect. Dis.* 19: 511–517, 1987.
17. Hooper, E. AIDS in Uganda. *Afr. Aff.* 86: 469–477, 1987.
18. Schapiro, M., Crookes, R. L., and O'Sullivan, E. Screening antenatal blood samples for anti-human immunodeficiency virus antibodies by a large pool enzyme-linked immunosorbant assay system: Results of an 18 month investigation. *S. Afr. J. Med.* 76: 245–249, 1989.
19. *Annual Report of the Medical Research Council*, p. 17. South Africa, 1988.
20. Mohammed, F., et al. HIV infection in Nigeria [letter]. *AIDS* 2: 61–62, 1988.
21. Chen, J., and Mann, J. M. Global patterns and prevalence of AIDS and HIV infection. *AIDS* 3(Suppl. 1): S247–S252, 1989.
22. Mann, J. M. Global AIDS in the 1990s. Unpublished document. Global Program on AIDS/Dir/89.2. World Health Organization, Geneva, 1989.
23. Liomba, N. G., et al. Comparison of Age Distribution of Anti-HIV-1 and AntiHBc in an Urban Population from Malawi. Abstract No. W.G.027. Fifth International Conference on AIDS, Montreal, 1989.
24. Somse, P., et al. Les aspects épidémiologiques des affections lieés aux VIH1 et 2 en République Centrafricaine. Abstract No. W.G.028. Fifth International Conference on AIDS, Montreal, 1989.
25. Turshen, M. *The Politics of Public Health*, pp. 219–241. Rutgers University Press, Rutgers, N.J., 1989.
26. Kenegeay-Kayondo, J. F., et al. Anti-HIV Seroprevalence in Adult Rural Populations in Uganda and Its Implication for Preventive Strategies. Abstract No. T.A.P. 111. Fifth International Conference on AIDS, Montreal, 1989.

27. Dolmans, W. M. V., et al. Prevalence of HIV-1 antibody among groups of patients and healthy subjects from a rural and urban population in Mwanza region, Tanzania. *AIDS* 3: 297–299, 1989.
28. Mertens, T., et al. Epidemiology of HIV and hepatitis B virus (HBV) in selected African and Asian populations. *Infections* 17: 4–7, 1989.
29. Stoneman, C. *Zimbabwe's Inheritance*. St. Martin's Press, New York, 1982.
30. Batezat, E., and Mwalo, M. *Women in Zimbabwe*, pp. 9–12. Sapes Trust Jongwe Printers, Harare, Zimbabwe, 1989.
31. Central Statistical Office. *Report on Demographic Socio-economic Survey of the Communal Lands. Permanent Sample Survey Unit Programme (ZNHSCP). Report No. 1 to 5*. Zimbabwe, 1984/85.
32. Riddell, R. *Report of the Commission of Inquiry into Incomes Price, and Conditions of Service*. Government of Zimbabwe, Harare, 1982.
33. Callear, D. *The Social and Cultural Factors Involved in Production by Small Farmers in Wedza Communal Area, Zimbabwe*, p. 22. Division for the Study of Development, UNESCO, Paris, 1982. [Cited in reference 37.]
34. Thiesen, R. J. *Agro-economic Factors Relating to the Health and Academic Achievement of Rural School Children*. Tribal Areas of Rhodesia Research Foundation, Salisbury [Harare], 1975. [Cited in reference 37.]
35. Day, S. Prostitute women and AIDS: Anthropology. *AIDS* 2: 421–428, 1989.
36. Larson, A. Social context of human immunodeficiency virus transmission in Africa: Historical and cultural bases of east and central African sexual relations. *Rev. Infect. Dis*. 2: 716–731, 1989.
37. UNICEF. *Children and Women in Zimbabwe: A Situation Analysis*. Government Printers, Harare, Zimbabwe, 1985.
38. Cameron, D. W., et al. Female to male transmission of human immunodeficiency virus type 1: Risk factors for seroconversion in men. *Lancet* 2: 403–407, 1989.
39. Secretary for Health. *Annual Report, 1988*. Government Printers, Harare, Zimbabwe, 1989.
40. Bassett, M. T., et al. HIV Infection in Urban Men in Zimbabwe. Abstract No. Th.C.581, Sixth International Conference on AIDS, San Francisco, 1990.
41. Kreiss, J. K., et al. AIDS virus infection in Nairobi prostitutes: Spread of the epidemic to East Africa. *N. Engl. J. Med*. 314: 414–418, 1986.
42. Schoepf, B. G., et al. AIDS in society in Central Africa: A view from Zaire. In *AIDS in Africa*, pp. 211–235. The Edwin Mellen Press, Lewiston, N.Y., 1988.
43. Condom use on the increase. *The Herald* (Harare, Zimbabwe), September 6, 1989, p. 1.
44. Mbivzo, M., and Adamchak, D. J. Condom use and acceptance: A survey of male Zimbabweans. *Cent. Afr. J. Med*. 35: 519–558, 1989.
45. Stein, Z. HIV prevention: The need for methods women can use. *Am. J. Public Health* 80: 460–462, 1990.
46. Ngugi, E. N., Plummer, F. A., and Simonsen, J. N. Prevention of transmission of human immunodeficiency virus in Africa: Effectiveness of condom promotion and health education among prostitutes. *Lancet* 2: 887–890, 1988.
47. Ngugi, E. N., and Plummer, F. A. Health outreach and control of HIV infection in Kenya. *J. Acquired Immunodeficiency Syndromes* 6: 566–570, 1988.

CHAPTER 7

Human Immunodeficiency Virus and Migrant Labor in South Africa

Karen Jochelson, Monyaola Mothibeli, and Jean-Patrick Leger

The purpose of the study described in this chapter was to identify whether migrant mineworkers are vulnerable to the human immunodeficiency virus (HIV) and, if so, how the spread of disease can be limited. A recent study by the Chamber of Mines concluded that "80% of employees are not, as commonly believed, promiscuous, and therefore not likely to spread the infection. . . . [W]ith proper housing and feeding and the generally responsible behavior of the vast majority of mineworkers, we believe that the industry and its employees play a very minor role in the spread of HIV infection in South Africa" (1). In contrast, the hypothesis of this study is that the migrant labor system may encourage high-risk sexual behavior and that it can efficiently transmit diseases over a broad geographic area. Migrants' frequent and lengthy absences from their homes disrupt their familial and stable sexual relationships. In a lonely and hostile environment and separated for long periods from their wives, some migrants may seek sexual relationships with women in nearby towns. Migrancy also subjects marriages to great strain, and divorce or abandonment deprives women of economic support. With access to few opportunities on the labor market, some women may choose prostitution as the only means of economic survival.

The most common form of transmission of HIV is through sexual intercourse. Studies of homosexual (2) and heterosexual males (3) and Nairobean female prostitutes (4, 5) with HIV infection or AIDS reveal that the risk of contracting the infection depends principally on the number of unprotected sexual contacts in

Originally published in the *International Journal of Health Services* 21(1): 157–173, 1991.

which an individual engages, rather than the mode of intercourse or an individual's sexual orientation. Prior infection with sexually transmitted diseases (STDs), which increases susceptibility to HIV or infectivity of infected persons, is also significant (5), and as discussed below, the incidence of STDs is high among migrant workers on the mines. This study examines only heterosexual relationships among migrant workers in the mining industry. Homosexual relationships do occur in single-sex hostels on the mines but are unlikely to involve unsafe sex. Moodie's (6) research shows that these relationships tend to be monogamous, and men do not have sexual contacts with multiple partners as has occurred elsewhere (3). Moreover, intercrural sex is practiced, which involves thigh contact rather than anal penetration.

Geographic mobility, migration, and widespread population displacement have also been identified as significant risk factors in the transmission of HIV (7, 8). The role of the migrant labor system in transmitting diseases over a wide geographic area as workers carry diseases they have contracted in towns back to their homes has been documented for tuberculosis (9) and might also hold in the case of STDs. This is particularly significant in South Africa, where migrant labor is an integral feature of the South African labor market and the mainstay of the mining industry. In South Africa in 1986, 2.6 million workers were officially registered as migrants from areas within South Africa excluding the "independent homelands" (1,365,000), Bophuthatswana (348,000), Ciskei (104,000), Transkei (339,000), and Venda (55,000). A further 378,000 foreign migrant workers come from Lesotho (138,000), Mozambique (73,000), Malawi (31,000), Botswana (28,000), Swaziland (22,000), Zimbabwe (7,000), and Zambia (2,000). The country of origin of a further 75,000 registered foreign workers is not classified (10). In addition, large numbers of migrant workers and refugees are not officially registered. For example, in 1987 it was estimated that there were 150,000 unregistered work-seekers and 70,000 refugees from Mozambique in South Africa (10, p. 17). The mining industry employs 625,000 black migrant workers. Almost all these miners are not allowed to bring their families to the mining areas and are housed in single-sex hostels.

The size of the migrant population indicates the potential future significance of HIV infection. However, the findings of this exploratory research project are tentative, and its statistical basis does not allow us to make significant generalizations. Thus the descriptions of relationships and experiences of a small purposively selected sample cannot be considered representative of migrant workers as a whole and should not be generalized to the entire migrant workforce. Nevertheless, our preliminary findings point to the devastating and destructive effects of the migrant labor system on the lives of migrant workers and their families. This study indicates the need for further research and prevention strategies that recognize the socioeconomic determinants of disease patterns and hence the limits of purely educational campaigns.

SEXUALLY TRANSMITTED DISEASES AND HIV: OLD CRISIS, NEW VIRUS

HIV is a new manifestation of a historic problem—an epidemic of STDs. Venereal diseases were unknown in southern Africa before colonization. Industrialization, particularly the rapid growth of the mining industry with the migrant labor system it created, led to the emergence of new diseases. By the 1930s and 1940s gonorrhea and syphilis were rampant in urban and rural populations in South Africa. Kark (11) related this high prevalence directly to the migrant labor system and argued that prostitution resulted from the separation of husbands from their wives and families. Today, STDs are an important health problem among mineworkers. The incidence of STDs in this workforce has increased substantially since the mid-1970s (Table 1). The figures may be even higher than those given in Table 1: a survey of 429 mineworkers showed that of those with an STD, 30 percent had consulted a mine doctor and 41 percent had seen a private general practitioner (1, p. 12). A study of 240 migrant mineworkers attending an STD clinic in a Transvaal mining town in 1986 showed that 49 percent had contracted an infection from a regular girlfriend, 33 percent from casual sexual contacts, and 15 percent from local prostitutes. The geographic source of the contacts varied: 55 percent of the men acquired their infection locally, 20 percent in Lesotho, 10 percent in Botswana, 5 percent in KwaZulu, and 3 percent in

Table 1

Comparative STD morbidity rates on Anglo American mines, including inpatients and outpatients, 1978–85[a]

	STD morbidity rate, per 1000 employees per year				
Year	Gold mines in the Transvaal	Gold mines in the Orange Free State	Collieries in Natal	Collieries in the Vaal	Diamond mines in South Africa and Namibia
1978	51.19	39.61	128.04	48.43	58.44
1979	55.39	50.54	134.01	64.24	50.54
1980	67.21	62.22	123.55	62.34	90.30
1981	70.05	63.18	112.78	63.28	98.71
1982	69.89	60.37	108.52	74.57	82.31
1983	73.10	65.21	96.15	91.47	62.97
1984	85.23	69.36	109.61[b]		63.02
1985	104.41	76.11	173.01[b]		87.69

[a]Source: Anglo American Medical Department Annual Reports, 1973–83; Anglo American Medical Department Records 1985–86.

[b]Rates for Natal and the Vaal combined.

Transkei. The remaining 7 percent contracted infections in Ciskei, Malawi, Swaziland, and Johannesburg (12).

Statistics on the current prevalence of STDs in urban and rural populations are also a source of concern (Table 2). The high prevalence of STDs is an indication of the potential extent of HIV transmission. But the number of recorded AIDS and HIV cases is still relatively low. The Chamber of Mines conducted an HIV screening program in 1986. Over 300,000 blood specimens were collected from black and white employees on gold and platinum mines. A sample of 29,961 specimens was tested according to territory of origin and racial group (13, 14). The prevalence of HIV antibody positivity among migrant workers from Lesotho, Mozambique, Swaziland, and South Africa was low, and was high amongst workers from Malawi (3.8 percent) and Botswana (0.34 percent) (Table 3). In 1986, blood specimens were taken from 1,200 women living in areas surrounding mines. Ninety-four women were believed to be prostitutes. The results on all 1,200 women were negative (14, 15). The Chamber of Mines has not undertaken a similar screening survey since 1986, but in 1987 tested Malawian miners and patients attending STD clinics (Table 3). The HIV disease prevalence among Malawian migrants rose from 3.8 percent in 1986 to 10 percent in 1987 and was 21 percent by 1989 (16). HIV prevalence has increased among mineworkers from all countries attending STD clinics. On the basis of its 1986 study, the Chamber estimated that 1,093 mine workers in 1986 (17) and over 2,000 workers in early 1988 (18) were seropositive.

The first two AIDS cases in South Africa were diagnosed in December 1982 (19). By April 1990 the figure had reached 386 (20) (Figure 1). The trajectory of the HIV epidemic in South Africa demonstrates "Western" and "African"

Table 2

STD prevalence in the South African black population, various years

Year	Sample frame	Sample description	STD prevalence
1969–70[a]	Urban hospital	587 men and women	17% syphilis
1978[b]	Urban family planning clinic	186 women	10% gonorrhea
1985–86[c]	Urban hospital	6287 pregnant women attending antenatal clinic	6% syphilis
1985–86[c]	Urban hospital	1625 pregnant women, mostly rural, wives of migrants	16% syphilis

[a]Source: Dogliotti, M. The incidence of syphilis in the Bantu: Survey of 587 cases from Baragwanath Hospital. *South Afr. Med. J.* 45: 8–10, 1971.

[b]Source: Hall, S. M., and Whitcomb, M. A. Screening for gonorrhoea in family planning acceptors in a developing community. *Public Health (London)* 92: 121–124, 1978.

[c]Source: Venter, A., et al. Congenital syphilis—who is at risk? A prevalence study at Baragwanath Hospital, Johannesburg, 1985–1986. *South Afr. Med. J.* 76: 93–95, 1989.

Table 3

HIV prevalence according to country of origin in samples drawn from the general migrant mineworker population (1986) and from mineworkers attending STD clinics (1987)[a,b]

	General population of mineworkers (1986)		Mineworkers attending STD clinics (1987)	
Country of origin	No. tested	No. HIV-positive	No. tested	No. HIV-positive
Malawi	3,165	119 (3.76%)	466	83 (17.8%)
Botswana	2,063	7 (0.34%)	1,269	7 (0.55%)
Lesotho	2,246	2 (0.09%)	5,230	5 (0.10%)
Mozambique	2,152	2 (0.09%)	1,298	7 (0.54%)
Swaziland	1,885	1 (0.05%)	846	2 (0.24%)
South Africa	18,450	4 (0.02%)	16,784	14 (0.08%)
Total	29,961	135 (0.45%)	25,893	118 (0.46%)

[a]Source: reference 14.
[b]The Chamber of Mines did not issue statistics for the general population for 1987.

transmission patterns. In the United States and the United Kingdom homosexual and bisexual men and intravenous drug users are identified as the major high-risk groups, with the sex ratios of infected persons biased toward men (21). In Africa HIV infection has resulted principally from heterosexual intercourse and affects males and females in equal ratios (22, 23). In South Africa the majority of AIDS cases have been among white homosexual or bisexual males, while the most significant mode of transmission among black men and women is heterosexual (Table 4). The low number of officially recorded AIDS cases seemingly gives little cause for alarm, but this probably reflects the early stages of the epidemic in South Africa and inconsistent case reporting. An indication of the future magnitude of HIV infection in South Africa and the significance of heterosexual transmission is evident in the number of HIV-positive persons. The total number of HIV-positive blood donors was 2,300 by January 1988 (19, p. 457). Screening of pregnant women at antenatal clinics in the southern Transvaal region showed that between May 1987 and October 1988, the prevalence of HIV among African women increased from 0.036 to 0.217 percent, highlighting the growing heterosexual transmission of the disease (24). The number of black persons with HIV infection is predicted to increase to between 45,000 and 63,000 by the end of 1990 (25).

The predominance of heterosexual HIV transmission is clearly important when considering the impact of the migrant labor system on sexual relationships. The following section examines how male migrants, their casual lovers, prostitutes, and their respective families may be particularly vulnerable to contracting HIV infection.

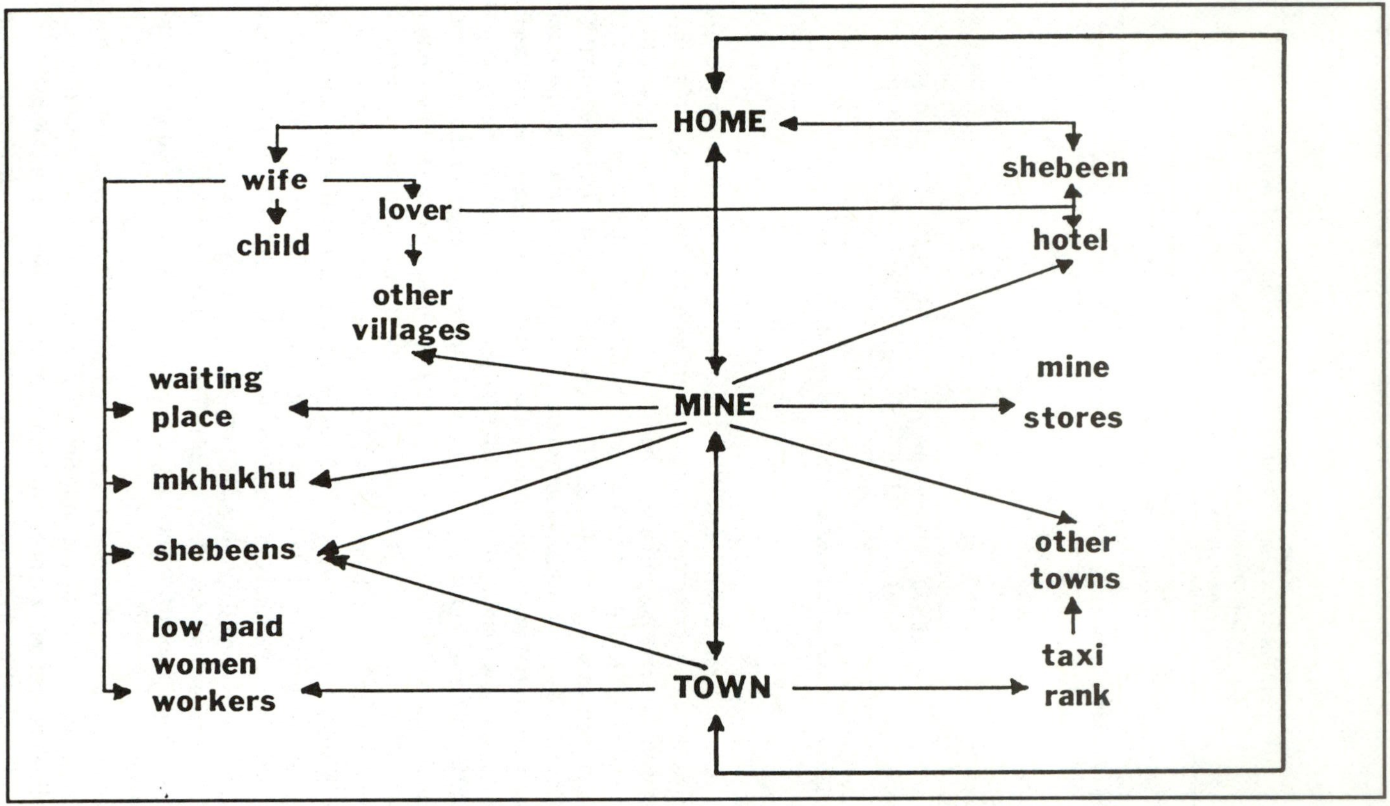

Figure 1. New AIDS cases in South Africa for each year, 1982–89. Source: AIDS Advisory Group, April 24, 1990.

Table 4

Breakdown of South African AIDS cases according to transmission category, population group, and gender, 1990[a]

	No. of AIDS cases									
	White		Black		Asian		Colored			
	M	F	M	F	M	F	M	F	Total	Percentage of total
Homo-/bisexual	211	—	2	—	3	—	8	1	225	58%
Heterosexual	7	2	48	57	—	—	1	1	116	30%
Transfusion	9	4	3	—	—	—	1	—	17	4%
Hemophiliac	9	—	3	—	—	—	1	—	13	3%
Intravenous drug user	1								1	—
Mother to child	—	—	8	6	—	—	—	—	14	4%
Total	237	6	64	63	3	—	11	2	386	100%
Percentage of total	61%	2%	17%	16%	1%	—	3%	1%	100%	

[a]Source: reference 20.

THE MIGRANT LABOR SYSTEM AND HETEROSEXUAL RELATIONSHIPS ON THE MINES

Research Methodology

Fieldwork comprised in-depth interviews conducted in a large mining town in South Africa during April and May 1988. The interviews were conducted during the 1988 government AIDS public education program and shortly after the distribution of management AIDS pamphlets on the mines. Interviews were conducted by two of the authors (white female and black male) in Sesotho with simultaneous English translation, and were later transcribed into English.

Interviewees were selected through strategic informant snowball sampling (26), a technique familiar to anthropologists and sociologists seeking to examine particular descriptive aspects of social organizations or communities. Initial informants introduced the field researchers to informants who shared similar life experiences. Such purposive sampling is useful for collecting qualitative and descriptive data, but weakest in determining the distribution of the research variables in the general population. The most significant check on data quality was the repetitiveness and consistency of informants' observations. Interviewees were asked about their familial, marital, and sexual experiences and their perceptions of the general experience of migrant mineworkers, their wives, and unmarried women with children. They were also questioned about their STD history, condom usage, beliefs about AIDS, and attitudes to AIDS prevention programs. Twenty interviews were conducted with mineworkers employed on two mines in the area, who frequented prostitutes or engaged in casual sexual relationships. Thirteen men were from Lesotho, three from the Transkei and eastern Cape, three from white-owned farms in the Orange Free State (OFS), and one was born in an OFS urban township. Their ages ranged from 21 to 45, though the majority were in the 25 to 35 age group. Fifteen men (75 percent) were married. Twenty-four interviews were conducted with women living in the area who supported themselves through prostitution or by taking sexual partners. Ten women (42 percent) were from Lesotho, seven were born in townships and farms in the eastern Cape, and seven in small townships and on farms in the OFS. Ages ranged from 19 to 46, with half in the 31 to 40 age group. Fourteen women (58 percent) had been married and 20 (82 percent) had children.

Social Consequences of the Migrant Labor System

The mineworkers we interviewed believed that the migrant labor system had harmed their family lives. Conditions in the single-sex hostels, they felt, were alienating: "It is lousy in the hostel," said one worker, "We are locked in like cattle in a cattlepost." Hostels are usually surrounded by security fences and have limited and supervised exits. There is no privacy in the hostel: respondents lived in rooms sleeping 12 to 16 men on bunk beds, and complained about open toilets and showers. Hostel living is a world of continuous queueing for showers, for meals, and to wash work clothes, even queueing for drinks before going to sleep.

Separation from their wives and children is an unremitting source of anxiety for mineworkers. Since the 1970s the labor force has stabilized: the average length of service has increased dramatically as the vast majority of workers now renew their annual contracts rather than, as previously, accept a limited number of short-term contracts. Unemployment has escalated in the rural areas, and more stringent mine employment policies make it extremely difficult for a miner to regain employment if he has a break in service. Those whose homes are not too distant from the mines undertake more frequent trips home over weekends. Migrants say it is still often difficult to tear themselves away from home to return to the hostel and to work:

> I go home once a month. My wife is not happy with us meeting only once a month. At times when I'm home on a weekend I loaf for two days because I feel I cannot part with her. When I arrive at the mine they charge me [that is, lay a disciplinary charge]. . . . [M]anagement complains that while I loafed and spent time with my wife production lagged. I'm told that if my wife is too beautiful I must go and stay with her and they will employ other workers.

After work, miners face the lonely hours of the evening. When workers describe how they spend their leisure time, the dominant theme is the need to escape the mine environment, to bury anxieties about work and separation from home.

Alcohol and marijuana are important outlets, as one interviewee explained: "I drink. Most of the time I think about my wife, I want to be next to her. I ask is she using the money I sent her in the right way. I think about the children and their education. So I drink to forget my worries" (27). The need to escape loneliness, the uniformity of male company, and grim hostel environs encourages some men to seek the company of women. Workers we interviewed sought casual or long-term relationships and felt that they could not remain celibate while separated from their wives for lengthy periods: "After washing my work clothes I go out [of] the hostel because it's lonely there and there is nothing to while away this loneliness. I go to the *likotaseng* [domestic worker quarters] to look for women."

The Relationship Network

Undoubtedly many men remain faithful to their spouses. Those who specifically seek sexual relationships, such as the men who were interviewed, engage in relationships that may be broadly divided into three categories: cash transactions with prostitutes (*matekatse*); casual, short-term relationships with unmarried women (*baratani*) or married or divorced women (*linyatsi*; singular form, *nyatsi*); and longer-term though not necessarily permanent relationships involving domestic obligations for both parties, in which the man is referred to as *monna* and the woman as *mosadi*, or as husband and wife (6, p. 245) (Table 5).

The areas in which men seek women appear to constitute established and extensive networks connecting hostels and their surrounding towns with the far-flung rural areas from which miners are recruited, as illustrated in Figure 2. A

Table 5

Male interviewees' relationships with women in urban and rural areas at the time of the interview, April/May 1988

Type of relationship[a]	No. of men
Prostitute and/or casual sexual contact	1
Prostitute and/or casual sexual contact and 1 partner	5
Prostitute and/or casual sexual contact and 2 partners	4
Prostitute and/or casual sexual contact and 3 or more partners	2
1 partner	1
2 partners	2
3 partners	0
4 or more partners	3
Inadequate information	2
Total	20

[a]A note on terminology: "prostitute" refers to a sexual relationship involving a cash transaction only; "casual sexual contact" refers to a short-term relationship without monetary obligations; "partner" is used to denote a relationship with a *nyatsi* or *mosadi*, that is, secondary and primary relationships.

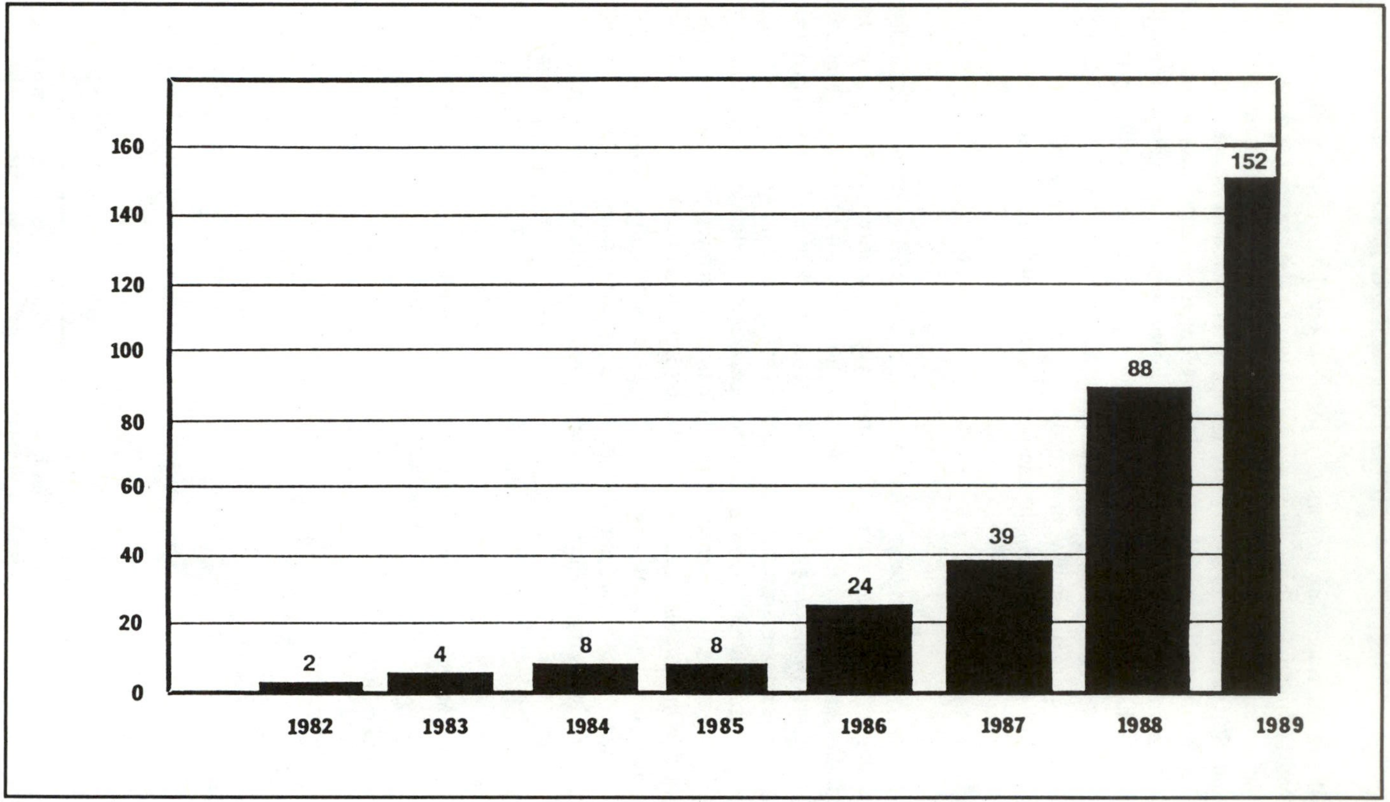

Figure 2. The partner network. The "waiting place" and *mkhukhu* (plural form, *mekhukhu*) are explained in the text.

worker may seek women at the "waiting place," an area outside the hostel gates where visiting wives wait for their husbands, and which miners pass daily on their way to the hostel. Female prostitutes who frequent the waiting place may go to a different mine every day of the week. Paydays are staggered on each mine, and they are familiar with these schedules. On payday a woman may accept up to ten clients. Miners also seek out prostitutes who wait for customers at the taxi ranks and shopping centers in white suburbs, or who drink with them at mine stores or in township shebeens. Other men visit the *mekhukhu* (squatter settlements on white farms) where the women sell alcohol and food and play dance music. At one mining town, a particular area in the veld (fields) near the hostels is a well-known pick-up point. Its name, *Lifofaneng*—the Airport—evokes the alienation that accompanies casual encounters. As one interviewee explained: "it was called *Lifofaneng* because it was a game of hit and run. You produce the money, have sex and go away immediately. Then the next man followed."

The relationship network extends beyond the mine locality. Population census statistics for magisterial districts with large mining populations show that each region is characterized by unequal male to female ratios. For example, Witbank, a coal and steel area, has a ratio of men to women of 17:10. In other magisterial districts the imbalance is more extreme. For example, the ratio in the gold mining areas of Klerksdorp is 22:10 and in Virginia and Carletonville is 50:10 (28). With such artificially created social imbalances men go further afield to seek relationships: "You'll find that near here I can't get a girlfriend because girls are few and men are many. You'll find that perhaps I'll get a girlfriend at a nearby town." Sometimes a few friends will visit one man's partner in a nearby town and she will arrange for them to meet women. Occasionally this traffic in women is more organized. A mineworker, popularly named Malukisa (one who fixes up immediately), ran a matchmaking service for ten years. He organized groups of mineworkers and ferried them to a large metropolitan township on weekends. There he introduced the men to women who did not have partners. Interviewees also recounted how some workers engage in casual encounters on their journey home from the mines. For example, certain hotels in Maseru, the capital of Lesotho, are "famous for their women" and rent out rooms by the hour.

Migrant Labor and Prostitution

The interviews suggest that the women who provide migrant mineworkers with sexual services come from socially and economically marginalized groups in rural and urban areas. Fourteen interviewees had been married. Half the marriages had lasted less than five years. In the absence of male financial support, reliance on lovers and prostitution to supplement low-wage income may become necessary for survival. We identified three groups of women according to the circumstances that forced them to choose to enter prostitution. The first group (17 percent of interviewees) comprised women who either had been abandoned by their husbands (who left them to live with other women) or had left their husbands following years of physical abuse or inadequate financial support. The second group (33 percent) consisted of women who had originally been abandoned by their *baratua* (lovers) when they became pregnant. They had to seek work to support themselves, their children, and, in several cases, other family members. Five of these interviewees had grown up in rural areas and decided to leave low-wage farm work to seek higher wages in towns. The third group (42 percent) were wives of migrant mineworkers and had entered South Africa illegally from Lesotho. The collapse of their marriages and their entry into prostitution were related to the way the migrant labor system interacts with women's subordinate and dependent social and economic position in rural Sotho society (29, 30).

The most frequently stated reasons for separation were lack of financial support by a husband due to his infidelity, and abandonment when a husband took a partner at a mine. Friction also arose when a husband suspected his wife of taking a partner. A lonely wife may seek a *nyatsi* not only for companionship but also for money, which she can spend without accounting to her husband or use to meet subsistence needs when remittances do not arrive (29, p. 153). If a husband suspects that his wife is involved in an extramarital affair he may beat her or make her leave the home. Women who return to their parental homes following divorce or abandonment are among the most economically disadvantaged and socially isolated in rural communities (29, pp. 31, 214, 259–298). They lose their rights to a homestead, to the remittances of their husbands, and to fields and livestock, and become entirely dependent on their fathers and brothers. These women, in particular, may decide to migrate to towns in Lesotho or illegally to South Africa to find means of support (31). With access only to insecure and poorly paid jobs, many women do not seek employment and rely on informal economic activity ranging from hawking and beer-brewing to prostitution.

The decision to provide sexual services is usually an economic one. Women talk of "spanning donkeys" (*hopana dipokola*) or "spanning oxen" (*hopana dikhomo*) when describing prostitution. In other words, women harness men's desires to work for and support them. Taking sexual partners is a way to supplement meager salaries, or replace them. One woman said she began "spanning" because of desperate economic circumstances: "I worked for six months and saw that it's better to span. I [could send] home money for my children to get something to eat. Just think what it is like if you have no place, no money, no husband." This decision is difficult as another respondent explained: "Other women said the way to make life better was by spanning donkeys. I was angry but decided to do it because I could find no work."

Interviewees' descriptions of their sexual relationships suggest that a typical pattern is one where a woman has a primary partner and enters prostitution or takes secondary partners (Table 6). This provides a degree of emotional and economic security. If abandoned by her primary partner, a woman can still depend on her secondary partners for financial support. For example, one woman found a

Table 6

Female interviewees' relationships with men at the time of the interview, April/May 1988

Type of relationship[a]	No. of women
Primary partner and prostitution	12
Primary partner and 1–6 secondary partners	3
Primary partner only	3
Prostitution only	2
Inadequate information	4
Total	24

[a]See footnote *a*, Table 5.

monna on the mine who gave her R80 (R2.50 to the U.S. dollar) per month, and she washed his clothes and cooked for him. She had three other *linyatsi* who respected her primary partner and visited her on days when they knew he was not present. Each man paid her between R10 and R20 every time he slept with her. She stayed with her *monna* for almost two years, though the other men changed frequently. These relationships, she said, made her "happy" because she "had money for her children." Paradoxically, some interviewees recognized that their misfortune was related to the effects of migrancy on their marriages but that their survival too depended on the migrant labor system. One woman said: "If there were no hostels we would die of hunger. We live because of the hostel system."

Sexually Transmitted Diseases and Condom Usage

Nine of 17 male interviewees (53 percent) who were asked about STDs said that they had been infected with an STD at least once. Only one man had informed his sexual contact, while the rest had not returned to the woman they thought had infected them. Few women interviewees said they had ever contracted an STD.

Condoms are recommended as a barrier to HIV and certain STD infections. However, few interviewees were accustomed to using condoms. Thirteen of 18 male respondents who were asked about condom usage said they would not use condoms. Similarly, in a survey of 429 mineworkers, 66 percent never used condoms (1, p. 21). Their reasons ranged from fears that it would interfere with sex and ignorance about using condoms, to distrust of mine management directives to use condoms, which they perceived as a further incursion into and control over their personal lives. As an interviewee explained: "I don't get the satisfaction [with a condom] you get from having sex naturally. . . . The reason why we don't take up the management's advice is because he doesn't satisfy us on many things but wants us to use condoms." Interviewees who used condoms said they did so because they distrusted their partners, or as a means to avoid recurrence of STD infections.

Three of 17 female interviewees who answered the question on condom usage said they used condoms with their clients. One woman said she feared venereal disease and she told men who refused to use condoms to go elsewhere. Two women depended on male customers who supplied them with condoms from the mine. The view of most women interviewed was that clients would refuse to use condoms because they felt they had paid for "natural" sex.

Ignorance about the transmission of STDs and AIDS was apparent among interviewees. Many interviewees had "heard about AIDS," but few knew that the virus was transmitted sexually. Male respondents who suggested monogamy and condom usage as forms of protection said they would not necessarily follow this advice themselves. Accusations of racism and implicit distrust of managerial initiatives led some interviewees to dismiss mine pamphlets as untrue. One worker said: "I did not believe management's pamphlets because he has locked us up in a hostel away from our wives. If these pamphlets were true they would give us at least four days every month to be with our wives." One woman blamed whites, and three women blamed other ethnic groups for the disease. A Mosotho woman explained: "I think Basotho men don't have AIDS. I don't have sex with other race groups. I think AIDS is common among Shangaans and amaXhosa workers, even Bapedi. . . . People told me that if you have sex with many men of different race groups you get AIDS." Blaming other groups is a common response to HIV infection. It implies that the individual or the group with which a person identifies is not at risk, and hence that changing sexual practices is unnecessary.

Discussion

Our research suggests that the migrant labor system has shaped high-risk relationships. Separated from their wives and families, a proportion of men may assuage loneliness and anxieties about home and work and seek sexual relief by finding sexual partners. Based on the descriptions of past and current relationships of a small purposive sample of male interviewees, it appears that there is a group of men who have multiple relationships with changing partners. They are usually reluctant to use condoms despite previous STDs.

Female prostitutes are also known to be at high risk for contracting and spreading HIV infection. Marriage promises a woman a degree of economic security. Divorce and abandonment—often related to the strain that migrant labor imposes on a marital relationship—deprive women of economic support. Relationships with primary and secondary partners or prostitution may be a means to supplement low wages or may be the only source of income. Some of these women may of necessity be involved in multiple encounters with different men. Dependence on clients who are generally reluctant to use condoms increases these women's vulnerability to developing STDs and HIV infection.

Drawing on our interviews, it appears that the migrant labor system has institutionalized a geographic network of relationships for spreading STDs (Figure 2). This network suggests that once HIV enters the heterosexual mining community it will spread into the immediate urban area, to surrounding urban areas, from urban to rural areas, within the rural areas, and across national boundaries. The government policy of repatriating HIV carriers is a vain attempt to keep out rather than confront the problem. The virus is already present in the local black heterosexual population, and the migrant labor system is likely to play a part in hastening its spread.

The maturation of an STD epidemic is complex. Our data may illustrate one end of the spectrum of behavior where multiple partners and frequent partner change are common. This group may represent a "core" population involved in high-risk activity, and these individuals may well be the first to contract HIV infection and act as major carriers. As the disease enters other more stable groups, the rate of transmission of the disease will slow down (32, 33). Further research using large-scale representative sampling is necessary to investigate the experiences of a wider range of migrants, differing levels of vulnerability to infection, and the size of groups most at risk.

COMBATING THE HIV EPIDEMIC

The results of this study indicate that HIV transmission cannot be curtailed unless the social conditions facilitating its spread—the migrant labor system, vulnerable family relationships, low-wage work for women—are transformed. A focus on individual behavior overlooks the social and economic factors that may facilitate the transmission of STDs and HIV. Rather than condemn individual behavior, a strategy must situate sexual behavior in its social context. This involves, first, an appropriate education program run by empathetic groups, and second, reexamination of social structures conducive to high-risk behavior.

The South African political terrain creates added difficulties for health educationists. A government HIV program will meet with extreme suspicion from the black community and be associated with past racist population control initiatives (34). On the mines, education by management and medical personnel is linked to management control. A program that advocates monogamy and celibacy in the absence of a marriage partner is unlikely to be favorably received by migrant workers. Our interviewees believed that since the mines depend on migrant labor, and as they perceive multiple relationships and prostitution as social consequences of migrant labor, management's concern about HIV must be insincere or have sinister motives. A message of monogamy aimed at women who engage in prostitution or take several partners due to economic necessity is similarly unlikely to be meaningful.

Rather than the development of a sensitive public education program, racist scape-goating has been most evident. AIDS has been characterized as a new *swart gevaar* (black peril) sweeping down from the north with African National Congress (ANC) guerrillas (35) or through apparently healthy workers (36, 37). Foreign migrant workers have been designated a "reservoir" of infection capable of contaminating the entire country (38, 39). These explanations informed the 1987 health regulations that introduced compulsory HIV testing of foreign labor recruits and repatriation of all HIV- positive foreign workers (40). Public debate has focused on the "promiscuous" behavior of individuals and social groups. A newspaper editorial claimed that the "public has little sympathy with most of the main risk groups." It concluded that "until science cracks the virus's code one hopes that the most profound effect AIDS will have will be to tidy up the world's morals and accidental procreation" (41). This callously implies that those who are infected with the virus deserve it and should deal with the consequences without sympathy from society.

The shortcomings of official education programs and the necessity for grassroots-controlled education programs are recognized by progressive organizations in South Africa. The National Union of Mineworkers resolved at its Health and Safety Conference in August 1989 to campaign against dismissals, discrimination, and retrenchment of HIV-positive workers; to negotiate with management on the nature of its education program; and to launch a union HIV education campaign (42). In April 1990, the ANC, unionists, community leaders, and progressive health workers resolved at a health conference in Mozambique to establish a national AIDS task force headed by the ANC to develop an appropriate strategy for South Africa (43).

Education is an immediate response to the AIDS epidemic, but ultimately the central problem—the migrant labor system—has to be confronted. Male and female interviewees felt that unsafe sexual behavior would continue as long as families are divided. One worker suggested: "I think the only ways of normalizing the present situation would be for all mining houses to house miners with their families at the workplace." A woman suggested that people should "be given houses at the workplace where they will live with their families in order to prevent divorces and many sicknesses."

If HIV is ignored, the results for individuals, communities, and industry are potentially devastating. Repatriation of HIV-seropositive migrants, insensitive education programs, and separation of families due to the migrant labor system do much to ensure that South Africa's path to an HIV epidemic remains unhindered. As a National Union of Mineworkers pamphlet concludes: "In the long term we have to fight for living conditions which allows us to live in stable communities. . . . Only under these circumstances will we no longer be driven into casual sexual relationships by loneliness and craving for physical affection. We need to fight for an end to migrant labor and [for] family housing" (44).

REFERENCES

1. Ijsselmuiden, C., Mashaba, W. Z., and Padayachee, N., Chamber of Mines. *Interview Survey of Black Mineworkers' Awareness of AIDS and Sexually Transmitted Diseases, and of Behavior Patterns Potentially Affecting Transmission of These*. Chamber of Mines Research Organization, Consultancy Report Project No. G119B(TEO3) HRL No. 4/89, 7. Johannesburg, June 1989.
2. Shilts, R. *And the Band Played on: Politics, People and the AIDS Epidemic*. Penguin Books, New York, 1987.
3. Clumeck, N. Heterosexual promiscuity among African patients with AIDS. *N. Engl. J. Med.* 313: 182, 1985.
4. Johnson, A. M. Heterosexual transmission of human immunodeficiency virus. *Br. Med. J.* 296: 1017–1020, 1988.
5. Kreiss, J. K., et al. AIDS virus infection in Nairobi prostitutes. *N. Engl. J. Med.* 314: 414–418, 1986.
6. Moodie, D. Migrancy and male sexuality on the South African gold mines. *J. South. Afr. Stud.* 14: 228–256, 1988.
7. Hooper, E. AIDS in Uganda. *Afr. Aff.* 86: 469–477, 1987.
8. Dawson, M. H. AIDS in Africa: Historical Roots. Paper presented at the Canadian Association of African Studies, 17th Annual Meeting, May 11–14, 1988.
9. de Beer, C. *The South African Disease: Apartheid Health and Health Services*, pp. 1–14. Southern African Research Services, Johannesburg, 1984.
10. South African Institute of Race Relations. *Race Relations Survey 1987/88*, pp. 312–313. Johannesburg, 1988.
11. Kark, S. L. The social pathology of syphilis in Africans. *South Afr. Med. J.* 23: 77–84, 1949.
12. Dangor, Y., et al. Causes and treatment of sexually acquired genital ulceration in southern Africa. *South Afr. Med. J.* 76: 239, 1989.
13. Brink, B. A., and Clausen, L. The acquired immune deficiency syndrome. *J. Mine Med. Officers Assoc. South Afr.* 63: 15, 1987.
14. Brink, B. A. The Epidemiology of HIV Infection in the Mining Industry. Paper presented at the Conference on AIDS: Perspectives on the Problem and its Management, Johannesburg, September 10, 1987.
15. Martino, O. Prostitutes. Paper presented at the AIDS Congress: Strategies for Southern Africa '88. Johannesburg, April 29–May 1, 1988.
16. Martini, O. AIDS in the Mining Industry. Paper presented at the AIDS Conference, Johannesburg, 28 June, 1989.
17. *Business Day*, September 7, 1987.
18. *Business Day*, April 12, 1988.
19. Ijsselmuiden, C. B., et al. AIDS and South Africa—towards a comprehensive strategy. Part 1. *South Afr. Med. J.* 73: 457, 1988.
20. AIDS Advisory Group, April 24, 1990.
21. Guinan, M. E., and Hardy, A. Epidemiology of AIDS in women in the United States: 1981 through 1986. *JAMA* 257: 2094–2096, 1987.
22. Imperato, P. J. The epidemiology of the acquired immunodeficiency syndrome in Africa. *N. Y. State J. Med.* 86: 118–121, 1986.
23. Quinn, C. Q., et al. AIDS in Africa: An epidemiological paradigm. *Science* 234: 960, 1986.
24. Shapiro, M., et al. Screening antenatal blood samples for anti-human immunodeficiency virus antibodies by a large-pool enzyme-linked immunoabsorbent assay system. Results of an 18-month investigation. *South Afr. Med. J.* 76: 245–247, 1989.

25. Padayachee, G. N., and Schall, R. Short Term Predictions of the Prevalence of HIV Infection among the Black Population in South Africa. Paper presented at the AIDS Symposium of the South African Institute for Medical Research, Johannesburg, December 1, 1989.
26. Smith, H. W. *Strategies of Social Research: The Methodological Imagination*, p. 118. Prentice-Hall International, London, 1975.
27. Moodie, D. Mine culture and miners' identity on the South African gold mines. In *Town and Countryside in the Transvaal*, edited by B. Bozzoli, pp. 176–197. Ravan Press, Johannesburg, 1983.
28. Central Statistical Services. *Population Census 1985. Industry by Development Region, Statistical Region and District*. Report No. 02-85-03. Pretoria, 1985.
29. Gay, J. Basotho Women's Options: A Study of Marital Careers in Rural Lesotho, Chapt. 3 Doctoral thesis, University of Cambridge, 1980.
30. Showers, K. A note on women, conflict and migrant labor. *South Afr. Labor Bull.* 6: 54–57, 1980.
31. Gay, J. Wage employment of rural Basotho women: A case study. *South Afr. Labor Bull.* 6: 40–53, 1980.
32. Sabatier, R. *Blaming Others*, p. 74. Panos Institute, London, 1988.
33. Schoub, B. D., et al. Epidemiological considerations of the present status and future growth of the acquired immunodeficiency syndrome epidemic in South Africa. *South Afr. Med. J.* 74: 153–157, 1988.
34. Brown, B. B. Facing the 'black peril.' The politics of population control in South Africa. *J. South. Afr. Stud.* 13: 256–273, 1987.
35. *Star*, August 9, 1988.
36. *Business Day*, April 20, 1988.
37. AIDS—The African horror. *Inside South Africa*, June 9, 1987.
38. *Business Day*, September 4, 1987.
39. *Sunday Star*, July 5, 1987.
40. *Government Gazette* No. 11014, Reg. No. 2438 and Reg. No. 2439. Pretoria, October 30, 1987.
41. *Saturday Star*, July 16, 1988.
42. National Union of Mineworkers. *Resolutions. Second Health and Safety Conference*, pp. 1–4, Johannesburg, August 26–27, 1989.
43. *Weekly Mail*, April 20, 1990.
44. National Union of Mineworkers. AIDS! An Issue for All Workers. Pamphlet. Johannesburg.

SECTION IV

Solidarity and AIDS

Introduction

Nancy Krieger

If you had AIDS, what would you do? Take a moment. Think about it. Answer this question.

If your partner or your lover or your spouse had AIDS, what would you do? If your mother or father, your brother or sister, your aunt or uncle, or your child, had AIDS, what would you do? If your best friend or your other friends or your neighbors had AIDS, what would you do? And if you were dying of AIDS—or if all these people in your life were dying of AIDS, one by one, or many all at once—*what would you do*?

Perhaps more than any other disease in recent history, AIDS has taught a cruel and crucial lesson: the constraints on our response are as deep as our denial, as entrenched as the inequities that permeate our society, as circumscribed as our knowledge, and as unlimited as our compassion and our commitment to human rights. Elaborating on these themes, the three chapters in Section IV consider three widely divergent yet intimately connected topics: AIDS in Cuba, AIDS in Brazil, and global AIDS prevention in the 1990s. Together, they caution that if we persist in treating AIDS as a problem only of "others," *no* country will be spared the social and economic devastation that promises to be the cost of our contempt and our folly. Solidarity is not an option; it is a necessity. Without conscious recognition of the worldwide relationship between health, human rights, and social inequalities, our attempts to abate the spread of AIDS—and to ease the suffering that follows in its wake—most surely will fall short of our goals.

Originally published in the *International Journal of Health Services* 21(3): 505–510, 1991.

AIDS IN CUBA

Chapter 8, "Human Immunodeficiency Virus in Cuba: The Public Health Response of a Third World Country," provides a thoughtful, clear, and thorough description of the epidemiology of AIDS in Cuba and the country's evolving efforts to develop a comprehensive program for the control of its human immunodeficiency virus (HIV) epidemic. Throughout, the three authors—Sarah Santana, Lily Faas, and Karen Wald—carefully delineate the encouraging as well as troubling aspects of Cuba's multifaceted campaign. An example of what a poor and socialist country can achieve in terms of providing health care for all, Cuba has guaranteed this right to all persons infected with HIV. At the same time, however, the Cuban government's initial strategy to control AIDS relied upon regressive measures: persons infected by HIV were isolated from the rest of Cuban society. This was done despite the knowledge that AIDS is not a casually transmitted disease. By seeking to understand what led Cuban health officials to adopt this approach—and why they are now moving away from quarantine and toward integrating HIV-infected persons back into their families, workplaces, and communities—the authors offer invaluable insights into the ways in which ideological convictions shape not only health policy but also the overall relationship between a government and its citizens.

According to Santana and colleagues, Cuba's AIDS program has five key components: (*a*) protecting the blood supply, (*b*) mass screening of the general population and "high-risk groups" (including persons who have worked abroad or had sexual contact with foreigners), (*c*) mass education, (*d*) isolation of all persons infected by HIV (ill or not) and their removal to a sanitorium (with those interned guaranteed health care, full salaries, and also social support for their families), and (*e*) clinical research to develop effective treatments. While Cuban health officials stress that quarantine was adopted as only a preliminary strategy to take advantage of the "epidemiologic opportunity" afforded by the initially low numbers of HIV-infected persons in Cuba, the evidence offered by the authors suggests more fundamental issues may be at stake: the Cuban belief in individual sacrifice for the good of the nation, combined with the Ministry of Health's apparent distrust of the Cuban population's willingness or ability to adopt safer sex practices (despite the fact that condom sales have soared).

Most telling of all, however, is the observation that while the Cuban government now emphasizes personal responsibility for curbing the spread of AIDS, the quarantine policy has led most citizens to believe that the state is taking care of everything. Moreover, despite Cuba's renown for its creative mass campaigns, educational efforts have been further undermined by the government's hedged and often paternalistic approach to AIDS. As documented by the authors, flaws include: (*a*) excessive reliance on AIDS educational materials produced abroad; (*b*) underutilization of the country's cultural and artistic talent, as well as expert sex educators, in the design and implementation of the AIDS education campaign;

(*c*) increasing emphasis on physicians, rather than the mass media, as the primary source of AIDS education; and (*d*) the omission of AIDS as a topic for study group discussions within the many mass organizations to which most Cubans belong. In the end, Santana and colleagues note that despite all these defects, Cuba has managed to provide health care to and prevent the impoverishment of people infected by HIV, feats that many wealthier nations have not even begun to achieve. The question we are left with is whether Cuba's accomplishments had to be accompanied by the coercion of quarantine. The evolving answer fortunately seems to be "no."

AIDS IN BRAZIL

If Cuba represents one example of a Third World country's response to AIDS, in which government programs have distorted the relationship between individual and collective responsibility for AIDS prevention, then according to Herbert Daniel, one of Brazil's leading AIDS activists, Brazil is the nightmare we all hope to escape. In Chapter 9, "We Are All People Living with AIDS: Myths and Realities of AIDS in Brazil," Daniel offers a searing indictment of the insufficient and outrageous response of the Brazilian government, media, and society to a rapidly escalating epidemic of already overwhelming proportions. In a land where extremes of wealth and poverty surpass imagination, AIDS has been downgraded to a "second class" epidemic, denied even the desultory treatment accorded the "great epidemics of history that," as Daniel pointedly remind us, "have never been eliminated."

Daniel's essential thesis is that while AIDS was anticipated in Brazil through voyeuristic and homophobic reporting of the epidemic's spread within the United States' gay community, no serious efforts were ever undertaken to prevent AIDS from taking root. Instead, the threat was minimized, as if Brazil were somehow immune to this "foreign" disorder. When AIDS did surface in 1983, the official response, according to Daniel, was to adopt an abstract, inappropriate, and ideological "Western" model, in which only stigmatized "others" and "minorities" were at risk of HIV infection. Using this model, and the logic that the exception proves the rule, Brazilian health authorities subsequently downplayed the significance of the sale of contaminated blood in HIV transmission, and likewise ignored the rising rates of AIDS among Brazil's one unarguable majority group: the poor. With wonderfully mordant humor, Daniel illustrates the consequences of the health officials' strenuous efforts to force the "facts" of AIDS to fit the false model's predictions. One striking example details their pitiful attempts to reduce the richly varied sexual relations in Brazilian society to the anemic and limited Anglo categories of "heterosexual," "bisexual," and "homosexual."

Beyond alerting us to the perils of preconceptions, Daniel's chapter also stands as an extremely powerful statement by a self-identified person with AIDS regarding the need to affirm life and to embrace solidarity as the principle upon which our response to the epidemic must be based. To Daniel, the context is clear: we *all* are people living with AIDS precisely because we live in this age of AIDS. Using the metaphor of Highland, Virginia—where, in a protest against establishing a home for abandoned AIDS babies, one woman wrote: "AIDS IS A WORLD PROBLEM, SO WHY BRING IT TO HIGHLAND?"—Daniel illustrates how Highland is not only present in every Brazilian town where persons with AIDS have been vilified, discriminated against, and denied necessary treatment, but is also present within all of us whenever we try to assert that AIDS is someone else's problem. In this time of crisis, Daniel argues, it is sheer folly to discriminate against persons infected by HIV and to obstruct their participation in efforts to curtail the epidemic's spread. According to Daniel, the necessary response to AIDS is solidarity, not because it is poetic, but because no other response will suffice. Herbert Daniel died in 1992.

AIDS PREVENTION IN THE 1990s

The theme of solidarity likewise anchors Chapter 10, "Global AIDS: Critical Issues for Prevention in the 1990s." Written by Dr. Jonathan Mann, who until recently headed the World Health Organization's Global Program on AIDS, this chapter argues that meeting the challenge of the growing pandemic requires not simply the application of current concepts and strategies, but the development of fundamentally new approaches as well. Efforts to formulate an affordable vaccine or to develop new low-cost drugs are not the only tasks we face. As importantly, we must also reassess the underlying concepts and values that guide our work and strengthen the political resolve needed to translate our ideas into realities. It is to these issues that Mann directs our attention.

Beginning with the topic of "behavior," Mann notes that while present-day epidemiologic and basic science research have created a coherent explanation of how HIV transmission occurs, our understanding of "risk behaviors" remains woefully inadequate. Hampered by linear, deterministic models of sexuality that intuitively are at odds with our experience of sexuality, we can neither capture the nuances of sexual decision-making, nor account for why—in the absence of known changes in established "risk factors"—HIV transmission rates are rising in some regions and stabilizing in others. To address these problems, Mann suggests we turn our sights to other fields, including the emerging discipline of "chaos," in which models based on nonlinear dynamics have yielded new approaches to understanding how patterns can be detected in seemingly random behavior (1). Other "behavioral" challenges cited by Mann concern the conduct of people who do AIDS work, and include not only resolving the tension now arising between the first and second generation of AIDS workers, but also enhancing both groups' creativity and commitment while preventing burn-out and bolstering essential long-term management skills.

Turning next to political factors affecting AIDS prevention programs, Mann highlights the growing contradiction between the activism and ideas of community-based organizations and the complacency and denial of national political leaders who control urgently needed resources. To move the AIDS agenda forward, Mann suggests AIDS activists should forge alliances with other groups also seeking to change deficient health and welfare policies; as a model for future coalition-building efforts, he cites the recent passage of a national disability bill in the United States that included legislation about, but did not focus exclusively upon, HIV-infected persons. Above all, Mann urges that our work be premised upon the concept of "globalism," in which solidarity and respect for human rights and human dignity are conceived as the necessary foundation for AIDS interventions in an increasingly interdependent and highly mobile world. To Mann, AIDS has precipitated a crucial breakthrough in our understanding of the inherent link between health and human rights; we cannot ignore how discrimination and inequality have fueled the epidemic's spread. And to those who might counter that idealistic appeals are at best a weak strategy, Mann concludes with the forceful reminder that it is precisely these values that have inspired people to change the world and that also give "our struggle against AIDS its human meaning, and its individual and global message."

REFERENCE

1. Gleick, J. *Chaos: Making a New Science*. Viking Penguin, New York, 1987.

CHAPTER 8

Human Immunodeficiency Virus in Cuba: The Public Health Response of a Third World Country

Sarah Santana, Lily Faas, and Karen Wald

Cuba's response to the epidemic of human immunodeficiency virus (HIV) infection merits attention for many reasons. First, it is a costly and comprehensive effort in a poor country whose socioeconomic, political, and health delivery systems allowed early, integrated, countrywide action. Second, the epidemiologic characteristics of HIV antibody-positive persons in Cuba are somewhat different from those in other Latin American countries. Third, it provides experience in the screening of large numbers of healthy individuals. Fourth, it could broaden the knowledge of the natural history of the disease given the long-term follow-up of asymptomatic HIV antibody-positive persons identified early. Finally, Cuba is the only country admitting into sanatoria both ill and healthy HIV antibody-positive individuals. This chapter will describe the Cuban program and venture some thoughts on its successes and failures.

The Cuban program includes five components integrating preventive and treatment approaches:

1. Protection of the blood supply to prevent new infections and identify seropositive carriers.
2. Widespread screening to identify seropositive individuals.

Originally published in the *International Journal of Health Services* 21(3): 511–537, 1991.

3. Educational programs for the general population, for specific high-risk groups, and for seropositive individuals and their friends and families in order to interrupt the transmission chain and prevent new infections.
4. Treatment of seropositive persons through a "sanatorial regimen" that includes partial isolation. This institutionalization has the double purpose of providing the best quality of medical care and living conditions possible and interrupting transmission by preventing contacts with new sexual partners.
5. Clinical research to evaluate the performance of different treatment protocols in both symptomatic and asymptomatic patients.

BACKGROUND

The Cuban program and the Cuban HIV epidemic must be studied within the socioeconomic, political, cultural, and ethical context of Cuban society. Cuba is quite different from other socialist countries in culture and history, and from other Latin American countries in its political, ideological, and economic systems. The epidemiology of HIV, the factors affecting who becomes infected, as well as the measures undertaken to control the epidemic are very much determined by this context.

Cuba is a small island country in the Caribbean with an area of 110,000 square kilometers and a population of approximately 10.5 million, 67 percent of whom are 15 to 64 years old, with an excess of males in most age categories. The male:female ratio ranges from 1.01 to 1.04 for all age groups except for those aged 50 to 64, who show a ratio of 0.992 (1).

A revolution overthrew dictator Fulgencio Batista in 1959. In 1961 the government officially declared Cuba a socialist state. Education and health services are free; housing and food costs represent a very small percentage of household income (2). Malnutrition, acute poverty, and many infectious diseases have been eradicated (2, 3).

Some social ills affecting the patterns of HIV transmission in other countries, such as intravenous (IV) drug abuse, are nonexistent. Others, such as prostitution, are minimal. Individual prostitutes work mostly in Havana and nearby tourist centers and have been estimated to number in the hundreds (4). "Pimping" and running a prostitution house are illegal, but prostitution itself is not. Because the prostitution trade is not in money but mostly in consumer goods available only with foreign currency, and because premarital and extramarital heterosexual relations are commonly accepted among the Cuban population, clients of prostitutes are mostly foreigners (4, 5). Although occasional gay prostitutes exist, gay prostitution is not widespread (6). All these conditions affect the pattern of transmission of HIV, which is very different from that observed in countries where prostitution and IV drug abuse are common. The most common risk factor for HIV in Cuba is having had sexual relations with a foreigner or with someone who had sexual contact with a foreigner (7).

Homosexuality is not illegal, but there is a strong cultural bias against it. During the last 20 years the state has not actively persecuted homosexuals, although they are still victims of unofficial social discrimination. There are no gay bars and baths where casual sexual activity occurs. Places where people pick up both heterosexual and homosexual partners exist, but they are rare, especially outside the largest cities.

Travel into and out of Cuba has been routinely controlled and monitored since 1960. The state can identify most Cuban residents who have traveled abroad (8). Cuba has large numbers of citizens studying or working abroad with civilian delegations in over 30 countries, and troops mostly in African countries (9). Serving abroad is looked upon as an honor; it is those the society wants to reward and those committed to its goals and ideology who travel and have contact with foreigners. Therefore, the individuals at highest risk of infection are not minorities or "underclasses" of the society as in many other countries.

Cuba has a single, unified health system (10) locally administered, with professional oversight at the national level. It has a widespread network of primary health care centers and family physicians, secondary and tertiary care hospitals, and research institutes. The health profile of the population is more like that of a developed country than a developing one, with low infant mortality, low fertility, low rates of infectious diseases, and high cancer and cardiovascular disease rates. Over 95 percent of pregnant women receive prenatal care, and 98 to 99 percent of newborns are delivered in hospitals. There is very high utilization of primary and secondary health care services (10, 11) (Table 1).

The health care system is based on certain operational principles, unchanged since 1961 (12, 13):

1. Health is the responsibility of the state and the right of the people.
2. Care must be comprehensive, integrating curative and preventive services.
3. Care must be free and accessible to all.
4. Social services, health care, and the socioeconomic development of the population are to be coordinated.
5. Popular participation in the health system is fundamental.

Although the health delivery organization has changed throughout these last 30 years, it has been a rational development built upon the solid bases of these principles (14). The system has gradually evolved through different stages, culminating in a primary health care system that relies on a network of community-based health teams (family physician and nurse) backed by extensive secondary and tertiary care institutions (14, 15).

The population is well organized in each community. Over 85 percent of residents belong to one or several mass organizations such as block associations, the Federation of Cuban Women, associations of small peasants, students associations, etc. (11, 16). These groups traditionally work in health activities such as

Table 1

Selected health indicators of the Cuban population[a]

	1960	1970	1980	1985	1989
A. Percentage population over 65 years of age	4.8	5.9	7.3	8.0	8.5
B. Mortality rates per 1,000 population, by age					
Under 1[b]		38.7	19.6	16.5	11.1
1–4		1.3	1.0	1.0	0.7
5–14		0.5	0.5	0.5	0.4
15–49		1.0	1.7	1.2	1.7
50–64		9.3	8.8	9.4	8.8
65+		52.9	47.3	49.6	48.4
Total		6.6	5.7	6.4	6.4
C. Percentage of deaths over 50 years of age	60.8	65.9	76.7	78.2	80.1

	1972–74	1982–84	1986–88
D. Mortality rates per 100,000, 10 main causes of death[c]			
Heart disease	196.2	170.2	176.4
Malignant tumors	122.6	113.4	114.0
Cerebrovascular disease	71.1	57.6	59.7
Influenza, pneumonia	45.2	37.8	33.8
Violent deaths (accidents, suicides, homicides)	60.2	67.7	65.0
Diabetes	12.6	13.1	22.3
Perinatal conditions	21.2	12.2	9.0
Congenital anomalies	9.4	8.4	7.8
Asthma, bronchitis, emphysema	14.1	7.5	8.3
Kidney and urinary tract diseases	10.8	6.8	7.2
Mortality per 1,000, all ages, age- and sex-standardized	6.8	5.9	5.1

	1962	1970	1985	1989
E. Mortality rates per 100,000 population, other selected causes of death				
Direct maternal mortality[d]	118.2 (1960)	70.4	30.8	29.2
Acute diarrheal diseases	57.3	17.7	4.3	2.7
Infectious and parasitic diseases	94.4	45.4	11.6	8.6

Table 1

(continued)

	1965	1985	1989
F. Incidence per 100,000 population, selected reportable diseases			
Typhoid fever	3.0	0.6	0.5
Tuberculosis	63.5	6.7	5.5
Leprosy	4.2	3.5	2.9
Diphtheria	8.0	0.0	0.0
Whooping cough	26.6	1.9	0.7
Tetanus	6.5	0.1	0.1
Tetanus neonatorum	1.3	0.0	0.0
Measles (1989, 12 cases)	118.8	28.6	0.1
Malaria	1.6	0.0[e]	0.0[e]
Meningococcal meningitis	0.3	8.0	3.7
Gonorrhea	8.9	361.0	381.9
Syphilis	29.7	62.8	82.2
Poliomyelitis[f]	—	—	—

	1960–65	1970–75	1980–85	1985–90
G. Life expectancy, years	65.10	70.93	73.59	73.97

	1974	1980	1987	1989
H. Low birthweight rate, percentage of live births	11.7	9.7	7.9	7.3

	1970	1975	1980	1989
I. Health services indicators				
Average yearly well visits per child under 1 year	3.0	6.1	8.3	11.0
Average ambulatory visits per person (all ages), excludes emergency room	2.5	2.7	3.1	4.4
Average obstetric visits per delivery	7.0	9.5	11.4	15.8
No. of physicians	6,512	—	15,247	34,752[g]

[a]Source: MINSAP Annual Reports, 1980, 1985, 1987, 1989.
[b]Per 1,000 live births.
[c]Rates age- and sex-standardized to the 1983 population.
[d]Per 100,000 live births.
[e]There have been no domestic cases for many years, only a few imported ones.
[f]Polio has been eradicated in Cuba since annual immunization campaigns were begun in 1962.
[g]10,359 are family physicians.

health education and follow-up of the chronically ill. This, together with the large proportion of the population reached by the health system, makes it possible to have mass health-oriented campaigns with very high participation and acceptance by the population. These campaigns include immunizations, blood donations, and cervical cancer and HIV screening (11, 16, 17).

The emphasis in Cuban education at all levels is on self-sacrifice, the common good, and the subordination of the desires of the individual to the needs of the nation. Most people actually behave this way, either out of conviction or out of peer pressure. Part of this collective mentality is the expectation that the government will take care of all health needs, individually and collectively, and protect society from any public health threat. These factors seem to influence the apparent lack of resistance to admission to the sanatoria and the seeming societal consensus about this measure (18).

METHODS

The work described in this chapter is a synthesis of our extended research in periods of varying duration throughout 1986–1990. We are foreign and native-born women, completely fluent in Spanish. Since some U.S. researchers distrust data provided by the Cuban government, regardless of how detailed and explicit (19, 20), we made extreme efforts to assure the accuracy of the information reported here. Nonofficial sources were interviewed independently of government officials, not only to confirm or deny government-provided information, but also to gather additional data. Some of the interviews are part of an anthropologic study to be published by one of the authors (LF) separately.

The Cuban Ministry of Public Health (MINSAP) provided access to sanatoria, patients, physicians, and other health professionals working with HIV antibody-positive individuals, as well as epidemiologic and surveillance data on HIV infection. Over 40 Cuban health officials were interviewed, including the following: the deputy minister for hygiene and epidemiology; the national director of epidemiology; the director of the national laboratory processing all screening and diagnostic tests in the program; clinicians working with symptomatic and asymptomatic HIV-infected persons at the sanatoria; psychologists attending to these persons and their families; epidemiologists at the provincial level; nurses tracing sexual contacts of HIV antibody-positive individuals and/or working with patients in the sanatoria; family physicians practicing in different settings; and the director of the national center of hematology and immunology. Pharmacies in Havana, chosen at random, were surveyed for availability of condoms on two occasions, in 1988 and in 1990. This was done without the participation of Cuban health officials. Statistics and figures were provided by MINSAP. We reviewed most television programs aired up to December 1989 and a sampling of educational articles in the press, brochures, handouts, and posters.

Over 50 interviews covering topics such as screening procedures, diagnostic tests, knowledge of the disease, safe sex behavior, and opinions on the Cuban program were carried out with persons working in foreign relations, film making, economics, psychology, and literature, as well as with students, Cuban and foreign sailors, immigrants, taxi drivers, manual laborers, pregnant women, and sexual contacts of HIV antibody-positive persons. These were not a random sample of the Cuban population, but samples selected for ease of access (people known to us) or because they potentially belonged to high-risk groups (persons unknown to us prior to the interviews, such as customers of bars in Havana, sailors at the waterfront, taxi drivers, foreign tourists who frequented prostitutes, young university and high school students, and persons selected at random in buses, stores, queues, etc.). We arranged all of these interviews individually and privately without the participation or escort of Cuban government officials.

Interviews were also conducted with family and friends of persons admitted to the sanatoria and with 21 sanatoria residents themselves regarding the conditions under which HIV antibody-positive individuals lived, and the procedures by which they were identified and admitted to the sanatoria. A few of these conversations took place in the presence of various types of health workers (physicians, nurses, social workers). The great majority of these interviews, however, took place without any participation of Cuban officials, and many were conducted outside health facilities. Also interviewed were five U.S. residents who visited friends living in the sanatoria on several occasions between 1986 and 1990.

In general, we found that the factual information provided by Cuban officials was true, and the opinions voiced by them were generally those of most of, but by no means all, the people interviewed.

EPIDEMIOLOGY OF HIV IN CUBA

The rates of HIV infection in Cuba are quite low. As of October 1990, the total number of identified seropositive individuals was 497. This represents a seropositive prevalence of approximately 0.47 per 10,000 inhabitants. Average annual incidence (1986–1990) is 0.102 per 10,000 population (21).

In 1989, 120 HIV antibody-positive persons were identified among 2,808,222 screenings, a prevalence of 0.43 per 10,000 tests. In 1988 the prevalence of newly identified seropositives among screened persons was 0.48 per 10,000; in 1987 it was 0.85 per 10,000; and in 1986, the year screening began, it was 1.49 per 10,000 (22). (Army recruits in the United States showed a prevalence of 1.48 per 1,000 persons screened for the entire period 1985–1987 (23).)

These steadily decreasing rates are a common phenomenon, to be expected as screening culls the population of older infections. With each successive screening, only persons infected very recently remain in the pool. Also, from 1986 to 1988 the screening universe was gradually enlarged to cover lower prevalence groups (first only blood donors and travelers abroad were included, then other groups were gradually added such as all hospital admissions and general populations in certain areas; see the later discussion of screening). Thus, the prevalence of seropositivity in the entire screened population could appear to have decreased, even if among specific high-risk groups it had not (although in Cuba these high-risk groups seem to also have decreasing prevalence; see Table 2). Once the screening universe has stabilized and screening intervals become regular, a decrease in prevalence could be interpreted as the result of lower transmission rates. It is still too early to tell.

A better measure is the incidence rate of seropositivity. Cuba has not experienced the exponential increase seen in other areas of the world, either in asymptomatic HIV infections or in AIDS cases (21) (Table 3).

HIV infection in Cuba is largely a male heterosexual disease (Table 4). Of the 497 seropositive individuals, 362 (73 percent) are males and 135 (27 percent) females. Of the males, 212 (59 percent) have classified themselves as heterosexual and 150 (41 percent) as either bisexual or homosexual. These figures are confirmed by information provided by both gay and straight residents of the sanatoria and their families and friends. The proportion of HIV-seropositive persons who classify themselves as bisexual or homosexual has been steadily, although slightly, increasing every year.

The male:female ratio is 2.68 and has remained constant throughout the epidemic; it was 2.65 in October 1988 and 2.66 at the end of 1989. Among heterosexuals the ratio is 1.6. The most likely explanation for the excess of men among this subgroup is probably the greater opportunity for their exposure, because it is mostly males who travel abroad. A differential transmission rate between men and women seems an unlikely explanation since there is evidence in the Cuban data that transmission from male to female is more efficient than that from female to male. Only 5.6 percent of male contacts of seropositive women were found to be infected, whereas 12.1 percent of female contacts of seropositive men tested positive (7). Another explanation for such a high male:female ratio among heterosexuals is that some men who are bisexual or homosexual may have deliberately misclassified themselves as heterosexual. This is possible, although gay residents of the sanatoria told us that they do not think this is likely.

The rate of seropositivity among pregnant women in 1987 was 0.38 per 10,000. In 1988 it was 0.30 per 10,000, representing six individuals. In 1990 seven more seropositive pregnancies were identified (7, 21, 22). Because of the high percentage of women who receive early prenatal care, seropositive pregnancies are identified early and women can have therapeutic abortions. This has contributed to the low pediatric HIV rate.

Table 2

HIV screening: Number of screening tests and number of HIV-positives, by population group screened and year, Cuba, 1986–1987[a]

							Cumulative totals to:			
	1986		1987		1988		Dec. 31, 1988		Sept. 30, 1990	
Population group	Tests	Pos.	Tests	Pos.	Tests	Pos.	Tests	Pos.	Tests	Pos.
Blood donors	304,856	12	491,884	6	584,954	2	1,381,694	20	n/a	34
Pregnant women			79,063	3	203,218	6	282,281	9	n/a	16
Hospital admissions			99,348	2	554,522	12	653,870	14	n/a	35
Patients with STDs[b]			9,552	0	95,986	9	105,538	9	n/a	40
Contacts of other HIV+ persons	552	17	350	34	415	21	1,317	72	n/a	132
Internationalists	241,983	54	93,926	19	89,019	22	424,928	95	n/a	130
General population screenings		n/a		n/a		n/a		n/a	n/a	29
Presented with clinical symptoms		n/a		n/a		n/a		n/a	n/a	9
Others	56,370	16	106,485	11	413,838	22	576,693	49	n/a	72
Total[c]	603,761	99	880,608	75	1,941,952	94	3,426,321	268	8,832,726	497

[a]Sources: references 7, p. 492; 21. n/a, data not available.
[b]Sexually transmitted diseases.
[c]In later tables the total for 1988 is reported as 663,761, with the group labeled "Others" reporting 116,370.

Table 3

Number of HIV antibody-positive individuals and AIDS cases, by year of onset of symptoms, Cuba, 1986–1990[a]

	HIV+		
	No.	Rate, per 100,000 population	No. AIDS cases
1986	99	0.97	14
1987	75	0.73	17
1988	94	0.90	20
1989	120	1.14	12
1990 (Oct.)	109	1.38 (annualized)	6
Total	497	1.02 (average)	69[b]

[a]Sources: references 7, 21, 22; personal communications, Dr. Hector Terry, April 1990, and Drs. R. Torres and A. Martinez, October 1990.
[b]Includes 38 deaths; total Group IV (CDC classification) = 94.

Table 4

Number of HIV antibody-positive individuals, by age and sex, Cuba, January 16, 1990[a]

Age, years	Male	Female	Total
0–14	1	2	3
15–19	25	7	32
20–24	93	36	129
25–29	58	27	85
30–34	37	15	52
35–39	33	14	47
40–44	21	4	25
45–49	9	0	9
50–59	8	2	10
60 +	0	0	0
Total	285	107	392
Total, Sept. 30, 1990[b]	362	135	497

[a]Sources: references 21, 22.
[b]Age breakdown not available for 1990.

Table 5

Number of HIV-seropositive persons, by exposure category, cumulative totals, Cuba, September 30, 1990

Category	No. HIV+
Sexually acquired infection	
Heterosexual	325
Bisexual or homosexual	150 (all males)
Infected from blood or its by-products	
Domestic	5
Foreign	2
Hemophiliacs	2
Prenatal or perinatal infection	3
Under study	10
Total	497

Of a total of 16 seropositive pregnancies, four were carried to term, resulting in three pediatric cases. One of them, a girl (now deceased), was born before the beginning of prenatal screening.

Nine seropositive individuals have been infected by blood or blood products (Table 5). Of these, seven are domestic cases (two hemophiliacs), apparently infected before 1986; two were infected abroad, including an occupational case (7, 21, 22).

The most common route of HIV transmission in Cuba is sexual. As of October 1990, when the total number of seropositives was 497, 475 (95.6 percent) were infected sexually. Ten individuals (2.1 percent) were under study and their source of infection had not been identified. Of those who were sexually infected, approximately 60 percent were infected by sexual contact with a foreign person, either in Cuba or abroad (22). Therefore, the remaining represent a first, second, third, and, in some transmission chains, even a fifth generation of Cubans infected by Cubans in Cuba. It is this type of transmission that can be expected to increase and that the Cuban program hopes to end by its widespread screening, and its educational and sanatorial programs.

Three general patterns are discernible among Cuban HIV-seropositive persons. The first pattern, occurring primarily in the easternmost provinces, shows the majority of infections acquired abroad, and is primarily a heterosexual pattern. A second pattern is observed in the central provinces, where infections acquired from other Cubans in Cuba predominate, with those acquired abroad in second place. The third pattern, observed in Havana City, does not show a predominance of any particular group (21). These latter two patterns show a higher percentage of bisexual and homosexual infections, which follows from the higher number of contacts declared by homosexual or bisexual individuals when compared with heterosexuals (see below).

Since the first case was diagnosed in 1986, 94 seropositive individuals have been classified as belonging to the Centers for Disease Control's Group IV (24). These include 69 individuals with AIDS and 38 deaths. The most common conditions resulting in the immediate cause of death have been opportunistic infections (*Pneumocystis carinii* pneumonia, candidiasis, histoplasmosis, cytomegalovirus infection, toxoplasmosis, cryptococcal and cryptosporidial infections) and cerebral atrophy (one of these cases presented dementia as the first symptom). Only two cases of Kaposi's sarcoma have been observed (21, 22, 25).

Among the 69 AIDS cases, the incubation period has ranged from a minimum of 5 months to a maximum of 12 years, and survival after diagnosis has ranged from 1 month to over 3 years (the latter value attributable to patients still alive). Based on 335 persons whose date of infection was known, a Kaplan-Meier survival analysis showed a 65 percent cumulative probability of having an incubation period of 11 years or more. This was true for both women and heterosexual males, but for bisexual and homosexual males the incubation period corresponding to the same 65 percent probability was shorter: 6 years. The average survival after a diagnosis of AIDS (not just HIV seropositivity) is 19 months, with an 80 percent probability of dying before 30 months. This holds true for all AIDS patients, regardless of sex or sexual orientation.

Cuban investigators venture as a possible explanation for the difference in incubation periods, the higher number of sex contacts declared by the bisexual and homosexual patients, who thus may be subject to more repeated infectious challenges to their immune system than the heterosexual patients. Once AIDS develops, however, there seems to be no difference in survival (21, 22, 25).

According to the figures provided by the Cuban authorities, as of April 1990, 122 HIV infections were directly attributed to travel to Africa, either because the person was infected there or because he or she was infected by someone who had traveled there. Over 350,000 Cubans have served in Angola in military or civilian capacities, and thousands more in other parts of Africa (8, 9, 26). As of December 31, 1988, among the 424,928 internationalists tested, there were 95 seropositives, a rate of 2.0 per 10,000 (7). There does not seem to be evidence to support the fear that Cuba's foreign aid activities in Africa would produce an explosive HIV epidemic at home, although it has been an important source of infection. Presently, Cubans in Angola are tested before they return to Cuba so that their HIV status is known to them and to the health authorities before their arrival (27).

Like everywhere else, in Cuba certain behaviors define groups at higher risk of HIV infection. Persons who have had sexual relations with a foreigner are the largest defined group. Prostitutes seem to be at higher risk for this same reason (the estimate by the staff of the sanatoria is that perhaps ten of the HIV-positive women are prostitutes). Two other groups show high prevalence: blood and blood products recipients and persons with a previously diagnosed sexually transmitted disease (STD). (Syphilis and gonorrhea have been increasing, but it is unclear whether or not this is a reporting artifact.) Blood donations have been screened for hepatitis B using an ELISA (enzyme-linked immunosorbent assay) since 1988; the prevalence estimated among blood donors in 1989 was 1.2 percent (28). There are no other common behavioral risks such as use of IV drugs. Because there are no studies on the average number of partners of HIV-negative persons during any time period, we cannot say that promiscuity is a risk factor in Cuba, although it stands to reason that it should be. The average number of contacts declared for tracing by seropositive persons in Cuba (time periods vary) are as follows: among male homosexuals, 9; among male heterosexuals, 3.4; among females, all heterosexual, 3.7 (7). Two factors may be artificially raising the average of the females and lowering that of heterosexual males. In the case of the females, the average includes the women who probably were prostitutes, who have a higher number of declared contacts; and in the case of the heterosexual males, all averages exclude contacts abroad.

In a case control study done among seropositive and seronegative female contacts of HIV-positive individuals, the number of sexual contacts, trauma during intercourse, and anal intercourse were all significantly associated with infection. Only 3.4 percent of female contacts of bisexual males were infected, whereas 12.1 percent of the female contacts of heterosexual males were HIV-positive (Table 6). This difference may be explained by the higher frequency of heterosexual contacts reporting anal intercourse (53 percent) compared with the contacts of bisexual males (0 percent) (7).

Table 3 shows cases by year of onset of symptoms. Given the screening and surveillance in place since 1986, time from infection to diagnosis of HIV seropositivity has become shorter. All 109 HIV-seropositive persons identified in 1990 were infected in 1989 or later. There is virtually no lag in reporting once a case or carrier is diagnosed, given the centralization of the program and the traditionally strong and uniform reporting system.

Table 6

Percentage of HIV-seropositives among traced sexual contacts of seropositive individuals, by sexual preference, Cuba, 1986–1988[a]

Index seropositive individuals	Male contacts			Female contacts			Total		
	Total	Pos.	%	Total	Pos.	%	Total	Pos.	%
Homosexuals	562	31	5.5	158	6	3.4	720	37	5.1
Heterosexuals (M and F)	161	9	5.6	436	53	12.1	597	62	10.4
Total	723	40	5.5	594	59	9.9	1,317	98	7.5

[a]Source: reference 7, p. 499.

DEVELOPMENT AND COST OF THE CUBAN HIV CONTROL PROGRAM

The National Commission for Control of AIDS was established in 1983. Its objectives were to ascertain the level of HIV infection in the Cuban population and to develop a program for the diagnosis, management, and epidemiologic control of the disease. Surveillance had been instituted in 1983 in all hospitals. No cases were identified before the beginning of screening. The first AIDS case (not the first HIV antibody- positive individual) was identified in 1986, presenting premortem at the hospital and not through screening.

In 1985 Cuban health authorities began planning, training personnel, and purchasing equipment to carry out widespread HIV screening. By the end of 1985 all the elements were in place to begin the program. Part of the difficulty in establishing the program was that, as with other health measures, Cuba was committed to making the test available in all provinces at the same time, so that the measures would not be applied differentially by area.

Cuba's response to the HIV epidemic has been no different from its response to any other health crisis. Almost every health worker interviewed, at all levels of the health hierarchy, immediately mentioned the dengue epidemic as an analogy to the HIV epidemic. MINSAP has a very strong surveillance program with virtually complete coverage of the country and responds to rising numbers of cases of any disease immediately. Thus, an increase in gastroenteritis, measles, or meningitis in a municipality or province is immediately detected and measures taken. Even when there may not be much that health authorities can do, the population is informed that MINSAP knows and is doing everything possible to deal with the situation. This happens again and again, whether the disease is conjunctivitis, dengue, or HIV infection. It is with this mind-set that Cuban health officials speak of the "epidemiologic opportunity" they had to prevent the spread of HIV when it had not yet infected many persons.

The Commission decided to first screen and protect the blood supply. Because the disease was clearly sexually transmitted, all persons exposed to possible intimate contact with foreigners were screened, regardless of their sex or sexual preference. Prisoners were tested on the assumption that high promiscuity in the prisons could cause rapid spread of the disease if introduced in that population.

The costs of the preventive and treatment aspects of the HIV program have been very high, especially for a poor country such as Cuba. According to figures provided by MINSAP (29), approximately U.S. $3,000,000 were spent during the first screening year (1986) on equipment, reagents, and other necessities that had to be imported from capitalist countries and thus purchased with foreign exchange.

Since then Cuba has produced its own screening tests (ELISA and Western blot), reducing its foreign expenditures (Table 7). The approximate cost of one

Table 7

Foreign exchange expended yearly on the HIV screening program, Cuba, 1985–1990[a]

	Expenditures, U.S. dollars
1985–86	3,000,000
1987	1,000,000
1988	400,000
1989	300,000

[a]Source: personal communication, Dr. Hector Terry, March 1990.

day's stay in a sanatorium is 42 Cuban pesos (30). This represents approximately 6.5 million pesos a year (and does not include screening or education, or the residents' salaries, which they continue to receive). Cuba's health expenditures for 1989 were 1,015,600,000 pesos ($97 per person), approximately 12 percent of the national budget, and a 3.7 percent increase over the previous year. Although total HIV costs represent about 1 percent of the Cuban health budget, there has been no competition among other programs for these funds. HIV expenditures have been new additions to the budget (31). (At official exchange rates, the Cuban peso varies between U.S. $0.75 and $1.00.)

BLOOD SUPPLY

In 1983 the importation of blood and blood products from countries with reported AIDS cases was halted. Officials report that Cuba is now self-sufficient in its blood supply. Since May 1986 all blood donations have been screened (27).

There have been seven domestic transfusion-associated cases, infected before 1986. Of these, two are hemophiliacs; there are approximately 500 hemophiliacs in Cuba (22). As of October 1990 approximately 2,500,000 units of blood had been screened and 34 of them (0.136 per 10,000) had been found to be HIV-positive (see Table 2) (7).

There are approximately one half million blood donations in Cuba yearly, 80 percent of them from men, 50 percent of whom are between 20 and 40 years old (27). Thus, at the beginning of the program, testing blood donations was a relatively quick way to reach a large sample of sexually active males, in addition to ensuring the safety of the blood supply.

Even though persons who have traveled abroad and other individuals at high risk of HIV infection are advised not to donate blood, there is no self-exclusion mechanism by which, upon donation, such individuals can identify themselves as high risk. This adds an additional measure of risk to the blood supply. Persons who suspect they may be HIV-infected but do not want to ask for a test explicitly may donate blood as a way of finding out their HIV antibody status. We have personal knowledge of one such person.

The testing of blood donors is not anonymous. Seropositive donors enter the process of confirmatory tests, contact tracing, and sanatorium admission following the same protocols as those identified through other screening methods.

SCREENING

Population Screened

By October 1990, 8,832,726 screening tests had been performed, identifying 497 seropositive persons (four seropositive to HIV-2 virus). Thus, in order to identify one seropositive individual, 17,772 tests were done (21, 22).

Cuban epidemiologists estimate that a substantial number of tests are repetitions. Many persons have been tested more than once, some several times since 1986. Almost 2 million of the tests have been on blood donors (400,000 to 500,000 per year). A very high percentage of persons donate every year, so their blood has been tested yearly. People working in certain trades are rescreened periodically, sometimes at semiannual intervals. Seronegative contacts of seropositive persons are tested multiple times. The approximate number of persons tested is estimated to be between 5.5 and 6.5 million. This is between 78 and 92 percent of the population aged between 15 and 64.

The screening program began by testing blood donors in 1986 and gradually expanded to cover other population groups. At the present time, the groups being screened are as follows (the first six groups are the same population groups sampled for anonymous screening by the CDC in the United States in order to estimate seroprevalence) (32):

- Blood donors.
- Pregnant women.
- Adults admitted to hospital.
- Persons diagnosed with other sexually transmitted diseases.
- Prisoners.
- Army recruits.
- Cubans who have traveled abroad since 1975 or have frequent contact with foreigners, e.g., workers in tourism or foreign relations.
- Sexual contacts of seropositive individuals.

- The adult population of specific municipalities where clusters have been discovered, where there is a high incidence of STDs or where specific high-risk conditions prevail, such as active tourist centers.
- Foreign students attending school in Cuba.
- Foreigners who live in Cuba for extended periods of time.

These last two groups are not reported here. Seropositive foreigners living or studying in Cuba are returned to their country.

Screening is periodically repeated at least once yearly in continually exposed groups such as workers in the tourist industry—for example, hotel personnel and taxi drivers. Others are tested every time they return from a trip abroad. At the individual level, seronegative sexual contacts of seropositive individuals are closely followed, counseled, and retested every three months. Foreign tourists and diplomats entering Cuba are not screened (33).

Consent

Persons screened because their blood was drawn for other types of procedures, such as during prenatal care, hospital admission, diagnosis and treatment of STDs, or blood donation, are not asked for explicit consent to perform HIV antibody testing. In these cases the test is treated as routine. Those tested in workplace or neighborhood screening sessions consent implicitly by submitting to the test, since they know the test is being performed. During screening of the general adult population in specific municipalities and workplaces, some persons absolutely refuse to be tested (for example, 130 in Old Havana and nearly 3,000 in Sancti Spiritus). They are not forced to provide a blood sample, but they are counseled about safe behavior on the assumption that they may be seropositive (34). However, it is clear that pressure from peers, neighbors, co-workers, and health officials is very strong, and many who would have preferred not to be tested have, nevertheless, agreed to it.

HIV-seropositive pregnant women are counseled but not coerced to have a therapeutic abortion (27, 34, 35). There is little if any stigma associated with elective abortions in Cuba. Even though the numbers and rate of abortions have decreased greatly in the last 10 years, the use of abortions as birth control was widespread in the 1960s and early 1970s, and still is among the young (31, 36, 37, 38).

Screening and Diagnostic Tests

ELISAs are used as screening tests. They are administered and processed at the provincial level in 45 diagnostic centers (these are epidemiology and hygiene centers that are part of the health system and are not used or established solely for

HIV testing). The Cuban-developed kit is similar to that produced by Burroughs Wellcome, using a direct competition method.

A central, national reference laboratory is responsible for quality control. Cuba sends its test kits abroad for evaluation and compares them periodically with eight foreign commercial kits. Several such evaluations have been carried out in foreign countries, including Sweden and the Soviet Union, with good results. Domestically, Cuba also periodically validates its tests by using foreign reference sera and commercial kits as well as sending Cuban sera abroad for testing in other countries. Twice yearly, different sets of standard reference sera, some domestic and some foreign, are randomly chosen by computer at the national reference laboratory. These are then coded and sent to all provincial laboratories for analysis. Sera from negative ELISAs are periodically tested by Western blot and radioimmunoprecipitation assay. This on-going evaluation of tests is at times impaired by the lack of foreign exchange and the United States' trade blockade of Cuba (39).

After a person has first tested positive by ELISA, another assay is performed on a second blood sample with an ELISA kit that uses a different method. If the second test is positive, a third one is performed at the central laboratory, proceeding then to confirmatory Western blot (reading bands for p24 and p41) and radioimmunoprecipitation assay.

The national laboratory reports a low false-positive rate after the third ELISA. This seems to be borne out by reports in the United States (23, 40). The Cuban test kits show a sensitivity of 100 percent, and a specificity of 98.3 percent, 98.83 percent, and 98.93 percent in Cuban and foreign trials that included sera from persons with other immunodeficiency syndromes (39, 41). Using the lowest specificity estimate, no more than 31 false positives would be expected after the third ELISA when screening 6,408,656 persons in a population with a prevalence of 0.611 persons per 10,000 *tested* (the estimate of the situation prevailing at the end of 1988). Since different ELISAs are used as second and third tests, with even higher specificity than the Cuban test, this would actually be an underestimate of false positives (40). Further testing of these persons with Western blot and radioimmunoprecipitation assays would eliminate all false positives. Because HIV prevalence among those screened in Cuba is so much lower than that among U.S. army recruits, the predictive value of a positive test is lower (92.7 percent) than that reported for the U.S. recruits (99.5 percent) (23). Among subgroups of the Cuban population with higher prevalence, such as travelers abroad or persons with STDs, the predictive value would be higher.

The Cuban reference laboratory has never found a negative confirmatory diagnostic test when the three ELISAs were clearly positive. Negative or ambiguous Western blots have been seen only among those with borderline ELISAs near the cut-off point. Persons with borderline positive results in Western blot (some protein bands show, but not others) and other diagnostic tests are followed in the community under very strict confidentiality, providing them with intensive counseling and support until a definitive diagnosis is made, in some cases more than one year later. Cuban officials emphasize the extreme care they take in confirming beyond any doubt the seropositive status of a person, since the consequences are so serious. For some individuals the correct diagnosis has required tests for HIV-2, simian immunodeficiency virus, and, if HIV is suspected from their clinical illness but they show no HIV antibodies, a virus isolate is done. Only two cases have been ultimately diagnosed as HIV-infected and consequently institutionalized. The rest had other diagnoses (39, 41).

TREATMENT: THE SANATORIAL REGIMEN

Admission Process

Persons confirmed to be HIV antibody-positive are interviewed by specialized physician and nurse epidemiologists in order to explain to them their condition and begin to plan their admission to a sanatorium. The individual's personal circumstances are taken into consideration, including family, employment, resources, housing, etc. All persons continue to receive a full salary, although they do not continue to work at their workplace. If they are unemployed, they are paid a stipend. Special attention is given to any domestic or economic problems, so that new housing is provided for the family should they need it, and children may be placed in better or nearer schools or their entry into a desired special school facilitated. A spouse's employment situation may be improved or changed as needed, and psychiatric and counseling services are provided to the family. Everything is free of charge.

The utmost care is taken in terms of confidentiality; all blood samples are identified by number, with the name code available only at the national ministry. Only two persons per province (the epidemiologist and the public health nurse assigned to the case) are privy to the identity of each seropositive individual. Sexual contacts traced, whether ultimately seropositive or seronegative, are not informed who provided their name. Contact-tracing personnel are chosen from among the most experienced staff in the program against STDs. Many of them were trained before 1980 by personnel from the CDC in Atlanta, Georgia.

The individual decides whether or not to tell family, friends, and co-workers of his or her HIV status. For persons who do not want to inform others, health officials provide elaborate and apparently effective alibis so that the persons' absence from their jobs and neighborhoods is not attributed to their HIV status. For example, in some cases individuals appear to be transferred to another province to work, or to have gone abroad to study. These "covers" will not be good forever, but they seem to have worked for the time being.

We were pleasantly surprised at the extreme confidentiality and care taken with the privacy of HIV antibody-positive persons, since neither the popular culture nor the manner of practice in Cuba places much importance on privacy. (Other patients are normally interviewed and examined in semiprivate areas, conversations of the most intimate nature go on in waiting rooms and hallways, women have sonograms in group sessions, and it is common to see people carrying on an intimate conversation from the sidewalk to a second-story balcony—nobody seems to mind.)

Treatment

The residents of the sanatoria have a special diet and exercise regimen. Pathogens are cultured periodically from different sites in each resident's body, and the person is treated for all infections, even asymptomatic ones. Constant surveillance and a close patient–physician relationship lead to prompt treatment of opportunistic infections, following internationally accepted protocols. Pentamidine, AZT, acyclovir, and interferon are used preventively and for cases classified as CDC Group IV (42).

According to reports from residents, the sanatorial regimen can increase or alleviate their stress. Some of the residents say that knowing their HIV status and having everything in their lives taken care of, as well as being able to relate closely to other HIV-positive people, has helped them relieve stress and cope with their illness. Even for these residents, however, the psychological distress produced by separation from family, friends, and work is considerable. The problem has been partly addressed by improved access to the world outside the sanatoria. Others say the stress of knowing they are HIV antibody-positive is worse than anything else, and that they would rather not have known.

Life in the Sanatoria

Cuban health officials have been changing and adapting the sanatorial system as it became clearer that there would be no effective curative agent or immunization available in the short run and that people would continue to be carriers for a long time. The goal now is the eventual reintroduction of still-infectious individuals to their communities after a period of separation rather than after a cure or after the population is protected by immunization. Cuban officials have always described the sanatorial regimen as "dialectic," something subject to change and evolution as the conditions changed. It has so far lived up to that concept.

Living conditions have become more permanent and comfortable. Residents of the sanatoria have moved to larger and better facilities since the inception of the program in 1986, now living in apartments housing two to four individuals per unit, with what in Cuba are considered luxuries such as air conditioners and color televisions. Five other sanatoria have been built in the central and eastern provinces of the country so that seropositive persons from those areas can live closer to their families if they choose.

The institution is staffed with health professionals specifically trained to work with HIV-positive individuals. The residents receive periodic medical exams, and specific physicians are assigned to each person to assure rapport and continuity of care and management. They follow the same family physician system as the rest of the Cuban population and are under close epidemiologic surveillance; their special diet and exercise regimen is supervised. The facilities seem to have well-developed recreation programs, and the residents can continue their university studies in the sanatorium.

Some residents who have trades or professions that can be practiced individually, such as writers, artisans, physicians, nurses, office workers, accountants, economists, or computer programmers, work in the facilities. However, most residents are limited to institutional-type arts and crafts, and "make work" activities. The lack of productive work in the institution is a serious problem for people who live in a society that holds work and service to others as the highest honor and a person's most important function in life. This, however, is slowly changing, and a few residents already attend classes at the university or continue to work outside the sanatorium.

Residents return to the community for visits, to attend parent–teacher conferences, and for block association meetings. Family and friends can visit them as often as they wish, and residents go home on the weekends, some accompanied by their families (parents, siblings, spouses, children), some chaperoned by medical students. These chaperons cannot prevent behavior leading to new infections, but have a strong inhibiting effect on the resident, since they act as observers. The only residents who leave the facility without company are couples considered stable, who leave together. Cuban law provides for a 50 pesos fine for unauthorized leave from the sanatoria, and imprisonment if a person *knowingly* infects another one.

Spouses are admitted into the sanatorium if seropositive. If they have not seroconverted they continue to live at home and visit their mates whenever they choose. The couple is counseled, but they are not prevented from engaging in sexual relations. Gay couples are treated in the same way as heterosexual couples, whether they are both seropositive or not. There have been cases of couples, discordant in antibody status, who have divorced, and the positive mate has then remarried a seropositive person in the sanatorium.

Seropositive children are admitted into the institution with their parents. Seronegative ones, even if newly born, live outside with relatives.

Although admission into the sanatorium is considered obligatory, one case of refusal has come to our attention. In that case, a woman with small children remained at home, closely monitored by the medical staff.

Reactions to the Sanatorial Regimen

Conversations with the residents revealed a sense of mutual support and caring among the HIV carriers and AIDS patients. While a strong sense of community is common in Cuba, it is especially strong in the sanatoria, and many residents said it was a major psychological factor in helping them cope with their illness. The fact that some of the doctors and nurses at the facility are HIV-positive adds to this sense of community.

No one wanted or liked to be there, but there were all levels of acceptance of the situation. Three internationalists (persons who do civilian and military duty abroad) said they were "at peace with" (had accepted) their situation because they "got the disease doing a good thing for the country," so they were not sorry or ashamed, just sad. They saw their residence in the sanatorium as another sacrifice for their country. Others felt that the semiconfinement of the sanatorium was unwarranted precisely because of their proven record of individual commitment and sacrifice to the common good. Some saw the program as an excessive application of governmental control, no matter how well-treated they may be. They all felt that the staff were doing their best. Most agreed that easier access and the hope of returning to their communities was very beneficial to them.

Some residents worried about unsafe behavior by others when they begin to live outside again. All the women residents interviewed stated that men in general were not to be trusted in their sexual behavior and therefore needed institutionalization. They felt that most women could behave in a manner that would not spread their infection, and could live in the community.

Although many felt they were now ready to behave responsibly outside, many did not and freely admitted it. The patients are categorized by the staff (psychologists, physicians, chaperons, nurses) by degree of reliability, considering among other factors their family situation.

MINSAP is constantly moving closer to returning many HIV-positive persons to their homes in the community and to their regular jobs, using the facilities only for ambulatory care.

Most families are eager to have the patients back at home. No one expressed fear of rejection by their closest relatives. Family loyalty is one of the strongest components of Cuban culture, rejecting an ill son or daughter is completely unacceptable socially. Several residents said they had felt rejection (*rechazo*) in the treatment by their neighbors, but it had been subtle enough that they themselves did not know whether it was real or in their own imagination. One said some neighbors had stopped speaking to him. Others said the neighbors were helpful. All felt the state should step up the educational efforts in the neighborhoods to help them adjust when they return home.

One recurring distressing complaint, especially given the cultural attachment to family, was the problem of seropositive women who were separated from their children. In a culture where several generations still live in the same household, and motherhood is greatly revered, this separation is very, very painful, especially when many of these women were monogamous and infected by their husbands.

Indirect evidence of the acceptance by the patients, their families, and the society of the "sanatorial regimen" is the relative discretion of the families and the population in publicizing and/or criticizing the existence of the sanatorium abroad. The general public in Cuba has known of the existence of the institution since 1986, and yet there have been none of the pleas on behalf of the patients nor the publicizing of details of their lives that have been carried out by the families and friends of inmates in Cuban prisons. Debate on the pros and cons of the sanatoria is limited to residents, their families, and staff at MINSAP, where the evolving consensus tends toward the return of some residents to the community. None of those interviewed outside these groups expressed disagreement with the policy, even though most Cubans tend to openly express their disagreement with many governmental policies, as long as their criticism does not appear to be doubting the fundamentals of the Revolution or of socialism.

EDUCATION

The educational component of the HIV prevention program addresses three different population groups: seropositive persons and their families and friends, the general public, and those in high-risk professions (for example, those in the merchant marine or the military, civilians whose work takes them abroad, and people in the tourist industry).

Accounts by health professionals and seropositive persons themselves describe as excellent the educational efforts directed at the residents of the sanatoria and their families. The long-term relationship established between seropositive persons and the health care workers facilitates an effective educational process, which includes printed materials, films, videos, live talks, and one-to-one sessions with the seropositive persons and their families and friends.

The AIDS/HIV preventive education for persons in high-risk occupations has consisted of talks, printed materials, and videos. The content emphasizes monogamy at home and celibacy abroad, and, in a lesser way, the use of condoms. We are not aware of studies done to evaluate these efforts.

The education of the general public has been large in scale, but probably not maximally effective. Radio programs in the hundreds have been broadcast. An estimated 6 to 7 million people have watched 33 television programs about HIV. Newspaper and magazine articles about AIDS are published every week, and we easily confirmed that literally millions of fliers, booklets, and informational materials are distributed through workplaces and schools in many areas of the country (43). The Cuban educational materials have been factual and non-hysterical. They have succeeded in teaching the population that HIV infection is a disease that can affect everybody, not just gay men (which was the early impression, given the descriptions of the disease coming from abroad, mainly the United States).

The Cuban health system seems the ideal one to implement widespread and imaginative educational programs, tailored specifically to its population. MINSAP can command the full cooperation of all the media and, when necessary, of other state institutions such as the Ministry of Education. The educational component of the Cuban program to control HIV infection has all the elements of a high-quality and imaginative program, but they seem to be disconnected and uncoordinated.

There are some excellent programs, such as a pilot one in the Bureau of Health Education in Pinar del Rio, which work with elderly groups, adolescents, prisoners, and newly married persons. HIV/AIDS education is integrated into these programs. The National Sex Education Working Group has years of excellent experience in sex education. AIDS/HIV is incorporated in its sexuality talks and radio programs. However, the members of this group, as expert sex educators, have not been included in the planning and implementation of the national HIV education program directed and executed by MINSAP (44).

There is outstanding talent in the country in film production, posters, and other commercial art, which has been used in an exemplary manner in cultural and political propaganda. Yet MINSAP has not brought these talents to bear on health education in general or AIDS/HIV education in particular. Many of the television programs use Spanish translations of totally inappropriate American or European film clips, or panel formats in which physicians answer questions posed by either callers or journalists. One very popular program addressed the transmission chains from individual to individual in understandable, graphic terms, and another showed documentary footage about the sanatoria. These are the exception rather than the rule. Many of the pieces in the written press are dense and use medical terminology, thus rendering them inaccessible or boring to many persons.

An educational program for high schools did not start until September 1988. There have been no widespread study groups on the issue among the many mass organizations, even though almost everything that happens in the country gets discussed in this framework. Surveys and studies have been conducted to determine educational preferences of the population, but the results have not been used to design programs (43, 45). The population prefers television programs, movies, and radio shows, yet, more and more, the responsibility is being left to the family physician. The family physicians in the neighborhoods, schools, and workplaces have been given a large part of the responsibility for educating the population. Not all schools and workplaces have family physicians. In many cases the physicians' information is incomplete or they have misconceptions—these are young physicians just beginning to learn about sex education themselves (44). Conversations with physicians confirmed this.

MINSAP figures show that almost everyone in the country has at least heard a talk or radio program or seen information on the television. Our interviews corroborated this. However, the knowledge about the disease among those interviewed was scant. Some said that since seropositive individuals are in the sanatoria and not among the general population, they did not need to protect themselves. In a 1989 survey of midlevel technicians, only 59 percent of those interviewed knew there was no immunization against AIDS (43, 45). The rationale expressed by Cuban health officials for the establishment of sanatoria is based in part on the belief that sexual behavioral change would take too long to achieve, given the sexual mores and culture and the machismo of the Cuban population. In the meantime, the probabilities of seropositive persons infecting others had to be diminished.

The educational materials are deemed to be in accord with the country's sexual culture. They promote behavioral change in terms of emphasizing monogamy, "knowing" your partner, and not having casual sexual encounters. Condom use is mentioned, although not emphasized. Other "safe sex" practices are not mentioned or considered culturally appropriate. The belief that the sexual behavior of Cubans (males and females) cannot be changed is belied by condom sales, which increased by 38 percent during the first 5 months of 1988 compared with the same period in 1987 (46). We found most pharmacies well stocked with condoms. KAP (knowledge, attitudes, and practices) surveys have been carried out since 1987, covering 245,000 persons in different settings (schools, workers in service and manufacturing, and others), which show that teenagers and young adults are much more accepting of condom usage than those over 21 years old (43, 45). This was corroborated by our interviews. All of 15 university students interviewed at a coffee shop in Havana (ages 16 to 19) carried condoms with them, made in Mexico or China. Whether or not they actually used them is another matter.

Cuban health authorities have tried to keep the HIV program as centralized as possible in order to protect individual confidentiality. As a result of this centralization, they have been slow to incorporate their best educators, survey specialists, artists, film-makers, and propagandists into HIV public education. It is ironic that a country that has won international prizes for posters and films, and whose population is accustomed to ubiquitous creative and imaginative theater, music, art, and literature, is using either translated foreign materials or mediocre national copy in this most important educational effort.

Public education about HIV began later than all the other components of the program. This may have allowed some infections to occur that should have been prevented. In fact, when interviewed, one of the internationalists in the sanatorium said that had he known about the disease when he left for Africa in 1986, he would not have become infected.

Cuban health officials themselves emphasize that ultimately only education affecting behavior will prevent infection. At every turn, the educational campaign on HIV waged by MINSAP insists on the importance of responsible individual behavior and the limited ability of the state in this situation to protect the population. But most people outside the sanatorium seemed to feel that they were protected by the measures taken to isolate seropositive persons.

Many of the shortcomings of the educational component of the HIV program, however, are not specific to it, but apply to health education in general. As with other health education efforts, Cuba produces a large volume of material, programs, and all sorts of activities, at great cost in human and material resources. The campaigns, however, need to be better designed and targeted so that they show results that translate into reduced incidence of the diseases and conditions they attempt to combat.

Among the Cuban population, perhaps it is the lack of awareness of and emphasis on individual responsibility in disease prevention that sets the stage for the less than optimum performance of health education in general, and specifically around AIDS. Contrary to the situation in the United States (47), in Cuba the population has the generalized attitude that assumes the state will take care of whatever problems arise. Collective solutions are offered and executed for all sorts of diseases, whether it is immunizations for measles or changes in the fat composition of milk. The health of the individual is a societal problem, so there is little precedent for placing the burden of prevention on individual behavior.

RESEARCH

Cuban scientists have been evaluating different treatment modalities for persons with AIDS and experimental preventive protocols for asymptomatic HIV carriers. Most of these trials have not yet concluded, and numbers are very small, since the universe of HIV-positive individuals is so limited.

One of these trials examines the use of interferon in preventing asymptomatic HIV carriers from developing AIDS. Preliminary results were reported at a conference on Interferon and Biotechnology in Havana in the spring of 1989, by Dr. Pedro Lopez Saura, director of the Biological Research Center in Havana: 11 of 18 HIV-positive patients with hepatitis B eliminated the hepatitis virus after treatment with interferon and developed their own antibodies against the disease. In three of six patients, HIV antigen could not be isolated again after administration of interferon. Other similar studies are in progress.

DISCUSSION

AIDS seems to be a disease that, like an X-ray, highlights the flaws and weak points of every society. In many countries persons with AIDS are homeless, have lost their jobs and salaries, have trouble paying for their health care, are shunned by family and friends, and depend on "the kindness of strangers" and private and religious organizations to survive. Most countries have not developed a comprehensive program to control HIV infection and to provide care and treatment to persons with AIDS. Cuba, a poor, small country, has developed an HIV and AIDS program, treating this disease in the same manner it would any other.

When examined within Cuba's socioeconomic, political, and cultural context, it becomes obvious, as Cuban health officials themselves state, that many aspects of the Cuban strategy to control the HIV epidemic, although logical and successful, are not exportable, especially to other third world nations. Such a program requires a quick and flexible response from a single national health system with equal access to all, high utilization by the population, and well-organized communities. It requires acceptance by the population of mass screening, and the ability of the health system to command the cooperation of other social institutions for the purposes of educating the public and to require that social welfare benefits be extended automatically and immediately to cover AIDS/HIV-affected persons. It also requires the technological and economic capacity to manufacture and/or import the necessary equipment, techniques, and pharmaceuticals to screen the population and provide treatment for those infected.

It is not the purpose of this article to discuss the ethical issues at play in the treatment of HIV carriers and AIDS patients in different countries. But the personal and societal costs of the freedom of HIV carriers and AIDS patients in other countries and the costs of the care that these persons receive in Cuba cannot be ignored. The Cuban program needs to be placed in the context of Cuban culture and society. Cuban AIDS patients are provided with all their medical and material needs, whether or not their family and friends are supportive. The "sanatorial regimen" has helped isolate them from possible prejudice and discrimination. In exchange, they have been required to live in an institution with only limited and supervised contacts with the rest of the world.

Each society has a different way of balancing individual versus collective rights when faced with phenomena it perceives as threatening to its health and integrity. Thus, the behavior allowed or required of a member of the community and the efforts expended to control the "threat" are different in each society. They depend on the perceived seriousness of the threat and the relative value placed on collective versus individual well-being. The behavior allowed or required of a member of a Mennonite congregation in Pennsylvania, or a resident of a small town in Holland, is very different from what is allowed or required of an individual in New York City or Amsterdam.

In Cuban society, great sacrifices are demanded of individuals in the interest of their perception of a strong and healthy society—not only in the case of persons with AIDS, but in all situations. This attitude, although reenforced by the socialist state, has its roots in traditional Cuban history and culture. A phrase from the Cuban national anthem (which dates from the middle of the 19th century) best sums up this attitude: "to die for the motherland means in fact, to live." In exchange for this sacrifice of privacy and individual freedom, the society provides the individual with a large measure of security, so that housing, health, jobs, education, and a safe environment are guaranteed and depend not on isolated individual actions, but on collective ones.

Institutionalization of HIV carriers is not an exportable model for many reasons. It is only possible early in the development of the epidemic, since it is not feasible (economically, socially, or politically) to institutionalize large numbers of persons in this manner. Cuban HIV-infected individuals, in contrast to those in other countries, are not members of any minority group. The only thing they have in common with each other is HIV infection and, in many cases, sexual contacts with foreigners. They are not IV drug abusers; they are not an ethnic, racial, sexual, or religious minority; they are not poorer or richer than the rest of the population. Therefore, there is no danger that institutionalization will be applied differentially to any group.

The goals of the Cuban HIV program are to interrupt transmission by preventing new infections and to provide the best medical and supportive care possible to those already infected, in the hope that this will prolong their lives until an effective therapeutic agent is discovered. The Cubans truly feel that these persons deserve the full support of the society and have devoted large amounts of resources (especially for such a poor country) to these goals.

The Cuban program is constantly under modification. Technical advances in treatment and screening are adopted as soon as possible. Educational efforts are constantly expanding, and new methods are incorporated yearly. The sanatoria themselves are under constant review and will soon be functioning, at least for many if not all HIV-positive persons, as back-up ambulatory facilities for receiving care and support, not as permanent residences.

It remains to be seen whether the Cuban program succeeds in lowering or stabilizing the rate of HIV transmission in the country. Questions need to be asked in the specific Cuban context in order to evaluate the performance of the program. It is already evident that the screening program has been successful in identifying HIV-seropositive persons before they develop AIDS symptoms. Only nine of the 497 seropositive persons have presented at a health facility with symptoms. (Others have been screened during hospital admission and found to be seropositive, but their admission was not HIV-related.)

Has the educational program succeeded in making HIV antibody-negative persons aware of their own responsibility for protecting themselves and preventing further spread? Does knowledge of HIV status encourage responsible sexual behavior, whether a person lives in a sanatorium or not? Will the persons that avoid testing for fear of institutionalization become a serious source of new infections in the population, or will they practice good prevention, even if evading the screening test? Has the sanatorial regimen been an important factor in preventing new infections, or has it been counterproductive by reenforcing unsafe sexual behavior in the population, which mistakenly relies on it as a measure of control? Have early identification, treatment, and optimal living conditions improved survival among HIV antibody-positive individuals regardless of the stresses of institutionalization? Is the low prevalence observed in successive screenings a real effect of diminished transmission rates, or an artifact produced by the groups that are being regularly rescreened?

Cubans do not pretend that all transmission will be stopped by their evolving program. But they may have been able to reduce transmission enough to prevent an exponential increase in infections. Cubans think they may have gained enough time to allow for improved educational methods to affect transmission and for the possible development of immunizing and/or curative agents in the future.

REFERENCES

1. MINSAP. *Annual Report, 1989*. Ministry of Public Health, Havana, 1990.
2. Benjamin, M., et al. *No Free Lunch—Food and Revolution in Cuba Today*. Institute for Food and Development Policy, San Francisco, 1984.
3. Gutierrez Muniz, J. A. *La economia cubana y la atencion infantil—aspectos basicos, 1959–1983*. Editorial Ciencias Medicas, Havana, 1984.
4. Manuel, L. El caso Sandra. *Somos Jovenes*, September 1987.
5. Interview with tourists and prostitutes, February and March 1990.
6. Informal interviews with gay men, 1986–1990.
7. Terry, H., et al. Programa de control del SIDA. Informe resumen del ano 1988 y acumulado. *Rev. Cub. de Higiene y Epidemiol.* 27: 491–503, 1989.
8. Terry, H., and Rodriguez, R., Division of Epidemiology, MINSAP. Personal communication, June 1988.
9. Grundy, P. H., et al. The distribution and supply of Cuban medical personnel in third world countries. *Am. J. Public Health* 70: 717–719, 1980.
10. Santana, S. Whither Cuban medicine? Challenges for the next generation. In *Transformation and Struggle, Cuba Faces the 1990's*, edited by S. Halebsky and J. Kirk, pp. 251–270. Praeger, New York, 1990.
11. Rios Massabot, E., and Tejeiro, A. Perfiles de salud. *Rev. Cub. de Medicina General Integral*, Suplemento, 1987.
12. MINSAP. *Diez anos de revolucion en salud publica*. Editorial Ciencias Sociales, Havana, 1969.
13. MINSAP. *Organizacion del sistema unico de salud*. MINSAP, Havana, 1970.
14. Santana, S. The Cuban health system: Responsiveness to changing population needs and demands. *World Development* 15: 113–125, 1987.
15. Gilpin, M. Cuba: On the road to a family medicine nation. *Fam. Med.* 21: 409, 1989.
16. Escalona Reguera, M., and Aguero Benitez, N. La participacion popular en la gestion estatal en Cuba. *Rev. Cub. de Administracion de Salud* 5: 211, 1979.
17. Monzon Torres, L., et al. El medico de la familia y su vinculacion con la comunidad. *Rev. Cub. de Administracion de Salud* 13(4), 1987.
18. Wald, K. *Los hijos del Che*. Extemporaneos, Mexico, 1986.
19. Zimbalist, A. Twisting statistics to attack Cuba. *Cubatimes*, January/February 1985.
20. Eberstadt, N. Did Fidel fudge the figures? *Caribbean Rev.* 15(2): 5, 1986.
21. Torres Peña, R., et al. Situacion del SIDA y la infeccion por VIH en Cuba, 1990. Paper presented at the III National Congress of Hygiene and Epidemiology, Havana, October 1990.
22. MINSAP. Programa de control del SIDA. Informe resumen hasta el 16 de enero, 1990. Unpublished report. MINSAP, Havana, 1990.
23. Burke, D. S., et al. Measurement of the false positive rate in a screening program for HIV infections. *N. Engl. J. Med.* 319: 961–964, 1988.
24. Centers for Disease Control. Revision of the CDC surveillance case definition for AIDS. *MMWR* 36, Suppl. 1S, 1987.
25. Martinez, A., and Torres, R., epidemiologists at the Santiago de las Vegas Sanatorium. Personal communication, October 1990.

26. Azicri, M. *Cuba: Politics, Economics and Society*. Pinter Publishers, London, 1988.
27. Rodriguez, R., National Director of Epidemiology. Personal communication, June 1988.
28. Muzio, V., and Galban Garcia, E. Report on the Situation of Hepatitis B in Cuban and Vaccine Research. Paper presented at the III National Congress of Hygiene and Epidemiology, Havana, October 1990.
29. Terry, H., Vice-minister for Hygiene and Epidemiology, MINSAP. Personal communication, March 1990.
30. Llanos, R., sanatorium economist. Personal communication, April 1990.
31. National Department of Health Statistics, MINSAP, April 1990.
32. Centers for Disease Control. Quarterly report to the Domestic Policy Council on the prevalence and rate of HIV and AIDS in the U.S. *MMWR* 37: 223–226, 1988.
33. Terry, H., and Rodriguez, R. Personal communication, 1988 and 1990.
34. Sanchez, S., epidemiologist, MINSAP. Personal communication, 1988.
35. Interviews with seropositive women, 1990.
36. Alvarez Vazquez, L., and Alvarez La Jonchere, C. *Cuba: fecundidad, diferenciales, contracepcion y abortos en zonas seleccionadas*. Instituto de Desarrollo de la Salud, Havana, 1978.
37. Hollerbach, P., and Diaz Briquets, S. *Fertility Determinants in Cuba*. National Academy Press, Washington, D.C., 1983.
38. Rios Massabot, E., National Director of Health Statistics. Personal communication, 1986.
39. Machado, F., Director, National Reference Laboratory, Havana. Personal communication, June 1988.
40. Schwartz, J. S., et al. HIV test evaluation, performance and use. *JAMA* 259: 2574–2579, 1988.
41. Fernandez Yero, J. L. Desarrollo y perspectivas de la tecnologia SUMA en el estudio de pesquisajes masivos. Paper presented at the III National Congress of Hygiene and Epidemiology, Havana, October 1990.
42. Millan, J. C., clinician at sanatorium. Personal communication, 1988.
43. Terry, H. En beneficio de todo el pueblo. *America Latina*, No. 1, pp. 10–15, January 1989.
44. Kraus, M., National Sex Education Working Group. Interview, October 1989.
45. Farinas, A. T. Surveys 1987–1989. In *MINSAP, Programa de controld del SIDA, cronologia 1983–1989*. MINSAP, Havana 1989.
46. Rodriguez, R. Personal communication, 1988.
47. Freudenberg, N. AIDS prevention in the U.S.: Lessons from the first decade. *Int. J. Health Serv*. 20: 589–599, 1990.

CHAPTER 9

We Are All People Living with AIDS: Myths and Realities of AIDS in Brazil

Herbert Daniel

The AIDS epidemic did not take Brazil by surprise. To the contrary, its coming was announced by many—physicians, scientists, journalists, and politicians. The press, more or less following the international news columns, especially those of the United States, had been carrying important items on the subject since 1982. The prevailing mood at the time was one of perplexity tinged with a sense of the exotic. The first reports drew for most of their information on American and European publications, but local stories were also sought. A "scientific" report in *VEJA* on July 17, 1982, told of the research of a professor in Bahia who asserted on the basis of his clinical experience that the infection could be traced to the abuse of injectable feminine hormones and "infected" silicone by homosexuals, at a time when, pursuing a theory of infection by a new virus, French scientists were already isolating LAV (later renamed HIV, human immunodeficiency virus). Needless to say, ideas of this kind, which proliferated at the time, disappeared soon after, swept away by the cleansing action of common sense. Others came to take their place, however, proving that "blaming the victim" is an indelible part of human nature. The press, which fueled most of the public debates, played up the more striking and enigmatic side of the epidemic, and especially the almost direct association the disease seemed to forge between the twin taboos of sex and death. (In its issue of June 15, 1983, *VEJA* carried a feature under the title "O enigma que mata" (The killer enigma). AIDS was depicted as a mystery, something beyond the technological capacity of the modern world, with death as its salient practical feature.)

Originally published in the *International Journal of Health Services* 21(3): 539–551, 1991.

In Brazil, where homosexual society is less organized than in the United States and Western Europe, the fact that AIDS in these regions affected mostly gay men aroused ambiguous emotions that did little to attract either serious or responsible journalism. By about 1983, all that remained was to expect confirmation of the presence of the disease in Brazil, and the press needed only the name of the first "victim" to produce headlines already composed in advance. In 1983, these headlines were printed, as Brazil witnessed its first AIDS case. During this year a veritable upsurge of press interest focused on what was then objectively referred to as the "gay cancer" or "gay plague."

This expectation was not merely sensationalist. There was real concern about the possible impact of the new epidemic. Many alerts were sounded, warnings given, predictions offered, and announcements made. But none of this resulted in any preventive action being taken. No measures were set into motion—especially not by the health authorities—to confront an epidemic that no one doubted would arrive in the country.[1]

The fact that AIDS arrived before AIDS, that is, that the epidemic preceded the disease, actually resulted in the adoption of an inappropriate ideological model that has guided Brazil's responses to the epidemic up to the present. It is the features of this model that I will discuss here. The principal characteristic of the predominant model of AIDS generated in Brazil, and relied upon by the government and the people, is not, I think, that this is a disease of gay men, or of the very poor, but a disease of "others," of strange and foreign people. There would not be any reason to expect that Brazil would follow the American epidemiological model, except for incorrect information and cultural colonialism. The epidemic "seemed to have come" from the United States, thus its model would be a copy of the "American Model." In this way, there was no criticism, either of the characteristics of the model or of its mechanical application. An effort to understand this model is an important part of the effort to dispel some of the myths that have contributed to government immobility and brought suffering and despair to many who suffer more from the imposed model of AIDS than from the terrible effects of HIV.

I speak more than anything else from the standpoint of one who lives with AIDS. I have learned to live with a disease that is not like any formal model. I know that freeing myself from the model has been essential to my own survival, for it was a struggle against legal death imposed by a view that, in other countries as well as in Brazil, makes the person with AIDS a pariah. Important as this is to the individual, I think it is just as important to society to cast off the model and its preconceptions and attempt to integrate into the community the millions of Brazilians who already have AIDS today. But there are millions more who give no credence to the disease because they feel it has no bearing on their daily lives, and

[1] See the Appendix for some background information on Brazil.

they, too, must be protected from it. This stance of solidarity seems to me the best vantage from which to talk about the possible impact of AIDS in my country. I also believe that this discussion is at bottom just one more attempt to answer the fundamental question of our time as we confront the HIV epidemic: How does one live with AIDS?

AIDS BEFORE AIDS

The first impact of AIDS in Brazil was surely on the public imagination. Actually, it arrived in the form of a "feature section" virus (1), which was not without appreciable long-term effects. Indeed, even today, I believe, the predominant ideas about AIDS bear traces of the earliest reactions to the prospect of the epidemic.

Even before any doctor had recorded a single verifiable case of AIDS, the press, especially the yellow variety, was heralding the arrival of the "gay plague" in Brazil as inevitable. A kind of expectation was generated and fanned, and there was even some fatalism. Not a few blew their alarmist trumpets to herald the arrival of punishment for sinners at last! Though there was discussion of how important AIDS could become in a country where public health was catastrophically deficient, and the epidemics of infectious and parasitic diseases had never really been brought under control, the main point is that no one doubted that AIDS would arrive. This epidemic, which was both real and remote, both deadly and sexual, both concrete and mysterious, was discussed as if it were a midway freak, a disease of "others," and not without an irony that frequently flared into the most merciless mockery.

The first banner headline on the "gay plague" in Brazil surfaced in a newspaper called *Folha de O POVO*. This headline was not followed by any actual news story, but rather merely printed as a joke for lack of any event with which to scandalize the paper's readers. The headline read: "Gay plague leaves all the faggots closed-assed"[2] (2). The problems with this headline were notable. To begin with, the wording implied that there was panic among homosexuals in Brazil. There was none. Homosexuals in the large Brazilian cities could scarcely believe at that time that the epidemic could possibly affect them in any way. Second, the irreverence of the press and the unheeded concern of some health professionals, intellectuals, and politicians, and also in a way the indifference of the homosexual community, reflected a conclusion that AIDS was not actually a matter of concern to anyone.

In studying this prehistory of AIDS in Brazil it may be asked why the country did not prepare itself to check the epidemic when it first surfaced, since it was

[2] This headline is written in a vulgar and extremely insulting language. It is quoted in the text specifically for its grotesque humor and for the profound disrespect that is contained therein.

crystal clear that it would become very important here. The new epidemic certainly stirred great agitation; why did this not generate any action? What I will argue is that adopting an abstract and imported model, lacking definitions drawn from actual conditions in Brazil, proved to be a way of doing nothing at all.

Today, almost a decade later, when the cases are counted in the tens of thousands, it is disquieting to observe that there is a kind of collective anesthesia, made evident by the scant interest in AIDS from the new administration that took office in March 1990—as if nothing more could be done in the face of an increasingly disastrous situation. To this day the government has taken no action on the epidemic, continuing the five-year record of inaction and indifference of the previous administration. There is today absolutely no national program for controlling the epidemic. The service set up by the previous administration in the Ministry of Health in 1986, when there were already more than 1,000 reported cases of AIDS, was a symbolic gesture. And so it remains. The idea that AIDS is inevitable, almost a kind of price to be paid for the modernity of our cities, the idea that it is not quite a Brazilian disease but something foreign or strange, has remained almost unchanged from the view that prevailed at that nearly forgotten time when AIDS arrived in Brazil. It is good not to forget what happened then, for we are experiencing the consequences of the attitudes that we took or failed to take at that time.

AIDS IN BRAZIL: A FALSE MODEL IN SEARCH OF "FACTS"

In societies in which modern means of communication predominate, rumor always moves faster than fact. Often, when a fact arrives it is interpreted in the light of a rumor, which manages to become more real than the fact. That is how it was with AIDS. More than once, the truth about this disease in Brazil had to be validated as true by the "model" we had imported from the more industrialized countries of the north. An epidemic was announced that "resembled" the American one; an epidemic was expected that would follow the Western pattern; the preconceived model was looked for in doctors' offices and local epidemiological tables. Since it is not difficult to find the outcome of what an analysis is expected to produce, we ended up with a model that gave us an epidemiological pattern just like that of the first world. In Rio de Janeiro and New York, in São Paulo and San Francisco, it was the same AIDS.

Above all, AIDS came to be regarded as a foreign disease in several senses. First, in the lowest sense of xenophobia: it was a disease of American gays; second, in the sense that it did not fit the pattern of traditional epidemics (if there has ever been anywhere an epidemic that could be described as "traditional"). Absurd as it might seem, this argument was repeated to satiety, even by government authorities, who asserted several times that AIDS was not a priority on the list of the country's common public health disasters.

To these authorities, AIDS at best was nothing more than an epidemic of "minorities," almost a problem of a few rich and well-provided-for homosexuals. So long as AIDS was wreaking havoc only in these allegedly well-defined "risk groups," there was no reason to sound the alarm, no reason to alert that shapeless mass known as the "general public." It is important to note that, according to the official arguments, what made AIDS less important was not that it was a disease of homosexuals but that it was a disease of "rich" people. Several official declarations were released to the effect that according to official statistics the disease in Brazil attacked the upper crust, which flew in the face of the experience of all community groups and health professionals concerned with the epidemic in the country.

It was with the North American's minimal and medical definition of AIDS, disguised in the durable bogeyman costume of the "risk group," that AIDS was first investigated in Brazil. A 1988 study of the first 500 cases reported in Rio de Janeiro showed clearly how the model was generated by the survey's own questionnaire (3). One of the most persistent questions was about "risk trips" (which included trips abroad, chiefly to New York and San Francisco). A "risk trip" was not always reported, but at times the answers were humorous, such as that of a traveler who described as a risk a trip he had made to an extremely placid inland city where he supposedly had commerce with prostitutes. In any event, that the case could be attributed to contagion from outside the country served as some degree of reassurance.

There was considerable difficulty in fitting those first 500 cases into such "risk groups" as, for example, "homosexuals" and "bisexuals." This terminology can scarcely be said to describe the common sexual practices between men in Brazil (4), which present more ambiguities than are dreamed of in the philosophy of an epidemiology borrowed from a society such as that in North America, where there is actually a gay community. The rich Brazilian sexual culture is not easily categorized along the lines established by science, between homosexuals, heterosexuals, and bisexuals, that actually establishes a necessary link of almost cause and effect between desire, the sexual act, and a sexual identity that comes from these. In Brazil, there are much more fluid criteria for establishing sexual identities. Men that have sexual relations, occasional or frequent, with other men continue to consider themselves "men," "heterosexual" and "macho," playing the active role in sexual relations. The social constructions that frame relations between the same sex can only be called "homosexual" from a distance. On the other hand, there is nothing similar to a "homosexual" or "gay" community, in terms of the European and North American models (2, 5–7).

Given these realities, no wonder the questionnaire responses of the first 500 people with AIDS could not be codified easily. Usually the questionnaires were turned in with the space for sexual practices studded with erasures. First a checkmark would be entered in the space for "heterosexual"; then that would be erased and another, clearer checkmark placed in the space for "bisexual," and then a circle drawn around the word "homosexual." And there were also arrows, marks, and lines in different colors and intensities, attesting to the extreme uncertainty of interviewer and interviewee. There was no lack of expressions of dissatisfaction on the part of the interviewers, who in addition to those three words, made a point in entering a "promiscuous" in the case of a homosexual.

In addition, there was also humor, some of it obscure to the interviewers. For example, one patient confessed to promiscuity, to having relations ten times a day, sometimes with cats, monkeys, and parrots.[3] The interviewer was unacquainted with the common parlance of "fairies"—that is, gay-identified men—in Brazil, and missed the patient's joke (8). The result was a fanciful instance of promiscuous bestiality that was actually no more than a colloquial leg-pull.

A remarkable development from this inglorious study began to emerge with the appearance of cases of "heterosexuals" suspected of sexual contagion, in which next to the word "heterosexual" the term "promiscuous" was written in red pencil.[4] The advent of the "promiscuous heterosexual," first seen in early 1987 (though it has not developed any further, since cases of "promiscuous heterosexuals" are much rarer than others), demonstrates the logic of the preconceptions that animate the model. This mystery figure lost interest for the researchers, but the basic idea remained that promiscuity was one of the ways of acquiring AIDS.

Meanwhile, despite the difficulties, the model of AIDS adopted in Brazil continued its undistinguished career of agreeing with the "Western" model. A brutally real situation succeeded in interjecting one specific local feature. As it happened, at least one in five (20 percent) of the AIDS cases recorded in those first five months of the epidemic had been caused by the use of tainted blood or blood products. The issue of blood emerged then as a purely specific feature of the Rio de Janeiro model. This pointed the finger at a traditional public health catastrophe, which was the use of contaminated blood supplied by an immoral trade that controlled the blood market throughout the state. The very magnitude of the numbers and the distribution of those cases in the society refuted the model on which the epidemiological research records were patterned. But it was all viewed as a kind of exaggeration of one particular case, a kind of exception that proved the rule of the "Western" model.

The tragedy that struck hemophiliacs and all other recipients of transfused blood in Rio in particular and in Brazil in general was insufficient to incite a

[3] The expression "cats, monkeys, and parrots" comes from a popular way to identify the family, with all its institutions, through an ironic and allegorical enumeration of all the members, close and distant relatives, and even the prized animals. So this enumeration of the most common domestic animals means, metaphorically, a certain excess, or "a bit of everything." It is almost a way of saying "etc." in a humorous way.

[4] "Promiscuous" refers to persons who have a high number of sexual partners and who do not practice safer sex.

searching reappraisal of our epidemiological methods. It was sufficient, however, to sharply alert the general public to the AIDS situation and generate a considerable mass movement to protect the blood of the Brazilian people, and strong enough even to secure the writing of important aspirations into the Constitution then being voted on. Today it is unconstitutional to trade in blood in Brazil. So far, however, this very well-intentioned law remains unenforced by the public health authorities.

In summary, the adopted model anesthetized awareness of the social problem revealed or exacerbated by AIDS. It continues to function as a camouflage: specific social and human problems can be blamed now on an enigma and a mystery. In the light of this false model, "knowledge"—such as information acquired in medical and epidemiological research studies—becomes pure superstition, and the epidemic continues its course, unfettered.

AIDS AS "SECOND-CLASS" EPIDEMIC

In a perversion of policy, the false model ensured that AIDS would be downgraded to a second-class epidemic, lacking the significance of the great epidemics of history that have never been eliminated. It is clear that nothing has ever been done about those other epidemics. And when it first appeared, and in the years that followed, AIDS was deemed such a small problem that even less provision was made against it.

Today two points stand out when we consider the AIDS situation in Brazil. First is the growth of the epidemic to massive proportions. The growth of the number of cases is beginning to generate complications with regard to the care of people with AIDS, especially because as AIDS starts to become more treatable, the question shifts from merely forced and painful survival—mere lingering in a hospital bed—to the complex issue of LIVING WITH AIDS. And also growing, at a runaway pace, is the number of carriers of the virus who are receiving no care at all and lack even the basic information they need to deal with their own situation. Second, growing alongside the epidemic is the increasing impoverishment of people with AIDS. We live in a country where most of the population is needy and bereft of all social services. It is inevitable that AIDS claims the largest number of people from this majority of the poor, mainly because they have no access to resources—whether material or symbolic: not only no hospitals, but also no education or information to help them cope with the disease.

In a few years we will very probably be speaking of AIDS as a typical third world disease (including the third world pockets in more industrialized countries). It will then be just another "traditional" epidemic. Just as it is now being treated by the authorities in Brazil, AIDS will be viewed as traditional by the world's medical community, a second-class epidemic, and by then the situation will be beyond saving, for, as it says in the Bible, mending cannot be done with old rags.

THE WORLD IS A LITTLE COUNTRY

In Highland County, Virginia, there was a tremendous discussion about AIDS when E. Kübler-Ross wanted to set up a home for abandoned AIDS babies there. Much of the local community opposed the project, which could have hurt tourism, business, and some other Christian sentiments and values I no longer remember. While the controversy raged, the local newspapers received many letters from readers (9). In one of them a woman who was probably very well-informed wrote in block capitals "AIDS IS A WORLD PROBLEM." Amidst all the confused and prejudiced arguments of the local readers, this seemed a breath of the fresh air of wisdom. But the woman went on to ask: "SO WHY BRING IT TO HIGHLAND?"

Where is the world? Where does humanity start? AIDS, as a crisis of world society and the hallmark crisis of modern civilization, actually asks these questions in the most pragmatic way possible.

There can be no doubt that powerful ethnocentric sentiments prompt all societies to blame diseases on others. A familiar case is syphilis, which for Neapolitans is the French disease, and for the French the Neapolitan disease. Examples abound. And AIDS has added to the list of ethnocentric and racist interpretations. This is not the place to discuss the efforts to discover the origin of the virus. Whatever discoveries science may have made, my point is that there was always the certainty that the virus was alien, from outside, that is, from the third world, and before the third world, from the most alien world of all—wildlife, nature. Even when there were no proofs, this was the overriding conviction. The AIDS virus became much stranger after the dispute among scientists over who had discovered it (10). It is well to note that these historical discoveries can clear up some matters, but do not change the story of the epidemic as it is unfolding today. They in no way alter the fact that it began in large cities of the Western world as the epidemic we know today.

In any case, I mention this to underscore the general need to make a disease such as AIDS something necessarily alien, that entered society from "outside," the result of a "foreign" practice. One scientist studying the epidemic in its beginning was certain that American homosexuals had created, in saunas, bars, and other unsanitary sex establishments, a "sexual third world," as he called it, where diseases could multiply freely (11). It must never have occurred to this scientist that this sexual world was patently a product of the first world, of its large cities, of which the metropolises of the third world were only poor imitations.

In reality, the AIDS epidemic is provoking a major economic breakdown, especially in third world countries. Brazil, for example, knows it does not have the means to surmount this crisis. In any case, no country can surmount the AIDS crisis if the epidemic is regarded as nothing more than a health crisis that can be dealt with by efforts put forth by the government and the health system. Nor will we succeed if we cling to the official AIDS model in which pain—both physical and moral—becomes an element of an economy that designates as "society" only those who can produce, and removes from that core of citizenship those who cannot produce yet (children) and can produce no longer (the aged and the sick). In this view, production and the production of profit become the soul and essence of the citizen. Thus the city of men is the city of profit, of the quest for it and worship of it. Human activity for production and reproduction outside this universe of the reproduction of consumer values is not a measurable economic quantity, and hence possesses no real human attributions. The irony is that if we fail to consider these "unmeasurables," the social and economic devastation brought about by AIDS and the response to this epidemic will be beyond reckoning.

If the epidemic is seen as a vast crisis of society, then it is obvious that measures against AIDS must be focused on a clear idea of citizenship and hence of solidarity. To deal with this disease, we must rally major resources in the community. If AIDS is viewed only as a private, "individual matter," or even only as the attribute of "groups," the most that will happen is an effort to provide care in order to minimize the problem. There will be no mobilization of the community so long as the disease is not seen as a global problem, a collective obligation.

From a cold analytical standpoint it might appear that ideas of solidarity are effective merely in a humanitarian sense, an attitude that is more poetic than practical. More than poetic, however, and for good reason, solidarity is primarily a political attitude, a conception of democracy as a day-to-day condition, a definition of citizenship.

Here the effectiveness—or rather the ineffectiveness—of the abstract model adopted for AIDS exposes its economic consequences. First, it does not control the epidemic and allows it to follow a course that will make it impossible to do anything later on except to tally up the losses. Second, the person with AIDS is viewed as legally dead, and all that is left to do is to wait for him or her to die. The relegated sufferer is not enlisted in an effort of primary importance, which is to prevent the epidemic. Surely the mobilization of people who live with HIV is vital (in more than one sense) for lessening the impact of the epidemic on a community. The model discriminates instead of encouraging participation. For these reasons alone, solidarity is a necessary response in this epoch of AIDS.

AIDS AND aids: LIVES BEFORE AND WITH

Who is living with AIDS? At least whoever can be diagnosed as having the opportunistic diseases that result from the immunodeficiency caused by the human immunodeficiency viruses. But since the discovery of the tests, we have known about the seropositive individual who carries the antibodies to the viruses in her or his body and lives with few or minimal symptoms of that long-term infection. Those who may be classed in the general category of virus carriers are many, in the millions (worldwide, the World Health Organization refers to

6 million at the beginning of the 1990s, but also to 10 million (12); we will assume that the figure lies somewhere in between). Many more are linked to these carriers by the most diverse human bonds: they are parents, children, brothers, relatives, lovers, spouses and sweethearts, friends and acquaintances, neighbors or—simply and complexly—CONTEMPORARIES. These are the many millions more that the virus has encountered in its path. Who can say that those people, directly involved as they are, are not living with AIDS? Here I am certainly not talking about a medical definition, but about a very complex social structure that requires a new term to try to encompass the vast field of intended meaning. I am talking about "aids," a common noun that refers to a complex of epidemics with a far wider social impact than a mere diagnosis that may be made on an individual body or even on millions of such bodies.

To determine who is living with aids today is a problem that cannot be solved in the laboratory. No blood test can determine who is living with aids. It can detect antibodies or viruses in the bloodstream, but not the established antibody of solidarity and its varieties—and of its contraries—in the stream of life today. HIV is following its biological course. Another complex of virulences (entering into the game of the usual metaphors of the aids age, we could simply call them ideological viruses) has spread through the social structure of aids, developing it into a three-dimensional photograph of contemporary civilization. Thus, it is no metaphor to assert that, on the planetary scale, humankind is seropositive. It is a historical and political axiom that merits an extensive explanation.

In its medical, epidemiological, and sociological sense, AIDS (used in the broad sense, as covering the whole infectious process caused by the HIV retrovirus) has set off a health crisis without precedent and has thus become the direst challenge to science at the end of the century. Aids, however (understood here as the whole breadth of the social structure that I label with the term in lower case letters), is not a problem of science or health. It is in fact a crisis of society. The terms of the equation that can express it are political and ideological unknowns, and at its root is the complex idea of solidarity.

The AIDS model overlaps with highly distinctive features of modern life: the economic and political unification of the planet, and the sharpness of its economic and political divisions; the physical world is progressively smaller and its social distances ever greater; the change in the power of medicine, in which we are already witnessing the demise of the clinic; the innovation of technologies of power; the new emergence of widespread rights. Human beings have made up a new body and new sex that dwarf the soul of the shopkeeper. It is still hard to determine how many bits there are in a modern soul.

I HAVE AIDS, I'M ALIVE

They say that telling one's story can save lives. Perhaps because it creates an awareness of risk, perhaps because it mobilizes solidarity, and perhaps simply because it breathes life into some benumbed feeling. I have many doubts about that. I am not sure that telling anybody's story is all that effective and redeeming. In my lifetime I have seen that experience itself never educates nor enhances until it has passed through the screen of the critical consciousness. I do not, therefore, aspire to that purpose. I have decided to write about living with AIDS to say just one thing: I'm alive. No, this is not going to help save lives. Not even mine. No, telling the story is not going to help save lives. But it may improve some, or improve life in general. That is why people write, else it would make no sense just to add one's trivialities to the general fund of triviality.

I know that many are telling immensely detailed stories about all the contests that are being waged inside their bodies. Some approach life with the virus as a kind of battle, and know they are going to "lose" the war. I cannot see myself as contending with a biological virus. I do not think I am ever going to lose any war in this way. I am certain, first of all, that aids would defeat me if I entered into the metaphor of war, and then if because of it I made a vain attempt to fool myself or it. AIDS—here I mean the opportunistic diseases that the immunodeficiency caused by HIV allows to supervene—can kill. Certainly it causes many hardships, and can even go so far as to immobilize mc totally or partially for a long time—either temporarily or permanently. But this is par for the course in the disease. It would defeat me not by killing me, but if I abandoned the awareness that I LIVE with it and must adapt to certain circumstances of life imposed by it. This approach to aids (here I mean the complex of its dimensions) enables me to respond to the principal preconceptions that make the AIDS sufferer the favorite decedent of our time.

I do not claim to have a solution for anybody who has to deal with aids, but I am certain that the solution can only be found if those who live with it start to take a hand in solving the problem of the epidemic. As individuals we are very unlikely to find anything to alleviate our burden, though matters become much easier if we are more aware of aids. For those who see AIDS only as a war, the only armistice they can envisage is a cure, which depends on a peace treaty that must be signed by others as well as oneself, since battlefields do not sign treaties. The war unfolds in the form of an effort by physicians contending with the virus and the operation of other more or less sophisticated technologies in the arsenal of that little war.

I am not a battlefield. I am not a landscape, but rather the presence that matters in this landscape that my body has become in this illness. There is no chance for victories or defeats on this field. There are other possibilities—of wisdom or stupidity, love or hate, greatness or meanness, solidarity or persecution.

I am having in my days of life, in these days of my life, in these days of my life in which I have discovered that life is the discovery of fragility, in these days of my life in which life has become a presence that is not pornographic or obscene in any way (to the contrary, it is always on stage, like a good actress who steals many of the best scenes), I am having the life that the day offers and I am able to live—with an avidity not at all uncertain but certainly undirected, like a hunger that should have started a millennia ago if I had only known millennia ago the millennial pleasures of each second that the intensity of the living moment provides and prepares.

THE WORLD OF LIFE—ALMOST THE END

The extraordinarily weighty argument of the woman of Highland County inevitably reminded me of a Woody Allen film in which a child suffering from anxiety is taken by his mother to a psychiatrist because of his strange ideas. The child is bewildered because it has discovered that the universe is expanding. Its mother scolds it and tells it that it has nothing to worry about because Brooklyn is NOT expanding.

I do not live in Highland. I have always lived in countries—if I ever lived in any—where the world's problems happen at my doorstep, at the end of my street, within a radius of 100 meters around my navel, inside my threshold. I have always been in places where the world's problems have always intruded upon me not just through the window of the television set or the diffident pages of the newspapers. These problems have taken immediate form in real people and the inevitable movements of things and beings around me. They have become real coalescences of the whole planet within my own body cells.

I am a citizen of the third world, but I am certain that Highland is not far away. Highland is today, and everywhere. It is a little town deep in the state of Rio de Janeiro where a young woman who had been the domestic servant of a homosexual was "accused" of having AIDS and then of spreading her virus by mixing her blood in the children's ketchup in supermarkets. It is a little town in the Northeast where a homosexual was driven out under several charges, including that of having been seen "touching several fruits at the open-air market" with the obvious intention, as his accusers charged, of spreading the plague through the tropical fruits. Highland is in the downtown area of the cosmopolitan city of São Paulo, where O Grupo pela VIDDA (Group for the Value, Integration and Dignity of the Person with AIDS), of which I am a member, encountered enormous difficulty in renting a room for its headquarters, because its members have AIDS. Highland is one of the places where the AIDS epidemic is at its worst—with the tactic of making the epidemic a coldly economic matter of health. Highland, which that woman wanted to keep uninvolved with the world aids problem, is one of the innumerable capitals of the epidemic in the world. Highland is within us. This is the treatment of our distress and of our defeat by the epidemic of emotional plagues of our time.

I am taking inventory of a collective pain. The pain becomes laceration when fertilized in the garden of indifference, in the landscape of intolerance.

Highland, in the end, is Brazil as well, where the "dead" die more often than the rich, and will die of AIDS much faster than the rich. Where we have no sure count of the number of AIDS cases because the figures are not just muddled, but falsified as well (13). Where we do not know what AIDS is doing because there are no surveys. Where people with AIDS die at the doorsteps of hospitals that were neglected during the years of the authoritarian military regime and are today powerless to cope with the catastrophic breakdown of public health throughout the country. Where the people do not believe in AIDS because the information they receive refers to a metaphorical disease that is full of mysteries. Where even today it has yet to be PROVEN even to gay men that there is such a thing as an AIDS epidemic, and not just a CIA plot to wipe out all gays, or a device of the newspapers to encourage their persecution. Where there is need to educate physicians who know nothing about the disease, and teachers, prelates, and authorities, to make them see that AIDS is not a punishment from heaven. Where $200,000 worth of AIDS test materials are thrown out because they have passed their expiration date, where another unspecified quantity of AZT,[5] also expired, is discarded because it was all bought by the Ministry of Health but got lost in the corridors of the blasted bureaucracy. Where people die of opportunistic infections for which there are no available cures because of bureaucratic problems in the importation of experimental drugs by scientists and physicians. Where no legal aid of any kind is provided for people with HIV, and the legal department of an organization such as O Grupo pela VIDDA has to handle the legal affairs of hundreds of persons in order to defend basic legal rights acquired by the population decades ago, at least on paper, and especially in matters of employment. Where citizenship is regarded as a luxury, and the carrier of the virus is condemned to a silent form of legal death with the kind complicity of the government authorities. Where health authorities say in the press that AZT should not be purchased for patients in public hospitals because "they're going to die anyway."

But this is also a country where thousands of people rally heroically in community organizations without funds or support so there will be more than just despair. I am writing a testament not only of pain, not merely of compassion. In speaking of those who are holding on, of the revolt of dignity, I must say that every string of calamities adds to the outline for a strategy of solidarity. The world is everywhere. And the better world is the better one we will build in our hearts by making our arms into roots, and linking ourselves each to the other.

A response on behalf of LIFE entails programming ranging from funding to meet the material needs of a growing population, to the mobilization of social and human resources to guarantee the full exercise of those people's rights as citizens. Aids cannot be spoken of as a problem ON the planet. The epidemic is a fact OF the planet. This fact is a part of the struggle for the "defense of life." The fight against aids is an ultimate democratic political aim on the same order of

[5] AZT, azidothymidine, is increasingly used to treat AIDS and is beginning to be given to people who are infected by HIV but are not symptomatic. A year's prescription for AZT in the United States costs a minimum of $3,000 to $5,000.

importance as the defense of life on the planet. The issue of human rights, viewed in its larger dimension as a broad democratic matter calling for the practice of solidarity, is the greatest challenge of the 1990s, mainly in countries such as Brazil, where democracy is still a very fragile plant.

We are living and learning with AIDS and with aids. We can infect every country on the planet with the most extreme and inexorable epidemic known to humanity: LIFE. Let us hope that this will be our great economic impact, so that in the coming century we may be remembered as more than just contemporaries of infamy—as the precursors of a world in which the human condition is not just the triumph of the absurd. There are still millions of stars of flesh to surprise the most cosmic moments of love.

LONG LIVE LIFE!

APPENDIX

Brazil, with approximately 150 million inhabitants, covers a very large territory, with pronounced regional differences. Since the end of the Second World War, an important and modern industrial reserve has been developed. Presently, the country has much natural raw production, a strong industrial output, despite the crisis of the 1980s, and plentiful natural resources. It cannot be said that it is a poor country, quite the contrary—it is a rich country inhabited by a very poor population. Although it is among the largest industrial economies of the world, Brazil has the third worst index of income distribution. The country also suffers greatly from an external debt of approximately $120 billion, the greatest in the third world.

From 1964, Brazil was dominated by a military dictatorship that instituted a model of economic growth that centralized income and put the country in the worst crisis of its history. The slow democratic opening that has been witnessed since 1985 has not yet resolved any of the most severe social problems of the country. The country is investing less and less in health service. There was a gradual abandonment of the public health care network and an intense privatization of health services during the military regimes, which together led to an enormous deterioration of all services. The majority of the population does not have basic care. So, the country has been affected by all the illnesses that characterize industrial and urban development, without ever having resolved the health problems that are tied to economic decline and underdevelopment.

It is said that in the Brazilian heart beat both myocardial arrest and Chagas' disease (trypanosomiasis), in the stomach are found both hunger and gastric ulcers. The situation is so serious that the incidence of illnesses such as Hansen's disease (leprosy), tuberculosis, Chagas' disease, and malaria is increasing at an alarming rate. In the most developed part of the country, in the Southeast, principally in Rio, epidemic outbreaks of meningitis are frightening the population, as is the emergence of a dengue epidemic and hemorrhagic dengue, which is particularly lethal.

REFERENCES

1. Carrara, S. Um Virus So nao Faz Epidemia (A single virus does not make an epidemic). *Communicacoes do ISER* (Rio de Janeiro) 4: 17, December 1985.
2. Daniel, H., and Miccolis, L. *Jacares e Lobisomens, dois ensaios sobre a homosexualidade, Rio*. Achiame, 1983.
3. Guimaraes, C. D., Daniel, H., and Galvao, J. *O Impacto Social da AIDS no Brasil* (The Social Impact of AIDS in Brazil). Associação Brasileira Interdisciplinar de AIDS, 1989.
4. Parker, R. Acquired immunodeficiency syndrome in urban Brazil. *Med. Anthropol. Q.* 1: 2, June 1987.
5. Fry, P. *Identidade e politica na cultura brasileira, Rio de Janeiro*. Zahar Ed., 1982.
6. Fry, P., and MacRae, E. *O que homosexualidade, São Paulo*. Brasiliense Ed., 1983.
7. Trevisan, S. *Devassos no Paraiso: a homosexualidade no Brasil, da Colonia a stualidade, São Paulo*. Max Limonad Ed., 1986.
8. Fatal, P. *INVICTA, AIDS Aqui*. GAPA/RJ, Rio de Janeiro, 1988.
9. Kübler-Ross, E. *AIDS, O Desafio Final*. Editora Best Seller, São Paulo, 1988.
10. Leibowitch, J. *Um Virus Estranho de Origem Desconhecida* (A Strange Virus of Unknown Provenance). Record, São Paulo, 1984.
11. Grmek, M. D. *Histoire du SIDA*. Médecine et Sociétés Payot, Paris, 1989.
12. World Health Organization. Update: AIDS cases worldwide. *Weekly Epidemiol. Rec.*, July 1990.
13. *Boletim da ABIA*, 2, 3, 4. Associção Brasileira Interdisciplinar de AIDS, 1989.

CHAPTER 10

Global AIDS: Critical Issues for Prevention in the 1990s

Jonathan M. Mann

The identification of critical issues for HIV/AIDS in the coming decade is based on an assessment of the pandemic (including predictions for the 1990s) and an evaluation of experience in prevention and control during the past decade. From the viewpoint of late 1990, the pandemic remains volatile, dynamic, and unstable. HIV (human immunodeficiency virus) infection, now estimated to involve at least 8 million people (5 million in Africa, 2 million in the Americas, 0.5 million each in Europe and Asia), is continuing to spread in already affected areas and is spreading, sometimes slowly yet relentlessly, to areas of the world previously unaffected or little involved in the pandemic. The conservative World Health Organization estimate for the 1990s suggests a tripling of the number of new HIV infections during the 1990s compared with the 1980s, along with a tenfold increase in new AIDS cases (of which about half will represent persons already infected during the 1980s) (1). This prediction must be considered conservative, especially in view of the spread of HIV in Southeast Asia during the period 1988–90.

The global effort to prevent HIV infection is unprecedented and remarkable, yet also dramatically inadequate. In October 1987, AIDS was discussed at an extraordinary session of the United Nations General Assembly, marking the first time a specific disease was considered by the world's highest political institution. In January 1988, a World Summit of Ministers of Health on AIDS Prevention assembled the largest ever number of ministerial delegations (over 100) to discuss AIDS programs (2). By late 1988, national AIDS programs, developed in

Originally published in the *International Journal of Health Services* 21(3): 553–559, 1991.

collaboration with the WHO Global Program on AIDS, had been initiated in virtually all countries.

The community, national, and international effort against AIDS has shown that social and political commitment could be rapidly mobilized in response to a new health threat. Innovative and creative programs also demonstrated that prevention can be accomplished through information and education, when linked with specific health and social services, and carried out in a climate of tolerance and nondiscrimination (3). The oft-cited experience in San Francisco merits its own renown, even if more recent data suggest a rise in recidivism regarding safer sex practices (4). In a group of gay men whose exuberant lifestyle led many to doubt the possibility for substantial behavior change, the full and courageous commitment to education, services, and nondiscrimination led to a rapid decline in the incidence of new HIV infections, from over 10 percent annually in 1980–81 to less than 1 percent by 1986 (5).

Yet the full and sustained application of these programs and policies has been beyond the capability of most communities and countries around the world. Incomplete or inadequate HIV prevention programs reflect most commonly a failure to obtain sufficient, or sufficiently sustained, social and political commitment to AIDS. Denial of the realities of the HIV/AIDS pandemic, at the personal, national, and international levels, has been a severe and persistent problem. As a result, even in the most severely affected areas of the world (e.g., sub-Saharan Africa, Thailand, the Caribbean, the United States), official policies and commitment on AIDS stops substantially short of a full mobilization of available resources.

This chapter proposes critical themes for the future of efforts to prevent HIV infection by considering areas that will require fundamental changes. From this perspective, it is assumed that many specific challenges of AIDS will be met through application of concepts, resources, or strategies that have already been developed. For example, the scientific quest for a vaccine to prevent HIV infection will likely succeed, through the further development of existing approaches or new approaches within the existing research effort. However, several challenges can be identified that seem highly unlikely to be resolved, or even adequately addressed, without more fundamental changes. In each instance, the deeper change required has involved concepts and values, yet these ideas will also require social and political will for successful implementation. In each instance, it is the power of ideas about individuals and society, rather than the development of new technologies, that appears critical.

From this perspective, critical issues for prevention during the 1990s can be grouped under three headings: behavior, societal action, and globalism. Two topics under "behavior" include study of risk behavior and behavior of those involved in the AIDS prevention effort. "Societal action" refers to collective behavior regarding HIV/AIDS, and under the heading of "globalism," solidarity and human rights will be discussed.

BEHAVIOR

Behavior, individual and collective, is already, and will increasingly become, recognized as the major challenge for public health in the future. To illustrate with a possibly counter-intuitive example, the challenge of protecting the global environment is fundamentally a problem of human behavior. While knowledge about how the internal combustion engine generates exhaust that is transformed into photochemical smog is important, the more basic questions involve social attitudes about driving, economic issues about how the workforce and workplace is organized, and political philosophy. Human behavior is the key to protecting the rainforest, dealing with toxic wastes, and, to restate the obvious, preventing nuclear war. It is one of the glories of our generation that we have seen and learned that technology, no matter how elaborate or sophisticated, is ultimately subject to human behavior; Three Mile Island and Chernobyl both illustrated the ultimately critical importance of the so-called "human factor."

In seeking to prevent HIV infection, enormous effort has been devoted to studies of "risk behaviors." The application of existing epidemiological methods to the study of HIV infection has yielded substantial information about those behaviors that are linked with risks of HIV transmission (6). In addition, studies have more recently identified several biological factors (e.g., genital ulcer disease, other sexually transmitted diseases, stage of illness in the partner) that strongly influence the likelihood of HIV transmission during a risk behavior (7). More recently, attention has been given to the social, economic, and political context within which risk behaviors exist (8). Collectively, these epidemiological studies have created a coherent view of HIV transmission, for application by those working to prevent HIV infection.

However, for purposes of HIV prevention, a sufficient understanding of risk behaviors has not yet been developed. The existing model of behavior upon which these studies are ultimately based is highly deterministic and linear. The deterministic model of sexual behavior disaggregates the presumed steps or elements of decision-making on sexual behavior, each of which is presumably susceptible to quantitative measurement. Yet the study of behavioral determinants of risk behavior, using standard concepts and classical methods, may have reached its limit.

This crisis in conceptualization of individual behavior has been provoked by the HIV/AIDS pandemic's insistent focus on sexual behavior. The urgent need to consider sexual issues related to HIV prevention unveiled a stunning level of ignorance regarding sexuality in most if not all societies. From the practical viewpoint of those responsible for HIV prevention programs, a critical gap has emerged between available information and information needed to design effective interventions to prevent sexual transmission of HIV.

In the confrontation between knowledge developed within existing frameworks for study of sexual behavior and the practical demands of HIV/AIDS prevention programs, a major catalytic element is awareness of substantial unpredictability, and uncertainty, about sexual behaviors. The relative simplicity of the behavioral measures collected through surveys of knowledge, attitudes, and practices (KAP surveys) conflicts with the intuitively felt complexity and dynamic quality of sexual life. For example, how well do existing models take account of changing environmental or situational factors? A heterosexually monogamous man may behave differently (seeking sex with men or women) during a business trip abroad; a willingness to exchange sex for money or goods may vary with prevailing economic conditions; sexual behavior of a newly divorced person may differ substantially from predivorce patterns; and finally, the details of seduction, sexual approach, and negotiation about sexual acts (including condom use) remain unobserved and unobservable through use of existing concepts and measurement techniques about sexuality.

Therefore, to advance further, detailed observational studies and innovative concepts and methods will all be required. In such cases, innovation often results from application of methods or ideas from other disciplines; in this case, the emerging concepts of "chaos" in the physical sciences may offer insight into the kinds of observational studies and research that can seek patterns in apparently unpredictable events (9).

At the individual level, the chaos model suggests an alternative to applying simple deterministic rules to behavior prediction. Observations of what seem to be unpredictable actions may lead to identification of the nature and power of forces that affect individual sexual practice. However, a second level of analysis will also be required, for individual behavior cannot be understood in isolation from its social, economic, and political contexts.

At the social level, it may be important to study the forces that act to alter societal sexual behavior patterns dramatically, leading to accelerated HIV transmission (as in physics, a stable current of fluid running through a channel can become chaotically turbulent as a result of relatively minor changes in the channel). There is field evidence that rapid changes in HIV incidence, both accelerating and decelerating, can occur in the absence of known explanatory factors. For example, recent observations in sub-Saharan Africa include the apparent stabilization of HIV prevalence in populations of Kinshasa, Zaire, at a level of 5 to 7 percent (10), which is relatively low considering the rate of increase documented from 1980 to 1984. In contrast, continuing rapid increases in seroprevalence are documented in Senegal (11) and in Côte d'Ivoire (12).

The challenge is clear: a revolution in epidemiological study of behavior may be required to close the gap between available information and the information on behavior that is needed for HIV prevention.

The second area of behavior that may require fundamental conceptual change involves the people involved in HIV/AIDS work. The first generation of AIDS experts and activists has been joined by a second; the basic challenge is to maintain high levels of commitment and creativity, while ensuring sufficient "institutionalization." This problem is particularly evident in the many non-governmental, community-based organizations that have arisen in response to AIDS. After the first few years, management skills may be increasingly important for the survival of the founders' ideals. Strategic development of the people working in AIDS programs, including innovative ways of preventing burnout and linking different organizational skills without sacrificing personal commitment and creativity, is a major challenge.

With increasing experience, AIDS-focused community organizations are recognizing the complexity of HIV/AIDS prevention and care issues. This awareness has led to efforts to seek alliances within the health and social community, as when the major umbrella organizations for AIDS groups in the United States developed a highly successful linkage with other agencies seeking social justice for all categories of disabled persons. In this manner, a highly desirable law against discrimination toward disabled persons was passed through a coalition; the legislation included, but did not focus exclusively upon, concerns of HIV-infected people.

It has also become clear that different nations have varying tolerance and ability to foster strong and diverse community-based responses to a health problem such as HIV/AIDS. The linkage between community-based response and political structure may provide important insight into social organization.

SOCIAL ACTION

Societal action is the second area that may require a fundamentally new approach. Public complacency and denial about the realities of the slowly (sometimes not so slowly) growing HIV/AIDS pandemic threatens the social and political commitment needed to confront AIDS. Denial has been a consistent and enduring phenomenon in this pandemic, in every country. In most countries, a consistent pattern has been observed, involving relative denial by the political leadership, in contrast to expressions of action and activism among community-based groups. As a result, the locus of action on AIDS has shifted the balance of initiative toward the community and away from the national government. While this development has useful implications for meeting short-range health and social service needs for HIV prevention and care, the longer-term consequences of a widening separation, not to say divorce, between communities and national political leadership remain uncertain. From an optimistic viewpoint, community-based organizations' attitudes on health may act to change dominant political paradigms and narrow the distance between health realities and public policies.

However, there is evidence that complacency is increasing worldwide. Political attention is being drawn away to other, often pressing social issues, and budgets for national or international HIV/AIDS prevention and care are stabilizing, rising slowly or actually declining. The need to develop sustained commitment is clear;

collective complacency and denial must be better understood and strategies to address these threats to continuing commitment to HIV must be developed.

GLOBALISM

Finally, the question of globalism is paramount for the future effort to prevent HIV infection. Globalism has several dimensions, but can be summarized as a need for solidarity and a respect for human rights and dignity.

Solidarity is fundamentally different from charity. Charity is ultimately optional, an appeal to good works in the sharing of resources. Solidarity is based on the understanding of interdependence and a recognition that excessive differences among people create a fundamental instability for the entire system. Solidarity in 1990 requires a community and a global orientation, for the objective conditions of the modern world involve transcendence of national boundaries (1).

In more practical terms, solidarity requires that the gap must be reduced between rich and poor (within and between countries) in their capacity to prevent HIV infection and to reduce the personal and social consequences of HIV infection and disease. Paradoxically, scientific progress has exacerbated this gap, for the new advances in early diagnosis and management of HIV infection and disease (e.g., zidovudine, aerosolized pentamidine) are virtually unobtainable and unaffordable, and therefore essentially irrelevant to most of the world's population that could benefit from these agents. Looking to the future, it will be essential that when (or if) an AIDS vaccine is developed, it be designed with the concept of the "world population in need" in mind, rather than being conceptualized to meet only the "market demand."

Solidarity is based on objective conditions of the modern world, in which the quantitative increase in movement of people and goods has transformed the cliche of the "global village" into a reality. However, solidarity is also founded on the unifying and universal principles of human rights and dignity. The Universal Declaration of Human Rights, unanimously adopted by the United Nations General Assembly in 1948, provides the formal expression and definition of human rights. Since 1948, key international covenants and conventions have refined and expanded on these basic principles. Thus, through the work of many dedicated individuals and organizations, the world today can understand and promote human rights in a conscious and consistent manner.

Experience in HIV/AIDS prevention and care during the past decade has demonstrated the relevance of human rights to health. Discrimination and prejudice appear to reduce the effectiveness of HIV prevention programs, by discouraging those most in need of prevention support and services from participating in prevention programs. In addition, those discriminated against, in any society and for any reason, are usually socially marginalized. As a result, they may be at increased risk of HIV infection, for a number of reasons: diminished access to health and social services; less influence on educational program development and resource allocation; and reduced social, economic, and political ability to take appropriate measures to protect against HIV infection. Therefore, discrimination and denial of human rights and dignity is a double threat to HIV prevention and to public health. The recognition of this linkage between human rights and health is a major advance in the history of society and health (1).

Of course, there is a basic unity or harmony among the concepts developed in this chapter: behavior, solidarity, human rights, and globalism. The essential message about the future of AIDS prevention and control is that the major challenges cannot be separated from the major public health and social issues of our time. It is often said that HIV/AIDS is a disease that reflects our modern world; equally, the way out of the crisis of AIDS is linked inextricably to the social, economic, and political evolution of our world. President Havel of Czechoslovakia has demonstrated and written about the "power of the powerless" and the strength of people who are determined to "live in truth" (13). These concepts, like those of globalism, solidarity, and respect for rights and dignity, may seem idealistic or unrealistic, or simply "weak"; yet these ideas have torn down seemingly insurmountable walls and barriers.

As we carry forward our daily work and establish our plans for the next year and the next, we should not lose sight of the vision of solidarity and human rights that gives our struggle against AIDS its human meaning and its individual and global message.

REFERENCES

1. Mann, J. M. Global AIDS into the 1990s. *J. AIDS* 3: 430–442, 1990.
2. World Health Organization. *AIDS Prevention and Control: Invited Presentations and Papers from the World Summit of Ministers of Health on Programmes for AIDS Prevention*. Pergamon Press, Oxford, 1988.
3. Mann, J. M. The global picture of AIDS. *J. AIDS* 1: 209–216, 1988.
4. Stall, R., et al. Relapse from Safer Sex: The AIDS Behavioral Research Project. Paper presented at the Sixth International Conference on AIDS, San Francisco, June 21, 1990.
5. Winkelstein, W., et al. Homosexual men. In *The Epidemiology of AIDS: Expression, Occurrence, and Control of Human Immunodeficiency Virus Type 1 Infection*, edited by R. A. Kaslow and D. P. Francis, pp. 117–135. Oxford University Press, New York, 1989.
6. Heyward, W. L., and Curran, J. W. The epidemiology of AIDS in the United States. *Sci. Am.* 259: 72–81, October 1988.
7. Padian, N. Heterosexual transmission: Infectivity and risks. In *Heterosexual Transmission of AIDS*, edited by N. J. Alexander, H. L. Gabelnick, and J. M. Spieler. Wiley-Liss, New York, 1990.
8. Coates, T. J., et al. Behavioral factors in the spread of HIV infection. *AIDS* 2(Suppl. 1): S239–S246, 1988.
9. Gleick, J. *Chaos: Making a New Science*. Penguin Books, New York, 1987.
10. Quinn, T. C., et al. AIDS in Africa—an epidemiological paradigm. *Science* 234: 935–963, 1986.

11. M'Boup, S., et al. Emergence of HIV-1 in a High Risk Group from an HIV-2 Endemic Area (Senegal). Paper presented at the Sixth International Conference on AIDS, San Francisco, June 22, 1990.
12. Soto, B., et al. AIDS in Côte d'Ivoire: Progression of the Epidemic in West Africa. Paper presented at the Sixth International Conference on AIDS, San Francisco, June 21, 1990.
13. Havel, V. *Living in Truth.* Faber & Faber, London, 1987.

SECTION V

The Histories of AIDS

Introduction

Nancy Krieger

AIDS is a disease that continually challenges conventional approaches to understanding and preventing disease. From the start, AIDS appeared as an anomaly. First diagnosed in the United States, one of the richest nations on earth, AIDS was a new infectious ailment that contradicted all predictions of public health policy. At a time when biomedical institutions and the public health agenda were increasingly oriented to managing the chronic diseases of an aging population, AIDS felled young people—and especially young gay men. It raised the specter of a quickly spreading lethal disease, bringing to the fore fears of a plague like the epidemics of what had seemed the distant, and unrepeatable, past. Upsetting fundamental notions of "progress" as well as of propriety, AIDS thrust upon the public and public health professionals the uncomfortable awareness that current policies were inadequate to deal with this upstart disease.

To gain a better understanding, some turned to history to make sense of this new disease (1). History, it seemed, could serve as a guide: lessons from the past could be invoked to prevent errors in the present. Public health professionals, legal scholars, and AIDS activists visited and revisited the questions of quarantine and other methods of control of mass infectious diseases. In the media, discussion of past epidemics inevitably turned to the one central to popular accounts of disastrous disease: the bubonic plague, which devastated the population of Europe in the 14th and 15th centuries.

The invocation of history as a guide to action was not—and has never been—a simple matter of straightforward analogies. The two chapters that comprise the final section of this book thus explore the ways in which the history of AIDS has been cast and recast—with reference both to diseases of the past and to modern disease paradigms.

Chapter 11, "Thinking and Rethinking AIDS: Implications for Health Policy," by Elizabeth Fee and Nancy Krieger, critically examines the emergence and features of two paradigms that have been widely used to comprehend AIDS: the paradigms of AIDS as "gay plague" and, more recently, as "chronic disease" (2). The authors argue that although adoption of the chronic disease model may have helped counter some of the problems of the plague paradigm, it nonetheless has adversely affected the fight against AIDS. At issue are the ways in which the chronic disease model promotes individualistic and "lifestyle"—rather than structural—analyses of disease causation and further emphasizes the management of illness rather than the prevention of disease. Urging the adoption of a more comprehensive framework, the authors contend that AIDS must be understood and approached on its own terms: a disease that is at once communicable and chronic, requiring urgent efforts to interrupt its transmission as well as ensure adequate care of those already afflicted.

In Chapter 12, "Understanding AIDS: Historical Interpretations and the Limits of Biomedical Individualism," Fee and Krieger extend their analysis of the different historical constructions of AIDS. They dissect how the paradigms of AIDS as "gay plague" and as "chronic disease" have each been influenced by the typically unstated and reductionist assumptions of the biomedical model. This model presents disease as fundamentally a matter of cellular pathology, devoid of social context. Treating individuals as independent and statistically equivalent units, it ignores issues of power and fails to consider how people's membership in groups defined by their society's economy and culture inevitably shapes their experience of health and disease. Noting that the inadequacies of the first two constructions of AIDS become especially evident when considering the realities of AIDS in other regions of the world, where AIDS is neither a particularly "gay" disease nor one that has the luxury of being deemed "chronic," the authors describe some emerging approaches to understanding and preventing AIDS that seek to move beyond the limitations of the biomedical approach. They conclude by arguing that AIDS prevention strategies will succeed only if they confront the simplistic assumptions of the biomedical model.

Together, the chapters in this section make clear that the history of AIDS is neither a simple listing of chronological events nor an inevitable consequence of the biological properties of HIV. Instead, the ways in which we understand—and anticipate—the course of the epidemic are profoundly affected by our prior conceptions about other diseases, both those of the past and those that afflict us now. Although much remains uncertain about the long-term future of the AIDS pandemic, one conclusion is apparent: we can neither afford to rely only on conventional strategies for controlling disease nor continue to elevate biomedical interventions above all others and treat prevention as a second-class endeavor. To survive AIDS, we will have to formulate more effective prevention strategies, a task that will require developing new approaches for understanding disease, new research agendas, and new research methodologies. The history of AIDS is ours to make, not just interpret, and we can only improve our work by becoming critically informed about—but not constrained by—past and present approaches to comprehending and improving the public's health.

REFERENCES

1. Fee, E., and Fox, D. M. (eds.). *AIDS: The Burdens of History.* University of California Press, Berkeley, 1988.
2. Fee, E., and Fox, D. M. (eds.). *AIDS: The Making of a Chronic Disease.* University of California Press, Berkeley, 1992.

CHAPTER 11

Thinking and Rethinking AIDS: Implications for Health Policy

Elizabeth Fee and Nancy Krieger

The history of AIDS does not simply present itself as a chronological succession of events. It is a history that necessarily is constructed and that cannot simply be inferred from the biological properties of HIV or the pathological realities of disease.[1] The history of AIDS is a human affair, and is part of a cultural process of attempting to come to terms with a new and often terrifying series of events—of young people dying before their time, of the intermingling of sex and death—in a period in which the world itself is changing before our eyes and stability is an unlikely dream.

Centered on the bodily experiences of illness and death, the social meaning of the history of AIDS intimately touches upon our ideas about sexuality and societal divisions, social responsibility and individual privacy, order and instability, and above all, health and the prospect of happiness. Understanding how we respond to AIDS, how we think about this epidemic, is consequently important not only for what it reveals about the ways in which health policy is created, but also for what it implies about our ability to meet the challenge of future emerging diseases and longstanding public health problems. By thinking and rethinking the

[1] In this article we refer to AIDS as a disease and also to HIV-related diseases. The pathological events initiated by HIV, including the destruction of the immune system, are appropriately designated as a single disease process. This in turn permits the expression of various opportunistic infections and other disorders (e.g., Kaposi's sarcoma), which have been part of the changing case definition of AIDS elaborated by the Centers for Disease Control. These latter infections and conditions are referred to as HIV-related diseases. This somewhat confusing terminology is itself part of the historical process of the scientific construction and definition of disease.

Originally published in the *International Journal of Health Services* 23(2): 323–346, 1993.

history of AIDS, we may thus be able to deal more effectively with a larger array of unsolved health issues.

Within the United States, we see three main phases in the construction of the history of AIDS, with each having very different implications for health and social policy. In the first, AIDS was conceived of as an epidemic disease, a "gay plague," by analogy to the sudden devastating epidemics of the past; in the second, it was normalized as a chronic disease, similar in many ways to diseases such as cancer; in the third, we propose a new historical model of a slow-moving, long-lasting pandemic, a chronic infectious ailment manifested through myriad specific HIV-related diseases.

THE FIRST HISTORY: AIDS AS PLAGUE

At first, AIDS had no history. A strange set of events occurred that were, for the most part, ignored. Some apparently healthy young men exhibited rare opportunistic infections and then died; only a few physicians and epidemiologists were aware that something extraordinary was happening. Noticing that several of the young men were homosexual, the epidemiologists gave the phenomenon its first name, gay-related immunodeficiency disease (GRID). The epidemiologists became fascinated by an apparently exotic lifestyle that included drugs (poppers) and large numbers of sexual partners. As the numbers of reported cases grew, the disease began to acquire its social identity as a new epidemic, a "gay plague" (1, 2).

The dawning recognition of a novel disease, a "gay plague," touched two central social ideas. One was the idea of homosexuality as a social, political, and medical problem; the old association of homosexuality with disease was resurrected and reinforced in cultural perception. But even more powerful was the idea of a new epidemic disease. AIDS shocked the western medical world, appearing as a throwback to an earlier era of infectious and fatal epidemics. AIDS seemed to appear out of historical context, at once entirely new, but also old; it properly belonged to a distant and less comfortable past, before economic and scientific progress had combined to banish the ancient plagues. People in the western world had become familiar with a "modern" pattern of chronic diseases, a familiar litany that began with heart disease and cancer and included a long list of disagreeable but nonfatal illnesses. The chronic diseases were associated with aging, and many considered them the characteristic ills of affluent societies (3–5).

Mass infectious diseases had ceased to command the attention of health policy analysts in the advanced industrial world; for the most part, they were firmly relegated to the third world as diseases of underdevelopment. Even there, the worldwide eradication of smallpox seemed to suggest that it was but a matter of time, organization, and resources until the major infectious diseases would be eradicated. AIDS challenged this hubris, together with the assumption that the late 20th century division of diseases into infectious and chronic disorders naturally fitted an economic and geographic distribution, with the chronic diseases appearing in highly industrialized nations and serious infectious diseases in the less developed countries. AIDS appeared at first as a disease of the United States, Western Europe, and Australia. A disease of unknown origin, a silent, fatal infection that killed young men in the prime of life, it seemed to be associated with societies of affluence and perhaps even hedonism (6). AIDS, it was true, quickly appeared rampant in Africa, but there it appeared in a different guise—as a disease of heterosexuality and of poverty. There was some connection between the two, but it seemed to many that the phenomena of AIDS in Africa and America were quite distinct. At the same time, Americans suspected that AIDS had been born in Africa; the idea, once publicly discussed, was indignantly rejected by Africans. Nations were busy blaming each other for an epidemic that none wanted to claim (7).

As the statistics on AIDS cases mounted, its identity as an inescapable "plague" seemed confirmed. It appeared to mimic the frightening epidemics of the past: cholera, yellow fever, leprosy, syphilis, and the Black Death. The history of AIDS—the history that seemed relevant to understanding the new epidemic—would be the history of the epidemics of the past (8, 9). This somewhat arcane branch of medical history suddenly gained new social relevance; policy analysts, lawyers, and journalists all wanted to know whether past epidemics could provide some clues to the contemporary crisis. How had societies attempted to deal with epidemics in the past? The contemporary meaning of the plague was read in the face of AIDS (10).

This first reading of the history of AIDS accurately captured and reflected the fear and confusion surrounding the disease. It also provided a frame of reference for talking about the many ethical, legal, and health policy issues it raised. The history of plague implied, for example, a history of quarantines, and quarantines for those with AIDS was, at least in some circles, a serious policy proposal (11–15). The history of most past epidemics (at least as read by liberal historians) suggested, however, that quarantines were more an expression of social distress and fear than an effective measure for controlling disease (16, 17).

The new historical approaches to AIDS prompted by the plague analogy examined such contemporary issues as social discrimination against those groups perceived as the purveyors of infection: in past epidemics, those so stigmatized had been prostitutes, the poor, or minority racial groups; they had been Jews, or Irish, or Italians. The unreasoning prejudices of the past now seemed to be reflected in contemporary social discrimination against gay men and intravenous drug users. To a considerable degree, the history of past epidemics was read as a cautionary tale of the health and social policies that should *not* be adopted in these more enlightened days.

The perception of AIDS as a devastating epidemic discontinuous with the immediate past fed into the millenarian tendencies of the late 20th century. The relatively stable organization of social conflict in the postwar era was dissolving into uncertainty; the capitalist world was mired in economic crises, recession, debt, bank failures, long-term unemployment, and the collapse of an older industrial base; the communist world was fragmenting into a series of political, economic, and national crises that succeeded each other at breathtaking speed; environmental degradation and global warming seemed to many to threaten the final destruction of an exploitative world order. Popular books announced the "end of history" and the "end of nature" (18, 19). AIDS fed this late 20th century sense of overwhelming catastrophe and continuing apocalypse (6).

In this context, the infectious disease paradigm of equilibrium disturbed and paradise lost took on new meaning. Many who were ecologically minded viewed humanity's meddling with technology as having disrupted the niches of natural organisms, thus creating the possibilities for transmission of new diseases (20, 21). Conversely, conservative social commentators saw the problem not so much as one of technology but as one of deviance. They viewed the disease as the revenge of nature on liberal society and appealed to a lost world of "traditional values" and a more stable and authoritarian order (13; 22, p. 48).

The growing sense of crisis, fanned by a sudden outburst of media attention and by the ever-climbing statistics of those ill and dying, aided the widespread adoption of the historical metaphor of an inexorable "plague." The language of plague, of crisis, of epidemic was in turn adopted by a gay community that organized to demand social and political attention to the disease, financial resources to care for those affected, accelerated scientific research to develop a cure and preventive vaccines, and mass public education to help prevent further transmission of infection. In the face of seeming societal indifference, gay activists demanded a "War on AIDS," thereby adopting the military metaphor often used by government to indicate that it takes a problem seriously enough to devote significant financial resources to its solution (6, 23). (Thus, we have had a "war on cancer" and a "war on drugs" but not yet a "war on homelessness" or a "war on illiteracy.")

The growing sense of crisis eventually permeated the levels of the federal government, and money began to fuel a massive scientific effort first to identify and then to understand the viral mechanisms of the disease. With the new flow of funding for research, scientists readily turned their attention to the race for discoveries. The view of AIDS as epidemic fed scientific competition between laboratories and nations; the competition for research funds was encouraged by the perception that large profits would reward those able to produce the laboratory tests, vaccines, and pharmaceuticals so urgently needed to address the disease. The scientific competition to unlock the secrets of AIDS seemed at once more intense, more glamorous, and more hopeful than the long struggle to deal with diseases such as cancer. Infectious diseases were believed less intractable than chronic ills; the media waited breathlessly to announce new scientific breakthroughs.

In 1983, those waiting were rewarded with the announcement of the discovery of the viral cause of AIDS, not once but twice—by both French and American researchers (20, pp. 47–82). This is not the place to recount the international dispute that followed, nor the political compromise by which France and the United States agreed to share credit for the discovery and to divide the considerable royalties from the patented HIV diagnostic test (20, 24). Mirko Grmek's (20) account is persuasive, but for our purposes here, it is sufficient to note that the discovery of what would be called, by international agreement, HIV would transform both the scientific and the public perception of the epidemic. The identification and naming of the viral cause of AIDS seemed to offer the first real hope that it could one day be controlled.

The Health Policy Implications of the First Paradigm

The plague analogy reflected social fears and also helped fan them. A crisis mentality marked by panic and confusion had surfaced; angry parents pulled their children from schools where HIV-positive children were enrolled. Health departments closed gay bathhouses, describing them as a locus of contagion. Newspapers and magazines, including some prominent medical journals, published accounts that suggested the entire population was at threat, that AIDS could perhaps be spread by mosquito bites, by household contacts, or by kissing (25–27). Careful epidemiological statements about the unlikelihood of infection by casual contact failed to pacify much of the population who wanted definitive assurance that they and their families were not at risk. People began to fear infection from restaurant and service workers, from their coworkers in offices, and from public toilet seats. In this atmosphere of panic, many people with AIDS lost their jobs, their apartments, their health insurance, and even their friends (28). The mounting statistics being reported by the media suggested an exponential increase in cases and deaths, the inescapability of the epidemic, its potential spread from defined risk groups to the "general population," and the conviction that the fragile and burdened health care system would soon be overwhelmed.

The escalating public sense of crisis had met with government indifference to a disease that was killing gay men; the Reagan administration was already committed to cutting taxes and social expenditures, reducing health care costs, and turning over health and safety regulations to private enterprise (29). The confrontation between the Washington policy establishment and gay community and public health leaders prompted many to become involved in demonstrations, lobbying, and the creation of alternative services and clinics. The previous organization and growing sense of self-identity and power of the gay community in cities such as New York and San Francisco were now channeled into the struggle to redefine national policy so as to address the emergency.

The sense of emergency could work two ways: to generate funding for AIDS services and research or to make a case for Draconian methods of prevention and social policies of exclusion. In the first instance, the perception of a sudden, time-limited epidemic was used to justify the funding of AIDS services by taking money from other budgets, such as those for Native American health services and for other sexually transmitted disease programs (30, 31). Such transfers meant that overall health expenditures could be contained; the money for AIDS was only a temporary measure—until the emergency passed. In the second instance, immigration policies, requiring the exclusion of those who were HIV-positive, harkened back to an older conviction that diseases came to America from outside and could be avoided by identifying and refusing to admit the sick. Within the cities most affected, gay communities coped with the dying while conservative commentators pronounced the disease God's retribution on the sinful (31, p. 18). Within the state of emergency, relatively simple methods of prevention were developed to promote condoms and clean up the blood supply.

The emphasis on AIDS as a sexually transmitted disease and the consequent social and epidemiological interest in the sexual practices associated with viral transmission produced an extraordinary new willingness to discuss sexual activities in graphic terms, at least within scientific and health policy circles.[2] Public discussion of sexual transmission was more guarded, with some of the pronouncements about transmission through the exchange of bodily fluids so vaguely worded that the populace was probably more confused than enlightened by the information.

Despite the cautious approach to public description of sexual activities, AIDS did bring new kinds of visibility to the gay community. For the first time, large numbers of gay men (and women) were seen on television screens and in newspapers and magazines talking about AIDS, lobbying, fundraising, and articulating alternative views. Health policy was, for perhaps the first time on such a large scale, being made outside the usual professional circles. Professional boundaries became permeable as people with HIV- related diseases declared themselves de facto experts and began the process of renaming themselves, redefining their illness, questioning medical authority, criticizing government spokespersons, demanding new and more appropriate services and more effective drugs,

[2] One can, for example, trace the increasingly explicit use of language within the august pages of the *American Journal of Epidemiology*. Compare the clinical but quasi-graphic listing of sexual practices in the article by A. R. Moss et al. in 1987 (32)—oral insertive, oral receptive, swallow semen, oral-anal insertive, oral-anal receptive, rectal insertive, rectal receptive, urine exposure active, urine exposure passive, manual-rectal insertive, manual-rectal passive, use of dildos insertive, use of dildos receptive, douching—with the exhaustive listing of sexual practices in the article by R. A. Coates et al. in 1988 (33)—mutual masturbation, primary inserts penis in contact's mouth, primary ejaculates in contact's mouth, contact inserts penis in primary's mouth, contact ejaculates in primary's mouth, primary inserts penis in contact's anus, primary ejaculates in contact's rectum, contact inserts penis in primary's anus, contact ejaculates in primary's rectum, primary inserts finger in contact's anus, contact inserts finger in primary's anus, primary inserts tongue in contact's anus, contact inserts tongue in primary's anus, primary inserts object in contact's anus, contact inserts object in primary's anus, primary inserts hand in contact's anus, contact inserts hand in primary's anus.

and insisting on both their rights to confidentiality and their rights to public expression and influence (34). The gay community refused the diagnosis of "promiscuity" as the problem and insisted upon "safer sex" rather than celibacy. Taking responsibility for AIDS as a disease, they also refused the language of guilt and innocence and claimed a more scientific and more humanitarian view of the epidemic as the problem of containing a virus while protecting the interests of those already infected.

The Problems of the First Paradigm

The sense of AIDS as an immediately catastrophic epidemic, a sudden, unexpected, and disastrous return to a vanished world of epidemic disease, began to change in the late 1980s. People were not, in fact, dying as rapidly as had initially been predicted. It became clear that there was a long latency period; people lived with HIV infection for 10 to 12 years, and it was not the sudden killer it had at first been perceived to be. The sense of immanent epidemic was diluted because a relatively low proportion of the population was ill. One may, for example, contrast AIDS to the influenza epidemic of 1918 when 20 percent of the population became ill, of whom 2 to 3 percent died (i.e., 0.4 to 0.6 percent of the total population); now 0.1 percent of the population had become sick over a ten-year period (35). Once the first series of shocks over AIDS had passed, the society, like many of those infected, was learning to live with AIDS (36).

In the first epidemic of fear of AIDS, a tactic of many of those arguing for increased resources to be devoted to the disease had been to stress the fact that AIDS was not limited to the homosexual community but potentially threatened the whole population. If it had struck the gay population first, this was merely a contingent fact; AIDS in Haiti and in Africa was a heterosexual disease, and its spread to the "general population" was just a matter of time. The crisis could not be contained in gay bars and bathhouses but would soon spill out into America's suburbs, schools, and churches. The death of movie idol Rock Hudson in 1985 was, ironically, taken by many in the United States to mean that "anyone" could get the disease; for the first time ever, President Reagan spoke about AIDS (37, 38).

With the passage of time, however, the warnings about a brushfire epidemic had come to seem overly alarmist. The disease had indeed spread, but not in any perceptible way to suburban havens; instead, it had spread to inner city minority populations and specifically to those using injectable drugs and their sexual partners (39). Despite anecdotal newspaper stories about wealthy young white women who had contracted the infection, the epidemic had not deeply affected worried white communities but was largely contained within the several well-defined risk groups.

The transmission of HIV did not, after all, follow the plague model. Diseases like plague spread very easily, whereas it had become clear that transmission of

HIV is quite difficult. It requires direct contact between people, usually by choice or else by the anonymous but still intimate exchange of blood through transfusions. Once the blood supply had been made safe and people had been made aware of the need for caution in having sex or sharing drugs, AIDS began to be perceived as potentially containable. The population, initially hoping for a miracle cure, had been repeatedly told that a vaccine would take at least ten years to develop; people were thus learning to accept a longer time frame for the disease.

Another reason for a diminished sense of an epidemic emergency was the discovery of some apparently effective palliative treatments and the promise of more experimental therapies to come; there was now some prospect of hope for those infected. Hospitals, clinics, and other health care institutions were working out new ways of providing services for AIDS patients; the disease was no longer such an anomaly and was becoming a more routine and expected sector of health care delivery.

Perhaps most importantly, the groups affected were themselves refusing to look on the disease as a death sentence. Numerous people with AIDS (PWAs) were surviving for many years and were vociferously insisting that the previous emphasis on dying be replaced with a new more optimistic focus on "living with AIDS," with attention directed at those who were HIV-positive but not ill, and those who had symptoms but were nonetheless capable of enjoying life, working, participating in their communities, and experiencing a wide range of emotions and pleasures. They did not want to be locked into a politics of fear and rejected being labeled as the "victims" of disease.

Within the gay community, and to some degree the population at large, the emphasis on safer sex now became a long-term strategy for a long-term disease; health education programs continuously stressed the fact that the virus could not be casually transmitted, and this understanding lessened the immediate panicked reaction to those infected. The resistance to testing decreased as the tests could now be linked to some prospect of aid; if infection were diagnosed early, medical care and pharmaceuticals could help. The availability of palliative therapy, most notably AZT, then placed AIDS into the larger pattern of chronic diseases with their emphasis on screening and early intervention and, at least for some, the potential management of long-term disease.

THE SECOND HISTORY: AIDS AS A CHRONIC DISEASE

The second history is therefore the conceptualization of AIDS as a chronic disease. In this history, AIDS became normalized and appeared as one more chronic disease that had to be managed, as part of the usual way of doing business. This is a history that was constructed—and could only be forged—in relatively wealthy industrialized countries, such as the United States and Western Europe, that could afford to provide health services for other chronic conditions.

Central to this new history was a view of chronic diseases as maladies that either are not infectious or else are not easily transmitted, develop over a long period of time (with changes that can usually be detected by screening), entail a lengthy period of illness and associated use of health services, are not easily cured, and are often fatal in the long run. Classic examples include hypertension and other cardiovascular diseases, diabetes, and many types of cancer. Although anomalies have long been acknowledged—for example, cervical cancer may be linked to a virus; a myocardial infarct is an acute and often immediately fatal event (40)—the category of "chronic disease" nonetheless has been useful, particularly from the perspective of those who must live with these diseases and the people and institutions responsible for providing health services.

In the second history, the metaphors of war and balance retreated into the body and became internalized. Images abounded of the immune system as the body's "defense" against "external invaders," with a new array of pharmaceutical agents forming welcome auxiliary forces (6, 41, 42). The new emphasis on treatment and on "living right" in order to live with AIDS harkened back to older, humoral notions of equilibrium (43); popular self-help books on AIDS are replete with reminders about the need to manage stress and to live a "balanced" life, with a "balanced" diet, adequate sleep, and appropriate exercise (44–47).

Outside the body, the call for a "war against AIDS" was directed toward new therapeutic discoveries and became a front for societal inaction in preventing the spread of AIDS. Like the "war against drugs," the official "war against AIDS" (at least in the United States) bolstered the status quo; just as government funds poured into law enforcement agencies and prisons while programs to combat poverty and rehabilitate prisoners languished (48, 49), so too were federal monies increasingly directed toward prestigious and profitable clinical trials while Congress fought over the allocation of Ryan White funds for community-based AIDS services and prevention campaigns (50–52).

As a chronic disease, AIDS was to be contained within its boundaries, like a sore that festers but does not spread. In the United States, its history included sharp debates over whether AIDS could "break out" and create a widespread "heterosexual epidemic" (53, 54), as opposed to remaining within the communities of the dispossessed—gay men, injection drug users, hemophiliacs, the poor, and people of color, in all their intersecting permutations. Ensconced ever more firmly as a disease of "others," AIDS found its niche in the inner cities (55, 56), and as a "chronic disease" became yet another marker of chronic social inequalities that could be tolerated as long as only those "others" died.

The Health Policy Implications of the Second Paradigm

In the second history of AIDS, attention turned to the ability of the health care system to deal with this new chronic disease. Health policy professionals reasserted their expertise in a familiar domain (50), and succeeded in at least partly closing out the voices of the gay community and others newly entering the AIDS arena, for example, the African-American community, women with AIDS, and advocates of needle exchange (57). With budgets and scarce resources at stake, accuracy in estimates became paramount. Costs of care were calculated and recalculated (58, 59), while tallies of the number of persons infected with HIV were revised downwards (50, 60). Increasing numbers of hospitals developed specialized AIDS units, a sign of the institutionalization of the disease (50).

Attention and funding also shifted toward developing new treatments. Reacting to these changes, many AIDS activists plunged into political battles to speed the release of approvals for experimental drugs and to demand new, more inclusive protocols (61–63). Others continued to fight for improved health coverage and against discriminatory practices by the health insurance industry (64).

The emphasis on treatment also led to a rethinking of questions about HIV testing, including the conflict between individual privacy and mandatory reporting (65–69). Ethical objections to testing people when nothing could be done to ameliorate their health status lost their clout, and were replaced by arguments that people should—or must—be tested for their own good. With fears about casual transmission relatively assuaged, new concerns surfaced about the possible threat posed by long-living, asymptomatic HIV-infected persons whose jobs routinely involved exposure to other people's blood, as in the case of surgeons and dentists (70–73). Reminiscent of earlier, more hysterical "plague"-like debates about the likelihood of improbable transmission scenarios, the debate about infected health care workers nonetheless belonged to and epitomized this second history of AIDS: people infected with HIV were not simply going to vanish through early deaths, and instead had to be reckoned with from the long-term vantage point of managing chronic diseases.

The Problems with the Second Paradigm

The shift from a "plague" to "chronic" disease model involved much more than the recognition that people infected with HIV and ill with AIDS may require health services for an extended period of time. Each paradigm of disease carries its own assumptions, concerning such basic issues as etiology, prevention, and treatment. Although framed in biological terms, these assumptions nonetheless have a strong social core that cannot be divorced from broader social attitudes about individual versus societal responsibility for health.

In the case of AIDS, adopting this new paradigm did far more than direct our attention to issues not anticipated by the plague model. It also introduced all the fundamental assumptions and inadequacies of the chronic disease model itself. Because most chronic diseases are considered noncommunicable and because their etiologies typically are obscure, the conceptualization of AIDS as a "chronic disease" inadvertently undermined the sense of urgency required to sustain societal efforts to prevent HIV transmission. To reiterate the obvious, AIDS *is* a communicable disease whose transmission *can* be prevented; this basic fact is deemphasized by the chronic disease model. Moreover, much of the scientific research around chronic diseases focuses on disease mechanisms and not disease origins; it emphasizes screening and treatment over prevention, and prevention itself typically is framed as an individual responsibility (74). In the usual pattern for chronic diseases, the primary concern is with managing the symptoms of the ailment (and possibly curing the disease, if feasible); once appropriate remedies are found, concern about etiology and prevention recedes. This pattern may be seen, for example, in the cases of hypertension, diabetes, and cancer. The question becomes how to stop the growth of a tumor once it starts or how to lower lipid levels once they rise, rather than how to prevent the initial onset of disease. This pathological orientation may be good for the pharmaceutical industry, but it does little for primary prevention.

To the extent that prevention is discussed, the strategies proposed for most chronic diseases are thoroughly individualistic and rarely challenge the conditions of the production of disease (75–78). Not only is disease prevention translated into the realm of individual effort, but the only actions typically considered are those that can be implemented by solo individuals. Little attention is accorded to possible disease prevention strategies to be used between persons with unequal power, such as consumers versus food producers over pricing policies or workers versus employers over occupational hazards. This orientation reflects the dominant view of individuals as isolated atoms, rather than as persons who necessarily are carriers of the social relations of class, race, and gender that permeate the society of which they are a part (79). It is also far easier to counsel individuals about what they should eat (and blame them for poor choices) than to get the food industry to change the production and promotion of "junk foods," just as it is much less controversial to encourage people not to smoke than to try to prevent the growing of tobacco or to curb air pollution. Intended or not, these attitudes toward the causation and prevention of chronic diseases now affect our thinking about AIDS and, if not addressed, threaten to vitiate our still inadequate response to the HIV epidemic.

Perhaps not surprisingly, our approach to AIDS already has begun to be influenced by these troubling features of the chronic disease model. With the identification of HIV, scientific interest shifted to the laboratory and the gaze turned inward, to the actions of HIV within the body (1, 50). Relatively less attention was devoted to understanding the complex societal factors affecting the social production and reproduction of the epidemic. Social and scientific rewards go to those who successfully examine the mechanisms of disease within the body. It is also less politically controversial to look inside cells than to investigate the political economy of inner cities, the war on drugs, prostitution, and the oppression of gays, women, and people of color.

Another common assumption built into the chronic disease model is that most chronic conditions have a multifactorial etiology, but the diseases themselves are specific and typically are characterized by the organ they affect (e.g., heart disease, ovarian cancer). Moreover, most of the exogenous exposures contributing to their etiology are viewed as ubiquitous or containable, and not easily eliminated (74, 80). Nor can the endogenous factors, such as genetic constitution or hormonal milieu, easily be altered—although the challenge of doing so remains a major spur for much biomedical research today (81).

The consequent notion of "balance" between the host, agent, and environment that informs the chronic disease model is much more accepting and pessimistic about the long-term presence of etiologic agents than is the paradigm for infectious diseases. In the latter, the agent is perceived as a noxious invader whose attack signals the rupture of a prior equilibrium enjoyed by the host and environment; removing the agent and restoring lost innocence becomes the goal. In the chronic disease model, however, the focus is less on preventing exposure to or eliminating the agent than on the adaptation of the host to life with the agent. The objective becomes elucidating how the mechanisms of the host's body can be altered or modified so as to deal better with the presence of the agent. Obviously, adopting such a framework for AIDS could well be lethal.

Given the assumption of ubiquitous etiologic agents (both exogenous and endogenous), the key research question in the chronic disease framework becomes why some people are susceptible while others are not (81). This in turn has led to a vigorous search for genetic markers, a trend now emerging in AIDS research as well (82). To the extent that susceptibility is thought to be mediated by "stress" rather than solely by genes, much of the emphasis in the chronic disease paradigm is on alleviating people's reaction to stress, rather than eliminating either the stress itself or the noxious exposure (80, 83). It is easier for public health workers to modify people's responses to existing conditions than to challenge the "balance" of the status quo responsible for these conditions. Even in those instances where the exogenous agent is deliberately manufactured, greater priority is given to containment rather than eradication, as exemplified by the emphasis on "permissible exposure limits" over product substitution in occupational health (84, 85). And, consonant with this orientation, more and more of the research on chronic diseases is being directed toward factors primarily under the control of health care professionals, ranging from the efficacy of patient education to iatrogenic illness. The ultimate message is that the best way to change health is to alter aspects of the health care system itself.

Certainly, not everyone concerned about chronic diseases has this narrow approach to their prevention, management, and treatment (75, 78, 86). A minority public health voice is challenging the acceptance of social conditions that contribute to current levels of chronic disease. Emanating from the ranks of environmentalists, occupational safety and health advocates, opponents of tobacco and of alcohol abuse, and nutritionists, to name a few, its proponents have called for such measures as enhancing the regulatory and punitive powers of EPA

(Environmental Protection Agency) and OSHA (Occupational Safety and Health Administration), enacting bans on smoking in public spaces and workplaces as well as increasing taxes on tobacco and alcohol products, and altering incentives to encourage food producers and retailers to market healthier foods at lower prices (86, 87).

Even so, most of the emphasis in chronic disease prevention remains targeted at "lifestyle" risk factors, and especially at encouraging consumers to reduce their exposure to nonessential exogenous agents, such as "junk food," tobacco, and excessive alcohol and dietary fat. This strategy, moreover, works best with people who have disposable income and leisure time to read and deal with the multiplying instructions about how to keep healthy—not to mention living in safer neighborhoods, buying more expensive foods, and joining health clubs (74, 88). Conversely, it has been least successful when prevention efforts require challenging social relations as they really are, as exemplified by the persistence of diseases of poverty and those due to occupational and environmental health hazards.

Perhaps the best illustration of the weaknesses of the chronic disease model as a guide for health policy is provided by the history of anti-tobacco initiatives. In many ways, tobacco is the smallpox of chronic disease—it is the one agent that can be eliminated and that can be aggressively fought by public health professionals, precisely because it is a nonessential product. As such, it is the exception that proves the rule. Insofar as smoking was seen solely as something that individuals inflicted upon themselves, much of the public health effort was devoted to educating people about the hazards of tobacco (in great part by affixing warnings to tobacco products and advertisements) and to individualized smoking cessation interventions that only rarely succeeded. Efforts to encourage crop substitution were half-hearted at best, and tobacco corporations faced only minimal pressure to diversify their holdings. Only when tobacco-related chronic diseases were redefined as "communicable," courtesy of second-hand smoke and the recognition that passive smoking constituted a health threat to nonsmokers, did the public debate and its policy implications change radically (89–91). Prevention efforts dramatically gained in strength and finally were able to restrict the use of tobacco in the public sphere.

In sum, when we adopt the classic chronic disease model, we effectively embrace what might be termed a postmodern public health policy, with all of its trappings and flaws. In this postmodern world, one caught up in the fragmented dazzle of the global market that reaches everywhere, people are seen to exist only as passive consumers, not active producers, their lives a pastiche of splintered identities constructed from the random output of our "information age" (92). With the death of the author comes the end of accountability, and the defeat of the belief that systematic change can be achieved. Instead, priority is accorded to the productions of the media, which reign supreme as the ultimate symbol and purveyor of a "free choice" that isn't.

This too is the condition of contemporary chronic disease policy. Oriented to the market and the media, it consistently offers individuals the chance to choose between preselected options about how to live better, even if these choices typically are beyond the grasp of those who most need a change. Declarations on the need for prevention serve primarily as commentary upon, rather than concrete challenges to, the social conditions that give rise to disease, both chronic and acute, communicable and noncommunicable. Only in its refusal to cede "expert" status to members of the "lay public," and its desire to employ nonoverlapping, noncontradictory categories (for example, "infectious" versus "chronic"), does this paradigm retain important yet problematic vestiges of its "modern" origins.

At a time when AIDS has already been designated as the first "postmodern" disease (93), and has provided the text for reams of commentary and reflection upon contemporary society, it is particularly important that AIDS prevention policies not succumb to the fatal logic of the chronic disease model as construed in our postmodern world. We cannot accept an approach that cleaves the categories of "communicable" and "chronic," that insists on an "either/or" logic when "both/and" thinking is required. The failures of containment policies for communicable diseases already abound, as evidenced by the growing epidemic of drug-resistant tuberculosis, itself linked to the HIV epidemic (94, 95), by the reappearance of cholera in the western hemisphere (96), and by the rise of measles due to insufficient funding to cover the cost of vaccination (97, 98). Nor have individualistic strategies succeeded in reducing the incidence of most noncommunicable chronic diseases. It is time for another approach, and time to forge another history of AIDS.

THE NEED FOR A NEW PARADIGM: AIDS AS A CHRONIC INFECTIOUS DISEASE AND PERSISTENT PANDEMIC

The third history begins with the recognition that neither of the first two histories of AIDS—as gay plague and as chronic disease—adequately reflects the complex realities of HIV-related diseases. Indeed, AIDS challenges all of our categories. If a plague, it is a peculiarly slow-moving plague; if a chronic disease, it is a notably communicable chronic disease. The standard assumptions surrounding the categories of infectious and chronic diseases thus fail to capture the multiple dimensions of AIDS.

These are not merely semantic objections. The words matter. We propose that a more adequate conceptualization of AIDS must be based on the fact that AIDS is a chronic infectious disease. Neither of these terms, "chronic" or "infectious," can be eliminated or ignored. Their order is, moreover, important from the point of view of prevention and policy. By calling AIDS a chronic infectious disease (rather than an infectious chronic disease), we emphasize the aspects of etiology, transmission, and prevention as opposed to clinical management.[3] Indeed, we might well term AIDS a collective chronic infectious disease in order to emphasize the inadequacies of dealing with AIDS from a purely individualistic perspective; AIDS is, above all, about people in personal and social relationships. And by calling AIDS a persistent pandemic, we emphasize both the long time frame of the disease and its global impact. Changing our historical construction of AIDS thus means changing the policies we perceive as relevant, and our sense of the time frame for developing interventions and preventing disasters. At issue is the urgent need to overcome the limitations of current ways of rigidly dichotomizing so-called "infectious" and "chronic" diseases, for if we cling to outdated categories and approaches, we will undercut our efforts to prevent and ease the burdens of AIDS.

In moving toward a new paradigm, we need to acknowledge that the old categories of infectious versus chronic disease that prove problematic in dealing with AIDS break down in many other places as well. The distinction between infectious and chronic disorders provided the basis for an important polemic in the 1940s and 1950s, when epidemiologists and public health officials were persuaded that their older emphasis on infectious diseases was inadequate to the apparently noncommunicable chronic ills that afflicted the populations of the more developed world (99, 100); although that polemic was successful, the categories now serve as much to impede as to promote thinking about disease. Elizabeth Barrett-Connor (40) has already argued that the distinction is arbitrary and is detrimental to understanding the epidemiology of a wide variety of diseases. By cleaving the two realms, the traditional categories barely admit the possibility of chronic infectious diseases (such as tuberculosis and herpes zoster) and also suggest that we are somehow to think differently about latency, transmissibility, etiology (especially unifactorial versus multifactorial), and behavioral risk factors for "infectious" versus "chronic" diseases, thereby skewing the research questions asked and policies proposed.

The different orientations to time inherent in the infectious and chronic disease models have quite different implications for disease prevention policies. The older plague model fostered a general attitude of crisis, including Draconian approaches to prevention; the chronic disease model expanded the time frame but turned attention away from prevention toward disease management. The third and more inclusive model implies that we need long-range strategies for dealing with the disease, including more effective methods of prevention over the long haul as well as providing care and social support for those already infected and those already

[3] The terminology of "infectious chronic disease" places a disease in the general category of chronic illnesses, with the term "infectious" used as a modifier. By contrast, "chronic infectious disease" highlights the infectious character of the disease, modified by its chronic or long-term features (of both latency and period of infectivity). Our taxonomy thus draws attention to the etiology, mode of transmission, and possibilities for prevention rather than the more usual focus on pathology.

sick. It acknowledges, like the earlier plague model, the extraordinary disruption and devastation produced by an infectious disease that afflicts people in their prime productive and reproductive years. At the same time, it offers a less pessimistic approach for people who test positive to HIV since it implies that a positive blood test is not an immediate death sentence but the sign of a major problem that must be dealt with and lived with for many years, with adequate social services, counseling, and health care.

As we begin to develop these programs, we must recognize the failures of prevention in the traditional infectious and chronic disease models. On the infectious side, for example, the reemergence of tuberculosis shows that, while it is important to find drugs effective against pathogenic organisms, these may only provide a temporary respite, perhaps lasting for several decades, before old problems reassert themselves. Effective drugs should be used to buy time to address the social context of the production of disease, not merely be developed as ends in themselves while the social context of disease is ignored. People in the health field need to understand that we cannot expect to address all of our ills within the health care system; planning for prevention should not be focused on a single-minded search for a technical fix.

Our approaches to prevention of the noninfectious diseases have also been too narrowly conceived. Too often the framework of prevention has merely been to persuade individuals to become more educated consumers and to desist from consuming hazardous products. More and more community-based interventions are now challenging this limited approach (101–103). In occupational and environmental health, for example, community-based efforts have proved far more successful than individualized interventions. In the case of AIDS, community-based safe sex campaigns, needle exchanges as a community endeavor, mass leafleting of bars, and community health outreach workers are proving considerably more effective than earlier individualized approaches (55, 104).

Beyond this, AIDS has repeatedly demonstrated that people cannot be dealt with as isolated individuals as they are in both the infectious and chronic disease models, but must be addressed as members of particular communities with historically determined identities. Within the gay community, much thought and creativity has gone into the development and promotion of safer sex practices. But cultural patterns of cruising and sexual anonymity are directly related to historic patterns of discrimination (22); a longer-term strategy for preventing transmission of sexually transmitted disease must include the effective implementation of anti-discrimination statutes. By affecting both the character and institutions of same-sex sexual encounters, AIDS may well have long-term effects on the politics of identity within the gay community; just as identity politics were largely a reaction to social discrimination, so the weakening of discrimination can open up more political options (and diversity of social experience) within this or any other affected group.

The forms of male sexuality related to AIDS transmission are certainly not restricted to gay men; they are forms of male sexuality that have long been celebrated and promoted, and they are culturally reflected and reproduced in our ideas of masculinity, our child-rearing patterns, and the constant selling of sex as a commodity. We are also only beginning to come to terms with the hidden world of bisexual married men who are invisible to most AIDS programs, yet are crucially important for disease transmission precisely because of the levels of secrecy involved. It is also important to consider the needs of those men who have sex with other men but do not view themselves as part of the gay ("white") community. It may be more effective to reach them through churches, minority organizations, and trade unions, and to conduct outreach efforts in bars, truck stops, and areas known for prostitution. Within the more restrictive approach of marketing safer sex, sex stores and sex videos have begun the enterprise of making safe sex sexier, and condom manufacturers have started to develop more innovative condoms in a variety of colors and tastes (105).

The overwhelmingly individualistic biomedical orientation of the infectious and chronic disease models and their typical disregard for the particular health status of racial/ethnic minorities in the United States also has distorted our understanding of the full epidemiology and reality of AIDS. Much of the early writing about AIDS, for example, ignored its prevalence and unique characteristics among people of color. Patterns of homosexuality and heterosexuality are not, however, cultural givens; they have different social constructions within white and minority ethnic communities, and these differences need to be understood and appropriately addressed (106–110). Given the multiple social and economic difficulties that many of these communities face, the specific problems of AIDS need to be approached within an understanding of the issues of employment, education, housing, economic development, and the struggles against the drugs that are flooding inner city communities. Needle exchange programs, for example, should be allied with drug treatment programs and other initiatives that offer some hope for an alternative to long-term drug dependence (111, 112). Most of the issues that are critical for people with AIDS, such as housing and health care, are widespread problems throughout these communities.

The epidemiological categories of "risk groups" that are firmly embedded in the infectious and chronic disease models have also tended to mask the class basis of many health issues. AIDS and HIV-related diseases are no exception. Official AIDS statistics, for example, report cases classified by age, gender, race/ethnicity, and mode of transmission and do not provide any information on poverty or social class (113). The invisibility of class in the official data mirrors the invisibility of class in public understanding and public policy. For their part, most trade unions have not had AIDS education on their agendas. A few unions are, however, now starting to take up issues in AIDS eduction; the Service Employees International Union (SEIU), for example, recently broadened its needle stick injury prevention program to include general educational materials about safer sex and AIDS (114).

As we move away from thinking solely in emergency terms and in terms of static, individualistic "risk groups," with the health experts in charge of strategic planning for AIDS, it should be possible to develop more coalition-based planning and policy making by involving unions and community-based, minority, and gay organizations (115).

Similarly, the problems of AIDS among women have only recently received much attention (116, 117) with the lag attributable, in part, to the predominance of narrow constructions of AIDS. To date, women with AIDS have tended to be ignored and left out of programs because they did not fit easily into gay male groups, because their symptoms and constellation of infections did not fit Centers for Disease Control (CDC) guidelines, or simply because AIDS programs were specifically designed for men (118–121).

Just as AIDS shows the inadequacy of mutually exclusive categories of infectious and chronic diseases, so too it challenges the traditional distinctions and separations between maternal and child health, women's reproductive health, pediatrics, and infectious diseases. AIDS crosses all the boundaries and, especially for women with AIDS, the boundaries themselves are part of the problem of gaining access to care and social supports for themselves and their children. There are, for example, virtually no detox programs that will take pregnant women or women with children.

The traditional assumptions around chronic disease care involve a family structure in which women are available to provide care for a sick family member. The chronic disease model rarely deals with the familial incidence of disease or situations in which several generations within one household are affected by disease at the same time. In the case of AIDS, mother and children may all be ill; we are also seeing a new generation left orphaned at an early age (122, 123). Such a situation requires new forms of care for children and attention to the total impact of disease on the household, not simply on the sick individual.

AIDS also poses the issue of women's reproductive rights in dealing with disempowered women whose ideas about childbearing may not fit those of their physicians or other health professionals (124–127). Women with AIDS and women who use drugs have found their reproductive rights restricted in every possible way. On the one hand, the opposition posed between the rights of the mother and the rights of the fetus has led to generally punitive attitudes toward any mother who fails to abide by the increasingly rigorous standards of healthy motherhood; on the other hand, women are punished because of social resentment of the financial demands that they and their children may make on society (128). One response to the numbers of infants with AIDS has been to deny women's rights to bear children; health care professionals often assume that any pregnant woman with AIDS should have an abortion. The presence of disease does not, however, abolish a woman's right to control her body, nor does it mean that all women want to end childbearing. Women who want to have children despite HIV infection need to be supported in this choice through the provision of health care for themselves and their children; they are likely to need counseling, access to child care options, and assistance with housing. Coming to terms with these questions in the case of AIDS may prepare us for the many issues raised by the genetic screening tests that will soon be available to detect a multiplicity of genetic disease markers (129). In our preoccupation with the scientific potential of genetic screening, we have not devoted the necessary attention to the social meanings and conflicts that will be precipitated by the application of these technologies.

Nor is the problem of preventing AIDS in women simply a matter of encouraging women to buy condoms, that is, simply an issue of purchasing a barrier to infection (as the infectious disease model would propose) or of acting as a responsible consumer (in accord with the chronic disease model). Any serious approach to prevention must take into account women's general lack of power in relationships with men; the consequent relations between sexuality, economic dependency, and power; rape, coerced sexuality, and violence against women; and the fact that casual prostitution may be an important way of earning money in a world where women's labor is often not valued (118). Women's ability to protect themselves from HIV infection is part economics, part power, part physical danger, and part psychology; it requires social support and protection for women who try to "Just say no."

What Are the Health Policy Implications of This Third View?

When we conceptualize AIDS as a collective chronic infectious disease and persistent pandemic, following the third historical model, we can take the time necessary to develop more effective interventions. Whereas a classic, time-limited epidemic lasting a few days, weeks, or months allows time only for immediate, emergency measures, a longer time frame should enable us to address the myriad unanswered questions about sexuality and drugs, and thereby develop appropriate mass education methods targeted at multiple different communities (117, 130). We must also study the social context of sexuality and drug use patterns: the cultural meanings of sexuality, not simply numbers of sexual contacts, are an essential aspect of developing more effective forms of prevention (22, 131). For sexually transmitted diseases, we need a better understanding of the various reasons that people engage in risk-taking behaviors, of how to sustain changes in risk-taking behavior over time, of how people negotiate power within sexual relationships, and how to balance risk reduction against abolition of harm. We know very little about sexuality—what people like, what people think they want, what people do—and we must more effectively address the political resistance to gaining this knowledge. In the United States, the suppression of recent national sex surveys is a foolish and dangerous refusal even to gather the minimal data needed (132–134). We also need to rethink the standard patterns of prevention based on individual behavior and to start thinking about prevention in terms of people in relationships—including both the variety of sexual relationships, from anonymous to monogamous, and the larger social relations of race, class, and gender.

We have seen that AIDS has affected several defined communities such as urban gay men and injection drug users and that different health education and prevention techniques are required to reach diverse constituencies. We cannot assume, however, that HIV infection will be confined to these defined communities; while working on different methods of prevention in communities already heavily affected, we should also be developing effective prevention in communities not yet deeply touched by the disease. The longer time frame we now accept implies that we can learn ways of preventing infection before many more whole communities are devastated. Our strategies for prevention must extend to a longer future, with more effective planning; we are not at liberty to expect that the epidemic will soon be over.

The fact that AIDS is a chronic as well as communicable disease requires attention to reforming the health care system to deal more effectively with all chronic ills (29, 135). Most obvious, at least in the United States, is the need for a rational system of financing medical care; if this were properly addressed it not only would mean a better ability to cope with HIV-related diseases, but would clearly provide an essential part of the answer to dealing with other diseases as well. We are, perhaps, beginning to learn the importance of having affected communities involved in the process of planning and setting policy.

There are other matters that require continued attention. The problems associated with testing and screening for HIV have only in part been worked out and are still highly controversial, given the lack of social protection for those who test positive. We are also beginning to accept the need for more inclusive clinical trials—or at least, to question trials that arbitrarily exclude participants by race or gender. The problems and ethical issues involved in the testing of experimental drugs, the use of placebos, and the approval of new drugs are all important in AIDS; the process of confronting these questions within the context of an engaged community will help provide answers that are likely to be also applicable to other new (and old) diseases.

CREATING A THIRD HISTORY OF AIDS

In this second decade of AIDS, we have the chance to learn from the first decade, from the unique history of AIDS itself, and no longer need to rely upon prior and not necessarily appropriate models. In seeking a more unified conception of AIDS, we want to retain the strengths of both earlier models and use each to counterbalance the weakness of the other. If we can begin this process with AIDS, it may also open new possibilities for dealing with other conditions that may have been too narrowly boxed into either the infectious or chronic disease category. Challenging the rigid distinction between the infectious and chronic disease categories also tacitly questions the assumption of diverse patterns of disease characteristic of the first and third worlds. Just as it has recently been recognized that the chronic diseases are now widespread in third world countries (136), so we must also acknowledge the reappearance of the infectious "diseases of underdevelopment" (tuberculosis, cholera, etc.) in the industrialized world. Thinking clearly about health and disease requires more attention to the global interdependence of societies and economies.

AIDS also has reminded us that in general there are relatively few routes of transmission of disease, and that we have much to learn from the failures as well as the successes of preventing "old" diseases. The experience with AIDS should therefore not only help us to prepare for other emerging diseases, but also force us to address the "old" diseases whose very existence established the models used to construct the first and second histories of AIDS. As part of this, we must acknowledge that these "old" diseases and AIDS persist both in the United States and around the world not simply because of a lack of knowledge, but because of socially created political and economic obstacles, which can only be overcome by being publicly identified and directly tackled. By capturing the worst elements of both infectious and chronic diseases in the populations assaulted and in the failures of health policy, AIDS has become a protracted disorder of the dispossessed. It demands analysis of their situation in its totality and not simply as yet one more disease problem to be approached in the usual fragmented and incomplete manner.

As the histories of AIDS so clearly demonstrate, we naturally look for analogies from the past. In general, this is appropriate. It can also be grossly misleading. Prior constructions of disease—of plague, of chronic illness—have simultaneously enhanced and constrained our understanding of AIDS and our response to this new epidemic. Each has invited us to think and act in particular terms, using concepts and approaches shaped by past periods of history. Complementary if not mutually exclusive, these successive paradigms have demanded that we either wage war on a mass epidemic or else contain a chronic ailment.

AIDS, however, has defied efforts at neat categorization. Challenging our narrow taxonomies of disease classification, this new affliction has highlighted serious flaws not only in the application, but also in the assumptions of predominant disease prevention strategies. In one short decade, AIDS has changed from a disease with no history to one with a history in its own right, that is not merely derived from the past, but belongs to the present we occupy and the future we forge. As we think and rethink our way through this wretched and wrenching epidemic, we must be prepared to embrace its complexities and contradictions. Perhaps by doing so, we will make ourselves more open to responding to the demands of other emerging diseases, and more able to deal with the scourges of the past that haunt us still.

REFERENCES

1. Oppenheimer, G. M. In the eye of the storm: The epidemiological construction of AIDS. In *AIDS: The Burdens of History*, edited by E. Fee and D. M. Fox, pp. 267–300. University of California Press, Berkeley, 1988.
2. Shilts, R. *And the Band Played On: Politics, People, and the AIDS Epidemic*. St. Martin's Press, New York, 1987.
3. McKeown, T. *The Origins of Human Disease*. Basil Blackwell, Oxford, 1988.
4. Terris, M. Epidemiology as a guide to health policy. *Annu. Rev. Public Health* 1: 323–344, 1980.
5. Kunitz, S. J. Explanations and ideologies of mortality patterns. *Popul. Dev. Rev.* 13: 379–407, 1987.
6. Sontag, S. *AIDS and Its Metaphors*. Farrar, Straus & Giroux, New York, 1988.
7. Sabatier, R. *Blaming Others: Prejudice, Race and Worldwide AIDS*. Panos Institute, New Society Publishers, Washington, D.C., 1988.
8. Mack, A. (ed.). *In Time of Plague: The History and Consequences of Lethal Epidemic Disease*. New York University Press, New York, 1991.
9. Fee, E., and Fox, D. M. (eds.). *AIDS: The Burdens of History*. University of California Press, Berkeley, 1988.
10. Crimp, D. (ed.). *AIDS: Cultural Analysis, Cultural Activism*. MIT Press, Cambridge, Mass., 1988.
11. Gostin, L., and Curran, W. J. Legal control measures for AIDS: Reporting requirements, surveillance, quarantine, and regulation of public meeting places. *Am. J. Public Health* 77: 214–218, 1987.
12. Associated Press. Poll indicates majority favor quarantine for AIDS victims. *New York Times*, December 20, 1985, p. 14.
13. Buckley, W. F. Jr. Crucial steps in combating the AIDS epidemic: Identify all the carriers. *New York Times*, March 18, 1986, p. 27.
14. Panos Dossier. *The 3rd Epidemic: Repercussions of the Fear of AIDS*. The Panos Institute, Budapest, 1990.
15. Krieger, N., and Lashof, J. AIDS, policy analysis, and the electorate: The role of schools of public health. *Am. J. Public Health* 78: 411–415, 1988.
16. Musto, D. F. Quarantine and the problem of AIDS. In *AIDS: The Burdens of History*, edited by E. Fee and D. M. Fox, pp. 67–85. University of California Press, Berkeley, 1988.
17. Brandt, A. M. *No Magic Bullet: A Social History of Venereal Disease in the United States Since 1880*. Oxford University Press, New York, 1987.
18. Fukuyama, F. *The End of History and the Last Man*. Free Press, New York, 1992.
19. McKibben, B. *The End of Nature*. Random House, New York, 1989.
20. Grmek, M. *History of AIDS: Emergence and Origin of a Modern Pandemic*, translated by R. C. Maulitz and J. Duffin. Princeton University Press, Princeton, N.J., 1990.
21. Dubos, R. *Mirage of Health: Utopias, Progress and Biological Change*. Harper Brothers, New York, 1959.
22. Weeks, J. *Sexuality and Its Discontents: Meanings, Myths, and Modern Sexualities*. Routledge & Kegan Paul, London, 1985.
23. Kramer, L. A Manhattan Project for AIDS. *New York Times*, July 16, 1990, p. A-15.
24. Gallo, R. C. *Virus Hunting: Cancer, AIDS and the Human Retrovirus: A Story of Scientific Discovery*. Basic Books, New York, 1991.
25. Fauci, A. S. The acquired immune deficiency syndrome: The ever-broadening clinical spectrum. *JAMA* 249: 2375–2376, 1983.

26. Oleske, J., et al. Immune deficiency syndrome in children. *JAMA* 249: 2347–2348, 1983.
27. Leishman, K. AIDS and insects. *Atlantic Monthly*, September 1987, pp. 56–72.
28. Gostin, L. The AIDS litigation project: A national review of court and human rights decisions on discrimination. In *AIDS: The Making of a Chronic Disease*, edited by E. Fee and D. M. Fox, pp. 144–169. University of California Press, Berkeley, 1992.
29. Fox, D. M. AIDS and the American health polity: The history and prospects of a crisis of authority. In *AIDS: The Burdens of History*, edited by E. Fee and D. M. Fox, pp. 316–343. University of California Press, Berkeley, 1988.
30. Krieger, N. AIDS Funding: Competing needs and the politics of priorities. *Int. J. Health Serv.* 18: 521–541, 1988.
31. Krieger, N., and Appleman, R. *The Politics of AIDS*. Frontline Pamphlets, Oakland, Calif., 1986.
32. Moss, A. R., et al. Risk factors for AIDS and HIV seropositivity in homosexual men. *Am. J. Epidemiol.* 125: 1035–1047, 1987.
33. Coates, R. A., et al. Validity of sexual histories in a prospective study of male sexual contacts of men with AIDS or an AIDS-related condition. *Am. J. Epidemiol.* 128: 719–728, 1988.
34. Padgug, R. A., and Oppenheimer, G. M. Riding the tiger: AIDS and the gay community. In *AIDS: The Making of a Chronic Disease*, edited by E. Fee and D. M. Fox, pp. 245–278. University of California Press, Berkeley, 1992
35. Crosby, A. W. Jr. The influenza pandemic of 1918. In *Influenza in America, 1918–1976*, edited by J. E. Osborn, pp. 5–13. Prodist, New York, 1977.
36. Graubard, S. R. (ed.). *Living with AIDS*. MIT Press, Cambridge, Mass., 1990.
37. Brandt, A. M. AIDS: From social history to social policy. In *AIDS: The Burdens of History*, edited by E. Fee and D. M. Fox, pp. 147–171. University of California Press, Berkeley, 1988.
38. Fear and AIDS in Hollywood. *People Magazine*, September 23, 1985, pp. 28–33.
39. Des Jarlais, D. C., Friedman, S. R., and Sotheran, J. L. The first city: HIV among intravenous drug users in New York City. In *AIDS: The Making of a Chronic Disease*, edited by E. Fee and D. M. Fox, pp. 279–295. University of California Press, Berkeley, 1992.
40. Barrett-Connor, E. Infectious and chronic disease epidemiology: Separate and unequal? *Am. J. Epidemiol.* 109: 245–249, 1979.
41. Martin, E. Toward an anthropology of immunology: The body as nation state. *Med. Anthropol. Q.* 4: 410–426, 1990.
42. Haraway, D. The biopolitics of postmodern bodies: Determinations of self in immune system discourses. *Differences* 1: 3–43, 1989.
43. Green, R. M. *A Translation of Galen's Hygiene (De Sanitate Tuenda)*. Charles C Thomas, Springfield, 1951.
44. Kidd, P. M., and Huber, W. *Living with AIDS: Strategies for Long-Term Survival*. HK Biomedical, Berkeley, Calif., 1990.
45. Callen, M. *Surviving AIDS*. Harper Collins, New York, 1990.
46. Badgley, L. *Healing AIDS Naturally*. Human Energy Press, Foster City, Calif., 1987.
47. Asistent, N. M., and Duffy, P. *Why I Survive AIDS*. Simon & Schuster, New York, 1991.
48. Stark, P. 20 Questions on the war on drugs. *Oakland Tribune*, July 1, 1988, p. B-8.
49. Berke, R. L. Drug chief calls for a vast prison plan. *New York Times*, August 3, 1989, p. A-11.
50. Institute of Medicine, National Academy of Sciences. *Confronting AIDS: Update 1988*. National Academy Press, Washington, D.C., 1988.

51. Lambert, B. Big lab for AIDS to open in Manhattan. *New York Times*, January 21, 1990, p. A-17.
52. De Witt, K. On Capitol Hill, the battle for AIDS funds heats up. *New York Times*, November 9, 1991, p. 35.
53. Fumento, M. *The Myth of Heterosexual AIDS*. Basic Books, New York, 1990.
54. Bregman, D. J., and Langmuir, A. D. Farr's Law applied to AIDS projections. *JAMA* 263: 1522–1525, 1990.
55. Freudenberg, N. AIDS prevention in the United States: Lessons from the first decade. *Int. J. Health Serv.* 20: 589–600, 1990.
56. Drucker, E. Epidemic in the war zone: AIDS and community survival in New York City. *Int. J. Health Serv.* 20: 601–616, 1990.
57. Altman, D. Legitimation through disaster: AIDS and the gay movement. In *AIDS: The Burdens of History*, edited by E. Fee and D. M. Fox, pp. 301–315. University of California Press, Berkeley, 1988.
58. Scitovsky, A. A., and Rice, D. P. Estimates of the direct and indirect costs of acquired immunodeficiency syndrome in the United States, 1985, 1986, and 1991. *Public Health Rep.* 102: 5–17, 1987.
59. Bloom, D. E., and Carliner, G. The economic impact of AIDS in the United States. *Science* 239: 604–609, 1988.
60. Centers for Disease Control. Estimates of HIV prevalence and projected AIDS cases: Summary of a workshop, October 31–November 1, 1989. *MMWR* 39: 110–119, 1990.
61. De Parle, J. Rash, rude and effective, ACT-UP helps change AIDS policy. *New York Times*, January 3, 1990, p. A-12.
62. Gomes, L. AIDS drugs networks. *Oakland Tribune*, July 11, 1988, pp. B-1, B-7.
63. Cimons, M., and Duncan, L. 90 AIDS activists arrested at FDA protest. *Oakland Tribune*, October 12, 1988, p. A-5.
64. Henry, S. Redlining people with AIDS. *The Nation*, November 11, 1991, pp. 582–586.
65. Francis, D. D., et al. Targeting AIDS prevention and treatment toward HIV-1-infected persons: The concept of early intervention. *JAMA* 262: 2572–2576, 1989.
66. Rhame, F. S., and Maki, D. G. The case for wider use of testing for HIV infection. *N. Engl. J. Med.* 320: 1248–1254, 1989.
67. Levine, C., and Bayer, R. The ethics of screening for early intervention in HIV disease. *Am. J. Public Health* 79: 1661–1667, 1989.
68. Baker, R. Public health policy and the AIDS epidemic: An end to HIV exceptionalism? *N. Engl. J. Med.* 324: 1500–1504, 1991.
69. Angell, M. A dual approach to the AIDS epidemic. *N. Engl. J. Med.* 324: 1498–1500, 1991.
70. Hilts, P. J. Congress urges AIDS tests for doctors. *New York Times*, October 4, 1991, p. A-9.
71. Brennan, T. A. Transmission of the human immunodeficiency virus in the health care setting—time for action. *N. Engl. J. Med.* 324: 1504–1508, 1991.
72. Rhame, F. S. The HIV-infected surgeon. *JAMA* 264: 507–508, 1990.
73. Gerbert, B., et al. Possible health care professional-to-patient HIV transmission: Dentists' reaction to a Centers for Disease Control report. *JAMA* 265: 1845–1848, 1991.
74. Tesh, S. *Hidden Arguments: Political Ideology and Disease Prevention Policy*. Rutgers University Press, New Brunswick, N.J., 1988.
75. Navarro, V. *Crisis, Health and Medicine: A Social Critique*. Tavistock, New York, 1986.

76. Waitzkin, H. *The Second Sickness: Contradictions of Capitalist Health Care*. Free Press, New York, 1983.
77. Conrad, P., and Kern, R. (eds.). *The Sociology of Health and Illness: Critical Perspectives*. St. Martin's Press, New York, 1981.
78. Terris, M. The lifestyle approach to prevention: Editorial. *J. Public Health Policy* 1: 5–9, 1980.
79. Essed, P. *Understanding Everyday Racism: An Interdisciplinary Theory*. Sage Publications, Newbury Park, Calif., 1991.
80. Cassel, J. The contribution of the social environment to host resistance. *Am. J. Epidemiol.* 104: 107–123, 1976.
81. Hulka, B. S., Wilcosky, T. C., and Griffith, J. D. (eds.). *Biological Markers in Epidemiology*. Oxford University Press, New York, 1990.
82. Louie, L. G., Newman, B., and King, M. C. Influence of host genotype on progression to AIDS among HIV-infected men. *J. Acquir. Immune Defic. Syndr*. 4: 814–818, 1991.
83. Dressler, W. D. *Stress and Adaptation in the Context of Culture: Depression in a Southern Black Community*. State University of New York Press, Albany, 1991.
84. Berman, D. M. *Death on the Job: Occupational Safety and Health Struggles in the United States*. Monthly Review Press, New York, 1978.
85. Elling, R. H. The political economy of workers' health. *Soc. Sci. Med.* 28: 1171–1182, 1989.
86. Terris, M., et al. The health agenda for the 1990s. *J. Public Health Policy* 12: 14–36, 1991.
87. Catford, J. Heartbeat Wales. *World Health*, June 1988, pp. 24–25.
88. Martin, E. *The Woman in the Body: A Cultural Analysis of Reproduction*. Beacon Press, Boston, 1987.
89. Fielding, J. E. Smoking: Health effects and control, Part 1 and Part 3. *N. Engl. J. Med.* 313: 491–498; 555–561, 1985.
90. Chapman, R., et al. Why the tobacco industry fears the passive smoking issue. *Int. J. Health Serv*. 20: 417–427, 1990.
91. Breslow, L. Control of cigarette smoking from a public policy perspective. *Annu. Rev. Public Health* 3: 129–151, 1982.
92. Jameson, F. *Postmodernism or, The Cultural Logic of Late Capitalism*. Duke University Press, Durham, N.C., 1991.
93. Rosenberg, C. E. What is an epidemic? In *Living with AIDS*, edited by S. R. Graubard, pp. 1–17. MIT Press, Cambridge, Mass., 1990.
94. Centers for Disease Control. Tuberculosis and human immunodeficiency virus infection: Recommendations of the Advisory Committee for the Elimination of Tuberculosis (ACET). *MMWR* 38: 236–250, 1989.
95. Altman, L. K. Drug-resistant TB makes U.S. rethink elimination program. *New York Times*, January 28, 1992, p. B-6.
96. Brooke, J. How the cholera scare is waking Latin America. *New York Times*, March 8, 1992, p. 4.
97. Rosenthal, E. Measles reemerges, and with far deadlier effects. *New York Times*, April 24, 1991, pp. A-1, C-23.
98. Centers for Disease Control. Measles—United States, 1990. *MMWR* 40: 369–372, 1991.
99. Committee on Medicine in the Changing Order. *Medicine in the Changing Order*. New York Academy of Medicine, New York, 1947.
100. Gordon, J. E. Epidemiology—old and new. *J. Mich. State Med. Soc.* 49: 194–199, 1950.

101. Syme, S. L. Health Promotion: Old Approaches: New Choices, Future Imperatives. Paper presented at The New Public Health: 1990, Los Angeles, April 25, 1990.
102. Brown, E. R. Community action for health promotion: A strategy to empower individuals and communities. *Int. J. Health Serv.* 21: 441–456, 1991.
103. Freudenberg, N. *Not in Our Backyard! Community Action for Health and the Environment*. Monthly Review Press, New York, 1984.
104. Friedman, S. R., Des Jarlais, D. C., and Sotheran, J. L. AIDS health education for intravenous drug users. *Health Educ. Q.* 13: 383–393, 1986.
105. Watney, S. *Policing Desire: Pornography, AIDS and the Media*. University of Minnesota Press, Minneapolis, 1987.
106. Mays, V. M., and Cochran, S. D. Acquired immunodeficiency syndrome and black Americans: Special psychosocial issues. *Public Health Rep.* 102: 224–231, 1987.
107. Friedman, S. R., et al. The AIDS epidemic among blacks and Hispanics. *Milbank Q.* 65 (suppl. 2): 455–499, 1987.
108. Alonso, A. M., and Koreck, M. T. Silences: Hispanics, AIDS, and sexual practices. *Differences* 1: 101–124, 1989.
109. Rogers, M., and Williams, W. AIDS in blacks and Hispanics: Implications for prevention. *Issues Sci. Technol.* 3: 89–94, 1987.
110. Thomas, S. B., and Quinn, S. C. The Tuskegee Syphilis Study, 1932 to 1972: Implications for HIV education and AIDS risk education programs in the black community. *Am. J. Public Health* 81: 1498–1505, 1991.
111. National Commission on AIDS. *America Living with AIDS. Report of the National Commission on Acquired Immune Deficiency Syndrome*. Washington, D.C., 1991.
112. Hilts, P. J. AIDS panel backs efforts to exchange drug users needles. *New York Times*, August 7, 1991, pp. A-1, A-12.
113. Centers for Disease Control. *HIV/AIDS Surveillance Report*. Atlanta, Ga., monthly.
114. Ascari, E., Labor Occupational Health Program, University of California, Berkeley. Personal communication, April 2, 1992.
115. Navarro, M. Fighting AIDS, and fighting one another: As the battleground shifts, old and newer groups vie for scarce funds. *New York Times*, March 31, 1992, pp. B-1, B-4.
116. Centers for Disease Control. Acquired immunodeficiency syndrome—United States, 1981–1990. *MMWR* 40: 358–369, 1991.
117. Miller, H. G., Turner, G. F., and Moses, L. E. (eds.). *AIDS: The Second Decade*. National Academy Press, Washington, D.C., 1990.
118. Caravano, K. More than mothers and whores: Redefining the AIDS prevention needs of women. *Int. J. Health Serv.* 21: 131–142, 1991.
119. Rieder, I., and Ruppelt, P. (eds.). *AIDS: The Women*. Cleis Press, San Francisco, 1988.
120. Minkoff, H. L., and DeHovitz, J. A. Care of women infected with the human immunodeficiency virus. *JAMA* 266: 2253–2258, 1991.
121. The ACT UP/New York Women and AIDS Book Group. *Women, AIDS and Activism*. South End Press, Boston, 1990.
122. Gross, J. Collapse of inner-city families creates America's new orphans. *New York Times*, March 29, 1992.
123. Teltsch, K. Custody help for mothers with AIDS. *New York Times*, August 30, 1991, p. A-15.
124. Working Group on HIV Testing of Pregnant Women and Newborns. HIV infection, pregnant women, and newborns: A policy proposal for information and testing. *JAMA* 264: 2416–2420, 1990.

125. Levine, C., and Dubler, N. N. Uncertain risks and bitter realities: The reproductive choices of HIV-infected women. *Milbank Q.* 68: 321–382, 1990.
126. Arras, J. D. AIDS and reproductive decisions: Having children in fear and trembling. *Milbank Q.* 68: 353–382, 1990.
127. Anastos, K., and Marte, C. Women—the missing persons in the AIDS epidemic. *Health/PAC Bull.*, Winter 1989, pp. 6–13.
128. Bayer, R. L. AIDS and the future of reproductive freedom. *Milbank Q.* 68(suppl. 2): 179–204, 1990.
129. Hubbard, R. *The Politics of Women's Biology*. Rutgers University Press, New Brunswick, N.J., 1990.
130. Mann, J. M. Global AIDS: Critical issues for prevention in the 1990s. *Int. J. Health Serv.* 21: 553–559, 1991.
131. Singer, L. Bodies—pleasures—powers. *Differences* 1: 45–65, 1989.
132. Sex survey is dealt a setback. *New York Times*, July 26, 1989, p. A-7.
133. Hilts, P. J. Panel criticizes cancellation of study of teenage life. *New York Times*, September 25, 1991, p. A-2.
134. Millman, M. Needed: A Federal Kinsey report. *New York Times*, October 21, 1991, p. A-15.
135. Fox, D. M. Health polity and changing epidemiology in the United States: Chronic disease in the twentieth century. In *Unnatural Causes: The Three Leading Killer Diseases in America*, edited by Russell Maulitz, pp. 11–31. Rutgers University Press, New Brunswick, N.J., 1988.
136. International Bank for Reconstruction and Development. *World Development Report 1991: The Challenge of Development*. Oxford University Press/World Bank, New York, 1991.

CHAPTER 12

Understanding AIDS: Historical Interpretations and the Limits of Biomedical Individualism

Elizabeth Fee and Nancy Krieger

Perhaps more than any other disease, acquired immunodeficiency syndrome (AIDS) offers a complex and vivid example of the ways in which people create multiple, contested explanations of health and illness. A plethora of social, political, and scientific actors have advanced competing claims to knowledge about the causes of AIDS. People directly affected by AIDS, especially within the organized gay community, have laid claim to both scientific and experiential knowledge and have challenged professional prerogatives; religious leaders have professed superior understanding of AIDS based on moral and biblical injunctions; politicians and the media have adopted, manipulated, and sometimes avoided the issue of AIDS depending on the rest of their social agenda and appeal to constituents; and scientists and health professionals have asserted what they consider to be rational and accurate appraisals of the problems and policies of AIDS.

From this apparent cacophony of voices and warring interpretations, some larger themes and patterns emerge. The popular and scientific understanding of AIDS, at least in the United States, has, we argue, been shaped by successive and clashing historical constructions or paradigms of disease, which have in turn been

Originally published in *American Journal of Public Health* 83(10): 1477–1486, 1993, and reprinted here with permission from the American Public Health Association.

driven by our accumulating experience with AIDS.[1] In the first construction of its history, AIDS was conceived of primarily as a "gay plague," by analogy with the sudden, devastating epidemics of the past (6). In the second paradigm, AIDS was normalized as a chronic disease to be managed medically over the long term (7).

Although each paradigm certainly has captured important aspects of the AIDS epidemic, neither has proven fully adequate for understanding and preventing AIDS, and each has had its share of critics. By examining and extending these critiques, we believe it is possible to discern the emergence of an alternative paradigm that considers AIDS to be a collective chronic infectious disease and persistent pandemic, manifested through myriad specific diseases associated with human immunodeficiency virus (HIV) infection (8). This alternative paradigm emphasizes that AIDS is at once a social and biological disorder; its course cannot be understood or altered without attention to its social and political context.

Each of these three historical constructions of AIDS incorporates distinct views of the etiology, prevention, pathology, and treatment of disease; each tacitly promotes different conceptions of the proper allocation of individual and social responsibility for the problems associated with the AIDS epidemic. In our exploration of the contesting interpretations of AIDS, we have found that, although it is certainly possible to contrast scientific and popular views, it is perhaps more revealing to contrast individualistic vs. collective, and biomedical vs. social and historical, views of disease.

THE FIRST PARADIGM: AIDS AS GAY PLAGUE

Like the great epidemics of the past, AIDS first appeared as a sudden, fatal, and communicable disease (9, 10). It seemed to resurrect the true meaning of *epidemic*: a disease that spreads like wildfire, consumes lives, and then burns out, leaving devastation in its wake. Epidemiologists, the first scientists to lay claim to understanding the mysterious new ailment, were struck by its seemingly exotic preference for young, homosexual men; they therefore searched for causes in the behaviors or "life-styles" common to gay men. In the process, they looked for risk factors prevalent in this "risk group" and indicted life in the fast lane, including "promiscuity," "poppers" (amyl nitrate), and anal sex.

Fascinated by the details of gay male sexual behavior and culture, researchers at first ignored the cases of AIDS that did not fit the gay plague model, such as those

[1] For one of the earliest analyses of paradigms (referred to as "thought collectives") in medical history, see (1); for a seminal discussion of paradigms in scientific thought more generally, see (2). Both analyses consider paradigms shaped by—and paradigms shifts to be mainly driven by—factors "internal" to science (e.g., level of technology, anomalous observations). Since the 1970s, however, a considerable body of literature on the social history of science, including medicine and public health, has analyzed how societal factors typically deemed "external" to science (e.g., prevailing ideologies) shape not simply the application but also the essence of scientific thought. See, for example, (3–5).

among women and users of injection drugs. Indeed, the disease was initially termed GRID, the gay-related immunodeficiency disease, and those stricken who denied homosexual contacts were often assumed to be lying. The gay plague model was clearly challenged, however, by the first cases among blood transfusion recipients, hemophiliacs, and Haitian immigrants.[2] Thereafter, researchers began to speak of the "4-H risk groups": homosexuals, Haitians, hemophiliacs, and heroin addicts.[3] To epidemiologists, risk groups were simply neutral, empirical descriptions of individuals with common identities and/or behaviors associated with an increased, but not absolute, risk of developing the disease. In popular perception, however, all members of the identified risk groups were seen as potentially contagious; from there it was but a short step to perceive those populations as "responsible" for AIDS. This in turn led to the prevalent media descriptions of the "innocent victims" of disease, such as hemophiliacs and children; by implication, the others were "guilty" culprits.

The gay and lesbian communities rejected both these characterizations: as statistical risk group and as population of disease carriers. These communities had a recently formed, self-conscious sense of their social and political identity, forged in part out of a successful struggle with the medical establishment over the psychiatric definition of homosexuality as a pathological disorder. The epidemiologists' apparently neutral categories were perceived as an attempt to resurrect the earlier biomedical construction of homosexuality as a sickness (13, 14). This perception was heightened by the unmediated associations between homosexuality and disease that appeared in the declarations of right-wing ideologues, who lost no opportunity to castigate homosexuals in the name of "family values" and the "American way of life" (15, 16). Rejecting these attacks, the politically formed gay community began to challenge the scientists' right to define the disease, design research, and determine social policy (17, 18).

In 1983, the identification of HIV, the AIDS virus, led to a new phase of the epidemic, in which AIDS was clearly characterized as an infectious disease.[4] Once the virus was identified, scientists tended to lose interest in the social factors accompanying transmission. They instead turned to laboratory studies of the virus and its action within the body in the hopes of making new discoveries that would lead to patents, vaccines, and possibly a cure.

The identification of the virus also changed popular views of the proximate and ultimate causes of the AIDS epidemic. A virus was a familiar if vague entity in popular culture, used to explain or explain away all kinds of indefinite ills (21). By

[2] The first case of AIDS in a hemophiliac was diagnosed in 1982, and by early 1983, scientists recognized that AIDS was a blood-borne disease (11).

[3] After diplomatic protest over identifying an entire nation with the disease, Haitians were dropped from the official risk-group listing of the Centers for Disease Control and Prevention (12).

[4] The story of scientific competition over the discovery of HIV is briefly but effectively told by Grmek (19, especially pp. 47–82). For an incompatible account, see Gallo (20).

the same token, a virus was perceived as something easy to catch; the idea that AIDS was caused by a virus, along with vague announcements about bodily fluids, may well have increased fears of casual transmission of the disease.[5] Although numerous surveys found that many people could correctly identify how HIV was transmitted—via sex and blood—they also documented widespread magical thinking (23, 24). As in other societies, where anthropologists have often noted the existence of pluralistic ideas of disease causation, many people in the United States simultaneously embraced scientific, traditional, and folk explanations of AIDS, with little sense of contradiction.

Ideas of "magical contagion" led otherwise well-informed people to fear contact with AIDS patients. For example, one study found that most people would refuse to wear a sweater previously worn by an AIDS patient, even if it had been thoroughly cleaned and even when they knew that AIDS could not be transmitted in this manner (25). More generally, popular conceptions showed that the scientific search for biomedical risk factors, agents, and other proximate causes of disease had failed to satisfy the broader need for ultimate explanations—the "why" and not just the "how" of disease causation. Notions of germ theory, deep-seated moral convictions, and ancient ideas about "bad blood" and contagion were thus conflated into a rich brew of popular attitudes toward disease; the brightly colored pictures of viruses in popular magazines bore little relevance to these complex emotional responses to the epidemic.

Among health professionals, the identification of HIV seemed to clarify strategies for AIDS prevention. It shifted attention away from the early risk-group designations and highlighted the importance of risk behaviors, thus focusing attention on specific acts rather than on sexual identities.[6] Given the enormous scientific problems involved in developing a vaccine, public health professionals advocated technically simple and individually oriented methods of prevention—such as condoms—to block the transmission of HIV. Campaigns to promote condom use, however, were immediately opposed by a right wing that was dead set against nonmarital sex. This conservative intransigence, sustained as it was by the Reagan White House (26, 27), made the public health approach to AIDS prevention an especially difficult and frustrating task. At the same time, these very disputes broke taboos and greatly expanded the boundaries of public discussions about sexuality.

For injection drug users, clean needles were the public health equivalent of condoms (28). But the act of providing individuals with clean needles was

[5] Some studies have found that fear of AIDS increases with increased knowledge about the disease (22).

[6] The language of some new health education materials, for example, addresses men who have sex with other men, whether or not they identify as homosexual. The distinction between "high-risk behaviors" and "high-risk groups" does not, however, always confront the fact that high-risk behaviors are riskier among high-risk groups because of the greater prevalence of HIV.

problematic because many people perceived the distribution of needles and bleach as a possible encouragement of drug use (29, 30). Many African Americans were convinced that these programs were part of a long-standing, white-led genocidal policy against blacks, and the called instead for drug treatment programs and jobs (31, 32). By contrast, many conservatives simply wanted drug addicts thrown into jail.

Prevention methods to curtail blood transmission were similarly framed in individualistic terms. People were urged to refrain from donating blood if they had any reason to believe they were at risk for HIV infection; people needing blood were encouraged to store their own blood prior to surgery or to collect blood from family and friends, as if only strangers' blood were dangerous (33). This represented a break with the more traditional view of blood banks as a communal resource; blood was now increasingly seen as an individual possession.

Ultimately, the identification of HIV and the discovery of a blood test for HIV antibodies made possible the traditional approach to infectious disease control—identification of those infected, followed by isolation, quarantine, or other societal action to cut off transmission[7]—and led to battles over testing immigrants, blood donors, and individuals considered to be at risk (37, 38). From the biomedical and epidemiological point of view, the availability of a test meant that people could and should be screened; if individuals knew their serostatus, they would more readily change behaviors that put either themselves or others at risk (39). However, this logic assumed that sexual behavior was a function of rational calculation; it ignored the complex power dynamics of sexual relationships (40). By a similar calculus of risk, many health care workers argued that if they knew the serostatus of their patients, they could take appropriate precautions (41).

This general logic of the infectious disease paradigm did not consider the social reality of discrimination in health insurance, jobs, and housing that faced those diagnosed as HIV positive (42). It also ignored the ethical problem that, in the early stages of the epidemic, no therapy was available; testing exposed the individual to considerable social risk while offering no medical benefit. Gay men and lesbians fought testing initiatives in terms of individual rights to privacy and confidentiality—the most viable political terms of discourse in the United States—and thus challenged the assumption that infection was the only risk that needed to be considered.[8] When the blood test threatened to create a new social division between those categorized as seropositive and seronegative, the lesbian and gay communities rejected this division and led a collective fight on behalf of everyone deemed at risk.

[7] For a brief review of the issue of quarantines in relation to epidemic disease and AIDS, see (34) and (35). For a counterargument, see (36).

[8] For a discussion of the tensions between individual liberties and public health priorities, see (43).

THE SECOND PARADIGM: AIDS AS A CHRONIC DISEASE

In the United States in the late 1980s, several factors contributed to shifting the framework for understanding AIDS from a plague to a chronic disease model (44). First was the recognition of the lengthening time frame of the epidemic; unlike plague and cholera, AIDS was clearly not going to disappear quickly. Then, too, dire predictions about the massive spread of AIDS throughout the entire U.S. population—the threatened "heterosexual explosion"—had not been fulfilled. Indeed, statisticians were revising downward the early estimates of the number of HIV-infected persons (45).

Perhaps most importantly, people with AIDS were living longer than expected. For people infected with HIV, the emphasis changed to living with, rather than dying from AIDS (46). Researchers and health care professionals shifted the focus of their concern from etiology to pathology and from prevention to potential therapies. The development of palliative treatments such as axidothymidine (AZT) for people with AIDS (and, later, for those who were HIV positive) placed new emphasis on health services, as reflected in the growing numbers of dedicated AIDS units for both inpatient and outpatient care (47). Early worries about the financing of AIDS care have been at least partially addressed (48, 49); from the point of view of health services delivery, AIDS was becoming just another expensive disease, like cancer, with which the medical system could cope—especially if patients had adequate health insurance (50).

When first conceived of as an infectious chronic disease, AIDS was likened to such diseases as tuberculosis and syphilis (44). This argument was initially contested, but within a few years, the idea that AIDS was a chronic disease became widely accepted in the economically developed countries.[9] According to the standard chronic disease model, which was developed for conditions like cardiovascular disease and cancer that were thought to be noncommunicable, chronic diseases are debilitating and often fatal conditions that are slow to develop, persist for many years, and require long-term management (52, 53).[10] Research focuses on disease mechanisms, usually at the cellular level, and increasingly concentrates on genetic determinants (55, 56). Based on this understanding of disease, health interventions most commonly emphasize screening, early detection,

[9] By mid-1992, the concept of AIDS as a chronic disease was well established. As Lawrence K. Altman reports (51), scientists attending the Eighth International AIDS Conference said that "the world had to learn to deal with AIDS—the acquired immune deficiency syndrome—as a chronic disease for which solutions will be long in coming" and that "infection with HIV—the human immunodeficiency virus—is taking its place with heart disease, cancer, and many other chronic diseases." See also the discussion of AIDS as a chronic disease by Wallace and Everett (52).

[10] Since the late 1970s, however, increasing evidence has called into question the "chronic" versus "infectious" dichotomy because some chronic diseases (e.g., cervical cancer) may be caused by infectious agents and many infectious diseases (e.g., tuberculosis) have chronic as well as acute symptoms (54).

and treatment, not primary prevention; finding the right pharmaceutical cure represents the epitome of successful disease management (57).

Reconceptualizing AIDS as a chronic disease inevitably brought these prevalent assumptions about chronic diseases to bear on all aspects of AIDS research, policies, and programs. The federal government, politicians, and the media, having already grown weary of contentious prevention campaigns and elusive attempts to develop a vaccine, displayed a new enthusiasm for supporting basic scientific research. Funding now flowed for studies of the natural history of AIDS, AIDS pathology, and clinical trials. Scientists vied with each other in hot pursuit of pharmaceutical agents that could slow the course of AIDS and HIV-related diseases. The success of Burroughs-Wellcome in the marketing of AZT fed the enthusiasm and entrepreneurial excitement of scientists and investors alike.[11] By contrast, few research dollars were expended on studies designed to improve prevention, whether for vaccines or social interventions. Certain uses of federal research funds were even proscribed. The U.S. Congress, for example, canceled two national surveys of sexual behavior (59), and until recently, the National Institute on Drug Abuse refused to fund research evaluating the effectiveness of needle-exchange programs. Testing for HIV was now encouraged more as a means of drawing infected people into early treatment than as an incentive to modify behavior (60, 61).

With the growing emphasis on health care, interested physicians began to specialize in AIDS and assumed a more important role in the management of AIDS and other HIV-related diseases. Evidence suggests, however, that most doctors were ill equipped to advise their patients about HIV disease, let alone take care of people with AIDS. One study found that more than 80 percent of a national sample of primary care physicians—those who might be expected to be on the front lines of patient education—said they lacked information about AIDS (62). Other research reported that most physicians were reluctant to talk about the basic issues of sex and drugs, and often failed to take relevant medical histories or to offer appropriate advice (63, 64). These studies found that many doctors were uncomfortable about sexuality, nervous around homosexuals, disturbed by drug addicts, and generally uneasy with AIDS patient (65). Indicating that patients were likewise reluctant to discuss sex drugs with their doctors, surveys found that most people obtained information about AIDS from the mass media, family, and friends, and that fewer than 10 percent had ever discussed the disease with their physician (24, 66).

Wary of physicians' biases, HIV-positive people were not necessarily willing to assume that their doctors knew best. Some were attracted to alternative explanations of AIDS, including Peter Duesberg's widely publicized claim that

[11]The initial announcement that AZT therapy would cost $10,000 per annum led to energetic public debate and speculation about drug profits (58).

HIV was only incidentally related to AIDS (67). People with AIDS explored alternative therapies and unconventional drugs, often purchasing pharmaceuticals that were only available in other countries through underground "buyers' clubs." Many of the popular books about living with AIDS challenged the hegemony of Western medicine and drew on alternative traditions ranging from classical Chinese acupuncture to New Age spirituality (68–71). Most of these alternative traditions, like the biomedical model, placed the onus of staying healthy on the individual.

AIDS activists increasingly became concerned about access to health care and the development of new and experimental treatments. They sought to extend the official definition of AIDS, expand access to AIDS services for HIV-infected persons, speed up experimental drug approvals, and broaden participation in clinical trials to include women, people of color, and people with low incomes. Reflecting their success and also the growing understanding of the progression of HIV disease, the Centers for Disease Control revised its diagnostic definition of AIDS in 1991 to include T-cell counts and, in 1992, to include cervical cancer and pulmonary tuberculosis among HIV-associated diseases (72). In a step that also had significant implications for other life-threatening diseases, the Food and Drug Administration agreed to streamline its procedures for drug approval (73). Similarly, the National Institutes of Health, under pressure from women, minorities, and AIDS activists, began to require broader participation in clinical trials and research protocols (74, 75).

Reflecting the clash between the first and second paradigms of AIDS, other AIDS activists questioned the single-minded focus on treatment and emphasized prevention. Tensions existed between those concerned strictly with AIDS and those who believed that the epidemic could be addressed only in relation to the health care crisis, the military budget, poverty, and racial and gender discrimination (76). Because the older AIDS organizations were largely staffed by and served the interests of gay white men, the newer constituencies of women, people of color, and injection drug users (in their overlapping permutations) created organizations to meet their own needs—and in the process completed for the same limited pool of funds.

As the epidemic persisted, individuals and cultural groups explored the personal and social meanings of AIDS through writing, video and film production, theater, art, photography, and music (77, 78). Many rejected the exclusively tragic imagery of dying in favor of diverse representations of living with AIDS. Their work incorporated the voices, faces, and experiences of people with AIDS, in contrast to the scientific and policy literature that presented the views of professional authorities (79). Cultural workers held the subjective truths of those directly affected by the epidemic to be authentic knowledge, as valuable for understanding AIDS as any objective biomedical account.

As AIDS touched every aspect of public life, from art to politics to sports, increasing popular awareness of the disease led to growing acceptance of people with AIDS. When the basketball staff Magic Johnson announced he was HIV positive, he was warmly applauded for his honesty and bravery. But although the language of guilt was less often applied to people ill with AIDS, the distinction between innocent and guilty "victims" lingered, as seen in the general hysteria over infected health care workers (80, 81).

The heated controversy over the minuscule risk posed by seemingly healthy HIV-positive persons working at their usual jobs was, however, more than an expression of irrational fears. It highlighted the new dilemmas created by AIDS as a "normal" chronic disease; the question remained how people living with AIDS could be incorporated into the daily fabric of society. As made manifestly clear by the chronic disease model, AIDS was here to stay (82).

CRITIQUE OF THE FIRST AND SECOND PARADIGMS: LIMITATIONS OF INDIVIDUALISM AND THE BIOMEDICAL MODEL

Reconceptualizing AIDS as a chronic disease addresses several notables failures of the plague paradigm, particularly the lack of a long-term perspective, but this approach may ultimately prove catastrophic. In accepting the chronic disease model's emphasis on pathology and treatment, many scientists and health care professionals have lost sight of the fact that AIDS is both infectious and preventable. The mounting number of HIV-infected persons, estimated at 12.9 million worldwide in early 1992, suggests that it may be useful to reconsider whether either paradigm is fully adequate for preventing AIDS or dealing with its social consequences (83).

Questions about the utility of the traditional infectious and chronic disease models in understanding health and disease are not unique to AIDS. In the case of the infectious disease model, we now recognize that its early reputation for success in controlling epidemics was overinflated. Historians have argued that much of the decline in infectious diseases predates scientific medicine and may more correctly be attributed to improved sanitation, clean water supplies, better nutrition, and less crowded living conditions (84–86). For contemporary infectious diseases, the "magic bullets" of antibiotics and pesticides certainly provide relief and vaccines continue to reduce the incidence of many childhood infections, but these types of measures along have not been able to prevent the resurgence of heretofore controlled diseases such as tuberculosis, cholera, and malaria (87).

If the successes of the infectious disease model have been more limited than was initially believed, the chronic disease model has fared no better. Although the incidence rates of a few cancers (e.g., stomach cancer) have declined, often for unknown reasons, the rates for many other types of cancer are stable or increasing (88, 89). When the American Cancer Society claims to be winning the war on cancer, it is generally referred to improvements in treatment and survival, not to reductions in incidence (90, 91). Although accelerated by recent attention to smoking, exercise, and nutrition, the decline in mortality from coronary heart disease began before current campaigns for heart-healthy living—again, for reasons not fully understood (92). While preventive interventions based on the chronic disease model have stressed individually oriented dietary and behavioral modifications, it is unclear how much health behaviors have really altered.[12] One clear change is the decline of cigarette smoking, but in this case, recent initiatives to restrict tobacco use have moved beyond criticism of smoking as an individual bad habit to target passive smoking as a communicable hazard (93).

Many of the limitations in our concepts of infectious and chronic diseases, reflected in our shifting understanding of AIDS, ultimately stem from the underlying and unstated assumptions of the biomedical model. As several critics have argued, 20th-century biomedical models typically are reductionist; they put primacy on explanations of disease etiology that fall within the purview of medical intervention narrowly construed, focus on disease mechanisms, and view social factors leading to disease as being secondary if not irrelevant (94–96). Proponents of such models may even consider emphasis on societal factors such as poverty or discrimination to be unscientific and polemical. Despite lip service to multifactorial etiology, they seek parsimonious biomedical explanations highlighting the role of one or a few proximate agents, and they generally assume that biomedical interventions, operating on biological mechanisms, will be sufficient to control disease.

The biomedical model is also premised on the ideology of individualism. Adopting the notion of the abstract individual from liberal political and economic theory, it considers individuals "free" to "choose" health behaviors. It treats people as consumers who make free choices in the marketplace of products and behaviors, and it generally ignores the role of industry, agribusiness, and government in structuring the array of risk factors that individuals are supposed to avoid. There is little place for understanding how behaviors are related to social conditions and constraints or how communities shape individuals' lives. From this perspective, populations and subgroups within populations—including "risk groups"—consist merely of summed individuals who exist without culture or history. There is no acknowledgment of the fact that when "risk groups" succeed in identifying populations at risk of disease, it is because these risk groups typically overlap with real social groups possessing historically conditioned identities.[13]

[12]A small proportion of the population has made dramatic changes in dietary patterns and exercise; the majority, however, seems to have been little affected by health exhortations (53).

[13]A classic example of this problem concerns the use of race rather than racism to explain disease prevalence. Within the biomedical framework, researchers, treating race as a valid biological category (despite long-standing evidence to the contrary), count up all the statistics on individuals of one or another race to argue the association of race with disease. Instead, one might start with an understanding of racism as a socially structured relationship and then attempt to discern its consequences for population patterns of health and disease (97).

The problems with the biomedical model extend beyond its exclusive focus on biological and individual-level factors and concern fundamental issues of scientific objectivity and the production of scientific knowledge. The canons of scientific objectivity, as embraced by this model, tend to discount the views and experiences of patients, the "objects" of scientific research and medical practice.[14] Only scientists and physicians are seen as possessing the expertise to define disease and frame research questions; negotiation of these issues with those directly affected is rarely considered. This model assigns physicians the unique responsibility for conveying specific knowledge about disease to individual patients, and it tacitly assumes that access to medical care is universal. It regards patients' beliefs as mere superstitions or misinformation that can be overcome with therapeutic doses of factual information. Subjectivity and culture—of the scientists and health care professionals as well as of their patients—are deemed irrelevant to "truth"; scientific knowledge is held to be outside the bounds of social context.

The assumptions of the biomedical model as embodied in the paradigms of gay plague and chronic disease have shaped scientific knowledge about AIDS as well as the medical and public health responses to this epidemic. The biomedical orientation has led to an almost exclusive focus on HIV and the mechanisms—as opposed to the social determinants—of its transmission. As methodology, biomedical individualism has resulted in data being collected chiefly on individuals with or at risk of AIDS, and rarely on the social context of their lives. Working under the rubric of "objectivity" as defined by the biomedical model, scientists have failed to see how social biases affect the type of research questions they ask. Physicians and other health care workers have failed to see how similar assumptions shape the medical care they provide. And these assumptions, if not addressed, threaten to vitiate our still-inadequate response to the epidemic.

Ultimately, the biomedical model embodies an approach to analyzing disease that is fundamentally individualistic and sanctions only the physicians' or scientists' point of view. Profoundly ahistorical, it contains within itself a dichotomy between the biological individual and the social community, and then it ignores the latter. It tends to reduce individuality to the very constrained level of genetic constitution and susceptibility (102, 103). Reflecting an ideological commitment to individualism, the only preventive actions seriously suggested are those that can be implemented by solo individuals. Little attention is accorded to situations in which negotiation is required between persons with unequal power, as is often the case between sexual partners or between advocates of needle exchange and the police (104). Intended or not, these attitudes implicitly accept social inequalities in health and fail to challenge the social production of disease.

[14]Feminist analysts of science have addressed these issues for some time and with increasing sophistication (98–101).

In challenging the assumptions of the biomedical model, we are not suggesting that disease can be understood without reference to biology; the question, however, is what approach we should take: a biology abstracted from social conditions or a biology understood in relation to its social context? Similarly, in questioning the ideology of individualism, we do not question the importance of individuality. But rather than posit the abstract, atomistic individuals of the idealized market, we want to emphasize how individuals' lives are shaped by both personal history and the social groups to which they belong.

FEATURES OF AN ALTERNATIVE PARADIGM: AIDS AS A COLLECTIVE, CHRONIC INFECTIOUS DISEASE AND PERSISTENT PANDEMIC

The creation of an alternative paradigm begins with the recognition that the individualistic assumptions of the existing biomedical model are simply not appropriate to AIDS[15]; AIDS is, in essence, a social disease. For this reason, we propose calling AIDS a collective chronic infectious disease and persistent pandemic. The term *collective* emphasizes the inadequacies of dealing with AIDS from a purely individualistic perspective; AIDS is, above all, about people in personal and social relationships. The term *chronic* acknowledges the potentially prolonged duration of the disease and its requirements for clinical management and care. The term *infectious* is retained to highlight fundamental aspects of etiology, modes of transmission, and possibilities for prevention.[16] And by calling AIDS a persistent pandemic, we stress both the long time frame of the disease and its global impact.

Transforming our historical understanding of AIDS in these ways implies developing an alternative research agenda, changing the policies we perceive as relevant, and creating new strategies of prevention. This incipient process is already under way, if only in fragmentary forms. It may be helpful to step back and consider some of the general parameters of the alternative approach and then examine some of its concrete manifestations.

This emphasis upon a collective rather than an individualistic approach to disease means drawing on a different body of theory—one that stresses the social production of disease and raises questions about how the social relationships of class, race, and gender affect people's working and living conditions and thereby influence their health status.[17] It asks how patterns of risk are socially shaped

[15]The same, of course, could be argued for other diseases.

[16]The term *infectious chronic disease*, with the word *infectious* used as a modifier, places AIDS in the general category of chronic illnesses and emphasizes pathology and treatment (see 44). By contrast, the term *chronic infectious disease* highlights the infectious character of the disease, modified by its chronic or long-term features of latency and period of infectivity, and emphasizes etiology and prevention.

[17]The literature on this subject dates back at least to the late 18th century; see (105). For contemporary discussions, see (106–110); see also (111).

within a historical context and why people make unhealthy life-style choices. It is thus concerned with how contemporary historical processes contribute to inequalities in health.

In asking these questions, this approach challenges investigators to develop a critical self-awareness of their own social and historical context and of the disease paradigms that guide their research. It encourages public health professionals to conceive of research as a two-way process in which investigators and subjects can instruct and learn from each other. It reminds us that AIDS, like other diseases, cannot be understood or addressed solely within the parameters of the health care system. And it reemphasizes the truly public character of public health.

This alternate approach has already led to some new insights relevant to AIDS prevention. For example, one study of minority women's decisions about condoms used focus groups to uncover the personal and economic context influencing their choices and, in the process, challenged cultural stereotypes of black and Hispanic women's lack of power in heterosexual relationships (40).[18] Another study found that injection drug users were more influenced by their material circumstances, such as access to clean needles and a private setting for drug use, than by their perceptions of risk of contracting AIDS from dirty needles (112).

Much of the broadening base of AIDS prevention activities is now being directed by and for minority communities. To improve care for HIV-infected persons, several groups are producing new educational materials that inform health care workers about the variety of cultural beliefs and attitudes toward disease, sexuality, drug use, and treatment found among their clients (113). Recognizing the importance of basing health education campaigns on what people really believe, researchers have begun to document the plurality of popular conceptions about health and disease causation in order to make AIDS education materials more compatible with people's own modes of understanding (114, 115).

Many AIDS prevention programs now also challenge the assumption that the key to prevention lies within the medical setting (104). Ex-addicts, for example, run some of the most effective needle-exchange programs by operating illegally on street corners. Health education campaigns within the gay community have been creative—and controversial—in attempting to eroticize safer sex and thus change collective social mores with respect to acceptable sexual behavior.

Other prevention efforts go well beyond the boundaries of traditional health education directed of traditional health education directed at the "consumers" of health care. Nicholas Freudenberg thus includes legislators among the groups in need of behavioral modification (116). These more radical visions of health education recognize that the target population for policy changes should include employers, the courts, the media, and the government (117, 118). Nor need these

[18]The point is that the specific economic context and not some global culture affects decision making within relationships.

campaigns be conducted only by health-related groups. Levi Strauss provides an example of what one company can do to provide health education to its work force, implement enlightened antidiscrimination policies, include domestic partners in insurance coverage, and fund community-based AIDS prevention groups (119, 120).

These new prevention strategies begin to acknowledge that people at risk for HIV infection do not come in the discrete packages suggested by the original epidemiological formulation of "risk groups" (121). Instead, real people overlap these categories in many different ways, and a single category may include a multiplicity of diverse social groups. It has been recognized, for example, that gay men belong to a wide variety of subcultures that occupy different social spaces, including local gyms, leather bars, and Wall Street. More recently, AIDS outreach workers have been learning to draw finer distinctions among cultural groups and between those men who have sex with men and do—or do not—consider themselves part of the gay community (122).

Similarly, women with AIDS do not represent one homogeneous group. Some are white and some are women of color; some are working class, some are wealthy; some contracted HIV infection from their partners, some from drugs, and some from transfusions. All may face certain issues unique to women with AIDS, such as the need for treatment of gynecologic opportunistic infections, and many must deal with fears of maternal-fetal transmission, but their diversity makes it obvious that no single program can be designed to cover "women with AIDS" (123).

This alternative understanding of AIDS also implies changes in the ways we make health policy. AIDS has unequivocally demonstrated that populations affected by a disease—people who are usually relegated to the position of being passive recipients of services—can spur innovative and effective planning. AIDS activists initially forced a major shift in the old public health approach to infectious disease control: for example, constraints on or quarantine of those infected. The political strength of the gay movement engendered within public health circles a new sensitivity to issues of stigma, confidentiality, privacy, and informed consent, and it ultimately helped democratize health policy.

If the paradigms of gay plague and chronic disease have failed to account for the many facets of AIDS within the United States, their inadequacies become even more apparent when one considers the phenomenon of AIDS as a spreading and persistent international pandemic. In most Central African, Latin American, and Southeast Asian countries, AIDS can be characterized neither as a peculiarly gay plague nor as a chronic disease; most people with AIDS are heterosexual and few can afford the luxury of extended treatment (124–126). Within the United States, we may have much to learn from the AIDS campaigns being created in various economically underdeveloped countries, which of necessity stress prevention since expensive pharmaceuticals and high-technology medical care are of only marginal relevance to most of their inhabitants (127).

The infectious disease model is, however, unlikely to prove adequate for controlling AIDS in these regions. As in the United States, the individualistic assumptions of this model fail to take into account the real conditions of people's lives and the social and material bases of disease transmission (128). Recognizing this fact, the National Union of Mineworkers, for example, a powerful trade union working alongside the African National Congress, is developing community-based strategies against AIDS in South Africa (129). Highlighting the links between employer-enforced working conditions, single-sex hostels, and the exchange of sex for money, the union has made clear that preventing HIV transmission will require changes in the structure of work and not just in the delivery of health services.

UNDERSTANDING AND PREVENTING AIDS: A COLLECTIVE ENTERPRISE

In conclusion, there is not a single understanding of AIDS because it is not a single disease that can be objectively known and defined in a timeless manner. The understandings of AIDS are diverse and reflect not only our growing experience with the epidemic, nationally and internationally, but also the different social contexts of those who establish these meanings through their work, their lives, and their deaths. To understand AIDS is to comprehend that our knowledge at any given point in time is shaped not only by accumulating biomedical discoveries, but also by the presence or absence of the voices of the different groups affected by the epidemic. If we are to understand AIDS better and formulate more effective prevention and health care strategies, the experiences and views of those hit hardest by the epidemic must be made more central to the conduct of scientific research and the establishment of health policy.

Transforming our approach to AIDS will not be an easy task. The issue is not simply a conflict between scientific and popular conceptions of AIDS, between "correct" and "incorrect" understandings. Instead, as we have argued, the task involves a thoroughgoing critique of the effects of individualism and the biomedical model upon our explanations of disease, our research agendas, and our policy priorities. It requires a greater appreciation of the historical and social contexts in which AIDS occurs, and of the relationships between the different social groups connected by the course of the disease. By analyzing the changing constructions of AIDS, we can begin to challenge the conventional view that AIDS will be understood and solved by science alone, and we can thereby expand our strategies to prevent this wretched and wrenching epidemic from becoming ever more entrenched.

REFERENCES

1. Fleck, L. *The Genesis and Development of a Scientific Fact.* University of Chicago Press, Chicago, 1935.
2. Kuhn, T. *The Structure of Scientific Revolutions,* Ed. 2. University of Chicago Press, Chicago, 1970.
3. Rose, H., and Rose, S. (eds.). *Ideology of/in the Natural Sciences.* Schenkman, Cambridge, Mass., 1979.
4. Dickson, D. *The New Politics of Science.* University of Chicago Press, Chicago, 1988.
5. Rosenberg, C. E., and Golden, J. (eds.). *Framing Disease: Studies in Cultural History.* Rutgers University Press, New Brunswick, N.J., 1992.
6. Fee, E., and Fox, D. M. (eds.). *AIDS: The Burdens of History.* University of California Press, Berkeley, 1988.
7. Fee, E., and Fox, D. M. (eds.). *AIDS: The Making of a Chronic Disease.* University of California Press, Berkeley, 1992.
8. Fee, E., and Krieger, N. Thinking and rethinking AIDS: Implications for health policy. *Int. J. Health Serv.* 23: 323–346, 1993.
9. Oppenheimer, G. M. In the eye of the storm: The epidemiological construction of AIDS. In *AIDS: The Burdens of History,* edited by E. Fee and D. M. Fox, pp. 267–300. University of California Press, Berkeley, 1988.
10. Shilts, R. *And the Band Played On: Politics, People, and the AIDS Epidemic.* St. Martin's Press, New York, 1987.
11. Institute of Medicine, National Academy of Sciences. *Confronting AIDS: Directions for Public Health, Health Care and Research,* p. 60. National Academy Press, Washington, D.C., 1986.
12. Sabatier, R. *Blaming Others: Prejudice, Race, and Worldwide AIDS.* Panos Institute, Washington, D.C., 1988.
13. Weeks, J. *Sex, Politics, and Society: The Regulation of Sexuality since 1800.* Longman, London, 1981.
14. Stevens, P. E., and Hall, J. M. A critical historical analysis of the medical construction of lesbianism. *Int. J. Health Serv.* 21: 291–307, 1991.
15. Krieger, N., and Appleman, R. *The Politics of AIDS.* Frontline Pamphlets, Oakland, Calif., 1986.
16. Francis, R. A. Moral beliefs of physicians, medical students, clergy, and lay public concerning AIDS. *J. Natl. Med. Assoc.* 81: 1141–1147, 1989.
17. Padgug, R. A., and Oppenheimer, G. M. Riding the tiger: AIDS and the gay community. In *AIDS: The Making of a Chronic Disease,* edited by E. Fee and D. M. Fox, pp. 245–278. University of California Press, Berkeley, 1992.
18. Treichler, P. A. AIDS, homophobia, and biomedical discourse: An epidemic of signification. *Cultural Stud.* 1: 263–305, 1987.
19. Grmek, M. D. *History of AIDS: Emergence and Origin of a Modern Pandemic,* translated by R. C. Maulitz and J. Duffin. Princeton University Press, Princeton, N.J., 1990.
20. Gallo, R. *Virus Hunting: Cancer, AIDS and the Human Retrovirus: A Story of Scientific Discovery.* Basic Books, New York, 1991.
21. McCombie, S. C. Folk flu and viral syndrome: An epidemiological perspective. *Soc. Sci. Med.* 25: 987–993, 1987.
22. Flaskerud, J. H., and Nyamanthi, A. M. Black and Latina women's AIDS-related knowledge, attitudes, and practices. *Res. Nursing Health* 12: 339–346, 1989.

23. Elder-Tabrizy, K. A., et al. AIDS and competing health concerns of blacks, Hispanics, and whites. *J. Community Health* 16: 11–21, 1991.
24. Epstein, R. Patient attitudes and knowledge about HIV infection and AIDS. *J. Fam. Pract.* 32: 373–377, 1991.
25. Bower, B. Contagious thoughts. *Sci. News* .140: 138–139, 1991.
26. Meese, E. III. Memorandum for the Domestic Policy Council, Subject: AIDS Education. The White House, Washington, D.C., February 11, 1987.
27. Boyd, G. M. President urges abstinence for young to avoid AIDS. *New York Times,* April 2, 1987, p. 10.
28. Drucker, E. Epidemic in the war zone: AIDS and community survival in New York City. *Int. J. Health Serv.* 20: 601–616, 1990.
29. Des Jarlais, D. C., and Stepherson, B. History, ethics, and politics in AIDS prevention research. *Am. J. Public Health* 81: 1393–1394, 1991.
30. Anderson, W. The New York needle trial: The politics of public health in the age of AIDS. *Am. J. Public Health* 81: 1506–1517, 1991.
31. Dalton, H. L. AIDS in blackface. *Daedalus* 118: 205–227, 1989.
32. Thomas, S. B., and Quinn, S. C. The Tuskegee syphilis study, 1932 to 1972: Implications for HIV education and AIDS risk education programs in the black community. *Am. J. Public Health* 81: 1498–1505, 1991.
33. Murray, T. H. The poisoned gift: AIDS and blood. *Milbank Q.* 68(Suppl. 2): 205–225, 1990.
34. Musto, D. F. Quarantine and the problem of AIDS. In *AIDS: The Burdens of History,* edited by E. Fee and D. M. Fox, pp. 67–85. University of California Press, Berkeley, 1988.
35. Brandt, A. M. *No Magic Bullet: A Social History of Venereal Disease in the United States since 1880,* revised edition. Oxford University Press, New York, 1987.
36. Kleinman, L. E. To end an epidemic: Lessons from the history of diphtheria. *N. Engl. J. Med.* .326: 773–777, 1992.
37. Centers for Disease Control. Additional recommendations to reduce sexual and drug abuse-related transmission of human T-lymphotropic virus type III/lymphadenopathy-associated virus. *MMWR* 35: 152–155, 1986.
38. Altman, L. K. U.S. urges blood test for millions with high risk of AIDS infection. *New York Times,* March 14, 1986, pp. 1, 9.
39. Institute of Medicine, National Academy of Sciences. *Mobilizing against AIDS: The Unfinished Story of a Virus.* National Academy Press, Washington, D.C., 1986.
40. Kline, A., Kline, E., and Oken, E. Minority women and sexual choices in the age of AIDS. *Soc. Sci. Med.* 34: 447–457, 1992.
41. Zuger, A., and Miles, S. H. Physicians, AIDS, and occupational risk: Historic traditions and ethical obligations. *JAMA* 258: 1924–1928, 1987.
42. Gostin, L. The AIDS litigation project: A national review of court and human rights decisions on discrimination. In *AIDS: The Making of a Chronic Disease,* edited by E. Fee and D. M. Fox, pp. 144–169. University of California Press, Berkeley, 1992.
43. Bayer, R. *Private Acts, Social Consequences: AIDS and the Politics of Public Health.* Rutgers University Press, New Brunswick, N.J., 1991.
44. Fee, E., and Fox, D. M. The contemporary historiography of AIDS. *J. Soc. Hist.* 23: 303–314, 1989.
45. Centers for Disease Control. Estimate of HIV prevalence and projected AIDS cases: Summary of a workshop, October 31–November 1, 1989. *MMWR* 39: 110–119, 1990.
46. Graubard, S. R. (ed.) *Living with AIDS.* MIT Press, Cambridge, Mass., 1990.
47. Cotton, D. J. The impact of AIDS on the medical care system. *JAMA* 260: 519–523, 1988.

48. Scitovsky, A. A., and Rice, D. P. Estimates of the direct and indirect costs of acquired immunodeficiency syndrome in the United States, 1985, 1986, and 1991. *Public Health Rep.* 102: 5–17, 1987.
49. Bloom, D. E., and Carliner, G. The economic impact of AIDS in the United States. *Science* 239: 604–609, 1988.
50. Andrulis, D. P., et al. Comparisons of hospital care for patients with AIDS and other HIV-related conditions. *JAMA* 267: 2482–2486, 1992.
51. Altman, L. K. At AIDS talks, reality weighs down hope. *New York Times,* July 26, 1992, Sect. 1, pp. 1, 15.
52. Wallace, R. B., and Everett, G. D. Prevention of chronic illness. In *Maxcy-Rosenau-Last Public Health and Preventive Medicine,* Ed. 13, edited by J. M. Last and R. B. Wallace, pp. 805–810. Appleton & Lange, Norwalk, Conn., 1992.
53. U.S. Department of Health and Human Services, Public Health Service. *Healthy People 2000: National Health Promotion and Disease Prevention Objectives.* DHHS Publication PHS 91-50123. Washington, D.C., 1990.
54. Barrett-Connor, E. Infectious and chronic disease epidemiology: Separate and unequal? *Am. J. Epidemiol.* 109: 245–249, 1979.
55. Hulka, B. S., Wilcosky, T. C., and Griffith, J. D. (eds.). *Biological Markers in Epidemiology.* Oxford University Press, New York, 1990.
56. Louie, L. G., Newman, B., and King, M. C. Influence of host genotype on progression to AIDS among HIV-infected men. *J. Acquir. Immune Defic. Syndr.* 4: 814–818, 1991.
57. Centers for Disease Control. A framework for assessing the effectiveness of disease and injury prevention. *MMWR* 41(RR-3): 1–11, 1992.
58. Lohr, S. Market place: Wellcome's bet on AIDS drug. *New York Times,* January 16, 1987, p. 30.
59. Hilts, P. J. Panel criticizes cancellation of study of teenage life. *New York Times,* September 25, 1991, p. A2.
60. Francis, D. D., et al. Targeting AIDS prevention and treatment toward HIV-1-infected persons: The concept of early intervention. *JAMA* 262: 2572–2576, 1989.
61. Levine, C., and Bayer, R. The ethics of screening for early intervention in HIV disease. *Am. J. Public Health* 79: 1661–1667, 1989.
62. Gerbert, B., et al. Primary care physicians and AIDS: Attitudinal and structural barriers to care. *JAMA* 266: 2837–2842, 1991.
63. Gemson, D. H., et al. Acquired immunodeficiency syndrome prevention: Knowledge, attitudes, and practices of primary care physicians. *Arch. Intern. Med.* 151: 1102–1108, 1991.
64. McCance, K. L., Moser, R., Jr., and Smith, K. R. A survey of physicians' knowledge and application of AIDS prevention capabilities. *Am. J. Prevent. Med.* 7: 141–145, 1991.
65. Coverdale, J. H., et al. AIDS, minority patients, and doctors: What's the risk? Who's talking? *South. Med. J.* 83: 1380–1383, 1990.
66. Hingson, R., et al. Survey of AIDS knowledge and behavior changes among Massachusetts adults. *Prevent. Med.* 18: 806–816, 1989.
67. Booth, W. A rebel without a cause of AIDS. *Science* 239: 1485–1488, 1988.
68. Kidd, P. M., and Huber, W. *Living with AIDS: Strategies for Long-Term Survival.* HK Biomedical, Berkeley, Calif., 1990.
69. Callen, M. *Surviving AIDS.* Harper Collins, New York, 1990.
70. Badgley, L. *Healing AIDS Naturally.* Human Energy Press, Foster City, Calif., 1987.
71. Asistent, N. M., and Duffy, P. *Why I Survive AIDS.* Simon and Schuster, New York, 1991.

72. Centers for Disease Control. Review of draft for revision of HIV infection classification system and expansion of AIDS surveillance case definition. *MMWR* 40: 787, 1991.
73. Edgar, H., and Rothman, D. J. New rules for new drugs: The challenge of AIDS to the regulatory process. *Milbank Q.* 68(Suppl. 1): 111–142, 1990.
74. Alcohol, Drug Abuse, and Mental Health Administration and National Institutes of Health. ADAMHA/NIH policy concerning inclusion of women in study populations. *NIH Guide* 20: 1–2, 1991.
75. Alcohol, Drug Abuse, and Mental Health Administration and National Institutes of Health. ADAMHA/NIH policy concerning inclusion of minorities in study populations. *NIH Guide* 20: 2–3, 1991.
76. Carter, G. M. *ACTUP: The AIDS War and Activism.* Open Magazine Pamphlet Series, Westfield, N.J., 1992.
77. Crimp, D. (ed.). *AIDS: Cultural Analysis, Cultural Activism.* MIT Press, Cambridge, Mass., 1988.
78. Crimp, D., with Rolston, A. *AIDSDEMOGRAPHICS.* Bay Press, Seattle, 1990.
79. Goldstein, R. The implicated and the immune: Cultural responses to AIDS. *Milbank Q.* 68(Suppl. 2): 295–319, 1990.
80. Hilts, P. J. Congress urges AIDS tests for doctors. *New York Times,* October 4, 1991, p. A9.
81. Daniels, N. HIV-infected health care professionals. *Milbank Q.* 70: 3–42, 1992.
82. National Commission on AIDS. *Americans Living with AIDS. Report of the National Commission on Acquired Immune Deficiency Syndrome.* Washington, D.C., 1991.
83. Mann, J., Tarantola, D. J. M., and Netter, T. W. (eds.). *AIDS in the World: A Global Report.* Harvard University Press, Cambridge, Mass., 1992.
84. Dubos, R. *Mirage of Health: Utopias, Progress, and Biological Change.* Rutgers University Press, New Brunswick, N.J., 1959.
85. McKeown, T. *The Modern Rise of Population.* Academic Press, New York, 1977.
86. Szreter, S. The importance of social intervention in Britain's mortality decline c.1850–1914: A re-interpretation of the role of public health. *Soc. Hist. Med.* 1: 1–37, 1988.
87. Bennett, J. V., et al. Infectious and parasitic diseases. In *Closing the Gap: The Burden of Unnecessary Illness,* edited by R. W. Amler and H. B. Dull, pp. 102–114. Oxford University Press, New York, 1987.
88. Rothenberg, R., et al. Cancer. In *Closing the Gap: The Burden of Unnecessary Illness,* edited by R. W. Amler and H. B. Dull, pp. 30–42. Oxford University Press, New York, 1987.
89. Breslow, L., and Cumberland, W. G. Progress and objectives in cancer control. *JAMA* 259: 1690–1694, 1988.
90. Cairns, J. The treatment of diseases and the war against cancer. *Sci. Am.* 253: 51–59, 1985.
91. Bailar, J. C. III, and Smith, E. M. Progress against cancer? *N. Engl. J. Med.* 314: 1226–1232, 1986.
92. White, C. C., et al. Cardiovascular disease. In *Closing the Gap: The Burden of Unnecessary Illness,* edited by R. W. Amler and H. B. Dull, pp. 43–54. Oxford University Press, New York, 1987.
93. Chapman, S., et al. Why the tobacco industry fears the passive smoking issue. *Int. J. Health Serv.* 20: 417–427, 1990.
94. Navarro, V. *Crisis, Health, and Medicine: A Social Critique.* Tavistock, New York, 1986.

95. Waitzkin, H. *The Second Sickness: Contradictions of Capitalist Health Care.* Free Press, New York, 1983.
96. Terris, M. The life-style approach to prevention (editorial). *J. Public Health Policy* 1: 5–9, 1980.
97. Krieger, N., and Bassett, M. The health of black folk: Disease, class, and ideology in science. *Monthly Rev.* 38: 74–85, 1986.
98. Fee, E. Is feminism a threat to scientific objectivity? *Int. J. Women's Stud.* 4: 378–392, 1981.
99. Harding, S. *The Science Question in Feminism.* Cornell University Press, Ithaca, N.Y., 1986.
100. Hubbard, R. *The Politics of Women's Biology.* Rutgers University Press, New Brunswick, N.J., 1990.
101. Haraway, D. J. *Simians, Cyborgs and Women: The Reinvention of Nature.* Routledge, New York, 1991.
102. Yach, D. Biological markers: Broadening or narrowing the scope of epidemiology. *J. Clin. Epidemiol. 43*: 309–310, 1990.
103. Susser, M. Epidemiology today: "A thought-tormented world." *Int. J. Epidemiol.* 18: 481–488, 1989.
104. Freudenberg, N. AIDS prevention in the United States: Lessons from the first decade. *Int. J. Health Serv.* 20: 589–600, 1990.
105. Rosen, G. *A History of Public Health.* Johns Hopkins University Press, Baltimore, 1993 [1958].
106. Black, D., et al. *Inequalities in Health: The Black Report.* Penguin, Harmondsworth, England, 1982.
107. Whitehead, M. *The Health Divide.* Penguin, Harmondsworth, England, 1987.
108. Navarro, V. *Medicine under Capitalism.* Prodist, New York, 1976.
109. Laurell, A. C. Social analysis of collective health in Latin America. *Soc. Sci. Med.* 28: 1183–1191, 1989.
110. Krieger, N., et al. Racism, sexism, and social class: Implications for studies of health, disease, and well-being. *Am. J. Prevent. Med.,* 1993, in press.
111. Krieger, N. The making of public health data: Paradigms, politics, and policy. *J. Public Health Policy.* 13: 412–427, 1992.
112. Huang, K., Watters, J. K., and Case, P. Health Beliefs among Intravenous Drug Users: Predicting Compliance with HIV Prevention Behaviors. Paper presented at the 116th annual meeting of the American Public Health Association, Boston, November 13–17, 1988.
113. Polaris Research and Development. *Cross-Cultural Guidelines for AIDS Service Providers.* San Francisco, 1991.
114. Duke, S. I., and Omi, J. Development of AIDS education and prevention materials for women by health department staff and community focus groups. *AIDS Educ. Prevent.* 3: 90–99, 1991.
115. Walsh, M. E., and Bibace, R. Developmentally-based AIDS/HIV education. *J. School Health.* 60: 256–261, 1990.
116. Freudenberg, N. *Preventing AIDS: A Guide to Effective Education for the Prevention of HIV Infection.* American Public Health Association, Washington, D.C., 1989.
117. Brown, E. R. Community action for health promotion: A strategy to empower individuals and communities. *Int. J. Health Serv.* 21: 441–456, 1991.
118. Freudenberg, N. *Not in Our Backyard! Community Action for Health and the Environment.* Monthly Review Press, New York, 1984.
119. De Wolk, R. Coping with AIDS and death at work. *Oakland Tribune,* November 26, 1990, pp. A1, A2.

120. Associated Press. Levi's grants health benefits to unmarried partners in U.S. *Oakland Tribune,* February 23, 1992, p. A6.
121. Magana, J. R. Sex, drugs, and HIV: An ethnographic approach. *Soc. Sci. Med.* 33: 5–9, 1991.
122. Mays, V., and Jackson, J. S. AIDS survey methodology with black Americans. *Soc. Sci. Med.* 33: 47–54, 1991.
123. Carovano, K. More than mothers and whores: Redefining the AIDS prevention needs of women. *Int. J. Health Serv.* 21: 131–142, 1991.
124. Bassett, M., and Mhloyi, M. Women and AIDS in Zimbabwe; The making of an epidemic. *Int. J. Health Serv.* 21: 143–156, 1991.
125. Sepulveda, J., Fineberg, H., and Mann, J. (eds.). *AIDS Prevention through Education: A World View.* Oxford University Press, New York, 1992.
126. Panos Institute. *AIDS and the Third World.* New Society Publishers, Philadelphia, 1989.
127. Mann, J. M. Global AIDS: Critical issues for prevention in the 1990s. *Int. J. Health Serv.* 21: 553–559, 1991.
128. Panos Institute. *The Hidden Cost of AIDS: The Challenge of HIV to Development.* London, 1993.
129. Jochelson, K., Mothibeli, M., and Leger, J.-P. Human immunodeficiency virus and migrant labor in South Africa. *Int. J. Health Serv.* 21: 157–173, 1991.

Contributors

ROSE APPLEMAN is the nom-de-plume for Marcy Rein, who has written for a variety of alternative media for the past fifteen years, including *Off Our Backs, The Guardian,* and *San Francisco Bay Times.* Most of her writing on the politics of AIDS and the lesbian/gay community was done during the eight years she worked with *Frontline,* a national Marxist bi-weekly. She worked for four years with the San Francisco needle exchange program, Prevention Point, and is now managing editor for a Northern California activist monthly, *News for a People's World.*

MARY BASSETT trained as a physician and epidemiologist. Since 1986 she has taught at the University of Zimbabwe Medical School where she is a senior lecturer in Community Medicine. Her current AIDS-related activities include a school-based adolescent AIDS prevention program.

ANNE-EMANUELLE BIRN is a resident at the Pan American Health Organization in Washington, D.C. and a Faculty Associate at The Johns Hopkins School of Hygiene and Public Health in Baltimore, Maryland. She completed her doctorate at Johns Hopkins in 1993, where her dissertation was entitled, "Local Health and Foreign Wealth: The Rockefeller Foundation's Public Health Programs in Mexico, 1924-1951." She previously directed a project for the school placement of HIV-positive children at the Catalunya Health Department in Barcelona, Spain and worked at the Baltimore City Health Department, Division of School and Adolescent Health. Her current research interests include the history of international health and health and social welfare policy in Latin America.

DR. LAWANDA GREEN BURWELL holds the degree of Doctorate of Science in Maternal and Child Health from Harvard School of Public Health. She is currently a Grant Development Specialist for the Baltimore County Public Schools and an Associate to the Faculty of The Johns Hopkins University, School of Hygiene and Public Health, Department of Maternal and Child Health. Between 1989 and 1993, Dr. Burwell was the project director and subsequently the principal investigator of a perinatal HIV prevention demonstration research project, conducted by the Baltimore City Health Department and funded by the Centers for Disease Control. This project developed and tested community-based strategies for the prevention of perinatal HIV. From 1991 to 1992, Dr. Burwell was a policy consultant for the Baltimore City Healthy Start Program, a federal demonstration research project to reduce infant mortality. Dr. Burwell had the special assignments of liaison for evaluation research with NIG/NICHD, Division of Epidemiology, Statistics and Prevention Research; and The Johns Hopkins University, School of Hygiene and Public Health, Department of Maternal and Child Health Science Consortium.

KATHRYN CAROVANO is a senior program officer at the Center for Communication Programs of The Johns Hopkins University working on the AIDSCOM Project, in Washington D.C. In this capacity, she is involved in the development, monitoring, and evaluation of AIDS prevention communication programs in Latin America and is also responsible for AIDSCOM's Women and AIDS initiative. Prior to joining AIDSCOM, Ms. Carovano worked at the Overseas Development Council, where she was engaged in research and writing on U.S. foreign policy toward the developing world, with a focus on AIDS policy. Ms. Carovano received her M.A. in International Relations from The Johns Hopkins School of Advanced International Studies in 1985, and her B.A. from Middlebury College in 1982. She has carried out research and written on foreign policy in Latin America, and is currently involved in work focusing on women and AIDS in the United States and elsewhere.

HERBERT DANIEL was a writer and served as executive director of the Associação Brasileira Interdisciplinar de AIDS (Brazilian Interdisciplinary Association on AIDS, or ABIA), and president of the Grupo pela VIDDA (pela Valorização, Integração e Dignidade do Doente de AIDS: Group for the Value, Integration, and Dignity of the Person with AIDS). Mr. Daniel took part in the armed resistance against the military dictatorship in Brazil in the 1960s and 1970s, and was a political exile for seven years. He returned to Brazil after the amnesty of 1979, after which he became involved with libertarian causes, both as a writer of seven published books—novels, essays, and plays—and as a political and AIDS activist. Herbert Daniel died of AIDS in 1992.

ERNEST DRUCKER, Ph.D., is Director, Division of Community Health and Professor, Department of Epidemiology and Social Medicine, Montefiore Medical Center/Albert Einstein College of Medicine, Bronx, New York. He received his Ph.D. from the City College of New York in 1969. In his twenty-five years at Montefiore, Dr. Drucker has developed and directed programs in occupational health, primary medical care, drug addiction treatment, and AIDS. His research has focused on social problems and their health consequences: most recently, on the social epidemiology and geography of drug use and AIDS in the Bronx. Dr. Drucker is also involved in drug policy reform and in international associations for a public health and harm reduction approach to drug problems. His most recent project is the Social Epidemiology Research Laboratory—a computerized system linking health and social data sets on the Bronx. Dr. Drucker is a founder and Chairman of the Board of Directors of Doctors of the World, an international medical relief and human rights organization; a member of the Board of Directors of Housing Works, inc., an AIDS housing organization in New York City; and a member of the Board of Directors of St. Benedict the Moor, a community-based AIDS and drug rehabilitation program in the Mott Haven section of the South Bronx. Dr. Drucker is Editor-in-Chief of the international journal *Addiction Research;* Associate Editor of the *International Journal on Drug Policy,* and a member of the editorial board of the *American Journal of Drug and Alcohol Abuse.*

LILY FAAS is a candidate for the master's degree in anthropology at the University of Amsterdam. She is an R.N. (1986), and received a B.S. in anthropology at the University of Amsterdam in 1987. Ms. Faas is working in AIDS research in Amsterdam and has a strong professional interest in Latin American anthropology.

ELIZABETH FEE is professor of history and health policy in the Department of Health Policy and Management at The Johns Hopkins School of Hygiene and Public Health in Baltimore, Maryland. She is author of *Disease and Discovery* (1987), editor of *Women and Health* (1983), co-editor with Daniel M. Fox of *AIDS: The Burdens of History* (1987) and *AIDS: The Making of a Chronic Disease* (1991), and co-editor, with Roy M. Acheson, of *A History of Education in Public Health* (1991). She teaches courses in health policy, history of public health, and women's health.

NICHOLAS FREUDENBERG is a professor and the director of the Program in Community Health Education at Hunter College School at Health Sciences, City University of New York. He also directs the Hunter College Center for Community Action to Prevent AIDS, which provides training and consultation on AIDS prevention to low-income community organizations in New York City. He received his D.P.H. in 1979 and M.P.H. in 1977 from Columbia University School of Public Health, and his B.Sc. from Hunter College. He has published widely on AIDS prevention, health education, and community organization for health.

KAREN JOCHELSON is currently reading toward her doctoral thesis at St. Anthony's College, Oxford. She previously worked in the Sociology of Work Program at the University of the Witwatersrand in Johannesburg. Her research is on a history of sexually transmitted diseases in South Africa, and examines medical discourse and the making of class, gender, and racial identification. She has also published work on contemporary South African politics.

NANCY KRIEGER is an epidemiologist at the Division of Research of the Kaiser Foundation Research Institute, in Oakland, California, and is a lecturer in the Epidemiology Program of the School of Public Health at University of California at Berkeley. She co-authored *The Politics of AIDS* (1986), co-edited the series "AIDS: The Politics of Survival" (*International Journal of Health Services,* 1990-1991), and prepared the AIDS platform for the Health Commission of the National Rainbow Coalition and the 1988 Jackson presidential campaign. Her research focuses on issues regarding race, class, gender, and cancer, particularly breast cancer; other work concerns the history and theoretical underpinnings of epidemiology.

JEAN-PATRICK LEGER, M.Sc., is a researcher in the Sociology of Work Program at the University of the Witwatersrand in Johannesburg. His research is primarily concerned with the South African mining industry, in particular, issues in health, safety, labor, and the economics of gold and coal mining. Specific foci of his work are the accident experiences of workers in South Africa's uniquely deep gold mines and accident statistics in mining and manufacturing industry. He has undertaken research commissioned by the National Union of Mineworkers and the Congress of South African Trade Unions.

DR. JONATHAN MANN, M.D., M.P.H., is the François-Xavier Bagnoud Professor of Health and Human Rights and Director, François-Xavier Bagnoud Center for Health and Human Rights at the Harvard School of Public Health. Additionally, Dr. Mann is Professor of Epidemiology and International Health, and Director of the International AIDS Center of the Harvard AIDS Institute. From 1986-1990, Dr. Mann was founding director of the World Health Organization's Global Program on AIDS, based in Geneva, Switzerland, From 1984-1986, he founded and directed the Projet SIDA, a collaborative AIDS research project based in Kinshasa, Zaire, and involving the U.S. Centers for Disease Control and National Institutes of Health, the Institute of Tropical Medicine (Antwerp, Belgium) and the Ministry of Health, Republic of Zaire. Prior to working in Zaire, Dr. Mann was state epidemiologist and assistant director of the health department in New Mexico. From 1975-1977, he was an Epidemic Intelligence Service Officer with the Centers for Disease Control. Dr. Mann received his B.A. (magna cum laude in History) from Harvard College, his M.D. from Washington University at St. Louis (1974), and his M.P.H. from the Harvard School of Public Health (1980). Dr. Mann is the President of Doctors of the World, the U.S. affiliate of the French medical humanitarian relief organization Medecins du Monde. He is the Chairman of the Global AIDS Policy Coalition, an independent research and advocacy organization, and senior editor of its book, *AIDS in the World,* published in late 1992 by the Harvard University Press. Dr. Mann's interests involve public health and human rights at the national and international level. He is involved with specific issues, including: global thinking and action on health and human rights; pandemic recognition and response; global learning and exchange; women and health; the role of community-based organizations in health; and AIDS.

GLEN MARGO, Dr.P.H., recently served as director of AIDSCOM, a communications support program designed to assist organizations and individuals throughout the developing world to create and implement effective HIV prevention activities. AIDSCOM is funded by the U.S. Agency for International Development, and managed by the Academy for Educational Development in Washington, D.C. He previously served as Bureau Chief for Health Promotion and Education with the San Francisco Department of Public Health. His research focuses on homophobia, sexism, and racism, and he has worked extensively with community-based organizations, people with AIDS, their families and friends.

MARVELLOUS MHLOYI, Ph.D., is a demographer and a lecturer in the Sociology Department of the University of Zimbabwe Medical School. Her research interests include population policy and fertility, infant and childhood mortality, and the sociocultural dimension of AIDS.

MONYAOLA MOTHIBELI works in the Sociology of Work Program at the University of the Witwatersrand in Johannesburg. He is a former mineworker and was chairperson of his branch of the National Union of Mineworkers as well as of the important Carletonville region when he was dismissed during a strike in 1985. Since then he has been involved in research into safety, health, and labor action on the mines. Active in struggles against the apartheid regime since the 1950s, he is currently writing his autobiography.

SARAH SANTANA is a senior staff associate at the G. H. Sergievsky Center and a doctoral candidate in epidemiology at Columbia University School of Public Health in New York. She received her B.S. from the University of Massachusetts in 1971, and M.P.H. from the University of Illinois in 1977. Recent publications include "Whither Cuban Medicine? Challenges for the Next Generation," in *Transformation and Struggle: Cuba Faces the 1990's,* edited by S. Halebsky and J. Kirk (Praeger, 1990); and "Some Thoughts on Vital Statistics and Health Status in Cuba," in *Cuban Political Economy,* edited by A. Zimbalist (Westview Press, 1988). She has worked on topics relating to health in Central America and Cuba, and is currently doing research on ethnicity and infant mortality in New York City.

DR. JOHN STEPHAN SANTELLI is a specialist in Adolescent Medicine with an interest in the primary prevention of adolescent risk-taking behaviors. From July 1987 through September 1991 he was the Director of School and Adolescent Health Services at the Baltimore City Health Department and the Principal Investigator for AIDS Prevention for Pediatric Life Enrichment, a CDC funded, community-based program to prevent perinatal HIV infection. From September 1991 through November 1992 he worked with the Operational Research Section, Division of STD/HIV Prevention at CDC where he coordinated a multi-site evaluation of street outreach to injecting drug users and youth in high risk situations. Dr. Santelli is currently a medical epidemiologist with the Division of Preventive Medicine and Epidemiology at the Baltimore City Health Department and an Adjunct Assistant Professor with the Department of Maternal and Child Health, The Johns Hopkins School of Hygiene and Public Health.

KAREN WALD is a journalist from Oakland, California, who has worked as a foreign correspondent in Cuba for eight years. She is the author of *Children of Che: Childcare and Education in Cuba* (Ramparts Press, 1978), *Los Hijos del Che* (Extemporaneous, Mexico, 1986), and articles for the popular press. The HIV epidemic is among the issues she has been examining in Cuba.